MOSHE'S
CHILDREN

STUDIES IN ANTISEMITISM
Alvin H. Rosenfeld, editor

MOSHE'S CHILDREN

The Orphans of the Holocaust and
the Birth of Israel

—⚏—

Sergio Luzzatto
translated by Stash Luczkiw

INDIANA UNIVERSITY PRESS

This book is a publication of

Indiana University Press
Office of Scholarly Publishing
Herman B Wells Library 350
1320 East 10th Street
Bloomington, Indiana 47405 USA

iupress.org

© 2023 by Sergio Luzzatto

All rights reserved

Original edition: *I bambini di Moshe. Gli orfani della Shoah e la nascita di Israele*, Turin: Einaudi, 2018.
No part of this book may be reproduced or utilized in any form or by any means, electronic or mechanical, including photocopying and recording, or by any information storage and retrieval system, without permission in writing from the publisher. The paper used in this publication meets the minimum requirements of the American National Standard for Information Sciences—Permanence of Paper for Printed Library Materials, ANSI Z39.48–1992.

Manufactured in the United States of America
First printing 2023
Cataloging information is available from the Library of Congress.
ISBN 978-0-253-06587-2 (hardback)
ISBN 978-0-253-06588-9 (paperback)
ISBN 978-0-253-06589-6 (ebook)

CONTENTS

Main Characters vii

Acknowledgments xi

Maps xiv

The Black Box 1
1. Far from Where 9
2. Yehudit 47
3. Close to Where 77
4. Anabasis 92
5. The Drowned and the Saved 128
6. The House of Mussolini 160
7. A Republic of Orphans 186
8. Life after Death 218
9. Kibbutz Selvino? 245
10. In Israel's Waters 275
11. The Road to Jerusalem 308

If You Survive 341

Glossary 347

Guide to Abbreviations 351

Notes 353

Index 405

MAIN CHARACTERS

JEWISH FAMILIES OF EASTERN EUROPE

David Kleiner, fodder merchant in Kopychyntsi
Zippora Kleiner, housewife
Rivka Kleiner, kindergarten teacher
Moshe Kleiner, carpenter's apprentice

Meir Liberman, pharmacist in Rovno
Feige Liberman, pharmacist
Adela Liberman, student
Inda Liberman, student

Moshe David Lipkunski, blacksmith in Dugalishok
Sara Mina Lipkunski, seamstress
Pinchas Lipkunski, yeshiva student
Avraham Lipkunski, yeshiva student
Yekutiel Lipkunski, schoolboy

Henoch Wexler, ritual slaughterer in Janowo
Mindel Wexler, seamstress
Shaya Wexler, Zionist militant
Yosef Wexler, Zionist militant

Dov Wexler, student
Adam Wexler, schoolboy

Vilmos Weisz, director of distillery in Nagyszőlős
Terez Weisz, housewife
Bandi Weisz, student
Aliz Weisz, student
Hedy Weisz, student
Suti Weisz, schoolboy
Icuka Weisz, schoolgirl

Alter Kacyzne, writer and photographer in Warsaw
Hana Kacyzne, housewife
Shulamit Kacyzne, student

JEWISH FAMILIES OF WESTERN EUROPE

Heinrich Meyer, meat wholesaler in Cologne
Wilhelmina Meyer, housewife
Jacques Meyer, musician
Trude Meyer, student

ZIONIST LEADERS AND EMISSARIES IN PALESTINE

Pinchas Lubianiker, founder of the Gordonia movement
Yosef Baratz, founder of Kibbutz Degania
Berl Katznelson, director of the newspaper *Davar*
Enzo Sereni, founder of Kibbutz Givat-Brenner
Ada Sereni, coordinator of Aliyah Beth, Enzo's wife

JEWISH VOLUNTEERS IN THE BRITISH ARMY

Lova Eliav, student in Jerusalem
Yissachar Haimowitz, major of the 745th Company
Reuven Kohen, student in Tel Aviv

Reuven Donath, student in Haifa
Heinz Rebhun, electrician in Haifa
Menachem Shemi, drawing teacher in Haifa
Shalhevet Freier, student in Jerusalem
Moshe Unger, driver

ZIONIST LEADERS AND ACTIVISTS IN ITALY

Raffaele Cantoni, president of the Jewish community of Milan
Davide Mario Levi, commander of the Matteotti Brigades
Max Varadi, Zionist leader in Florence
Matilde Cassin, Zionist militant, girlfriend of Max Varadi

ORPHANS IN SELVINO

Nina Boniówka, orphan from Warsaw
Haim Luftman, orphan from Poznan
Yaakov Meriash, orphan from Kaunas
Shmulik Shulman, orphan from Lutsk
Lea Spivak, orphan from Sarny
Shalom Finkelstein, Jew from Lomza

ACKNOWLEDGMENTS

WRITING A BOOK ABOUT MOSHE'S children would not have been possible without the help of Moshe's first child: his daughter, Nitza. By sharing with me a transcript of the letters exchanged between her parents, even before they were deposited in the Yad Vashem archive, Nitza Zeiri Sarner gave me access to the "black box" of history: the details of the journey, ideological and psychological, that turned Moshe's military volunteer service into a redemption mission. After that, Nitza accompanied me in the search with an attention equal only to her discretion.

Nor could I have written the book without the help of Moshe's other children: his adopted children, the orphans reborn to life through their Selvino experience. During the years of research and writing, some of those orphans disappeared; may my words serve as a tribute to them in memoriam. Thanks to Adam Wexler, the contrarian of Sciesopoli (and to his wife, Dalia, and his son Henoch). Thanks to Avraham and Ayala Aviel (as children, Avraham Lipkunski and Inda Liberman): Sara and I will never forget their Tel Aviv takeaway pizza, which was better than any Neapolitan pizza. Thanks to Yitzhak Livnat (Suti Weisz), especially for our trip in the rain. Thanks to Yaakov Meriash for his dedication in the book on the cut tree and the new tree. Thanks to

Haim Sarid (Haim Luftman) for his brief and insightful emails. Thanks to Yocheved (Helga) Weintraub for the simplicity of her welcome to Rishon LeZion.

In Israel as in Italy, there were many people who wanted to share their legacy of memories, documents, and photographs with me. I am therefore grateful to express here the gratitude I feel for Tali Zeiri Amitai, Moshe's second daughter. For Noga Cohen Donath (in memoriam), and for her son Nir. For Yocheved (Helga) Weintraub, a child in Selvino, and for Alisa Varadi, daughter of Matilde Cassin. For Avi Shilo, Shmulik Shulman's son. For Miriam Rebhun, daughter of Heinz, and for Paola Reale, Eugenio Reale and Shulamit Kacyzne's granddaughter. And for the Selivino natives: Alberto Cortinovis, Giovanni Grigis, and Pierina Tiraboschi Ghilardi.

During the research, a generous and precious support came to me from the archivist Bernardino Pasinelli. One might say we came to discover and study this story together. And together we became passionate about Moshe's children, working so the reconstruction of their story also became, in some way, a small monument of memory. That obviously does not mean that Bernardino should be held responsible for the final result of my research.

The book owes a lot to Chiara Camarda. Without her subtlety as a translator from Hebrew, I really would not have known how to capture Moshe's voice, or the voice of the orphaned editors of the newspaper *Nivenu*.

In writing, I was able to count on some attentive and competent readers. I would like to thank them here, and I would add that they do not share any responsibility for the contents of the book. Thanks to Rosaria Carpinelli, an intellectual beachhead even before being a literary agent; to Enrica Bricchetto, who helped me a lot in finding the right tone; to Elena Loewenthal and Arturo Marzano, much more accredited specialists in Jewish studies than myself; to Walter Barberis and Andrea Bosco, editors and interlocutors; and to Ernesto Franco, who believed in it from the beginning, as always.

At Einaudi I found, as usual, a formidable team spirit. For the cover, the illustrations, the maps, and the index of names, I was able to treasure the work of Monica Aldi, Yara Mavrides, Viviana Gottardello, and Sara Latella. For the text and the notes, I was lucky enough to meet Claudia Canale, who read and reread me not only with infinite patience but also with rare sensitivity.

In Via Biancamano, Irene Babboni was the first reader of the first chapters of the typescript. A cruel fate prevented her from moving forward. May these pages of mine also serve, in their small way, as a tribute of gratitude and memory.

NOTE TO THE AMERICAN EDITION

The English version of this book corresponds in every way to the original version, published in Italian in 2018. For the splendid translation, I am deeply grateful to Stash Luczkiw.

Since the book's release in Italy, some particularly important studies have been added to the bibliography given in the notes. Among them, I limit myself here to pointing out: S. Kangisser Cohen and D. Ofer (eds.), *Starting Anwew. The Rehabilitation of Child Survivors of the Holocaust in the Early Postwar Years*, Jerusalem: Yad Vashem, 2019; R. Clifford, *Survivors. Children's Lives After the Holocaust*, New Haven: Yale University Press, 2020; R. Whitehouse, *The People on the Beach. Journeys to Freedom After the Holocaust*, London: Hurst & Company, 2020; G. Fantoni, *Storia della Brigata ebraica. Gli ebrei della Palestina che combatterono in Italia nella Seconda guerra mondiale*, Turin: Einaudi, 2022.

MAPS

1. The Republic of Poland in interwar Europe, 1918–1939

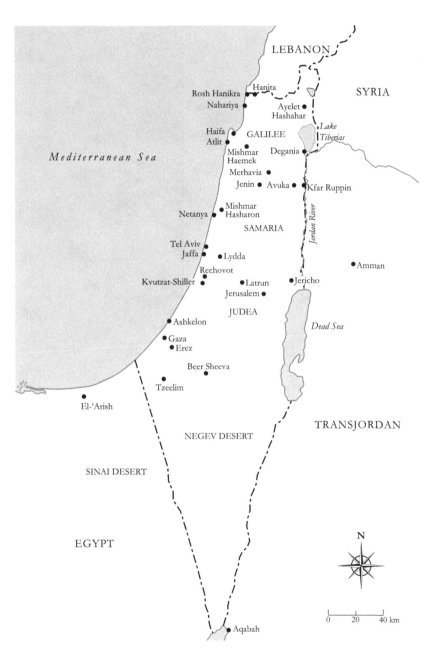

2. Palestine under the British Mandate, 1920–1948

MOSHE'S
CHILDREN

THE BLACK BOX

JERUSALEM, JUNE 17, 2014

It all looked easy on the map we checked before getting into the car. We would leave the house near Damascus Gate and simply follow the tram line to Mount Herzl. From there, Yad Vashem was only a few hundred meters away on the western slope. But as we were nearing Jaffa Gate, heavy morning traffic led us away from the tram tracks, and soon we were lost between one hill of modern Jerusalem and another. The GPS had been sitting in the glove box since we'd arrived in Israel partly out of laziness, partly out of presumption, and partly because Sara maintained that getting it up and working would make her carsick. The result was an unplanned tour of the city, more irritated than delighted, to see the bridge designed by Santiago Calatrava (a Calatrava bridge like all his other bridges), and we arrived at our destination half an hour late.

No problem. Nitza is patient, and a half-hour delay isn't going to ruin her day. She's come down specially from London with Martin, also for a musical festival they'll be taking part in all across Israel. Because today, at Yad Vashem, we'll be commemorating her father's story. Moshe Zeiri, born on June 15, 1914, in Kopychyntsi—part of the Austro-Hungarian Empire then, Poland between the two world wars, and Ukraine today—would have turned one hundred a couple of days ago. He was born just a few weeks before the outbreak of World War I. He was twenty when he came to Palestine from his shtetl in Galicia, where he had been trained as a carpenter—though he was a theater actor by vocation. A decade later, he would be serving with the British Royal Engineers, first in 1943 in Egypt; then in Benghazi, Libya; then in Naples in 1944; and then in Milan in 1945. Moshe was an ordinary sapper among the thousands of Jewish volunteers who had finally persuaded the reluctant British Army to enroll them so at least they could do something in Europe, and try to salvage the salvageable.

The hundreds of letters sent by Moshe to his wife, Yehudit—written on a regular basis from 1943 to 1946, throughout the entire duration of his service in the 745th "Palestinian" Company of Royal Engineers—are exceptional historical documents.[1] Yehudit remained on a kibbutz near Tel Aviv with their infant, Nitza. The missives offer a day-by-day account—live, as it were—of a liberation adventure that becomes, in the process, a nightmare revelation: the discovery that it is now too late, horrifically late, and that almost nothing remains to be saved.[2] But the letters also recount the relief of a further acknowledgment: the discovery that some of Europe's Jews have survived the Final Solution, and that they are not only saved Jews; they are also (in biblical terms) Jews who save. Redeemed, the survivor becomes a redeemer.[3] So Moshe Zeiri stops in Italy after the Liberation and settles in Selvino, in the mountains above Bergamo, at a former fascist vacation camp that will be called Mussolini House by the refugees, where he will welcome the youngest of the redeeming survivors from the bloodlands. Hundreds of Jewish children to be reborn, and with whom to be reborn in perhaps the most important orphanage in postwar Europe. Moshe's children.

At Yad Vashem, while Sara and Martin visit the museum, Nitza and I will go to the International Institute for Holocaust Research. We have an appointment with the director, who is as friendly and welcoming as she is contagiously energetic. When I phoned from Turin before leaving for Israel, the formalities lasted but a few seconds; I introduced myself, and as soon as I said a few words about Moshe and his letters to Yehudit, she was already inviting us to Yad Vashem. "So come with Nitza. We must absolutely do something about this!" Now she's taking us downstairs to the floor below the archive entrance, but first she asks me to find Sara and Martin, because she wants us all together. An initiation rite awaits us—a surprisingly public initiation.

We go down a first flight of stairs, then a second. We find ourselves in front of an armored door, like in a bank vault. There is a guardian, and the director hands him the identification card. After inserting the card into an optical reader, the guardian steps aside, and we enter a windowless room that serves as a vestibule to the storage area. If the people exterminated through the Final Solution are People of the Book par excellence, and if all of Yad Vashem is a shrine raised to the memory of the extermination, we are now in the very heart of the shrine. Here, millions of documents relating to the Final Solution are kept in different microclimates, depending on the type of paper used. There are millions of photographs, letters, diaries, artifacts, and testimonies, which together make up the Book of the Shoah.[4]

The director approaches a shelf and takes a black box. She places the box on a table, opens it in front of us. We see a small pile of yellowing cards, each in an envelope that looks like clear plastic. "This is an archival document like no other," she tells Nitza. "We keep them all like this. Each has its own custom-made box, and each sheet of each document is kept in an envelope made of a special material, so it can be better protected." She pauses for a moment before continuing steadily. "Your father's letters should

also be kept here. Because this is their place. Here, they can be preserved forever." "What about the letters my mother sent back to him from Palestine?" Nitza asks. "Those too, of course," she replies. Then she adds jokingly, "In Israel, you know, we make no difference between men and women!"

We leave the vault and go up the stairs. The director is guiding us to the digitization department. She asks us to speak in a low voice so as not to disturb the dozen young workers scanning documents. "Sheet by sheet, the originals of the letters from

Moshe and Yehudit will pass through one of these machines. Sophisticated, cutting-edge scanners. And once they go digital, your mother and father's letters will be placed in a black box like the others. All the scholars here at Yad Vashem will be able to read them on a screen. Back and forth, up and down, whenever and as often as they like. But no one will have access to the originals, except family members. Only you can, Nitza. And your children, and your children's children..."

Written on the lightest of paper (because of the war's shortages, as well as the hard and fast rules of the Royal Mail), Moshe's letters sent to the kibbutz in British Palestine are very fragile documents indeed. If Nitza and her siblings decide to give them to Yad Vashem, they'll need to be restored before being placed in their black box. The director now takes us to the restoration lab so we can see how Moshe's letters will be treated when they enter this temple of memory.

Five or six technicians in white coats restore the documents, coordinated by a manager who welcomes us with perfect English. "You're lucky today," she says with a smile. "Here we have a piece that the Yad Vashem archive recently collected, and on which we worked like crazy." There is another black box, also custom-made around some fairly large sheets of paper, each in its own transparent envelope. This is what remains of a diary kept in the Warsaw ghetto sometime between 1941 and 1943. The lady in the white coat shows us the photographs of the manuscript that the restoration laboratory initially received. They are a dirty and shapeless little heap, like a tattered bundle of what was once an ancient Greek papyrus, or a ball of rags abandoned on a Brazilian beach.

"In the ghetto, the manuscript was both flooded and burned." Seventy years later, at Yad Vashem, they were able to separate the sheets and restore them until they were legible. "But if our colleagues from the Shrine of the Book (the section of the Israel Museum where the famous Dead Sea Scrolls are kept) had not helped us, I doubt we would have managed." Are the pages

of the diary that escaped the ruin of the Warsaw ghetto really legible? "Actually, strange as it may seem, we don't understand the language in which it's written." Mostly in Polish, it seems. And in Yiddish, though transcribed into Latin letters. With the odd phrase in German and Russian. "So frustrating," the head of the laboratory admits, "to have reached this point and still not understand anything." But she won't give up. As we say goodbye, she tells us confidently, "Sooner or later we will manage. Sooner or later someone will find the key." Like a dilapidated Rosetta stone, the Warsaw diary awaits its Champollion in Jerusalem.

Moshe's letters need no Champollion. Written entirely in Hebrew, they are perfectly legible. They were translated by Chiara Camarda, a scholar born in Trapani, Sicily, whose passion for

Jewish studies had led her to Venice to work on her PhD, then to Jerusalem, and from there, who knows? Nitza's younger sister Tali, from a kibbutz at Erez near the Gaza Strip, patiently deciphered her father's handwriting where it was hard to read, producing a Word document that could be passed on to Chiara. So even before I first touched Moshe's correspondence at Erez, letters so neatly written on pages bearing a Palestine Company letterhead, I had already read and reread the Italian translations. I knew Moshe's still-private correspondence without ever having seen it.[5]

It reminds me of Amos Oz's epistolary novel, *Black Box*, although the book has nothing to do with Yad Vashem or with documents to decipher. And it makes me think of a passage in *Jews and Words*, written by Oz and his daughter Fania Oz-Salzberger, a professional historian: "We are not about stones, clans or chromosomes. You don't have to be an archaeologist, an anthropologist or a geneticist to trace and substantiate the Jewish continuum. You don't have to be an observant Jew. You don't have to be a Jew. Or, for that matter, an anti-Semite. All you have to be is a reader."[6]

ONE

FAR FROM WHERE

THE KLEINER FAMILY

The photograph says a lot about them. It was taken in Kopychyntsi, in 1925 or so. Moshe is eleven or twelve years old, and his sister, Rivka, is seven years older. The whole family posed in what was very likely the shtetl's only photography studio. It was the same one the Kleiner children went to every year, as schoolchildren, for the class photo (I recognize it from the backdrop with the fake birch landscape, the same in every photo I saw of Moshe as a boy).[1]

David Kleiner's gaze is that of a tired, unmotivated man close to the end: the incarnation of the Eastern European Jew who had barely survived his world of yesterday, pre–World War I *Galicia Felix*. Now it's the mother, Zippora, who supports the family. The illiterate Zippora is scarcely able to turn the pages of her prayer book on Shabbat and unable to express herself in any language other than Yiddish. But she is resolute, and that gaze of hers, fixed on the lens, attests to her force of will. From morning to evening, she engages in the shtetl's small-time commerce of hard-boiled eggs, corn on the cob, goose feathers, and old carpets to make ends meet, to allow the kids to study, thus making up for her much older husband's weariness. He has long stopped trading in fodder and only comes to life again when he boards the cart to visit the rabbi at the Hasidic court. Yes, this photograph almost says it all. Rivka—always the best in her class at the Polish school—feels uncomfortable about having parents too visibly antiquated, almost primitive, incorrigibly Yiddish. Moshe's mood is different from his sister's. He's less embarrassed. Serene, contented even. He's proud of his bearded old father in that black caftan and felt hat. Proud of his mother's piercing eyes and straight back.

Moshe's Galician childhood had not been easy. The fact that only Yiddish was spoken at home had made his passage, at the age of seven, from the Jewish private school to the Polish public one traumatic. The large school was next to the church, whose size was already disconcerting. Years later, Moshe could still recall vividly how every morning outside class, he silently prayed that the teacher wouldn't call on him. Ever. Even half a question was too much for him—anything spoken in Polish was incomprehensible. "I swore that if the miracle happened, I would be a good boy at home. I would obey my parents through and through. I would respect all the Commandments, and I would say my prayers."[2] Like the melamed, the old teacher at the Jewish school, his new Polish teacher always kept the ruler close at hand, and he wouldn't hesitate to rap the dunces on their knuckles. Besides, even when he did learn Polish, Moshe was still a lackluster pupil. The only subject he excelled at, with his melodious voice, was singing.[3]

Apart from family and school, his childhood was made difficult by the disaster Jewish villages in eastern Galicia had experienced during World War I and the postwar period. No historian has described that disaster more vividly than novice writer Isaac Babel. This Jew from Odessa traveled the length and breadth of the region on horseback in 1920 as a war correspondent for the Red Army, and in his salty Russian prose, he captured the experience in a collection of stories called *Red Cavalry*. For a century and a half after the eighteenth-century partition of Poland, the "Kingdom of Galicia and Lodomiria" had been part of the Habsburg Empire, together with the "Grand Duchy of Krakow" and the "Duchies of Auschwitz and Zator." The kingdom flourished economically, through border smuggling, grain and timber trade, and the growing business of oil extraction, and culturally, through the literary and scientific activity in Lviv. But with World War I—and then the Russian Revolution of 1917, the war of 1918–19 between the revived Poland and the newborn republic of Ukraine, and the war of 1920 between Poland itself and Soviet Russia—came the end of the Habsburg Empire and the decline of eastern Galicia. And with it, the misfortune of the Jews, who populated not only the sparkling Lviv but also the sleepy countryside's towns and villages.[4]

It is all too easy to imagine Moshe, born in Kopychyntsi in the fateful year of 1914, in that environment. As a child, he must have seen the very landscape depicted by Babel: the destroyed churches and crucifixes, the decapitated wooden synagogues, the wheat fields left uncultivated, the straight roads that no longer led to any fair. He saw an "insignificant, miserable and afflicted" Jewish population, peasants who sold pears in exchange for out-of-date money, shylocks in green stockings and robes, and bony men with "tragic yellow beards" who slowly swayed their heads at crossroads or lingered on the doorsteps of their houses, shrugging their shoulders "like birds with their wings clipped."[5] We might do better to mitigate this vivid depiction of Galicia's Jews in the 1920s with the more subdued colors of a thoughtful historian. On the one hand, there is the picture of a life made precarious by the new geopolitical map, whereby being Jewish in the ultra-Catholic and nationalist Republic of Poland was harder than being one in the tolerant Habsburg Empire. On the other hand, there is the picture of a life made dynamic by the infusion throughout the countryside as well as in the cities of a fresh, vital, contagious element: Zionist propaganda.[6]

On the road connecting Ternopil to Chortkiv, in the direction of the Carpathians, Kopychyntsi looked just like many of the other Jewish villages in eastern Galicia. The same ones that, during Moshe's childhood, were gaining literary dignity thanks to the talent of Shmuel Yosef Agnon, a novelist born in Buchach, a day's carriage ride from Kopychyntsi. As in any shtetl worthy of the name, geese ran through the streets in Kopychyntsi, and the poorest children walked around barefoot. That world was composed above all of smells, starting with the scents of the market: cabbage, onions, and pickled herring. During the winter, the Jewish shops along the main road in Kopychyntsi were filled with goods to sell for the Gentiles' holidays: cinnamon, ginger, and raisins. There was vodka, as well as cognac for the wealthier customers, the Polish or Ukrainian landowners who got out of their carriages wrapped in bear's or wolf's fur, with a retinue of haughty bookkeepers and portly farmhands.[7]

The Kleiner house was by the river. It was a small, recently built wooden house. There were two rooms, with a bed in each: one for Zippora and Rivka, the other for David and Moshe. But there was only one iron stove around which they gathered on winter evenings while potatoes baked in the embers. When Moshe went out into the yard with friends to play, he had nothing to wear but Rivka's old coat, the lining of which hung spitefully below the hem until it dragged through the snow.[8] The weeping willows also hung over the banks of the Nichlavka. "As a child, I always believed that the river was fed by the weeping willows' tears."[9] Daily life in the shtetl probably stirred fewer poetic memories in Moshe. Fortunately, some photos taken in the Kopychyntsi of the 1920s survived the death of the shtetl; they were taken by a Warsaw reporter with the eye of a sociologist and the pen of a writer, Alter Kacyzne, who saved a handful of these scenes for us. Two rope makers, father and son, trying to sell their miserable cordage. There is an elderly Orthodox Jew whose job, Kacyzne's caption explains, consists of hanging out in the market square from dawn to dusk, offering himself for any odd job.[10]

The Kleiners raised their children with a heavy hand. It took little for Moshe to get a smack; it was enough to just skip the afternoon prayers, or play on Saturdays, or sleep without the kippah.[11] But the memory of the blows received as a child would not cloud his memory of the most intense moment in family life: the holidays. David and Zippora were observant Jews, both outside and inside the home. Zippora was responsible for respecting the food prescriptions and keeping everything strictly kosher. David was responsible for the rest, including raising Moshe in the religion of his ancestors. "I can still see my father going out" to the synagogue (in Kopychyntsi, there were no fewer than six, for a Jewish population of 2,500), "his tallith under his arm, and me behind him, and my mother who said goodbye with a blessing." On Rosh Hashanah, the temple echoed sad melodies sung by David Kleiner and the other cantors, with Abraham Yaakov, Yehuda Yakar, and Avrami Peled sounding the shofar. On Yom Kippur, Zippora returned from the women's gallery transfigured: "after shedding torrents of tears, she felt better." For Passover, she bought her children new clothes. Once a year, Moshe could feel proud in front of the mirror.[12]

Alter Kacyzne also photographed Chortkiv, the Hasidic court where David Kleiner was a disciple. It was a court renowned far beyond the borders of eastern Galicia, in Volhynia, Podolia, and as far as Hungary and Russia. For more than a century, the followers of the Friedman dynasty had gathered here, and the whole life of the town revolved around the charismatic presence of the rebbe, or Hassidic spiritual leader.[13] It is hard to know whether Moshe's father, having reached Chortkiv—half a day's donkey ride from Kopychyntsi—focused only on the revered teacher, or whether his gaze widened to include the multicolored humanity of pilgrims, brokers, infirm, and beggars that could always be found at a Hasidic court.[14] A family legend has been passed down in which the old fodder merchant returned to the shtetl and went to bed for days, sick from all the excitement and consumed by his mystical encounter with the rebbe.[15] Another legend remembers the time when young Moshe had also been admitted into the presence of the teacher, and with his beautiful voice, he had sung for him. The rebbe blessed him and even went as far as predicting, "Perhaps one day you will sing with the Levites in the Temple of Jerusalem."[16]

PHOTO ALBUM

We will never hear young Moshe's voice. Not even the smallest written trace of him dating back to his life in Poland has been preserved in the family. As for the fragments of memory, evocative though they may be, they always risk distorting the picture—even more so in the case of the memory of the shtetl, a world not only lost but annihilated. So to give us back something of Moshe's early life, the photos are precious. They come to us more or less directly, having escaped the Shoah, because it is true that the Final Solution annihilated not only people but also things, including those very special things that are images of people and objects. So any story of the destruction of Europe's Jews, which, like this one, also wants to be a story of their salvation and redemption must also be a story of photos, even though a "groan of despair" emanates from each of those photos, just like the one that tormented Austerlitz, the hero of W. G. Sebald's novel of the same name.[17]

How many of the children at the Jewish school of Probizhna pictured in 1928 with their young teacher, Rivka Kleiner, became adults? How many of the Kopychyntsi boys pictured with Moshe in a group photo that can also be dated to the late 1920s made it?[18] To find photos of Jewish Galician childhoods or youths between the two world wars from which groans of despair do not emanate,

you have to look at the albums of those who managed to leave in time, especially the albums of those who saw the prospect of emigrating from Poland as not just a necessity but also an opportunity: the Zionist militants.

In their shtetl, in Kopychyntsi, Rivka and Moshe Kleiner had the good fortune of bonding with the Lubianiker brothers and sisters, a family destined to make a mark in the history of Zionism. Rivka knew Pinchas, the youngest of the Lubianikers, quite well. She often went to their house. It was not only an Orthodox Jewish household but also a bourgeois one, with many rooms and a piano in the living room. Born in 1904, Pinchas was only three years older than Rivka. But by the late 1920s, when she graduated and began her teaching career in Probizhna (a nearby shtetl), Pinchas Lubianiker would find time both to graduate from Lviv University and to found, with his brother Zelig and his sister Eva, a Zionist movement called Gordonia.[19] Some photos taken then and subsequently transported by Rivka far away, toward a new life, recount through images the sentimental education of a girl

whose solidarity with the Lubianikers changed her existence and profoundly influenced the fate of her brother, Moshe.

It began with the theater. The Lubianiker brothers had set up an amateur company, to which Rivka belonged. There were a dozen young men and women.[20] On the model of wandering companies, they traveled through the province of Ternopil offering popular audiences the typical Yiddish theater repertoire: a combination of acting and singing, unusual and cliché, lowbrow and highbrow, rooted and untethered, classical and experimental, sacred and profane.[21] It was the strange mixture of Hasidic tradition and Stanislavski-like modernity that in 1911 had struck the insurance clerk Franz Kafka in Prague.[22] It led him to discover a natural and spontaneous way of being Jewish previously unknown to him, pushing him to envy the existential condition of those *Ostjuden* so snubbed in the West. It made Kafka want to be reborn inside the skin of the "Jewish boy from Eastern Europe in the corner of the room, who's afraid of nothing."[23]

As an Eastern European Jewish boy in the corner of the room, Moshe was spellbound as he watched the rehearsals of his sister

and the Lubianikers' theater company in Kopychyntsi. When the cheerful brigade of amateur actors set off to stage some Romanian or Russian operetta in one of the neighboring shtetls, Moshe always found—to Rivka's chagrin—a way to tag along: the pestering little brother in a group of young men and women who together experienced, in addition to the Yiddish repertoire, a freedom of movement and promiscuity totally unknown (and presumably unwelcome) to their parents. Moshe's theatrical passion was so all-consuming that the fearless Jewish boy found a way to get all the way up to the stage, when the Jewish tour companies passed through the shtetl. These companies would perform in Kopychyntsi, in the barn of an inn along the main road—an inn that did not elude Alter Kacyzne's camera.[24]

The theater was an essential ingredient of Zionism. Followers of Theodor Herzl recognized show nights as the best way to both acculturate the masses and promote parallel actions. Propaganda for the Zionist congresses in Basel. Collections in support of the Jewish National Fund. Advertising for Tarbut, the new cultural organization, founded in Warsaw in 1922, which had given itself the mission of spreading the teaching of the modern Hebrew language to the four corners of Poland. In eastern Galicia, Tarbut

had been so successful that by the turn of the decade, one could hear children speaking Hebrew among themselves on the dirt roads of a shtetl.[25] In Probizhna, Rivka Kleiner, the kindergarten teacher, was among the animators of the local Tarbut. A group portrait, which the Zionists never missed the chance to take, amounted to much more than a souvenir photo.[26] They laid the first stones and served as collective identity cards.

If they managed to escape from the Shoah of Things, those group portraits today underscore the structurally youthful and sexually promiscuous nature of the Zionist experience: not only males and females together but also young people without fathers and mothers.[27] Because only by leaving their parents behind (parents were perceived as outdated, stilted, short-sighted), choosing (so to speak) to become orphans, and abandoning the family and shtetl community could the Zionists transform Herzl's dream—mass emigration to Palestine and the birth of a Jewish state—from giddy fantasy into arduous reality.[28]

GORDONIA

To compensate for the paucity of sources on Moshe's youth, literature comes to the rescue. Literature is fundamental. After all, so many aspects of Moshe Kleiner's upbringing can be found in an Israel Joshua Singer novel, or a Joseph Roth reportage, or a Bruno Schulz short story.[29] The mercantile drabness of the shtetl, the growing misunderstanding between parents and children, the mysterious enzyme released by the Hasidic tradition, the vital energy of the Zionist circle, the unprecedented alliance between brothers and sisters, the latent tension between Yiddish and Hebrew, the experience of apprenticeship in the agricultural colonies, the impatient wait for an emigration permit . . . If young Moshe's voice today is impossible to recover, the voices of those around him—if not the ideas stirring in his mind and the passions in his heart—resound from the shelves of any good bookcase.

The reporter from Warsaw, Alter Kacyzne—whose camera captured two Kopychyntsi rope makers in the 1920s, an idle Jewish handyman, and the stable of an inn converted into a theater—was perhaps the most profound interpreter of the polarity that ruled the existence of Poland's Jews at that time. On the one hand, there was the shtetl pole, represented by Kacyzne in hundreds of photographs sent by him to America to be published in *Forverts* (The Forward), New York's Yiddish newspaper, and thus saved from the Shoah of Things. It was the same pole represented by Kacyzne (with the pen instead of the Leica camera) in savory "provincial sketches" that *The Forward* refused to publish.[30] On the other side was the urban pole, represented by Kacyzne in the novel *The Strong and the Weak*. Because the modest horizon of the shtetl was far from exhausting the existential landscape of the three million Polish Jews. Most of them lived in cities, Warsaw or Łódź, Poznan or Lublin, Vilnius or Lviv.[31] And the young people who did not live there—half of the Polish Jews were under twenty—were eager to go there, only to discover the downside upon arrival.

From the literature, we can gauge the attraction and repulsion that the city exerted on the young people raised in the shtetl. And it was not just Warsaw, with so much variety in people and places that stemmed from it being a hodgepodge of different communities, businessmen and Talmudists, secular and Orthodox, Bundists and Zionists; the Jewish metropolis described by Kacyzne (who in turn had come from outside) was that of a "shadow people," former proofreaders recycled as brokers, talkative trade unionists, tireless tailors, visionary editors, impoverished widows of provincial singers, cynical timber merchants, sickly editors of revolutionary magazines.[32] There was Lviv too. This was the city where Moshe Kleiner wound up at fifteen or sixteen, on an unspecified day in 1929 or 1930. Lviv was the pride of the Jewish Galician intelligentsia, with its prestigious university, the Babel-like mixture of languages in the market square, the Viennese-style cafés on Karola Ludwika Street, the Hasidic oratories, the upper-middle-class neighborhoods, the hillside boulevards. Lviv was a political capital in vogue, a breeding ground for the most diverse Zionist movements. But Lviv as an economic capital was in crisis.

The Jewish traders, traditionally masters of wholesale and retail, struggled to get by, and half of the one hundred thousand Jewish residents lived on public subsidies. It was proof of how not only the Poland of the countryside but also the Poland of the cities, no longer able to rely on the Russian imperial market, was a precarious world on the verge of bankruptcy.[33]

According to family memory, Moshe left Kopychyntsi for Lviv soon after the death of his father. He had waited to become an orphan for real (at least by half) before taking Zionism's road of voluntary orphanhood. Fifteen years later, he would remember how he had taken up residence in Lviv, at the headquarters of Hechaluz, the Jewish organization that trained young people to emigrate to Palestine. "I was living there with the pioneers who were preparing for aliyah," to make the "ascent" to the Promised Land. "It was a long, narrow room, with the beds facing each other. I had taken refuge at the far end of the room, where I had only one neighbor."[34] In Lviv, Moshe attended a carpentry course at the Jewish Organization for Rehabilitation through Training (ORT), specializing in the vocational training of workers.[35] It is not clear whether he finished his studies and got a diploma. Learning a manual trade was certainly an integral part of a Zionist education in Poland at the time. As state trade legislation became increasingly antisemitic, the mastery of a craft would offer young Jews a guarantee for the future—far away in Eretz Israel.[36]

Founded by the Lubianiker brothers in 1923, the Gordonia movement owed its name to the ideologist Aharon David Gordon, who emigrated to Palestine at the turn of the century to practice a kind of Tolstoyan religion of work in the nascent kibbutz community. Compared to other Zionist movements, Gordonia had little that was socialist, much less Marxist. It corresponded to a nationalist political orientation, which interpreted the conquest of work as the conquest of land. For Pinchas Lubianiker—the most theoretical mind of that Kopychyntsi family—the founding principle of the Jewish state to come was not the class struggle but rather occupation of the land—that land for which Lubianiker brother Zvi had already taken up arms during World War I, enlisting in the Jewish Legion of the British Army and fighting with General Allenby's troops to free Palestine from Ottoman rule.[37]

By the time Moshe Kleiner moved into the last bed at the end of the Hechaluz dormitory in Lviv, Pinchas Lubianiker had already left Poland and joined Zvi in British Mandate Palestine. But the Lubianikers could count on a large contingent of activists from Gordonia in Galicia and Poland as a whole.[38] One of these was Moshe. Very likely—if you knew what to look for in the Polish or Israeli archives—you could find traces of his propaganda work, along with that of the other apostles who traveled throughout the cities and countryside of the republic to spread the word about the aliyah, to convince a maximum of boys and girls (if not their parents) that the best solution for the Jews of Poland was to prepare for emigration to Palestine no matter what the ultra-Orthodox Jews said about it on the streets of the shtetl or in the Talmudic school. The Orthodox believed that emigration was a scandal and that it would be the blackest impiety to cut short the biblical term of *exile* and return to the Promised Land before the advent of the Messiah.[39]

We see Moshe back in Kopychyntsi at work with his companions, two or three males and about fifteen females, in a spartan agricultural colony set up by Hechaluz. The girls—they stopped for a moment to smile at the photographer—are handling something I can't quite recognize. Seeds from some kind of plant? Whatever the case, these young Galicians are surely considering sowing the seeds for their future life. Because their friends have already settled in Palestine and written to them over and over that the Promised Land is arid and inhospitable, and mastering the art of working in the fields (something Polish Jews rarely did) is a necessary skill for survival. Nor was it just a question of planting trees, as the prophet Herzl had enjoined them during

his legendary trip to Palestine.⁴⁰ It was a question of redeeming the soil that two thousand years of Christian, Arab, and Ottoman neglect had made little more than a desert. It would be one of the accomplishments of those true pioneers of the kibbutz movement: the heroes of the fight against malaria, the inventors of drip irrigation systems for crops like wheat and barley, the cultivators of sparkling citrus groves by the coast.⁴¹

If he had to go from Kopychyntsi to Lviv for the Hechaluz meetings, Moshe didn't have enough money to pay for either the local train to Ternopil or the Habsburg-built Carl-Ludwig-Bahn, a railway route for the rich.⁴² To get to Lviv, Moshe had to go by cart, traveling a hundred or so kilometers and praying that the scrawny horse would make it. "I'm happy to hate bumpy roads," he would joke many years later. "I made the most of it in my youth, when I was travelling through cities and towns in Galicia on Hechaluz business."⁴³ Moshe was already a tireless worker. At times, his mother would steal up on him and bring him food, worried that he might skip his meal—like some *yiddishe mame* right out of a story. Other times, Zippora had to keep from running after him. In the family album, there is a photo that bears an inscription on the back: "After a meeting in Rivne, 1934."[44] Rivne was no longer in Galicia but in Volhynia—far away, too far for even the most solicitous of Jewish mothers.

ADELA AND INDA

There are no photos of Adela and Inda as children. Not one survived the Shoah of Things. We can only imagine them, apparently fortunate sisters, in the Rivne of the 1930s. Their shtetl was so important that it seemed like a big city, the economic engine of Volhynia. Forty thousand inhabitants or nearly, and more than half of them Jews. In proportion, it was the most Jewish city in Poland.[45] The Liberman parents chose to live in this city of industry and commerce after their university studies in Kyiv, where they had met during World War I. Meir and Feige were pharmacists. Once the girls were born—Adela in 1926, Inda in 1928—the Libermans managed to raise them to the best of their ability, without money problems. The pharmacy was prosperous, and they expanded beyond retail sales to distribute medicine throughout the province. The girls at 5 Spółdzielcza Street grew up in a well-to-do bourgeois household. They went to a private school and took piano and dance lessons from an early age.[46]

Given the lacuna of sources about Adela and Inda's childhood, literature comes to the rescue again. If there is a shtetl that each of us can imagine even without studying its history, it is Rivne. Fania Mussman, Amos Oz's mother, was born and raised there with her sisters before emigrating as a twenty-year-old to Palestine in the mid-1930s. In *A Tale of Love and Darkness*, Oz succeeded in the enterprise of returning a life to his mother's birthplace on the basis of stories he had heard as a child from his own mother before she took her own life. "The cinema in Rivne was owned by a German named Brandt. One of the pharmacists was a Czech by the name of Mahacek. The chief surgeon at the hospital was a Jew called Dr. Segal, whose rivals nicknamed him Mad Segal. A colleague of his at the hospital was the orthopedic surgeon, Dr. Yosef Kopeyka, who was a keen Revisionist Zionist. Moshe Rothenberg and Simcha Hertz Majafit were the town's rabbis. The Jews dealt in timber and cereals, milled flour, worked in textiles and household goods, gold and silver work, hides, printing, clothing, grocery haberdashery, trade, and banking. Some young Jews were driven by their social conscience to join the proletariat as print workers, apprentices, and day laborers. The Pisiuk family had a brewery. The Twischor family were well-known craftsmen. The Strauch family made soap. The Gendelberg family leased forests. The Steinberg family owned a match factory."[47]

Adela and Inda Liberman followed many of Fania Mussman's steps, with over a decade between them. They attended a Jewish school in Rivne. They participated in the activities of the Tarbut. They frequented local Zionist circles from an early age because their mother, Feige, was vice president of the town's Women's International Zionist Organization (WIZO). Before the outbreak of World War II, Adela studied in the same Hebrew gymnasium where Fania had studied. And one day in January 1939, at school, Adela heard a visiting writer from Palestine tell a story that she would never forget. It was a popular legend common to the folkloric cultures all over the world that a Jewish poet originally from Volhynia—the delightful Haim Nahman Bialik—had adapted a few years earlier for the use of Zionism.

It was the story of King David in the cave. The king of Israel was not really dead; he was merely asleep in a secret cave. And he was waiting for someone to wake him so he could return to the world stage and save the Chosen People. One day, two willing young men decided to look for this secret cave. After confronting many dangers, they managed to find it. And when the entrance opened in front of them, they were stunned by the magnificence of what they saw. In a room with gold walls, King David was lying on a bed of gold. Beside his head was his spear and a bottle of water collected in the garden of Eden. A candle burned at his feet. Hanging on the wall was the king's gilded harp, and on a gold table were his crown and scepter set with diamonds. King David extended his arms in the direction of the two young men so they could pour the sacred water of the bottle on his hands and thus awaken him. But the two were so stunned that they didn't react in time, and King David recoiled and shrugged. A terrible storm broke out, which drove the two young men out of the cave and cast them away to an unknown land. As much as they tried and tried again, they could no longer find the cave.[48]

AVRAHAM

Five hundred kilometers north of Rivne, where Poland bordered on Lithuania, Avraham—a little younger than Adela, the same age as Inda—was discovering the charm of Bialik's Hebrew verses as well. They were youthful poems composed in 1891, when the poet from Volhynia was an orphan who hadn't even turned twenty. He was a disciple of a Lithuanian Talmudic school, but he was impatient for life and new horizons. They were the first poems published by the man who would later become the national poet of the new State of Israel. Encouraged by the leaders of his Zionist youth group, Avraham Lipkunski discovered the poem entitled "To the Bird."[49]

> Welcome back to my window, sweet bird,
> Back from the wards of the sun,
> Let me hear the voice my soul longs for
> When you leave my winter home.

What could a bird returning north from that warm and wonderful land of Zion tell a Jewish child from Eastern Europe? What news could he bring to him of the Jewish brothers who had managed to reach the banks of the Jordan, the valleys of Judea, the mountains of Galilee? Had the God of the Book finally shown mercy on the people of Israel? Could the brothers who ascended to Palestine push their plows with joy? Could they pick the dates and almonds with their own hands? And what did the distant brothers know of all the sufferings that still affected the Jews of the Diaspora? The bird that reappeared at the window of the house in the north must have had an interest in migrating again, in leaving for the mountains and the southern desert. "Be happy you left my home. / Winged creature, had you stayed here with me, / you, too, would mourn my fate bitterly."[50]

Like his elder brother Pinchas, Avraham was a student at the yeshiva in Raduń. As a child, he fully participated in the spiritual climate that had made the Jewish towns in Poland, near the borders of Lithuania, the cradle of especially revered rabbinic dynasties and of a particularly self-aware Yiddish culture. The Lipkunskis lived in Dugalishok. It was not even a shtetl and more like a handful of houses along the road between Raduń and Eišiškės. It was renowned for its enchanting pine forest, in which Pinchas and Avraham—trained by their father—knew every tree and clearing. In the summer, the famous Hafetz Haim, the rebbe of the great yeshiva of Raduń, used to vacation in Dugalishok with his circle. The two Lipkunski brothers (their younger brother Yekutiel was still too small) frequented the minor yeshiva. Avraham's people were scrupulously orthodox, especially on their mother's side, the Rakowski family, and had ties to the more learned rabbis of Eišiškės. One of them, Yankl the harpsichordist, was related to Sara Mina Rakowski.[51]

The Lipkunskis had lived there for generations. In the nineteenth century, they were something like the lords of Dugalishok, where they owned many of the small plots. But the new century had not brought them fortune. Some members of the extended family, like so many other Jewish subjects of Russia's tsar, tried their luck overseas. In 1917, Gussie Lipman from Turner Falls, Massachusetts, had been able to send some money to a "Moses Lipkunsky" from "Dugalishok near Radun, Lida district, Vilnius governorate." It was none other than Moshe David Lipkunski, future father of Avraham.[52] A dozen years later—after marrying Sara Mina and giving birth to three children—Moshe David himself had embarked with his brother Yaakov Leib across the ocean—in their case, to Argentina.[53] A photograph has been preserved showing them on the deck of the *Andes* ocean liner in service on the Southampton–Buenos Aires route. The sign hanging from the lifesaver said in Polish, "Third Class Passengers."[54]

A photo of the Lipkunskis who stayed at home has also been saved. The photo was sent not only to Moshe David in Argentina but to his North American relatives as well, thus escaping the Shoah of Things.[55] The two older brothers, Pinchas and Avraham, do not have payot, or sidecurls, which wasn't the custom among Lithuania's Hasidic Jews. But their white buttoned shirts are already that of two little Talmudists. As for Yekutiel's sailor suit, it could reassure his distant father by testifying to their relative economic well-being. Sara Mina's modest clothing suits that of a Jewish mother (Orthodox Jewish, but not to the point of wearing the customary wig). Her long dress, though, has something soberly flirtatious about it. Her long, chaste sleeves are matched by an elegant collar that leaves her neck rather exposed.

In the Raduń photo studio, Sara Mina had good reasons to look into the lens like a woman who is sure of herself. She was far from being a dependent wife waiting for a money order from overseas. Shtetl mothers used to work hard to compensate for the unproductiveness of husbands devoted to the study of the Torah and Talmud.[56] In Sara Mina's case, it could not be said that her husband was a soul lost in the verses of the Bible or the lofty heights of Kabbalah. But Moshe David was gone, and no matter how much money he sent, there was never enough, especially with the two children already out of the house and attending the Raduń yeshiva. So Avraham's mother didn't stop for a moment. From morning to evening—and often at night—she ran the sewing machine, the Singer that she had proudly brought as part of her dowry. Like so many women in the neighborhood, Sara

Mina was a seamstres. Perpetually at work, and perpetually in competition to meet the demand of a clientele whose tastes were increasingly less provincial and more attentive to the latest city fashions.[57] A couple of times a week, she baked breads and sweets that she sold around the district for Shabbat. At times she had to pawn her gold ring or silverware to get by.[58]

Things got better after her husband's return from Argentina in 1935. Moshe David resumed his business as a blacksmith and farrier in Dugalishok, with moderate success. When they returned from the yeshiva for a few days with the family, it was a source of pride for Pinchas and Avraham to see how much respect the Christian peasants had for their father. On occasion they were even offered a ride home in the cart or on the sled.[59] But starting in 1935—after the death of Józef Piłsudski, the strongman of the Republic of Poland—the general situation of Poland's Jews worsened considerably. Several legislative measures were approved by the Sejm with the aim of sabotaging the economic activities of the Jews, to push them toward the path of emigration. As in Germany with the Nuremberg Laws, Poland also gave rise to a paradoxical convergence of interests between the antisemites and the Zionists: both judged that a mass exodus represented the only possible solution to the "Jewish problem." Also, from 1935 onward, Poland saw the rekindling of an endemic fever: the pogrom. Outbreaks of violence against the Jews multiplied in every province of the republic. Civil authorities were indifferent, and the Catholic Church kept silent.[60]

Organized Judaism reacted with little energy.[61] The only exception was the revisionist movement led by Vladimir Ze'ev Jabotinsky, the controversial Zionist leader, whose prized military experience was matched by a sinister admiration for Mussolini's Italy. Jabotinsky devised an "evacuation plan" that included the mass emigration of some 1.5 million Jews to Palestine: Polish Jews, but also Romanian, Hungarian, Austrian, Baltic, and German Jews—any European Jew who had reason to feel threatened by a general wave of antisemitism. Meanwhile, the ranks of Betar, the paramilitary youth organization that Jabotinsky had founded as early as 1923, grew visibly. The militants belonged to a younger generation than their leader, and for years they had paraded through the cities of Poland in black fascist-style shirts. Jabotinsky's recruits were more explicit than he was and quicker to recognize political violence as a constituent ingredient of the Zionist struggle.[62]

Too young to take up arms, Avraham Lipkunski was affiliated with the section of Betar that indoctrinated children. Wearing miniature uniforms and shooting toy guns, the Raduń yeshiva boy discovered Bialik's poem "To the Bird," which he quickly learned by heart.[63]

DOV AND ADAM

Before taking part in Betar proper, Shaya and Yosef—Dov and Adam Wexler's elder brothers—belonged to the juvenile section. What remains today is a portrait of them, taken by a traveling photographer, passing through Janowo around 1932. It shows the two younger brothers between Mindel, their mother, and Yosef, proud in his paramilitary uniform. Dov is wearing the white button-up shirt of a budding Talmudist, and Adam hasn't yet reached the age of three, when he can be admitted to the Jewish kindergarten.

Like Dugalishok, the village of Janowo was less than a shtetl. In the past, the local Jewish community had been quite large, but it had gradually thinned to a few dozen units. The rest were goyim, Gentiles—especially poor peasants. On the border between the provinces of Masuria and Masovia in northern Poland, Janowo's relatively stingy soil didn't offer much produce for its inhabitants, yet it was a village of some importance compared to the tiny surrounding villages. There was a police station and a firehouse in Janowo. There was a post office with a telephone. There was a public office that functioned as a registry, two bakeries, and the grocery store run by a Jewish family. The hospital, in contrast, was in Mława, thirty kilometers south toward Warsaw. Almost everyone went there by cart. The wealthiest took the coach run by Laypshe, Mindel Wexler's distant cousin. Laypshe was the only Jew from Janowo who wore glasses, Adam recalls. And on holidays, he had been the one who most often officiated at the ceremonies in the synagogue.[64]

But the synagogue was gone; it had burned down during World War I. There was, however, a Beit Midrash, a study house. It was

visible just behind the last few farms. It was nothing comparable to the Catholic church, of course, which dominated the Janowo countryside, with its red bricks and big black cross atop the bell tower. But still, it was better than nothing. Upon returning from captivity in Germany, Henoch Wexler had been in charge of preparing the study house. Shaya was about ten, Yosef was five or six, Dov and Adam were still to come. Henoch had been raised in a Hasidic family and couldn't stand the lack of a place of worship. The study house was divided into two parts. One part was reserved for prayer, and the other (when the water pipes worked) was used as a sauna, perhaps even a mikvah, a ritual bath.

Until the outbreak of World War I, Janowo had found herself in the extreme west of Tsarist Russia, on the border with the Prussian Empire. During the war, Henoch—like hundreds of thousands of the tsar's soldiers—had been taken prisoner by the Germans. He had been captured near Janowo and interned in an East Prussian camp. When the Germans discovered that he spoke Yiddish fluently, they used him as an interpreter to communicate with other Russian prisoners of Jewish origin. Perhaps also for this reason, upon returning from Germany after the end of the war, Henoch had brought with him a reputation as a Bolshevik.[65] He was a bit like Benjamin Lerner in I. J. Singer's novel *Steel and Iron*: not exactly a communist, but someone whose experience in the Babel of German imperial prisoner of war camps for Russians had opened his eyes to the opportunity to accomplish something in that world turned upside down—and not, as Orthodox Jews had been inclined, to simply suffer and pray and sing.[66]

Like almost all the inhabitants of Janowo, Henoch and Mindel Wexler had a wooden house. It was spacious, but part of it was sold to Christian peasants due to money problems. Mindel was a seamstress by trade. She was primarily the one to keep the household running—yet another example of the economic centrality of mothers in Hasidic families. Because if ever Henoch had ever been touched by the sacred fire of industry in Germany, that fever soon passed after the end of the war. He limited himself to traveling to a nearby village from time to time, where he pocketed a few handfuls of zlotys by serving as a shochet, a ritual slaughterer—though without the formal investiture of a rabbi. Otherwise, Henoch would stay in Janowo, in the study house. He pored over the Talmud. He read the newspapers. He played chess and passed his passion for it on to his two younger children. Much later, Adam would remember games played as a very young child. "I would play against my brother Dov. Usually, I lost—and I cried."[67]

Dov and Adam's first school had been old-fashioned, harsh, and severe, conducted by the village melamed. To imagine Adam as a schoolboy, the photographs sent by Alter Kacyzne to *The Forward* in New York are useful. "Son of the Shochet reading a book" is the caption on one of those photos. A young boy sits on a wooden bench, wrapped in his child's tallith, opening two tired and questioning eyes toward the Warsaw reporter, while his elbow rests on a book larger than himself.[68] That book is the alpha and omega of the Jewish school for children: the millennial effort of pronouncing and spelling out its words when one has hardly learned to speak; the millennial promise of redemption for the children of Israel by means of mastering the alphabet. After school, Dov and Adam did what they could to play with their Christian peers, to be accepted by them. To catch crayfish with the Malkowskis on the banks of the Orzyc, they even got over their squeamishness about handling the slimy little frogs they used as bait. But sooner or later, the time came when one of the friends reminded the two brothers that they were still just Jews, so they should get out of people's way and go to their Palestine.[69]

More trouble came to the Wexler family as a result of the laws on ritual slaughter enacted in 1936. Officially, regulations were intended to spare the animals unnecessary suffering and to ensure compliance with minimum standards of hygiene. In fact, the regulations were imbued with the antisemitism spreading more broadly throughout Polish society.[70] The example came directly from Hitler's Germany: in 1933, the approval of restrictive measures on ritual slaughter was one of the Nazis' first acts when they took power.[71] In smaller Jewish communities, such as those of Janowo and surrounding villages, ritual slaughter was banned altogether, forcing precarious workers like Henoch Wexler to choose between unemployment or breaking the law. Dov and Adam's father opted for the latter. With the complicity of some Christian farmers and butchers, he supplied kosher meat to the fellow believers in the surrounding area, under the counter. Once discovered, he spent a few weeks locked up in the Janowo police station jail. It wasn't so bad, and he was even able to make friends with a jailer, who at the end of his sentence visited the Wexler house one Shabbat. "He stared in amazement at the candles, the white tablecloth, the ritual challah bread, clearly wondering how it was possible to be Jewish."[72]

The Yiddish newspaper that Henoch received three times a week by post from Warsaw contained increasingly alarming news. The Gdansk corridor was a few dozen kilometers away, East Prussia a few dozen meters. It got to the point where the Hitlerjugend brown shirts came out to parade in front of the Janowo customs. One day Dov, by now at the Polish school, was punished by his teacher, Miss Jarzembowska, for misbehaving. He had to kneel in a corner of the classroom, just like his classmates did when punished. Dov refused, and the teacher sent him to the principal. A question arose, and even Białek, the priest, got involved. But rather than kneel like a Christian in church, Dov preferred to drop out of school. Another day, on the first trip of his life, Adam experienced worse. They had gone as far as Łódź, with their mother and Shaya, for an uncle's wedding. On the way back from Mława, they had already boarded Laypshe's coach when they were attacked by a gang of boys with stones and sticks. Fortunately, Mariusz, a Christian grocer they called "Half-portion," helped them. Weighing in at just under a hundred pounds, he managed to chase away the antisemitic thugs.[73]

Then Shaya was old enough to be called up for the draft. The Wexlers' firstborn did nothing to evade it. The Betar instructors never tired of repeating that any military experience could prove useful, in the future, to the needs of the Revisionist Zionists. "The whole house echoed with the name of Jabotinsky, whose every utterance was taken as the word of a God."[74] Or at least that was how Shaya and Yosef took it. They were more and more at odds with their father, Henoch, who was grooming them for projects other than Zionism, with its evacuation plan and aliyah in Palestine. Yosef, for example, with the voice he had, would have made an ideal liturgical cantor. But he wasn't the least bit interested. At first, Yosef had stubbornly worked as an apprentice in the carpentry shop of Rakowski, a Christian. Then he left home and Janowo. He moved to Łódź with his uncle David, a salesman. There too he maintained ties with Betar.

Dov and Adam were both full of admiration for their two older brothers. Shaya was impressive when he returned on leave wearing a real Polish army uniform. And Yosef was said to be making great strides in the big city as a Betar militant. They'd even heard that on the occasion of a visit by Jabotinsky to Poland, and of his passage through Łódź, Yosef had been chosen to serve as bodyguard.[75]

SUTI

In Eastern Europe, there was only one country where Jabotinsky's name was not on the lips of all the Jews, like the hero of a fable—or its villain. This country was Hungary.[76] In general, Hungary was the only country in Eastern Europe where Zionist propaganda did not find fertile ground—and this as early as the time of Herzl, who happened to be born in Pest. A bit like German Jews (and those in Italy), Hungarian Jews felt fully integrated into the society where they lived. They shared its culture, including Magyar patriotism. Or at least they had shared it until the dissolution of the Austro-Hungarian Empire and the cataclysm that followed. Then came the drama of the Béla Kun's communist revolution and the subsequent anti-communist reaction. Hungarian Jews became the target of both sides in the struggle. For the revolutionaries, the Jews were capitalists. For the reactionaries, they were Bolsheviks.[77]

The town of Nagyszőlős in Ruthenia had been Hungarian for centuries. Today it is called Vynohradiv, in Ukraine, or Transcarpathia if one prefers, on the Danube side of the Carpathians. Between the two world wars, it was a Czechoslovakian town called Sevlus. There were fifteen thousand inhabitants, one-third of whom were Jews; the other two-thirds were a mix of Magyars, Ruthenians, Slovaks, Ukrainians, Romanians, Germans, Bulgarians, and Roma—an exemplary concentration of Mitteleuropean diversity. Many Jews in Nagyszőlős knew Yiddish but preferred to speak Hungarian, even at home. They had experienced the Treaty of Trianon, which in 1920 had amputated the historical borders of Hungary and assigned Ruthenia to the newborn Czechoslovakia, as an injustice. The young Jewish fathers were veterans from the trenches of World War I, in which they fought under the banner of the double-headed eagle. The popular songs of their childhood, those to be taught to children on winter evenings, were Magyar songs. The newspapers they read were in Hungarian and still arrived by train from Budapest. Also, the Perényi, the local barons around whose fiefdom the Nagyszőlős's economy had always revolved, were 100 percent Magyar.[78]

The Weisz family lived next to the distillery. Only the park separated them from the baroque castle of the Perényi, on the slopes of the Black Mountain, right where the Carpathians flattened out among the vineyards and where the boundless plain opened up. Sándor's parents had been there since 1924, since Vilmos was hired as administrator of the estate and director of the distillery. In Nagyszőlős, everything belonged to the Perényi. The potatoes that the Ruthenian peasants gathered in summer in fields as far as the eye could see belonged to the Perényi, along with the melons, grapes, cherries, and strawberries. The tobacco works belonged to the Perényi, as did the herbs processed in the distillery during the winter, which of course contributed to the Weisz family's local reputation. Vilmos, Terez, and their five sons shone with reflected light: their proximity to the barons made them, so to speak, the noble Jews of the city. Sándor, known as Suti, was the fourth of the five siblings. Before him there were Bandi, the eldest son, and his two older sisters, Aliz and Hedi. After him came Icuka, the little girl of the family.[79]

Apart from the hassle of having to attend Czechoslovakian school while feeling Hungarian, the Weisz children had everything they could want in life. Occasionally they might hear some mean-spirited jokes about Jews and Palestine in the playgrounds or at recess. Beyond that, they could hardly have dreamed, in the Eastern Europe of the 1930s, of a more carefree and happier Jewish childhood. Summer swims in the Tisza, a river right out of a postcard. Mushroom picking and gorging on raspberries. Winter sled races on the slopes of the Black Mountain. The autumn or spring back and forth along Weborczy Street, the main thoroughfare. Sunday cinema. The popular songs sung by Vilmos accompanying himself on the violin. Piano lessons for Hedi, at the convent for nuns. Suti's stamp collection, which all his companions envied. The costumes of Purim (together with Hanukkah, the only holiday the family celebrated). Hebrew learned almost for fun, privately, while taking private math lessons. And that smattering of Zionism that would come to the boys from Aliz's boyfriend, a Betar militant.

Everything looks so remarkably in its place in the Weisz family portrait. The way parents and children gaze into the photographer's lens is so reassuring, so full of bourgeois self-awareness. Everything seems to correspond exactly to the words that Suti will pronounce as an old man: "I had a wonderful childhood."[80]

CHILDREN RUNNING

The first to leave was Rivka, in 1932 or maybe 1933. Once again I have to settle for fragments of information, shreds of family memory.[81] I don't even know for sure how Rivka got from Galicia to Palestine. Probably it was by way of the typical itinerary of those who made the aliyah from Poland: reaching the Black Sea through Romania, passing through Chernivtsi, Iași, Galata. I assume she wasn't alone and went with a group of other Zionists. In theory, they were mere visitors to the Promised Land, with tourist visas to circumvent the immigration quotas applied by the British administration of Palestine.[82] Did the kindergarten teacher Rivka Kleiner travel to the Black Sea by train, like the rich emigrants, or in horse-drawn wagons, as the poor did? Either way, everyone boarded in Constanța. She passed through the Straits, the Bosporus, and the Aegean. She then sailed across the open sea to the sacred shores of Eretz Israel.

A few years earlier, Shmuel Yosef Agnon—the future Nobel laureate, born a day's donkey ride from Kopychyntsi—wrote in his book *In the Heart of the Seas* about a trip similar to the one Rivka may have made. He described its physical stages but above all its symbolic significance. Biblical strength, but also biblical torment. Biblical strength because "suppose a man wants to go up to the land of Israel and does not go up, what if his soul should suddenly depart from his body and he be left lying like a dumb stone." But also biblical torment: "All the town went out to speed them on their journey, except the rabbi. For the rabbi used to say, Those who proceed to the land of Israel before the coming of the Messiah remind me of the boys who run ahead of the bridegroom and bride on the way to the bridal canopy." Agnon also described the implacable distrust that the Diaspora Jew, after two thousand years on the land, still felt for the sea. The fear of drowning. The terror of dying without a burial.[83]

In Palestine, Rivka initially lived in Tel Aviv, at the Lubianikers' home.[84] They were drawn together by solidarity between fellow villagers, the common memory of the shtetl, the amateur theater, and Gordonia. To think that Pinchas Lubianiker had come a long way since the time of Kopychyntsi. Three or four years after landing in Eretz Israel, he had already risen to the top of Mapai, the new political party dominant in the Jewish community of Palestine, led by David Ben-Gurion. Lubianiker had also climbed to the top of the Histadrut, the Zionist confederation of labor, of which Ben-Gurion himself was general secretary.[85] Much more than a mere trade union, the Histadrut was an imposingly monopolistic social service and patronage organ, the infrastructural key for the Jewish national project.[86] Lubianiker had worked to further Gordonia's Palestinian roots by committing himself to the kibbutz movement. He had been one of the founders (or refounders) of Kibbutz Hulda, in the central plain, along the Jaffa-Jerusalem railway line. And he had managed to place a contingent of Gordonia's followers in the legendary Kibbutz Degania near the Sea of Galilee.[87]

Kibbutz Ayelet Hashachar, where Rivka was hired as a teacher a few months after landing in Palestine, was also located in Galilee. Technically, she was an external hire, not an internal member of the kibbutz. This allowed her to get a slightly better salary—a few more Palestinian pounds to send to Poland via money order at the post office. It would help her mother, Zippora, still on the shtetl.[88] So Rivka started her second life doing the same job as she had done before, a kindergarten teacher, but with renewed motivation. There was the added incentive that came from the awareness of how important a kindergarten teacher could be in the construction of the new state. First of all, she taught Hebrew to children whose mother tongue was Polish or Yiddish, German or Russian. Moreover, she transmitted to those children an initial, categorically Zionist, idea of the history of the Middle East and Palestine.[89]

"If there is a country, a corner of the world, where a child has the chance to be honestly entrusted with our dreams and fears, our secret desires and our lacerations, this country could well be Palestine. Where a monument to the unknown orphan should be erected. So when you see a child running there in a field, under a real sky, try to imagine him living in a house in Lviv or Warsaw. That child whose hand you just shook might live in Pawia Street 17, apartment 58, or at 30 Franciszkańska Street, apartment 90. He might be one of fifty schoolchildren locked up in a smelly classroom on Grzybowska Street. Yes, I have not given up the hope of being able to spend my last years in Palestine, and of feeling nostalgic for Poland from there." Rivka had no way of knowing these words, which Janusz Korczak—the pediatrician who founded the Warsaw Orphan's House, the pedagogue whom all enlightened teachers in Poland venerated as a prophet, the storyteller who for thirty years had fascinated all Polish children, whether Jewish or Christian—had recently addressed to another educator, a young disciple of his who had emigrated to Palestine.[90] However, it is reasonable to assume that in the summer of 1934, Rivka heard the news from Kibbutz Ein Harod, seventy kilometers south of Kibbutz Ayelet Hashachar, that Janusz Korczak was coming to the land of Israel for the first time.

It must have meant something if, at the age of fifty-six, the legendary "Pan Doktor," who had never been a Zionist in public—far from it—had decided to visit the Jewish settlement of Palestine. The three-week visit, between July and August,[91] took place while the children of the orphanage were outside Warsaw at summer camp, when there was no need to keep up with them twenty-four hours a day, combining firmness with discretion in that republic of children that the Orphan's House in Krochmalna

Street had been trying to be for over twenty years, with its nascent self-governing organs, its job rotation criteria, and its model of peer education.[92] It must have meant something if Korczak found his way to Eretz Israel after having insisted so much on taking a very different path in Warsaw: the road of a humanism that was too integrally secular, too close to the Enlightenment to allow for a Jewish humanism. Obviously, it must have meant that even the Pan Doktor had resigned himself. They needed to leave. Poland was no longer a country for Jews.

NEW LIFE

In Moshe's case too, the exact date of his departure from Poland and ascent to Palestine is not known. It was roughly in 1935. In any event, it was winter, when the shtetl was snow white. I know this because there is a letter from him from a few years later in which the farewell from Kopychyntsi is mentioned in detail, in particular Moshe's farewell to his mother, Zippora. "I see her as I found her when I came back to say hello, before making the aliyah. The walls of the cottage shone like diamonds and precious stones from the snow and ice that covered them. I didn't feel pain, but anger. Anger at myself, at Rabbi Shaya, at the whole world, at the injustice of everything... And I didn't want to leave, but I couldn't help it. In fact, if I had stayed, I would have been an extra burden to her. She was always so worried about us, she took the bread out of her mouth to feed us. And yet, despite everything, I knew that if I stayed a little longer I would make her happy. She was so proud of me. I remember how she sat in the front row on the last night at my farewell concert. A concert that I had prepared especially for her."[93]

Who knows what Moshe sang that last night? I imagine the Hasidic melodies he had learned as a child from his father and the other cantors in the synagogue. The same melodies that, sung with his beautiful voice, had earned him the prophecy of the rebbe of Chortkiv: maybe one day, you will sing with the Levites in the Temple of Jerusalem. Moshe certainly packed his bags during a spike in the migration curve of Polish Jews to Palestine. There were seventeen thousand departures from 1930 to 1933, and fifty thousand departures from 1934 to 1937.[94] With an ongoing general economic crisis in Poland, the tendency of public opinion was to blame the Jews, and with an explicitly antisemitic climate reigning in the Sejm,[95] Moshe Kleiner was among those who concluded that enough was enough. Even though they were angry with themselves, with the rabbi, and with the whole world, all true Zionists had to make a clean break. There was really nothing left to do but set off into the heart of the seas, to the Promised Land.

Who knows whether Rivka went to pick him up at the port of Jaffa? It may have been like in a novel, where the big sister, who had the courage to leave first, goes to meet her little brother, and they don't even look like brother and sister anymore. Rivka is tanned, dressed lightly, and emboldened in her ways; her brother is pale, overdressed, and almost tentative. Meanwhile, the Arab porters—the first Arabs of his life—grab for the luggage, shout in their language, and haggle on the dock in that strange, unfamiliar heat, with the sharp light of Palestine cutting like nothing he'd ever seen. All of it is too much. It's more likely that Rivka stayed at Ayelet Hashachar, the kibbutz in northern Galilee, and that his Zionist comrades from Gordonia came to meet Moshe. They probably met not only Moshe but also a group of pioneers. Certainly, Moshe arrived together with his wife, Chava.

A wife? The family memory has handed down the fact that Moshe had signed a fictitious marriage on the eve of his departure from Poland, so as to allow a second person to benefit from the legal privilege his immigration certificate afforded. And here, once more we are in the realm of literature. Isaac Bashevis Singer would dedicate a whole novel, *The Certificate*, to the turmoil of a young Pole who has the chance to go to Palestine with

a wife of convenience and can't decide between three women: a humble worker, a decadent bourgeois lady, or an uninhibited communist.[96] Moshe's case was more pragmatic: he had married a colleague in Gordonia. Chava Schuminer came from the Sambir shtetl and was in fact the companion of another Zionist militant.[97]

On the eve of his departure, Moshe had also decided to change his name. Many did it at the time of the aliyah. A new life, a new name. Moshe chose to be called Ben-David: "son of David."[98] But shortly after arriving in Palestine (the exact date remained unspecified), Moshe changed it again, as evidenced by his identity card, issued by the British authorities in Tel Aviv, which finally guarantees a documentary foothold. It is the first archival trace of Moshe that is more than a mere photo.[99]

Moshe is no longer Kleiner, nor is he Ben-David. He is Moshe Ze'iry. (Soon, in the papers of the British administration, he will be Moshe Zeiri.) After all, there is no Pindaric flight in the choice of this new identity: in Hebrew, the adjective *zair* means small, like *klein* in German. If anything, it's his passport photo that appears to intimate a flight—Moshe's look seems to me singularly intense, magnetic, enthralling. I'm also struck by the forehead of this boy in his early twenties. I find it surprisingly marked, as if by a premature excess of thoughts and efforts. However, the identity cards of the British Mandate government did not provide any space to record the holder's date of birth, as if to suggest that even in the eyes of the London bureaucrats, arriving in Palestine was equivalent to being reborn. As for the date of the document's issue, it is only partially legible. The indication of the day and month, December 11, does not dispel the doubt about the year.

Moshe Zeiri stands five feet six inches tall. His eyes are hazel, his hair (which the passport photo shows is long, bohemian) is "chestnut." His build is average. As for "race," he is a Jew. By profession, he is a "labourer." He therefore corresponds to the prototype of the Zionist who, before emigrating from Europe, learned a trade for the future, because being reborn in Palestine almost by definition involves knowing how to wield a spade or pickaxe, to redeem the sacred soil. Moshe Zeiri's workplace coincides with his place of residence, Kvutzat-Shiller. A kvutza, strictly speaking, is a community of workers gathered in an agricultural cooperative. In practice it is a real kibbutz, but a small one. Moshe's kibbutz is located "near Rehovot" on the coastal plain south of Tel Aviv.

There, benefiting from both the proximity of the port of Jaffa and a particularly favorable microclimate, newly arrived settlers are miraculously cultivating citrus groves. German immigrants skilled in agronomy, Polish Jews with a talent for business, and a workforce of indigenous Arabs: this special blend of skills and experience will transform Jaffa oranges into a prized brand known throughout the world.[100]

TWO

YEHUDIT

HANUKKAH 1933

Trude and Rachel are acting in a home show, the kind the Meyers would put on to celebrate holidays. "Chinese dance," the writing on the back of the photo specifies. Disguised as a boy, Rachel woos Trude, who smiles back coyly.[1] There's a date. And it's not just any date, considering they are German Jews: "Chanuka 1933," the Festival of Lights, amid the darkness of Nazi Germany. When did the eight days of Hanukkah fall in the year 1933? From December 12 to 20.

On the eve of the Third Reich's first Christmas, cousins Trude Meyer and Rachel Berkowitz were both thirteen years old. They had reached the Jewish age of maturity that year during those disastrous months: the economic bankruptcy of the Weimar Republic, the peak of mass unemployment, the legislative elections called one after the other, the agitated count of National Socialist votes. But after President von Hindenburg surrendered to the little Austrian corporal, it got even worse. The April 1 *Judenboykott*, the state's sabotage of Jewish trade, set the tone. After that, at all institutional levels, from the central government of the Reich to the last of the provincial associations, a shower of antisemitic measures fell over half a million German Jews. In general, prohibition of access to civil service positions, restrictions on professional activities, limited numbers in schools and universities. In particular, hundreds of other bans, exclusions, and expulsions. In Cologne—the Meyer family's city, as well as home to Germany's oldest Jewish community—an example was set by closing the municipal sports facilities to Jews in March. Shortly thereafter, the Jews of Cologne were erased from the roles of the municipal administration. Between spring and summer, authorities throughout the land competed to solve the various other problems posed by Judaism. In Berlin, Jews were banned from visiting the beaches of Lake Wannsee. In Baden, the use of Yiddish at livestock markets was prohibited.[2]

Trude's father is a meat wholesaler, but he does not speak Yiddish in business negotiations. His language is German, both at work and in the family. Like most of Cologne's Jews, Heinrich Meyer belongs to an assimilated middle class. In the suburb of Ehrenfeld, where the Meyers have lived since before the war, the synagogue was recently enlarged to make room for Polish Jews who immigrated steadily to the neighborhood.[3] But although the synagogue is located on Körnerstrasse, a ten-minute walk from 31 Nussbaumerstrasse, Heinrich rarely goes there. When he does, it is usually to please his wife, Wilhelmina (the Löwendahls had grown up in a more traditional environment).[4] There is not even the shadow of a kosher diet in the Meyer household, nor a religious upbringing. If Trude and Rachel celebrate Hanukkah by acting and dancing, it is because the Meyers enjoy the festivities. And Hanukkah is a festival, isn't it? Even though, just outside the front door, the world is collapsing around Germany's Jews.

Who could have predicted this twenty years ago? In the summer of 1914—the same year that Jacques, Trude's elder brother, was born—Cologne's Jewish community was among the first in

Germany to declare their readiness to sacrifice for the "beloved homeland." They declared it, and they proved it. Offices were offered to accommodate refugees. Gyms of the Jewish Gymnastics Association were converted into military depots. There was patriotic mobilization not only of the Jews called to arms as conscripts or reservists but also of the intelligentsia, the rabbinate, and even the Zionists.[5] Born in 1880, Heinrich Meyer had served as a reservist on the Western Front: Landsturm Infanterie, Ersatz Bataillon Elsenborn. A photo from 1915 has been preserved in the family, which shows him smiling together with about twenty fellow soldiers, bowl in hand, queuing for his rations.[6] His driver's license, issued on April 3, 1915, has also been preserved. In the passport photo, Heinrich is wearing a bourgeois suit and looks like anything but a meat wholesaler. He has a sensitive, thoughtful expression, a cross between Thomas Mann and Stefan Zweig.[7]

Heinrich was then seriously injured on the Western Front, losing his sight in one eye. Others had fared worse. By the end of the hostilities, the number of German Jews who had fallen in World War I had reached twelve thousand, out of a total of one hundred thousand German Jews mobilized.[8] One of them, Benno Löwendahl—born in Cologne in 1890, with a law degree from the University of Bonn and a doctorate in law from the University of Greifswald[9]—was Wilhelmina's younger brother, Heinrich's brother-in-law. He had fallen on the field of honor on September 27, 1916.[10]

THEIR FAULT

It is likely that Trude Meyer is at the Jewish cemetery in Cologne on Sunday July 8, 1934, along with her parents, to commemorate Uncle Benno, whom she has never met. The cemetery is not far from their house on Nussbaumerstrasse, and there are many Jews in the city on the Rhine who have responded to the memorial. The men wear black, and the women are dressed in light colors. The funeral monument is an initiative of the Reichsbund judischer Frontsoldaten (RjF), the association for Jewish frontline veterans. "To our fallen," the inscription on the stone pyramid reads soberly. Beside it, inscribed on another stone, are the names and surnames of the hundreds of local heroes, including Benno Löwendahl.[11] The RjF is also preparing the publication of a book with a selection of the last letters of fallen Jews.[12] "We believe that this volume is particularly suitable as a gift for Rosh Hashanah, or for a bar-mitzvah, or for Hanukkah," the leaders of the RjF will explain in the bulletin of September 10, 1935, after its publication—five days before the Nuremberg Laws.[13]

By the time Trude has turned fifteen, very little remains of her former life: her comfortable and serene childhood in the 1920s, which the family album brings back through photos of trips to the sea, cousins all dressed up, picnics in the forest.[14] Heinrich

Meyer's wholesale trade did not take long to feel the effects of the antisemitic legislation, even though Jacques and Trude's father had managed to register it to a front man.[15] And the antisemitic school legislation overwhelmed Trude's daily life, even though there were dispensations for the children of veterans. Not yet expelled by law from public schools in the Reich, Jewish schoolchildren were discriminated against in practice: no more essays on German history, no films, no swimming lessons, no overnight stays with classmates on school trips.[16]

A competitive swimmer, Trude suffered from being banned from public swimming pools.[17] Thus the dream that Max Nordau—the Hungarian doctor, Theodor Herzl's right-hand man—had formulated of a "muscular Judaism" vanished around her. As did the dream of a "regeneration" of the Jews by means of the body before the mind, which would usher them into modernity as men (and women) more physical and athletic than cerebral and reflective.[18] Several other dreams also vanished around Trude. After the age of compulsory schooling, the daughter of Heinrich and Wilhelmina Meyer had to reduce her study ambitions. Not only did she have to put aside any concrete prospects of going on to university, but she also had to give up her more reasonably modest ambition of going to high school. Both the antisemitic legislation of the Nazis and the reaction of the Jews to that legislation pushed girls like Trude into vocational schools.

But the choice of what to study tore Jewish middle-class families apart, particularly with regard to their daughters. The parents advocated training in textiles as seamstresses, embroiderers, and upholsterers—professions that would be needed in the Germany of the Third Reich. The daughters preferred to see themselves as company secretaries, or as kindergarten teachers, to be out in the world, not locked within four walls with a needle in hand and foot on the pedal of a sewing machine. In practice, a growing percentage of girls dropped out of school. The Jewish welfare organizations considered it a priority to commit themselves to the future of the boys. As in Poland, the ORT in Germany worked above all on the professional training of shoemakers, designers, painters, carpenters, mechanics, and dyers. Deep down, there was still hope that a solution for girls would pop up, perhaps as marriage prospects, like in the old days. More or less absurdly, German Jews counted on the fact that even in the thousand-year Reich, there would be marriageable Jewish girls.[19]

According to the family memory, when she turned fourteen, Trude wanted to go to school to become a kindergarten teacher. Her parents, however, chose a vocational institute for her. (In the meantime, Jacques had left home to become a musician and would soon go to Latin America via Spain.) Trude then began attending Jewish youth associations. There, she got a glimpse beyond the embroidery courses and sewing workshops. She played sports—swimming and gymnastics—at the pools and gyms in Cologne reserved for Jews. She could share her adolescence, so much more difficult than her childhood, with girls and boys who were peers in their pariah status. To help her on this path was her cousin Hans Berkowitz, Rachel's elder brother. He was the one, with his twenty-year-old authority, who opened her eyes to the need young German Jews had to free themselves from their parents. It was he who spoke to her about the Maccabi movement, a bridge launched between the Jewish children of the East and those of the West. It was Hans who started his cousin on the road to Zionism.[20]

Even in Trude's case, the photo album is the only document from her first life preserved in the second. But also here, to remedy the silence of the sources, literature comes to the rescue: specifically, Lion Feuchtwanger's novel *The Oppermanns*, published in Amsterdam in 1933.[21] To get a sense of Hans and Trude's conversations in 1935 Cologne, you have to read the dialogue between the two Berlin cousins, Ruth and Berthold, imagined by

Feuchtwanger. You have to witness the settling of scores that made certain young Jews in Third Reich Germany the voluntary orphans of their parents. "Our fathers have had their day. They don't concern us, they have no right over us. Whose fault is it all? Theirs. They're the ones who went to war. They couldn't do better. They've chosen the most convenient homeland instead of the true homeland. My father is a very good person; yours is relatively first-rate too. But we must not allow ourselves to be misled by personal sympathies. To hell with the whole lot. We must go to Palestine. That's our place."[22]

NATURAL DIGNITY

In the Jewish settlement of Palestine, Hitler's seizure of power was immediately seen as a deadly threat to the Jews of Europe. The Führer had been chancellor in Berlin for less than twenty-four hours when *Davar*—the Histadrut's newspaper—called January 30, 1933, a bitter and fateful day, the advent of the "new Vandal" who would "uproot Judaism." A month and a half later, a *Davar* headline read, "For German Jews It's Time for the Shoah." In August, again in the Histadrut newspaper, the Russian-born rabbi and historian Ben-Zion Dinur, trained in prewar Berlin, was wary of considering Hitlerism a local and superficial phenomenon. He felt it was a profound current in European history, an antisemitic upheaval that had been going on for decades and could threaten the survival of the Jewish people.[23]

In contrast, the very gravity of the danger seemed an extraordinary opportunity to more than one observer, almost a godsend that might allow Jews to fulfill their fate of creating a Jewish settlement. Because there were degrees of aliyah. It was one thing to flood Palestine with derelict hosts of *Ostjuden*, Jews from Poland, Ukraine, the Baltics, and Russia, who brought nothing more than their pioneering enthusiasm and hoeing muscle to the Promised Land. Another thing was to fill Palestine with selected ranks of German Jews, *Westjuden*, who would bring scientific knowledge, technical skills, and boatloads of money to the Promised Land. Upon returning from a trip to Hitler's Germany, a *Davar* editor wrote to Berl Katznelson, founder and editor-in-chief of the Histadrut's newspaper, "The streets over there are paved with more money than we could ever dream of in the whole history of Zionism. We are facing an opportunity to build and prosper, as we have never had, and will never have again."[24]

Many German Jews were already leaving Germany (sixty thousand departures between 1933 and 1934), but only a small part chose Palestine as the place to rebuild their lives.[25] Hence the importance of the negotiations initiated by the German Zionists with the German government just after Hitler came to power and successfully concluded in the summer of 1933: the agreement on the transfer of a certain number of Jewish assets from Germany to Palestine, in the face of the emigrants' renunciation of all their other goods.[26] It was equally important to convince the German Jews that emigration to Palestine represented a credible—immediate and concrete—solution to the "Jewish problem" raised by Nazism. In particular, a solution for young people: boys and girls who grew up in Berlin, Hamburg, Cologne, or Munich could be embraced as adopted children in the Jewish settlements throughout the coastal plain, on the banks of the Jordan, in the valleys of Judea, or in the hills of Galilee. They would be welcomed all together, educated at school, and raised in a community.[27]

It was also necessary to not frighten the German Jews. They had to be convinced that in Palestine, it wouldn't all be agricultural commune, kibbutz, and socialism. For that generation of children, a future had to be envisioned that was relatively similar to what they would have had in Germany if Hitler and the Nazis had not decided to steal it from them. They had to be able to study mathematics, physics, chemistry, and biology, and then engineering, medicine, and veterinary medicine. There had to be music conservatories and physical education. All this was promised in the pages of *Jüdische Rundschau*, the German Zionist Federation's weekly publication, which Trude Meyer may have asked her parents to buy from time to time in Cologne at some point in 1934 or 1935. Trude certainly read it with her friends in the Jugend-Alijah, the Zionist youth association. They enjoyed the translations of Sholem Aleichem's stories from the Yiddish and pored over the Hebrew letters and drawings in the language textbooks. They daydreamed over the Lloyd Triestino ads, "Trieste-Haifa, the quickest and most comfortable way to Palestine": ships as they should be, traveling safely and cheaply.[28]

The Jugend-Alijah was founded—on the day of Hitler's appointment as chancellor—by Recha Freier, the charismatic and energetic wife of a Berlin rabbi. In the eyes of this visionary teacher, there was not a single minute to waste. A generation of Jews (Recha herself had three children), whom the Third Reich was depriving of any prospect for the future, had to be concretely prepared for the aliyah. It was a difficult wager, and not just because the British government of Palestine granted a limited number of immigration certificates. The gamble was further complicated by the social, cultural, and environmental distance that separated the young German Jews from their next world. Young people of bourgeois extraction, ignorant of Hebrew and enamored with the urban life, were asked to master the language of the Bible, equip themselves with a spade and pickax, and prepare themselves for a rural life. They were asked to change their skin even before being reborn.[29]

From Palestine, the Zionist leaders insisted on the sensitivity with which the immigrant selection process had to be carried out. The "material" (as they came to call it) needed to be chosen with care. And given the impossibility of welcoming everyone, it was necessary to assert the "cruel criterion" of Zionism.[30] An Italian

Jew, Enzo Sereni, who was former emissary of the Histadrut in Germany and a close collaborator of Recha Freier in the Jugend-Alijah project, became influential in Palestine and insisted on some knowledge of Hebrew. Mastery of the language would be the first requirement for obtaining the immigration certificate. Requirement number two was the willingness to undertake agricultural work in a kvutza or kibbutz, rather than hoping to get a clerical job in Haifa or Tel Aviv. Evidently, the application of the two parameters would reward the generation of children over that of the fathers: "children will be able to bring their parents into Eretz Israel, and not vice versa."[31]

The head of the Paris office of the Jugend-Alijah was a German philosopher not yet thirty years old, Hannah Arendt. In May 1935, she submitted an essay to the French weekly *Le Journal Juif*, a merciless analysis of a generational split in the Judaism of Germany. On the one hand, she said, there are the parents: men and women struck down by circumstances and now out of the game, "too obsequious or too insolent," people with "life behind them," with no future. On the other hand, there are the children who are "desperate" but not "destroyed," ashamed of their parents' ruin but ready to free themselves from it and impatient to get away. They were like the fifteen-year-old whom Arendt had recently received in her office, the first time together with his father. The boy stood there with his mouth shut while his father lavished her with the story of the family's misfortunes. But the next day, the fifteen-year-old returned alone, and without any irony, he declared himself an old Zionist. Arendt explained to him that he had no reason to be ashamed, that his condition was identical to that of all German Jews his age, and that the group experience, the preparation for aliyah, the separation from his parents, and the departure for Palestine would restore the "natural dignity" that history seemed to deny him.[32]

Meanwhile, in Berlin, Nazi officials specializing in Jewish affairs were doing their utmost to cooperate with the German

Zionists. They were convinced that the best way to solve the problem of the Jews in Germany was, quite simply, to accompany them to the exit. One of these officials, Adolf Eichmann, even studied Yiddish and Hebrew.[33] The Reich government encouraged the establishment of agricultural schools to prepare young people for emigration to Palestine.[34] Thus, Nazis, such as Eichmann and the SS security service, represented objective allies of Zionists such as Freier, founder and animator of the Jugend-Alijah. Between the beginning of 1934 and the end of 1935, about a thousand underage German Jews were authorized to emigrate to Palestine on their own, without their parents. Sixty percent were male, and 40 percent were female.[35] One of them, from Cologne, was Trude Meyer.

CHILDREN WHO BECOME LETTERS

In the photo on the immigration certificate, she has a child's face and looks younger than her fifteen years. Before taking her to the photographer, her mother must have tended to the girl's flawless hairdo. And who knows whether mother and daughter chose the dress together, the one with the lace collar, light-years from any pioneering clothing. Surely Heinrich Meyer had to put his signature on the contract with Jugend-Alijah: minors (the minimum age was just fifteen) couldn't leave without parental consent. The date on the certificate—issued by the Warsaw office of the Jewish Agency—is December 19, 1935, exactly two years after the theater performance at home, the Chinese dance with Rachel, for Hanukkah.[36]

Trude must consider herself lucky to have the certificate. From September onward, after the promulgation of the Nuremberg Laws, the number of requests from Germany soars, both for German Jews in general and for young people. The Jugend-Alijah is now registering three hundred applications per month. There is no way to accommodate them all, and Trude Meyer benefits from

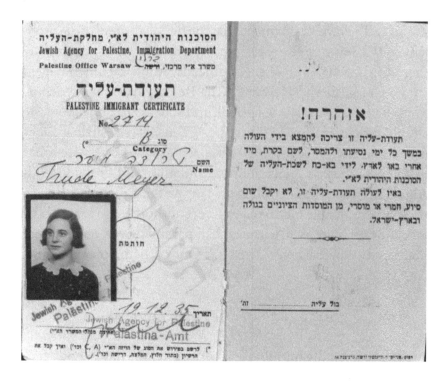

a rare opportunity.[37] True to form, Arthur Ruppin, the German sociologist converted into a Zionist leader, puts it bluntly:[38] The kids between the ages of fifteen and seventeen whom the Jewish Agency brought to Palestine are children of Israel removed from a "self-destructive existence ... Every child torn from that hell of hatred that today's Germany has become for Jews is a child saved and restored to life."[39]

We can only imagine the moment she said farewell to her parents. Heinrich and Wilhelmina might have accompanied her to the platform; the central station is not far from Nussbaumerstrasse. Or they might have said goodbye before that, entrusting her to the group leaders. We can imagine the agony of seeing her go, now that Jacques is gone too. Back then, the German Jews called them "children who become letters."[40] The next scene is

Trude's journey. The train from Cologne to Italy, passing through Vienna and Tarvisio. The arrival at the Trieste railway station. Accommodation in the dormitory in Via del Monte 7. The descent toward the port the following morning.[41] Boarding a Lloyd Triestino ship with its auspicious name, *Jerusalem*, along with 224 other "Jewish passengers" (seventy-two Germans, including Trude; the rest Poles, Austrians, Czechoslovakians, Lithuanians, Estonians, Latvians, Hungarians—a little of everything), as well as fifteen tons of iron and ninety-nine tons of various goods.[42] The departure is at exactly 1:00 p.m. on Christmas Day, Wednesday, December 25, 1935. There are six days of navigation, with stops in Brindisi and Larnaca, Cyprus. The arrival in Jaffa is on the morning of December 30. Then there is continuation to Haifa, with disembarkation by evening and the festive welcome of the Zionist militants on the pier.[43]

What was her impression of the land and people of Eretz Israel? What did she make of "the sand dunes, the motor pumps in the citrus groves, the rocky hillsides . . . the headlines in the newspapers and the cooperative dairy produce, the wadis, the hamsins, the domes of the walled convents, the ice-cold water from the *jarra*, the cultural evenings with accordion and harmonica music, the cooperative bus drivers in their khaki shorts, the sounds of English (the language of the rulers of the country), the dark orchards, the minarets, strings of camels carrying building sand, Hebrew watchmen, suntanned pioneers from the kibbutz, construction workers in shabby caps?" As I wonder about Trude Meyer's first glances over the people of Palestine and their surroundings, I will never find a better inventory than Amos Oz's page on the arrival, in 1934, of his mother, Fania Mussman, even though the latter came from Poland rather than Germany, and she joined her family in Jerusalem.[44] But as much as Oz helps with the questions, he can't even suggest the answers.

There is no trace in the family archive of the correspondence that Trude—the daughter who became letters—must have exchanged with her parents, who remained in Cologne. There are no reports on her journey, the landing, or the welcome from Maccabi militants, closely linked to those of Gordonia. Nor is there anything about her first moves to the land of Israel, her assignment to a small kibbutz just south of Tel Aviv, near the citrus groves of Rehovot: Kvutzat-Shiller. Whatever she may have shared with Heinrich and Wilhelmina about the first impressions of her new life escapes us: reassuring her parents about what worried them most, the impact with the language, the climate, the food; glossing over the surprises; avoiding references to what didn't actually correspond to the myth of the kibbutz. Starting with the alleged equality between men and women. There was very little equality—the kibbutz was a male-dominated microcosm where the body (and mind) of men mattered more than those of women.[45] Above all, she may have glossed over the biggest and most serious surprise: the existence in Palestine, apart from a Jewish settlement, of Arabs.

THE END OF INNOCENCE

Since Herzl's time, the Zionists' vision had been based on a singular combination of farsightedness and myopia. It was farsighted for their ability to predict the apocalyptic fate of Europe's Jews. It was myopic for their inability to foresee Arab resistance to the Zionist territorial project.[46] Made in Germany, the famous "blue boxes"—the tin containers in which donations destined for the Jewish National Fund were collected—from 1934 onward bore a map of Palestine drawn on them. On this map, there was no indication of natural or state borders, no limits to the Jewish reconquest of the Promised Land.[47] From the propaganda photos—a whole iconology of tents and backhoes, of reclamation and biceps, construction sites and crates of oranges—one cannot even claim that the indigenous Arabs were hidden or expelled. Rather, they represented a detail in the painting, a touch of color—the color of a half-exotic and half-pathetic humanity amid the overall triumphant picture of the Chosen People's reappropriation of Eretz Israel.[48]

Less than four months after her arrival in Palestine, Trude Meyer discovers that indigenous Arabs are not necessarily half-exotic, half-pathetic figures. An hour by bus from Kvutzat-Shiller, a fuse is lit in the narrow streets of Jaffa, and the fire quickly hits the boulevards of Tel Aviv. Hundreds of Arabs impoverished by the economic situation, exasperated by the continual landings of Jewish immigrants, and incited by the rumor that three or four of them were killed in Tel Aviv attack the police station and government offices. They throw stones at the buses and taxis, and they chase Jewish passersby while brandishing kitchen knives and sledgehammers. The first to fall on April 19, 1936, are Haim Pashigoda, Eliezer Bisozky, Haim Kornfeld, Victor Koopermintz, and David Shambadal—an office worker, a pensioner, two unskilled laborers, and an electrician, respectively. It is the beginning of the Arab Revolt that in the following days extends to the whole of Palestine, a revolt destined to last and to bring about the end of all innocence in the Zionist ranks.[49]

"Life, Papa, in this country as anywhere else, also involves the revolver, the knife, the bomb, and murder."[50] This is what the generation of children settled in Palestine will want to explain with increasingly hardened tones to their parents' generation. The Zionists' struggle for independence from the British Mandate is only part of the problem. It is perhaps not even the most delicate. The harsh reality of Palestine is that of a Jewish liberation movement bent on clashing with an Arab liberation movement. Inevitably, the operational tactics of the Zionists would be less marked by the magnanimous principles on which the movement had originally been founded.[51] And yet among the exponents of the older generation, there are those who did not wait for the trauma of the Arab Revolt of 1936 to raise the question of the growing distance separating the world of children from that of their fathers. Among the Zionist leaders of Palestine, there are also men like Yosef Baratz.

A Moldovan Jew, Baratz arrived in Palestine in 1907, little more than a teenager. He worked as a farmhand in the fields of Rehovot. Then he was a stonemason in Jerusalem, Tel Aviv, and Atlit, after which he settled in Galilee, on the shores of the Lake Tiberias, as a founding member of Kibbutz Degania. Bananas, grapefruits, fodder, dairy cows—from the 1910s to the 1920s, the agricultural community grew so much in productivity and reputation that it became known as "the mother of all kibbutzim." Aharon David Gordon, the ideologue of a much more nationalist than socialist Zionism, had chosen to live his last years in Degania, and starting from 1929, he had chosen to associate with Degania the network of small kibbutzim animated by Pinchas Lubianiker and affiliated with the Gordonia movement. But Baratz did not stop there. As an emissary of the Histadrut, he traveled to Russia, the United States, and Europe to channel human resources, economic aid, and political sympathies to Palestine. In the Jewish settlements, the mere mention of Baratz was tantamount to evoking the prototype of the Zionist paragon.[52]

The father of seven, Baratz had a broad and direct experience of the sabras, Jews born in Palestine to parents from the Diaspora.[53] And in 1933, writing in a magazine of the kibbutz movement, Baratz judged with surprising frankness what his generation had achieved in the area of raising children. "Our children are pragmatic," he pointed out, "and, perhaps put even more accurately, they are prosaic." They are interested in politics, involved in national public events, and react to terrorist incidents. "In contrast, they lack tenderness and a human attitude with respect to the elementary phenomena of everyday life. What is their attitude towards the poor, the aged, the Arabs, the sick?" In their prosaic concreteness, the children believe they correspond to the lesson of their parents, who had chosen to be reborn in Palestine as men and women of action, less absorbed by thought in comparison to their ancestors. But the parents did not know how to transmit to their children an essential quality, which had been typical of diasporic Judaism: the sabras lacked the traditional virtue of compassion.[54]

In another work, *The Story of Degania*, published in 1936, Baratz boasts the welcome reserved by his network of kibbutzim for young Jews fleeing Germany: "in the last three years, one hundred and fifty German boys and girls have found a home among us." (One of these girls, in Kvutzat-Shiller, is Trude Meyer.) On the same page, Baratz estimates the number of Gordonia youths integrated into the kibbutz network "from different countries of the diaspora" at 1,300.[55] (One of these young people, in Kvutzat-Shiller, is Moshe Zeiri.) And yet in his magazine article of 1933, Baratz described the ideological profile of those with whom the young people fresh from Europe are preparing to share their lives. In the sabras, "the national element is more developed than the social element. . . . Their love for this endangered homeland is increasing and at times awakens excessive patriotic instincts."[56]

THE HEBREW TEACHER

In Kvutzat-Shiller, Moshe Zeiri is a laborer. That is what was written in the document issued by the British authorities in Tel Aviv. And like almost all the members of the kibbutz, he works either in the citrus groves or for the citrus groves. He contributes to the virtuous dynamic that is making the fields around Rehovot a formidable economic reality, with Jaffa oranges to be grown and harvested by the tons, transported to the docks of the port, and then shipped to Liverpool as the best ambassador of the new Palestine: a small, dark orange ambassador, oval-shaped with a thick skin, almost seedless, and as sweet as any orange ever tasted. They were unlike their international competition: the sour oranges of Spain or California or South Africa.[57]

In Kvutzat-Shiller, Moshe is also the tarbutnik, the "cultural attaché," whom the kibbutz sabras tend to mock as a leftover from the past: a cloud-catching Jew, thoughtful rather than muscular, but whose work many ultimately recognize as necessary. Because without a house of culture more or less worthy of the name, without a reading room and a concert hall, even the busiest kibbutz on the coastal plain would risk resembling a place without a soul. True, the citrus groves require work all year round, not only from November to March, at harvest time, when Arab laborers climb the ladders with shears in hand and shoulder bags and remove the oranges from the tree one at a time and then entrust them to the Bedouin girls, who proceed toward the warehouse with the baskets on their heads, whereafter the Yemeni Jews do the sorting—all the best fruits for export, the rest staying—and the Eastern European Jews delicately wrap the oranges one by one, and one by one carpenters from Poland or Bohemia, Belarus or Moldova arrange them in packing crates, between layers of jute, closing the crates by tapping each nail with sacrosanct care, making sure not even one orange goes bad since that would risk spoiling them all. True, the citrus groves require continuous work from April to October, with the roar of diesel pumps extracting water from the wells, cleaning the concrete channels that carry water to the fields, clearing the irrigation furrows from rotten fruit and all sorts of debris. All this is true, but it is also true that one does not live on Jaffa oranges alone, nor does one live solely on evening committee meetings and plenary assemblies and communications from the treasurer and nocturnal changes of the guard and endless discussions about the refectory hours and where in the kibbutz the children should sleep. Now that the shtetl has been left behind, far away; now that life is missing not only the ringing of *their* bells, the bells of the Gentiles, but also the Sabbath buzz of men in caftans on their way to the synagogue, and the ubiquitous scent of sheep, and the muffled noise of carts in the winter snow; now more than ever, to fill the void, art and music, newspapers and magazines, books and mandolins are needed.

A tireless worker, Moshe Zeiri is also a Hebrew teacher. And that's how the teacher meets his pupil Trude Meyer. They would have met anyway. The kvutza has no more than two hundred members (there are almost a thousand at Givat-Brenner, the great kibbutz next door, founded by Enzo Sereni), so sooner or later, everyone gets to know each other. Still, they are smitten by each other in class, and the matchmaker is the Hebrew textbook and its author. In the eyes of sixteen-year-old Trude, the charm of twenty-two-year-old Moshe is perhaps fueled by his status as a teacher. Again, the aura surrounding the very figure of a Hebrew teacher—in Zionist culture perceived as a kind of pioneer in the unexplored territories of a new national identity—might have something to do with it.[58] Nor can one exclude that the Western Jewess from a good family, the bourgeois girl who grew up in Cologne in an assimilated environment, is experiencing further liberation from the world of her parents in the love for an Eastern Jew of modest origins raised in an Orthodox family and still imbued with the moods of the shtetl: Hasidic ditties, gefilte fish, pickles.

Initially the romance proceeds with small steps for reasons of prudence, to circumvent the social surveillance typical of every kibbutz, where nothing escapes anyone's eyes and the walls have ears. But it is also for reasons of character; both Moshe and Trude are shy. Years later, husband and wife will remember the inaugural season of their love as the time when they exchanged notes, communicating in writing rather than verbally: "We were in the same place, but we were too clumsy to tell each other things looking into each other's eyes." That "prehistoric period" was soon followed by the time of clandestine love, in Moshe's "tiny room . . . with the wind blowing through the cracks in the windows, the single bed, the table, the wardrobe, the trunk of books along the wall, and the boxes that served as chairs and storage for newspapers. . . . You fell asleep on my bed, wrapped in my arms with your clothes on, and we woke up after midnight and I secretly escorted you to the youth house, passing through the back so that the caretaker wouldn't see us."[59]

During that period of clandestine love, the girl from the youth house changes her name: Trude becomes Yehudit. Etymologically, the Germanic "strength" becomes the Hebrew "woman of Judea" (the documents issued by the British administration give the name in the English: Judith). And according to family memory, it was Moshe who chose the new name.[60] The Hebrew teacher demonstrates how tight his hold is not only on her heart but also on the very sense of identity his pupil is urged to develop. Notwithstanding the theoretical equality between the sexes that reigns in the kibbutz, Moshe immediately defines the power dynamics in his relationship with Yehudit. The girl renounces the name chosen for her by her parents in her first life and is reborn with a name assigned to her in her new life by her future husband. It is clearly a biblical name: that of one of the wives of Jacob's brother Esau. But it's also a telluric name, referring to Judea. It is a name rooted deeply in the soil of the Promised Land.

Beyond the names, Moshe Zeiri—the son of David Kleiner, cantor in the Kopychyntsi synagogue and disciple of the rebbe of Chortkiv—is among those who think that the Bible must finally enter the kibbutz: not as an instrument of religious proselytism, to restore faith to Jews so modern that they are under the illusion they can do without the Book, but rather as an instrument of national acculturation and identity cohesion. As a historical tale, no matter how legendary. As a foundation myth of the Jewish state to come.[61] Nor should only the Bible enter the kibbutz. Jewish holidays must also be celebrated as collective rituals intended to cement the sabra community and immigrants through a recognition of their shared roots. In 1933, it was Yosef Baratz (yet again) who emphasized the opportunity to introduce the celebration of Shabbat in every kibbutz in Palestine. Much more than a gastronomic custom consisting of a special Friday evening dinner, it would be a feast of the spirit, with readings from the Bible, the singing of traditional melodies with musical accompaniment, and the lighting of candles. Purim, Pesach, Rosh Hashanah, Sukkot, Hanukkah: following Baratz, Moshe will be more and more convinced of the added value of the holidays for the purpose of a complete realization of the Zionist ideal.[62]

LOVE IN THE TIME OF THE KIBBUTZ

Moshe was also a son who became letters. His were written in Yiddish, which Zippora, in Kopychyntsi, had to have read to her by a kind yet discreet soul, someone who could remedy the recipient's illiteracy without telling too many people.[63] Those letters have been lost, but it doesn't take much effort to imagine their contents. The son insisted with his mother that she take the giant step. What on earth was holding her to the shtetl? Why was she waiting to leave the ruins of Galicia, to plunge into the heart of the seas, to join him and Rivka in Eretz Israel?

In 1937, Kopychyntsi's municipal canteen, which distributed free meals to the poor, closed down. It was built in the aftermath of World War I by the Polish representatives of the American Jewish Joint Distribution Committee (known simply as the Joint), the same benefactors who had financed the restoration of Kopychytnsi's ritual baths.[64] Perhaps this is also why Zippora decides to go. After the canteen closed, the little bit of money sent by Rivka, the Palestinian pounds converted into zloty, is no longer enough for her to make ends meet. Or maybe not, and maybe the widow Kleiner is not that bad off; after all, she owns a house. Who knows? It is impossible to ascertain the exact date of Zippora's aliyah, her ascent to Palestine. Presumably it is by the end of 1937. Certainly it is by September 10, 1938. The photographs of Moshe and Yehudit's wedding, celebrated that day in Rehovot, show Zippora together with the spouses, as well as Yehudit's parents, Heinrich and Wilhelmina Meyer, who came to Palestine from Germany. Thus they realized—at least in their specific case—what Enzo Sereni had foreseen when he said the children will be able to bring their parents to Eretz Israel.

In the wedding photos,[65] the smiles for the occasion barely serve to mask the distance that separates the widow Kleiner from the Meyers, the Polish Jewess from the German Jews, a social and cultural distance that is reflected in their respective luggage. No one in the family remembers anything of Zippora's bags. It is as if leaving the shtetl, the *yiddishe mame* had indeed limited herself to shutting the door of the cottage by the river behind her. It is likely that Zippora brought something with her, but whatever it was must have seemed to her children—and then to her grandchildren—as obsolete or useless as the contents of Grandma Henny's *kifat* in David Grossman's novel *See Under: Love*, "a kind of box you tie up" with all the "stuff from Over There." Worn-out clothes. Worn shoes. A prayer book. The wooden plank on which, at the shtetl, sweets were prepared for Shabbat. And "what is most

important," "three bags full of goose feathers that she dragged halfway around the world in boats and trains braving terrible dangers," to make a quilt to keep her feet warm, but her children in Palestine had bought her a double quilt already made, "so the feathers stayed in the cellar where pretty soon they caught mildew and other cholerias."[66] How different from the furniture and objects that the Meyers could afford to bring from Cologne to Tel Aviv in 1937 or 1938, at the time of their aliyah: the Bauhaus-style dining table, the dressing table with mirror and small drawers, the sommier bed, horsehair mattresses, sets of pots and cutlery and glasses, coffee grinders, silver candlesticks for Hanukkah, and Meissen porcelain.[67]

And what a difference in the in-laws' living arrangements in Palestine. Zippora joins Rivka in Ayelet Hashachar in northern Galilee. As a first-rate cook, she is taken to work in the kitchens of her daughter's kibbutz.[68] There, she can get by without knowing Hebrew, only with Yiddish, and maybe even try to include some touches of Galician cuisine—chicken soup, chopped liver, fried fruit—into the refectory's Levantine diet. For Zippora, the only real worry must be the total disregard for the prescriptions of kosher cuisine. Heinrich and Wilhelmina, for their part, buy a house in Givatayim, a residential middle-class suburb of Tel Aviv full of small, single-story houses with two or three rooms, a veranda, and a section of garden. They live there together with the Julichs, another Jewish couple close to sixty who made the aliyah from Germany. Within a couple of years, Heinrich Meyer will be organized. There will be Hebrew courses for adults, as well as a new business almost identical to the old one: retail meat sales. He has a butcher shop and a decent turnover in a growing Tel Aviv neighborhood full of German Jews. Basically, everything is good, the only hitch being the increasingly heated protests of Jerusalem's rabbis against the trade of nonkosher meat.[69]

On the days when Moshe and Yehudit take the bus from Kvutzat-Shiller to visit the Meyers, Moshe speaks Yiddish with his in-laws, whereas Yehudit and her parents continue to speak to each other in German (and they continue to call her Trude).[70] For the rest, the two young spouses live with one foot in the present and one foot in the future. While working three jobs in the kibbutz—farmhand, cultural attaché, and Hebrew teacher—Moshe dreams of doing the job he feels he was born for, ever since the shtetl days and performances at the Kopychyntsi inn and impromptu tours with the Lubianiker brothers' amateur company: a theater actor. In Tel Aviv, there are now two important theatrical groups, the Ohel and the Habima.[71] Moshe dreams of attending the acting school of one or the other. As for Yehudit, she is preparing to attend a teacher training school that the kibbutz movement is setting up in Tel Aviv. She failed to become a kindergarten teacher in Third Reich Germany. In Palestine's Jewish settlement, she will succeed.

Five or six years later, Moshe—the husband who became letters—will remember with enchantment the first seasons of

his marriage to Yehudit, love in the time of the kibbutz. Studious love: like when they were newlyweds and, to escape the mosquitoes and scorching heat of their tiny apartment, would sit down to read behind the shower shack, next to the rabbit hutch, where at least a little wind would blow. Or they would go as far as the orange grove and read by leaning their backs against a tree trunk. Stolen love: "Here is the wardrobe with the big mirror in which I see myself, voluntarily or involuntarily, and it brings to mind how nice it would be to see your image, sneak behind you, put my hands around you and hold you tightly to me, to see your head turn and get a kiss while you keep your eyes closed." Gourmand love: like when Moshe, returning from guard duty, passed by the dovecote and somehow got a dove, a delicacy cooked quickly to "bring to you in the middle of the night," and "watch you half asleep, bent over on the plate to lick the tender bones."[72]

With respect to the political scene at the Jewish settlements, the dove—metaphorically speaking—is Pinchas Lubianiker, the most moderate of the Mapai leaders, the least willing to chase the party's hawks along the path of a radical interpretation of the "Arab problem." But even though Lubianiker managed to get himself appointed deputy secretary general of Ben-Gurion's party in 1938, the climate at the top of Mapai is increasingly that of an unrelenting struggle against the Arabs, in continual revolt since 1936. As such, the Zionist leadership systematically practices the "tower and palisade" tactic (and the British administration lets them). It multiplies the lightning-fast construction of new kibbutzim that correspond, in fact, to military outposts: dozens and dozens of fortified enclosures at the extreme edges of the Jewish settlement, around which to give birth to just as many colonies of settlers armed to the teeth.

On the border with Lebanon, the Kibbutz Hanita, founded in 1938, becomes the symbol of a new era of Zionism—the era no longer of working the land but of conquering the land. It is the era that Nathan Alterman, a young poet on the rise, seals with the verses of "Song of Platoons":

> Wait for us, my land, on your mountain paths,
> Wait for us in your vast wheatfields,
> Once your boys brought the peace of plows,
> Now their guns guarantee the peace.[73]

THE CHANCE OF A LIFE

As the crow flies, no more than fifteen miles separate Kvutzat-Shiller from the center of Tel Aviv—few, but still too many for Moshe to go back and forth from morning to night. So he writes to Yehudit about a letter a day, letters burning with nostalgia, passion, and love. Toward evening, when his housemates disperse among the thousand temptations of the big city, and he remains alone among the empty rooms and doesn't know what to do with his "tempestuous heart," he "inevitably" thinks back to Bialik's poem, "To the Bird." Who will give him wings to fly to the land of dates and almonds? "I would fly up to you, my dear, and lay my head on your lap, to calm the storm in me."[74]

In January 1939, Moshe Zeiri is given permission to leave the kibbutz and try to fulfill his life's dream of becoming a theater actor. He attends the Habima Theatre School. He thus manages to set foot inside a legend of Zionist culture, known by all the Jews of the world in step with the times, in Moscow, London, Warsaw, and New York. The theater made its own aliyah, reborn in the Promised Land after having established itself in the Russia of the Bolshevik Revolution as one of the ripest of Stanislavski's fruits. From 1935 onward, the inhabitants of Tel Aviv also saw Habima grow in the proper sense of the verb: piece by piece, the construction of an imposing theater hall in modernist style in the center of the city, on Rothschild Boulevard, coming to completion. It is yet another architectural jewel in a Jewish city that rose up—within thirty years—literally from the sand.[75]

Studying at Habima is equivalent to receiving more than a strictly theatrical training. Besides the lectures of directors and actors, Moshe has the opportunity to attend lectures on Jewish history, biblical philology, and Hassidic culture, and he enthusiastically writes about it all to Yehudit. How proud the principal of his Lviv vocational school would be! "I really should write to him, he was the only one who cared about my future on the stage."[76] Not that Moshe can afford to only be a drama school student. The kibbutz pays the tuition fees, not the maintenance fees in Tel Aviv. At the crack of dawn, Moshe is on time at the port of Jaffa, where he works as a docker and is paid by the day. In fact, the job literally sticks to him: "It's eleven in the evening, and as I write to you, my clothes still smell of the flour I unloaded from the ships: it's not a good smell, but I can deal with it."[77] In this respect, Moshe Zeiri appears to be a typical laborer in that unique Histadrut union. While not belonging to the economic elite of the Jewish settlement, he belongs, in some way, to its cultural elite.[78]

Moshe has no free time, so he doesn't take advantage of the boom of such a remarkably vital city as much as he could. At the end of the 1930s, Tel Aviv had 150,000 inhabitants (only 85,000 ten years earlier), one-third of the Jews residing in Palestine. Even though they are mostly Eastern European Jews, as many as in an Ashkenazi city, Tel Aviv has a Sephardic appearance. Surrounding the glittering signs of Allenby Street and the Bauhaus cottages of Rothschild Boulevard is a dirty, noisy, chaotic city, a cross between a Mediterranean port and a huge shtetl. It is a city of bazaars, small businesses, and dodgy deals, as well as restaurants where you eat anything at all hours, like in a Middle Eastern New York, and beaches where tanned Jews show off their muscles, like in a Los Angeles without Hollywood. As a child of Kopychyntsi, Moshe doesn't know how to swim. And he shares something of the kibbutznik's prejudice against Tel Aviv, the city of idleness and vice. At best, it's a city of traders and speculators rather than land workers, little more than a new Warsaw or Lviv.[79]

The sacrifices that Moshe imposes on himself reach the point of debilitating him. Sometimes he gets so tired and eats so little that he no longer has the strength or voice to act at the theater school. But more often than not, his letters to Yehudit convey the fever of an apprenticeship experienced as a chance in his life: even at the cost of carving out less time for returning to Kvutzat-Shiller, at the cost of sacrificing love. "I fear you will suffer, my darling, when I am absorbed in stage work. On the other hand, it is good that each of us has his own space for self-fulfillment," Moshe writes to Yehudit.[80] What more could he want than touring the land of Israel with Habima teachers and schoolmates, no longer staging masterpieces of the past—the Yiddish plays that enchanted the Eastern European Jewish boy in the corner of the theater hall—but masterpieces of the present and future, the texts of a Jewish theater that would serve as the foundations of a new national culture? What more could he want than to act in a theatrical performance of *King David in the Cave*, the folktale adapted by Bialik for Zionist purposes? And these are just the beginnings. Moshe thinks big for the future. Through an agreement between Kvutzat-Shiller and Givat-Brenner (the kibbutz next door, which is the largest in Palestine), he plans to found a kibbutz theater company. He makes contacts and prepares meetings. "I don't want to wait. I want to be seen as a revolutionary, as long as I can keep my independence."[81]

Moshe is thinking big during the first months of 1939, as the bells of history are preparing to ring for everyone, in Mandatory Palestine, in the Middle East, in the whole world. Released in May, the so-called White Paper of the British government—which prefigures the creation in Palestine of a single state, cohabited by Arabs and Jews—is taken by the Zionists as a genuine provocation. Although it manages to appease the Arab Revolt that broke out in 1936, it ignites the powder keg of a Jewish revolt no longer restricted to armed groups such as the Irgun, the terrorist wing of Betar.[82] On June 14, Moshe writes a letter to Yehudit about what he learned regarding Ayelet Hashachar, Rivka's kibbutz in northern Galilee, toward the Golan Heights. There was a fire on the kibbutz grounds. Firefighters, mostly Arabs, came in under the orders of a British officer. Members of the kibbutz feared that their underground weapons cache would be discovered. An Arab firefighter was suspicious and discovered the hidden arsenal. A British officer replied to the fire brigade, "I asked you to put out the fire, not to look for guns."[83]

After the outbreak of World War II, on September 1, 1939, the Zionists openly declare that Palestine is still an open question, that they will continue to fight the White Paper even in the midst of the struggle against the Axis powers. "We must help the British in the war as if the White Paper were not there, and we must oppose the White Paper as if there were no war," says David Ben-Gurion.[84] Then in Tel Aviv, the general staff of the Haganah, the clandestine army of Palestine's Jews, is organized. Meanwhile in October 1939, Vladimir Jabotinsky, the historical leader of

Betar—now tired and sick in his London exile—coordinates with the Irgun leaders to carry out a project as unrealistic as it is reckless: a general armed uprising in Eretz Israel.[85] More realistically, Jabotinsky meets with Berl Katznelson, the director of *Davar*, sent to London by Mapai to negotiate a common policy between Revisionist Zionism and Labor Zionism.[86] But Katznelson himself is doubtful. He is terribly pessimistic about the situation of the Jews: "We are orphans in this world. And as the world crumbles, our orphanhood intensifies."[87]

THREE

CLOSE TO WHERE

THE WEXLERS' RADIO

The Wexlers didn't wait until September 1, 1939, to leave the shtetl. Janowo was too exposed for Jews to stay there. It was right on the border between Poland and Germany, awaiting the arrival of the Wehrmacht tanks and SS trucks. In the fog of an April morning, it was time to close up the house. Before detaching the mezuzah from the door jamb, Henoch had loaded what the family held most precious onto Mr. Zawadski's cart, with the help of Dov and Adam. First of all, the sewing machine, the Singer that Mindel called her milk cow. Then the basket of tablecloths and sheets, and a smaller basket with sacred books. "The cart crossed the market square diagonally," Adam recalled decades later. They headed toward Mława, with Łódź as their final destination. In Mława, after the household goods were transferred from the cart to a truck, Zawadski refused to be paid. And yet he was a penniless peasant, and a Christian. The Wexlers had to insist that he accept at least a symbolic fee.[1]

Of that last summer of peace, Adam would remember almost nothing apart from the comings and goings of trains and the chicken incident. The Wexlers had settled in Kolumna, a holiday resort not far from Łódź, with the hope that Mindel would get the opportunity to earn something with her milk cow, by working as a seamstress. The village was along the railway line to Wrocław (at the time called Breslau), and Adam spent whole days contemplating the departures and arrivals of trains—a wonder he couldn't enjoy during the shtetl years. Less enthralling was the chicken incident. A Jewish boy of his own age, about ten years old, was sent around by his mother with a chicken in hand to find a shochet, a ritual slaughterer. Adam pointed to his father. Henoch, however, was not a slaughterer certified by the local rabbi. What ensued was a chorus of increasingly acrimonious voices gathering around the Wexler house, with dozens of Jews, men and women, screaming at the abomination while the crying chicken boy took refuge in his mother's arms. The boy pointed Adam out to the crowd as the one responsible for the bad advice. Meanwhile, the boy's mother brandished the impiously slaughtered chicken in Mindel's face and demanded material compensation for the offense. The incident ended when Adam's mother agreed to buy the scandalous chicken for six zlotys, double its market value.[2]

From mid-September onward—after having seen the waves of silver or dark green Luftwaffe planes flying overhead—the Wexlers lived in Łódź, at their uncle David's house. David was a shoemaker by trade, and this was the uncle with whom Shaya and Yosef had stayed before responding, as conscripts of the Republic of Poland, to the mobilization against the German invaders. But the soldiers Shaya and Yosef soon had to return to their uncle David's apartment. The Polish army was in disarray, and the armed forces of the Third Reich occupied Łódź almost without a shot being fired, amid the cheers of the Germans living in the city. After that, for a couple of months, the occupants behaved with relative restraint. For the Wexlers, the only immediate trauma was when Henoch was obliged to shave his beard. On the street, some Orthodox Jews were rounded up and forced to shave each other. "In the evening, when he came home, my father was a humiliated man." Henoch didn't speak for two days, he was "devastated by this first encounter with the Nazis."[3]

The order to concentrate within the limits of the Bałuty district became effective on May 1, 1940. At that time, there were 150,000 Jews locked up in the four square kilometers of Poland's second biggest ghetto by population. It was also the most isolated, totally cut off from the rest of the city of Łódź and the rest of the occupied country.[4] But compared to the majority of forced residents, the Wexlers had a significant advantage. Two close relatives—Henoch's brother and brother-in-law—held important positions in the Jewish administration of the ghetto, led by Haim Rumkowski. It was a complex system of relationships, opportunism, and exchange of favors.[5] So the apartment assigned to the Wexlers, at 37 Łagiewnicka Street, was a rather good accommodation compared to others. Furthermore, Uncle David's apartment was in the same building, and the one assigned to another of Henoch's brothers, Uncle Yankl, was not far away, at 6 Niecała Street. Later, again thanks to their high-ranking friendships, the Wexlers got to move to 61 Łagiewnicka Street, again with their uncle David.

The first tragedy strikes the family in the form of dysentery, and in a few days Yosef succumbs. Barely twenty years old, he is one of the 243 who die of dysentery in the two months of May and June 1940.[6] Yosef—the Betar militant in his mini-uniform as a child, who became Jabotinsky's bodyguard—was the idol of Dov and Adam's childhood. When Adam returns to school on the edge of the ghetto, in Smugowa Street, after the days of mourning, Yosef's Zionist past offers Adam one more reason to be enchanted by the speeches of his teacher Joshua. His usual teacher, Mrs. Ruda, has a substitute, and he has been to Palestine. He tells the children that it is a land where oranges cost less than potatoes and where the Jews are no longer afraid of anyone, because they have learned to take up arms.[7] There is a photo that survived the Shoah of Things, which I saw recently, and which allows me to visually imagine how the youngest of the Wexlers may have mourned Yosef's death. (Even his shorn hair, to prevent lice, was a source of shame for Adam.) In a ghetto school, a teacher with the Star of David pinned to her jacket collar stands by the wall near a map of the Middle East. Next to her, a shaved schoolboy points to the coast of Palestine with his finger. He is pointing to the Gulf of Haifa, and Mount Carmel.[8]

The school on Smugowa Street is the same one where Dawid Sierakowiak, the author of a sadly memorable diary of the ghetto, attends high school. So not much imagination is needed to get a sense of Adam's daily life at school. Just open Dawid's diary to the page of April 27, 1941. "The school is in a very small building, which barely fits the desks. There's nothing else (not even a blackboard). There's no changing room and we wear our coats in the classroom. We had five lessons today. During the last one, Rumkowski himself arrived, accompanied by Praszkier, Karo (the 'minister' of culture) and other ghetto 'dignitaries.' Rumkowski walked around the kitchen, tasted the soup (which was just delicious, probably made especially for him) and told the students about the difficulties they had encountered in opening the school, and that he will try to provide more for us. He asked us to work hard, keep clean and behave."[9]

After the summer of 1941—the summer of Operation Barbarossa, with the German invasion of the Soviet Union—there is no more school for Adam, nor for Dov, who is two years older and already works in a factory workshop on Zgierska Street, making nails for the boots of German paratroopers. The entire Łódź ghetto is a labor camp and constitutes a significant part of the Reich's war economy. The leader of the Jews, Rumkowski, knows this well. He knows that the productivity of the ghetto can stay the death sentence that awaits its inhabitants. Carrying out work that is functional to German war production may not be life insurance, but it offers a moratorium on deportation.[10] So in the Łódź ghetto, the stamp found on a work certificate—*Geprüft*,

"Checked," physically able—counts for a lot. At eleven, Adam is not yet old enough to apply for one. He nonetheless keeps himself as busy as he can, and as much as his mother will allow. With some neighbors, he tries to grow edible herbs on an abandoned piece of land at the edge of the ghetto, or he hauls wheelbarrows of coal scraped out of the landfills to be recycled as fuel.[11]

Above all, Adam listens to the radio. From the spring of 1942 onward—as deportations to the Chełmno extermination camp, sixty kilometers northwest of Łódź, take on a regular pace[12]— even the youngest of the Wexler brothers is authorized by the eldest, Shaya, to frequent the apartment of Mr. Lubinski, a neighbor of Uncle Yankl's. Shaya, who is part of a politically atypical half-Zionist, half-Bundist circle, has set up a radio listening station there, one of the very rare clandestine stations ever set up in that ghetto too isolated, too hermetically sealed off to put up any effective forms of resistance. The Wexler radio would go down in the annals of the Holocaust as a pathetically courageous attempt

among a few captives in the Łódź ghetto to defy the warlords of the thousand-year Reich.[13]

Shaya's group is headed by a Zionist militant, a certain Chaim Widawski. He's the one who has woven the network to which the Wexler brothers belong, along with their father, Henoch, the Bundist uncle Yankl, and his two sons, Shimek and Karol. The radio was assembled by an electrician, Wiktor Rundbaken, with spare parts collected in the ghetto. But the key figure of the clandestine radio post is Moshe Topel, a synagogue cantor who knows several foreign languages, so he can interpret what gets picked up on international frequencies.[14] There is huge news, and far from good. On the Eastern Front, the Germans are advancing toward the Caucasus, with Stalingrad besieged by the Axis forces. On the Southern Front, the Germans are pushing toward Egypt, with General Rommel's Afrika Korps arriving beyond Benghazi, a few hundred kilometers from the Suez Canal and even Palestine.

Each Jewish ghetto is also a world of voices, full of news— reliable or unchecked, reassuring or desperate.[15] The Łódź ghetto is no exception. Starting from Yitzhak Lubinski's apartment at

6 Niecała Street, the secret Wexler radio post spreads tidbits of news, each more shocking than the previous one. The Germans are said to be carrying out a systematic plan for the liquidation of all the Jews in Europe, in the east as well as the west.

SOSENSKI FOREST

September 1, 1939, had been very different in southeastern Poland than in western and central Poland. As a result of the Molotov-Ribbentrop pact, the invaders in both eastern Galicia and Volhynia were not the Nazis but the Bolsheviks, not the Werhmacht and the SS but the Red Army. That was also why the local Jews had reserved something like a welcome for the invaders. The Red Army resented the Poles much more than the Jews.[16] In any case, the authorities in the Soviet occupation zone did the best they could with respect to the Red Army. In Rivne, the county prefect had personally met the first column entering the city. Ternopil's county prefect went as far as using loudspeakers to invite the population to festively welcome Stalin's soldiers. In Kopychyntsi, a municipal official shouted to a small crowd of Soviet soldiers, Polish civilians, and shtetl Jews from the balcony of the town hall: "Gentlemen, Poles, soldiers, we will beat the Germans now that the Bolsheviks are on our side!"[17]

Nearly all of Poland's Jews found the Soviet occupier preferable—and not without reason—to the Germans, so much so that hundreds of thousands of them, coming from the German occupation zone, had chosen to seek refuge in eastern Galicia. One of these refugees was Alter Kacyzne, the multifaceted intellectual who had established himself as a poignant interpreter of Yiddish culture in Warsaw between the wars, and whose photographs had shown the Jewish villages of Poland to the readers of *The Forward* in New York. With his wife, Hana, and their only daughter, sixteen-year-old Shulamit, Kacyzne had fled from Warsaw and settled in Lviv, where he animated the circles of pro-Soviet intelligentsia.[18] While Shulamit was studying in high school and enchanting her classmates with her Warsaw sophistication, her father had volunteered to undertake, along with a delegation of writers, the ritual of a pilgrimage to Stalinist Moscow.[19]

At the time of Operation Barbarossa, none of this exonerated Alter Kacyzne from his appointment with the architects of the Final Solution. They were not only German architects: between the end of June and the beginning of July 1941, the pogroms of Lviv involved the coordinated effort of the Wehrmacht, the SS, and Ukrainian auxiliaries, along with Ukrainian and Polish civilians.[20] Kacyzne separated from his wife and daughter and tried to escape eastward. He didn't make it. He was killed on July 7 near Ternopil with a shot to the back of his head, and then he was dumped in a mass grave—an operational mode gaining ground as a standard Einsatzgruppen technique for solving the Jewish problem on the Eastern Front.[21] As for Hana and Shulamit, they remained in Lviv. Once locked up in the Zamarstyniv ghetto, they organized themselves to survive. They initially worked at the German citadel barracks, the mother as a maid, the daughter as an attendant in the hospital for Soviet prisoners of war. Shulamit then found employment at a Hungarian military post, and from there she was able to come into contact, outside the ghetto, with the Italian soldiers of the Army Group Rear Area Command, stationed in Lviv in support of the expeditionary force in Russia. An attractive eighteen-year-old, Shulamit spoke and wrote in Polish, Russian, Ukrainian, German and French. She obtained a false identity card with the name of Janina Dwojakowska and effortlessly managed to work as a translator at the offices of the Italian Command.[22]

In the Germans' eastward advance, Rivne and Volhynia came immediately after eastern Galicia. On balance, at the end of the war, the effectiveness of the local actions of the Einsatzgruppen proved extraordinary. More Jews were liquidated with a shot to the back of the head, and there were fewer survivors: only about 3,500, out of the 250,000 Jews who lived in Volhynia in 1939. Such an outcome would be clearly impossible had the German executioners not benefited from the intensive collaboration of willing Ukrainian executioners: nationalist militants, but also civilians and neighbors of the Jews.[23] In Rivne, the three days of November 7–9, 1941, were enough to liquidate 17,000 of them. That was the Sosenki forest massacre, which occurred about a month after the better-known massacre in Babyn Yar, near Kyiv—two of the sixty-four massacres of Jews perpetrated on the Eastern Front between September and December 1941.[24]

Four years later, in the autumn of 1945, Adela Liberman, a girl from Rivne who had just turned fifteen in November 1941, would recount the Sosenki massacre in her own words to a Polish commission of inquiry into German war crimes. With her sister, Inda, two years younger than her, at her side, she reported what she thought she knew about how events unfolded. On the afternoon of Thursday, November 6, the Jews of Rivne who didn't have a work certificate were summoned. At six the following morning, they were to present themselves in Grabnik Square, bringing food and their personal effects. They would be gathered in the Sosenki pine forest, and from there evacuated to a labor camp. At dawn on Friday the seventh, the Jews who actually came by the thousands to the darkness of the square headed toward the woods four kilometers from the city, escorted by German soldiers and Ukrainian auxiliaries. In Sosenki, the mass graves were ready, ten meters each. The shots were fired from atop the ridge, a first layer of about twenty corpses, a spray of carbolic acid, more shots, another layer of corpses, and another spray of carbolic acid. The children were stabbed with bayonets, so as not to waste ammunition, and thrown haphazardly on the corpses of the adults, thereby taking up less space. This continued for the whole day of Saturday the eighth until the early hours of Sunday the ninth.[25]

More than half a century later, the author of *A Tale of Love and Darkness* will also recount in his own words what happened in the Sosenki forest: "There, among boughs, birds mushrooms, currants and berries," Amos Oz, the son of Fania Mussman, will recount how the Jews of Rivne were liquidated by the thousands in forty-eight hours. Among them, "almost all my mother's classmates perished. Together with their parents, and all of their neighbors, acquaintances, business rivals, and enemies; well-to-do and proletarian, pious, assimilated, and baptized, communal leaders, synagogue functionaries, peddlers and drawers of water, Communists and Zionists, intellectuals, artists, and village idiots, and some four thousand babies. My mother's schoolteachers also died there, the headmaster, Issachar Reiss, with his charismatic presence and hypnotic eyes, whose look had pierced the dreams of so many adolescent schoolgirls, sleepy, absentminded Isaac Berkowski, hot-tempered Eliezer Buslik, who had taught Jewish culture, Fanka Zeidmann, who had taught geography and biology and also PE, and her brother Shmuel the painter, and pedantic, embittered Dr. Moshe Bergmann, who through almost clenched teeth had taught general and Polish history. All of them."[26]

Because they had no work certificate, Adela and Inda were careful not to go to Grabnik Square on the morning of November 7, 1941. After the massacre in the woods, they immediately joined their parents, Meir and Feige, in Zdolbuniv, a village not far from Rivne. During the two years of the Soviet occupation, the Libermans had been dispossessed of both the pharmacy and the pharmaceutical distribution company—intrinsically counterrevolutionary activities in the eyes of the Bolsheviks, activities that could have merited deportation to Siberia. Even before Operation Barbarossa, Meir had recycled himself as a pharmacist in the Zdolbuniv hospital, and Feige followed him, even though she was worried about separating from their daughters, who were trying to continue their studies in Rivne—Adela in the lyceum,

Inda in gymnasium. But after the Sosenki massacre, the priority of the Liberman family had become to stay united in the face of a future that threatened to be just as dramatic as the present.

In fact, not all the Jews of Volhynia were exterminated. In the winter and then in the spring of 1942 (when the Wannsee Conference near Berlin established a protocol for the Final Solution), it was clear to everyone, executioners and victims, that there was still work in the Reichskommissariat Ukraine to be finished. In Rivne, at least seven thousand Jews were crammed into a ghetto created in the northwestern part of the city.[27] And in Zdolbuniv itself, there was a small ghetto to keep the Jews who allowed themselves to remain alive—like the Libermans—within range of a Mauser.

"LISTEN, O ISRAEL"

In northeastern Poland, September 1, 1939, was still different from the other areas of the invaded and dismembered republic. The district of Lida, including the town of Raduń, had been occupied by the Red Army; but the nearby Eišiškės had been assigned to Lithuania, as was the city of Vilnius.[28] The Lipkunski family had thus found themselves divided by a border. Under the command of Soviet authorities, Moshe David and Sara Mina continued their lives as a blacksmith and seamstress, respectively, in Dugalishok together with their youngest son, Yekutiel. Pinchas and Avraham—the two older sons, fourteen and twelve, respectively—had reached Lithuanian territory to continue their Biblical and Talmudic studies in Eišiškės. Officially Pinchas and Avraham Lipkunski were considered two very young refugees: their names appeared on a list of the nine thousand Jews assisted by the Joint's Vilnius office in 1940.[29]

Homesick, Avraham chose to go back to Dugalishok. When it was time for his bar mitzvah—the Jewish ceremony marking a boy's entry into maturity, in which he would receive two cases of phylacteries from his mother and become responsible for his own destiny—his pride was accompanied by an inner conflict. On the one hand, Avraham wished to be reunited with Pinchas, his much admired older brother, and pursue with him the goal that Lipkunski's parents had always imagined for their children: that they become rabbis, honoring an established tradition of religious studies, which was the pride of the family. On the other hand, all Avraham wanted was to stay home, without having to attend the new secular and communist school of the Russians, as Yekutiel did. At thirteen, he wanted to hear his mother's voice humming Hasidic tunes as she worked on the sewing machine. At most he wanted to learn the art of forging a horseshoe from his father, in the shop, which would satisfy the surrounding Christian peasants and leave them full of admiration.[30]

Since June 1941, Operation Barbarossa resolved Avraham's inner conflict far too well. Doubts about the future lost their urgency in a present where the Red Army was dissolving under the assaults of the German armed forces, and where within a few months—on November 16—the Jews of Raduń would also be shunted off into a ghetto. After saying goodbye to Dugalishok, the Lipkunskis (including Pinchas, returning from Eišiškės) were assigned a one-room apartment on the lower part of Lida Street. Eleven of them had to live there: the five Lipkunskis, a family of four refugees from Eišiškės, and a certain Rivka along with her uncle Velvel, relatives from the Rakowski side. During the day, Pinchas and Avraham left the ghetto, escorted by guards, to do some sort of forced labor, such as chopping wood in the forest or clearing the streets of snow. In the evening, defying the curfew, they happened to reach, within the ghetto itself, the study house of Mordechai Beer, a rabbi who had been their teacher at the minor yeshiva in Raduń. They sought to pick up the sacred books again, to relive the life of the spirit.[31]

But in the Reichskommissariat Ostland, as elsewhere in occupied Poland, it is only a matter of time. Like all the Jews in all the ghettos, the Lipkunskis belong by law to the realm of the dying. On May 7, 1942, the Raduń ghetto is surrounded by Polish and Lithuanian auxiliaries, under the command of German soldiers, in preparation for its liquidation, scheduled for May 10. On the morning of that Sunday, Moshe David and Pinchas are picked up at the crack of dawn. With a hundred other good men, they are escorted to the cemetery of Raduń, a mere two kilometers away along the road to Grodno. They have to dig mass graves. Spring has now advanced, the thaw is complete, and excavations are proceeding swiftly. Left at home with his mother and Yekutiel, Avraham watches from the window as the ghetto inhabitants swarm toward the center of the town. A few more minutes, and it's the three Lipkunskis' turn to join the thousand Jews already gathered in the market square.[32]

Twenty years later, Avraham will offer public testimony of what followed: the slow march from the market square to the mass graves. On May 5, 1961, the former pupil of the small Raduń yeshiva will testify in a courtroom set up inside the People's House in Jerusalem. At thirty-four, he might well be one of the youngest witnesses at the Eichmann trial.[33]

—So there were a thousand of you who went?
—Yes, I was close to my mother. We walked together, with the children.
—Your mother in the middle, you and your brother at each side?
—Yes, that's how it was, I was on her right, my little brother on her left. That was how we went.
—What did your mother say?
—She said: say *Listen, O Israel*, say the prayer *Listen, O Israel*. We must die as Jews.
—And they all walked that way, praying to their God ... *Shema, Yisrael*?
—I repeated the words after her, but inside I rebelled, I did it reluctantly.... Because my idea ... my idea had always been ... at least one of us has to survive, one must stay alive ... *überleben*, to be able to tell ... tell what happened.[34]

The column proceeded without complaints, without hysteria, without resistance. Every now and then, a few shots were heard: German policemen or Polish or Lithuanian auxiliaries would kill those who could not march farther right on the spot. Alongside the three Lipkunskis walked a family of their acquaintances, the Koralniks. Shlomo, like Sara Mina, was also a tailor in Dugalishok. He had married Sheinke, the eldest daughter of a rabbi, and they had two children. Shlomo had been in Cuba for many years, where he'd emigrated to put some money aside. Like Moshe David, who had emigrated to Argentina, he had returned home—one may have said—only to be killed together with his wife and his children.[35]

At the cemetery, Jews are forced to kneel on the ground, with their heads down. Peering beyond them, Avraham glimpses a pit that seems immense to him. And next to it, along the heap of landfill, he sees the German machine guns aimed at the ridge. Row after row, entire families are pushed toward that ridge, one by one. There, all the Jews—men, women, elderly, children—are forced to undress. And there they are strafed by volleys of automatic weapons, falling into the pit like bowling pins. The time for the Lipkunskis is almost at hand when Avraham recognizes his brother Pinchas. He's still alive, working not far from the ridge, with other young people from Raduń. He has a spade in his hand, digging new pits. The mere sight of Pinchas—of Pinchas alive—suffuses Avraham with unsuspected energy, and he instantly makes the decision to escape. Without saying a word to his mother and Yekutiel, Avraham gets up and runs off. Climbing over heads, arms, knees, and feet, he runs to reach Pinchas's group. A German intercepts him and asks him what on earth he is doing. Avraham replies with the three or four words of German he knows: I'm a blacksmith, I'm a good blacksmith. The German lets him go. Avraham runs a few more meters and reaches Pinchas.

Today, I surf the internet from the computer on my desk. I rewatch the black-and-white video of hearing number 29 of the

Eichmann trial, in Jerusalem, at the People's House, May 5, 1961. At minute 15 of the YouTube video, the prosecutor turns to the witness, Avraham, and asks him for the sequel to the story:

—What happened to your mother and little brother?
—My mother was killed, she was shot, along with all the other Jews, at the edge of the mass grave.
—And your brother Yekutiel?
—My brother Yekutiel was also killed there that day. Only later did I learn that, for some reason, I was the only one to get out alive, and to be ... to be saved.[36]

FOUR

ANABASIS

PALESTINE 1942

Palestine is a strange place in 1942. On the one hand, it is the scene of an economic boom. Beginning in September 1939, the Jewish settlement's economy benefited enormously from World War II. Without being a war zone, Palestine is in fact a rear guard for the British armies mobilized in the Middle East and North Africa, to the full advantage of the Jewish economy, which must satisfy a growing demand for products and services. Even though the Jaffa orange industry is in crisis, this crisis is amply compensated by the production of what the British Army troops need: tents, parachutes, camouflage patterns, boots, ropes, tanks, hoists, tires, plastics, optical and measurement instruments, dry ice, chemical compounds, telephone and electrical cables, canned foods, and medicines. In parallel, the turnover of Solel Boneh, Histadrut's construction company, soars. It carries out engineering works—bridges, railways, camps—necessary for the British not only in Palestine but also in Egypt, Iraq, and Iran.[1]

On the other hand, the Palestine of 1942 is the site of a society that is traumatized and in collective labor. Well within the course of the year, between spring and summer, the risk of a German invasion becomes real: not so much from the northeast as from the southwest, from North Africa. In June, General Erwin Rommel's divisions are stationed a hundred kilometers from Alexandria, Egypt. In the Zionist circles of Tel Aviv, the possibility is openly considered that the British, should they lose Alexandria, might evacuate Palestine. Thus, the nightmare of seeing the Afrika Korps parade through the streets of the Promised Land materializes. All this as the news coming from Poland—however scarce and sporadic—no longer allows for any doubts about the systematic nature of the extermination of the Jews. Although quantifying the carnage is impossible, the scale of the ongoing tragedy is evident to anyone who wants to see it.[2] In the summer of 1942, the major Jewish newspapers devote one article after another to the subject.[3]

But the collective trauma of 1942 is also one in which those assessing the extent of the tragedy in progress regret not doing enough to remedy it. The trauma entails the guilt that the Zionists in Palestine feel with regard to the destruction of the Jews of Europe.[4] That is, for the destruction—in many cases—of their own families, for the extermination of their grandparents and parents and brothers and sisters and uncles and cousins and nephews. It is a sense of guilt all the more lacerating because it was etched into the psychology of Zionism even before the Third Reich, and before the Final Solution. Zionism as a break with the world of origin, an investment in the community of brothers to the detriment of the community of family and shtetl. Zionism as an ideology of voluntary orphans, ready to trade everything else for Palestine—parents, mother tongue, home, childhood.[5]

It is September 1942 when the Jewish National Fund receives the formal proposal from a delegate of the kibbutz movement to raise a special memorial to the destruction of the Jews of Europe, which will soon be called Yad Vashem, "a memorial and a name." In December, the Zionist leadership announces three days of national mourning, attended by over one hundred thousand people—a fifth of the total population of the Jewish settlement. The Jews of Palestine commemorate the Shoah dead when hundreds of thousands of them are still alive, locked up in ghettos or concentration camps, precariously hidden under false identities, or perilously free in the forests of Poland, Belarus, Moldova, or Ukraine. At the same time, the political leaders of the Jewish settlement are starting to wonder what the impact of the Shoah may be on the ultimate outcome of the struggle for independence. More or less cynically, they wonder if and how the massacre of the Jews with the yellow stars will contribute to the triumph of the Jews with the blue star: the Jews of Palestine gathered under the insignia of the shield of David.[6]

Beyond the tactics of David Ben-Gurion and the other Zionist leaders, 1942 sees a significant mobilization of volunteers. Thousands of Jews knock on the offices of the British Military Command in the Middle East to be recruited into the British Army's combat units, or at least its auxiliary units. Most of them are sabra, Jews born in Palestine. But there are also many Jews of recent immigration: Germans, Austrians, Poles, Bohemians, Italians. These young men (and women) are asking for the opportunity to do something. After having managed to escape from Hitler's Germany or Anschluss Austria, from post-Piłsudski Poland or 1938 Czechoslovakia or the Italy of the racial laws, they are now asking to return in the uniform of a British soldier, to add their stone to the building of a Europe liberated from Nazism, and to be able to return home to their former homes, in the towns and villages where they had grown up and from which they had fled. They want to touch with their own hands whatever might remain standing and find out if at least any of the family members left behind, parents or grandparents, brothers or sisters, uncles or nephews or cousins, had escaped persecution and annihilation.[7]

Under instructions from the London government, the British Military Command has long tried to discourage "Palestinian" volunteers (as they were then called). They are discouraged for political reasons, in that they do not want to give Ben-Gurion any leverage at the peace negotiation table. And they discourage it for technical reasons. The British foresee difficulties created by the presence of Jewish and Arab soldiers in the same units. They fear the opportunities that free access to military equipment would provide to Zionist militants, allowing them to procure weapons for later use in the battle for independence. However, in 1942 the command finally relents. It agrees to the creation of auxiliary units, composed of skilled workers—mechanics, carpenters, plumbers—mobilized in support of the combat units of the British Army. Thus autonomous companies were born, each made up of 250–300 volunteer soldiers under the command of a major (a "Palestinian," i.e., a Jew) and aggregated into the departments of the Corps of Royal Engineers.[8]

The 745th Company of Royal Engineers, "745th (Pal) Artisan Works Coy, R.E.," is one such auxiliary unit. And one of the volunteer soldiers is Moshe Zeiri, a carpenter from Kvutzat-Shiller, near Rehovot.

A TERRIBLE SOLDIER

"My sweetest daughter, best wishes on your first birthday, from your father, who is physically far away, but close in the heart. You know, it's like I see you in front of me. Even now that I am walking around here with a rifle on my shoulder, I always have your smiling face in front of me." Late April 1943 is during the Passover holidays, which coincide in the Jewish calendar with the birthday of Nitza, Moshe's little girl. But her father is far away; he has left for the war. When he writes to her mother, at the kibbutz (which he does several times a week, numbering the letters so Yehudit can verify that she has received them all), he cannot say exactly where he is because military censorship forbids him. In any case, he is in Egypt for now, at the training camp. "Spr. Zeiri M. 745 Art. Wks. Coy R.E.": Moshe doesn't know any English—he ignores the language of command—but he has learned what he has to write, in Latin characters, at the beginning of each letter. His company is the 745th, and "spr." stands for sapper, which in the Royal Engineers is equivalent to private. In World War II, Moshe Zeiri is a private.

Nitza was born the year before, on the third day of Passover; in the Christian calendar, it was April 5, 1942. Writing to Yehudit later, during the war and from a distance, Moshe will evoke in detail "that Passover" when they went to the hospital "on a spring night" (Nitza's very name is springlike: in Hebrew, *nitza* means flowering). "There was a full moon, mute and silent, the scents of cedar blossoms seeped through the ambulance window and filled the space of the night. How much joy in my heart! I was sitting bent over you, holding your hand in mine, I asked you to squeeze tightly whenever you felt pain, which you did several times. How happy I would have been had I been able to participate in your labor pains, to relieve you. And then the day that followed the night of prolonged waiting, the tension, the anxiety. My imagination's delirium, which made me go to the telephone to announce that my daughter was born. My visit to you while you were still there, and then the journey home. The car bumping along the potholed side road, and you grimacing with every jolt. But the little one was fine, lying on your lap; asleep, she didn't even care to enjoy the beauty that surrounded her, the green fields, the golden orchards, the expanse of the Judean mountains that could be seen from far away."[9]

Moshe was recruited as a volunteer in the British Army a few months after Nitza's birth, in the winter of 1942–43. He left Kvutzat-Shiller in January, and after a few weeks of training in Palestine, he reached a larger training camp in Ismailia, in the Egypt that evoked biblical memories. The 745th Company of the Royal Engineers was made up of workers and craftsmen enrolled in Solel Boneh, the Histadrut's construction company, and Moshe Zeiri was one of them. However, not all the volunteers were as unfamiliar with military matters as he was, and not all had such scant experience with weapons, limited to night guard duty at the turret of a kibbutz, where the only enemy lurking was the risk of falling asleep and the spine-chilling howls of hyenas or jackals. There were Jews from Palestine enlisted in the 745th with a much fuller resume in martial matters. Lova Eliav, for example, was a Russian Jew who had served in an artillery unit of the British Army in 1940 and who, however young, imposed himself on his fellow soldiers with the natural authority of an educated person; he came from a good high school in Tel Aviv and had studied history and sociology at the Hebrew University of Jerusalem.[10]

Decades later, Eliav himself—as a public figure of the State of Israel, a former Labor MP, and one of the best-known activists of the peace movement—would evoke the Moshe Zeiri of the 745th Company in the words used by others for Berl Katznelson: "A terrible soldier, but what a man!" Eliav would remember Moshe's slovenly appearance, his invariably wrinkled uniform, the cap worn haphazardly, the service weapon filthy with desert sand—in short, the total lack of military bearing. But Eliav would also remember the qualities that had made the soldier Moshe Zeiri, from the time of his training in Egypt, a unique character among the 745th. His unwavering motivation as a cultural animator, and his formidable ability to translate projects into reality. Moshe's determination to transform the company into a kind of kibbutz infiltrated into the British Army, where Palestinian soldiers maintained the minimal infrastructure needed in a home of Zionist culture: a space where they could listen to and sing traditional Jewish music, read books and newspapers in Hebrew—in short, where they could cultivate the mental garden of modern Judaism.[11]

Writing to Yehudit, Moshe did not hide from her how he felt out of place in an auxiliary unit of the British Army mobilized in the war. "People see me as a tarbutnik, a 'vegetarian' pacifist, with all the contempt this can imply in the eyes of old soldiers.

And I admit that if I ever had to kill a man, I would suffer for the rest of my life." Reprimanded by his superiors for his dirty weapon, Moshe felt the same as he had felt at the shtetl's Polish school when the teacher asked him to speak in a language other than his own. But other memories of childhood and youth served as a positive lesson: a Zionist militant in Galicia between the two wars, Moshe had learned how many great things could be done with little means, starting almost from nothing. So just two or three weeks after arriving at the Ismailia camp, eighty miles northeast of Cairo, Sapper Zeiri of the 745th had already "organized a 'synagogue'" (he used quotation marks, in the letter to Yehudit): "a club where we can read, listen to the radio or music, and enrich our lives."[12]

Yehudit didn't need too much imagination to conjure the club. It was an area of the mess hall partitioned enough to set it off as a separate space, with some wooden shelves and reading tables resting on containers filled with sand, a low table with newspapers in chronological order, a radio, a harmonium fixed up who knows how, and two or three lights in the right place. Yet what emerged was a pleasant, welcoming environment. "The other night I was there, lending out those few books that I'd brought with me, and it warmed my heart." But what Moshe most wanted to share with Yehudit, what had made him happiest, was the scene of the Yemeni janitor: a modest-looking type, with "big sad eyes, like a child," in charge of the camp kitchens. "He comes every night, to bring back a book and get another. And when I go to the mess hall, he always welcomes me with a smile and a little something as a gift, an extra slice of melon, a bigger piece of meat.... I was about to close up one night, I was tired and thirsty, and here comes the guy who serves me a cup of iced tea." How to explain Moshe's joy? "He reminded me of the characters in Y. L. Peretz, one of those poor illiterate men who serve scholars with water in the study house so that they can continue to teach them the psalms."[13]

Moshe also had other reasons to be proud of his military life, starting with that sign at the entrance to the camp—745th Solel Boneh Company—written "in large Hebrew letters." Yehudit may have been tempted to laugh, but the simple fact that you could see, at the Egyptian camp of the British Army, an inscription in Hebrew instead of English or Arabic, and see it not on a black background, like the others, but on a light blue background, the national color of the Jewish settlement, served to make them proud. In general, they could be proud of the atmosphere they breathed in the company. "The whole place looks like a kibbutz." The way of life in the camp was full of camaraderie, nothing hierarchical. The officers called the soldiers by name, and the soldiers had the right to reciprocate. Officers and enlisted men sat at the same tables; Sapper Zeiri dined next to Major Haimowitz, the commander of the 745th, as well as Yechiel Duvdevani, one of the more authoritative sergeants. Nor was it just a matter of convivial solidarity. Haimowitz and Duvdevani strongly supported the cultural initiatives promoted by Moshe: little piano recitals, Hasidic songs. One evening at the end of June 1943 may have been the most successful: a ceremony in honor of the "Heroes of the Ghetto." According to information considered reliable, a few weeks earlier the heroes of the Warsaw Ghetto had dared to rise up against the German occupiers, despite knowing that the ghetto revolt was fatally doomed to defeat and martyrdom.[14]

Among Moshe's comrades in arms, there were two by the name of Reuven mentioned in the letters to Yehudit: Reuven Kohen and Reuven Donath.[15] Reuven Kohen was a Jew of Bohemian descent. He had a middle-class family behind him, a first-rate general culture, and thorough knowledge of music. Moshe had started spending time with him to get some English lessons, and the student's admiration for his teacher—who became the company's interior designer—soon became something like veneration. Reuven Donath came from a family of Jews from Hungary on his father's side, Poland on his mother's side, but he was a

sabra. He was born in Palestine and had grown up in relatively privileged conditions. At first Moshe had felt some reservations toward him, distrusting the typical sabra cynicism. Over time, his judgment became more indulgent, and Reuven Donath would eventually become one of Moshe's favorite comrades.[16]

Reuven Donath owned a camera, and he enjoyed using it during his free time from training (the visit to the Pyramids was particularly memorable), about which he wrote to Matti, a friend who had remained in Haifa. This Reuven had a brilliant character and was also brilliant with his pen. He described the work of the Royal Engineers as an obtusely mechanical activity, in every way similar to that of Charlie Chaplin in *Modern Times*.[17] Heinz Rebhun, a Jew from Berlin, also owned a camera—a Voigtlander to be envied—and was also a volunteer in the Royal Engineers. Several photographs taken by Rebhun in 1943 have recently been published, and they help to imagine the real-life material and immaterial surroundings of Sapper Moshe Zeiri in North Africa: the dull profile of the camp tents, the mammoth trucks driving in the sand, the daily tasks of Solel Boneh's engineers, and their symbolic apparatus, as predictable as it is exhilarating.[18]

The best photo, which could easily have been composed as a souvenir, was of the men arranging six rifles into a Jewish star. "I would have liked to see Mussolini's face" in front of the spectacle of the fasces symbol turned into that "hated shield of David," Moshe wrote in a letter to Yehudit dated August 27, 1943.[19] By that time, the fascist regime had fallen in Italy, and the Palestinian volunteers of the 745th had already made their crossing of the desert.

THE FIRST CHILDREN

From Cairo to Tobruk, there are five hundred miles; it is another three hundred from Tobruk to Benghazi. Practically all of it desert. According to the historical diary of the 745th Company, the crossing of the Palestinian Royal Engineers took place between July 10 and 15, 1943.[20] Moshe first wrote to Yehudit about it on July 12, during a quick stop ("hard to write on my lap, no table here") and a second time, on July 16, from the Benghazi camp. In between, there were "enchanting vast spaces" as well as "distressing views"[21]: the lunar landscape of what had been, in North Africa, the endless clash between the Axis and Allied armed forces, before the latter prevailed in May of 1943, with the Tunisian campaign and the Italian and German surrender.[22]

Disturbing views aside, officers and soldiers of the 745th will remember the days and especially the nights—the endless nights of convoys through Egypt and Libya—as a time of high morale.

The great fear of a year earlier was far away, and the nightmare of the Afrika Korps on parade through the boulevards of Tel Aviv was gone. Erwin Rommel, the "desert fox," had left months ago for Berlin, leaving behind soldiers who for years had seemed indomitable and who were now crowding the prison camps of the British Eighth Army.[23] So all through the nights of July 1943, they sang on the trucks lined up toward Benghazi. And they competed to have Zeiri on board, next to the driver not because he had a driver's license—he didn't—but because he could keep any driver awake, and he improved the crew's mood with the grace of his voice and his contagious cheer. Moshe would sing "Let the Wind Hit You, Boys," a patriotic ballad by Nathan Alterman, which would soon become the company's unofficial anthem, and would accompany them on their anabasis.[24] It was a completely different "ascent" compared to the aliyah of the Jews toward the Promised Land. Here they rose up in arms from the coast of North Africa toward the heart of Europe, toward the bloodlands of the Final Solution.

Compared to the bulk of the British Army troops, Palestinian companies such as the 462nd, 178th, and 745th had an additional motivation in Libya: they were helping the Jews. They helped ancient Sephardic communities, which, during Italy's colonial rule in the twenties and thirties, had been relatively prosperous, but which had then suffered terribly, first as a result of the racial laws imposed by fascism and then due to the combined effect of war and the presence of the German occupation forces in Libya. Between 1941 and 1943, thousands of Jews from Tripolitania and Cyrenaica had been deported to the concentration camp of Jadu, where they had been decimated by hunger and hardship.[25] The rest of Libya's Jews, even if they escaped the trauma of deportation and internment, had witnessed the destruction of their world: the scores of synagogues in Tripoli, Benghazi, and Tobruk, as well as the Jewish schools of these and other cities, the workshops, stores, and houses.[26]

"Yehudit, you should see the misery here. Children so undernourished that every single bone pokes out from the skin. . . . The workers and artisans without tools, robbed by the Arabs while they were displaced. The houses and shops of Jews and Italians almost all looted and kidnapped by the Arabs, who now resell the entire booty." For the first time, in Benghazi during the summer of 1943, the volunteers of the 745th come into direct contact with the devastation of the Second World War and with the desolation of an impoverished, disoriented, Jewish community that, while not physically annihilated, has nonetheless been spiritually raped: "These Jews are refugees in their own country." In contrast, the miserable conditions of the local Jews feeds the fire of Zionist determination among the volunteers enrolled in the Royal Engineers; they resolve to work discreetly, without attracting the attention of the British Command, to transform the work of assistance into propaganda activities in a push toward emigration. Regarding these Jewish refugees in their own country, Moshe explained to Yehudit, "we have the duty to approach them," and "prepare them," and "lead them to Eretz Israel."[27]

However crucial adult education was, it was necessary to start with the children. These children returned to Benghazi from the countryside where they had been displaced with their families to escape the bombing, and then they wandered begging from one city street to another. So the volunteers of the first Palestinian companies who arrived there opened a Jewish school in the spring: eight classes for three hundred schoolchildren, boys and girls. They also quickly organized secret training seminars for adults. Shortly after his arrival with the 745th, Moshe Zeiri joins a group of educators engaged in a variety of teaching activities, such as Hebrew language, arithmetic, gymnastics, drawing, and singing. "All teachers are soldiers"[28]: in a group photo, the teachers of the Hebrew school in Benghazi, including Moshe, actually appear in uniform, alongside local administrative staff. Yet, there is no immediate understanding between Ashkenazi

and Sephardic Jews.[29] Moshe recognizes this: "For us, who come from Eastern Europe, it is difficult to put ourselves in the shoes of Jews like these, to understand their mentality."[30] Not to mention the thousand difficulties created by the British military administration, for fear that the Jewish school might become a hotbed of Zionist acculturation. Hence the attempt to impose teaching in Arabic, the request to provide adequate training for the trainers, and the orders to close and reopen the school in fits and starts.[31]

These are problems that Moshe Zeiri can put aside that August of 1943, when he gets a leave to return home to the kibbutz in Palestine, to Yehudit and Nitza. His leave is far too short, though, a few days in all, inaugurated by the disappointment of his very first meeting with his daughter: she is fifteen months old and does not remember ever having seen her father. She bursts into tears as Moshe rushes to pick her up. Nothing serious, of course. Nitza quickly understands that the gentleman in uniform has just come from the very city that her mother has been mentioning so often that the word *Benghazi* was one of the first the little girl learned how to pronounce.[32]

Sapper Zeiri stays just long enough to get a taste for family life, and then he has to return to Libya with the weight on his heart of those who depart from their loves and the bitterness in his mouth typical of soldiers toward those comfortably in the rear, away from the front, who don't want to know or understand. "They've forgotten the days when Rommel was approaching the borders of Eretz Israel and everyone was ready to take up a weapon in defense of the homeland. Now that the risk has passed, and people are starting to mind their own business and accumulating money, why bother with the soldiers?" Moshe would soon complain.[33] He wasn't wrong. The Palestine of 1943 was very different from that of 1942. After the great fear of a breakthrough by the Afrika Korps, the sigh of relief was accompanied, in the Jewish settlement, by a resumption of business as usual. The Zionist leaders began to measure their moves toward the British administration. Ben-Gurion relaunched his slogan: Fight the world war as if the White Paper didn't exist, and fight the White Paper as if there were no world war. Even the collective trauma of 1942, the acknowledgment of the Final Solution, turned into a form of habit. At a meeting of the central committee of the Histadrut in May 1943, the Shoah featured as the sixth item on the agenda.[34]

Compared to certain Tel Aviv Zionists, some of the British Army volunteers have a clearer perception of the enormity of the present. Writing to Yehudit in mid-September 1943, Moshe records the news of the "total and unconditional surrender of the Italians," and he comments, "We hope this is the beginning of the end."[35] A couple of months later, Moshe himself reports the news available, in the Benghazi camp, about the German occupation of Italy after September 8, about the uncertain beginnings of an Italian Resistance, and even about the participation in this Resistance of some Jews who went up to the mountains. All reasons, in Moshe's opinion, not to regret his choice to enlist as a volunteer in the British Army—indeed, to be proud of it. And now, with the prospect that had opened up in front of the Palestinian auxiliary companies, of following the Eighth Army beyond the island of Malta and the sea around Sicily to liberate Italy and maybe even go beyond the Alps, he would be counting the days. "Moments like these will probably never happen again for the rest of our lives."[36]

Meanwhile, the Hebrew school in Benghazi was working at full capacity. Among the volunteers of the Royal Engineers, a professional teacher from Tel Aviv helped form the group of amateurs. Didactic material came from Palestine, and the Americans of the Joint arranged to finance the expenses of the local staff.[37] As for Moshe Zeiri, he has taken on a variety of roles, as usual: "Instead of working in the carpentry shop, I work at the Soldiers' Club, I teach singing at the adult school, I teach Hebrew at the children's school." Moshe especially tried to develop the ability to lead a class without raising his voice and without resorting to punishment. He managed to accomplish a lot with little: cutting out the characters of the alphabet from cardboard, using the postage stamps of the Jewish National Fund to introduce the children of Libya to the geography of the Promised Land, asking a decorator soldier to paint educational posters. "For an amateur, I do pretty well," Moshe concluded.[38]

The soldier decorating the posters was Menachem Shemi, and in civilian life he was a drawing teacher in an elementary school in Haifa. But that wasn't all he did. In the 1930s, he had worked as a choreographer for the Habima Theatre in Tel Aviv, where Moshe Zeiri would later go to drama school. When Kibbutz Hanita was founded in 1938, he had painted images of both the refectory hall and the watchtower, as if to pay immediate homage to the symbolic place of the Zionist conquest. In 1938 and again in 1942, Shemi had won the Dizengoff Prize for painting, the highest artistic award in British Palestine.[39] In short, he was no run-of-the-mill painter as he moved with the weapons and baggage of the Solel Boneh Company. Moshe understood this perfectly after hanging out with him in the makeshift workshop that Shemi had carved out for himself in the Benghazi camp. When you sit down and watch him paint, he confided to Yehudit, you feel transported

many meters above all the down-to-earth people who surround us here.[40]

The inside of a camp tent. A circus in Egypt. Soldiers with an oriental tower in the background. A veteran. A carpenter soldier. A peasant soldier. Still life with gloves. The Jewish street in Benghazi. Muslim child on a cart. Hungry children. Jewish women in Benghazi. Women of Cyrenaica. Women and children on a street in Benghazi. Black village in Cyrenaica. Diggers. A landscape of Benghazi. Scene after scene, the oil paintings by Menachem Shemi during the summer and autumn of 1943 accurately illustrate first the Egyptian, then the Libyan world of the 745th Company. And they illustrate it so vividly that I wish I could convey the North Africa of Palestinian volunteers enlisted in the British Army with nothing but these canvases. I would like to suspend the verbal story and make room for one made up of images. Instead, I have to settle for a single painting, the one that most impressed Moshe:[41] *Black Washerwomen in Benghazi*.[42]

In mid-December 1943, it becomes clear to the men of the 745th that their engagement in Libya is coming to an end. Their company will be transferred to Italy. So Moshe Zeiri prepares to separate from the children of the Hebrew school in Benghazi, and he does so with mixed emotions. On the one hand, he is saddened by the prospect of leaving them. He suffers from seeing them cry at the announcement of his departure, and he is tempted to shed tears for them as well. He fears that the new teachers will prove inadequate, that the children will be left to fend for themselves, that the rabbis and Orthodox leaders of the local Jewish community may again condemn them to inaction, blocking the doors to a future in Palestine.[43] On the other hand, Moshe experiences the prospect of 745th Company's anabasis as exalting, because of what this means in terms of the historical mission of the Palestinian volunteers. To Yehudit, who urgently presses him to tell her when he will return on leave to Kvutzat-Shiller, Moshe replies that he has no intention of asking for any leave and that he didn't even give it a moment's thought.[44]

"What I want most is to arrive in Italy soon, and contribute to helping the refugees. Dry the tears of those who are left. Do something useful there too for the children of Israel. My dear, please understand me. You know what an immense task the Jewish soldier has today. After all, it is only now that he is beginning to carry out the mission that he had glimpsed when he volunteered: to reach whatever still survives of our world in the reconquered countries of Europe."[45]

NAPLES, 1944

Despite Moshe Zeiri's impatience, more than three months would pass before the 745th Company of Royal Engineers landed in Puglia at the end of March 1944, making its base in the Lucera

camp, in the province of Foggia. Taking advantage of these extended delays, Moshe ended up asking for leave time. After the entire company left Libya for Egypt in January,[46] Zeiri was authorized to spend most of February in Palestine. And this time Nitza did not cry when the gentleman in uniform hugged her. Also, with her father she could do fun things outside of the limited Kvutzat-Shiller routine. For example, she rode with him and her mother on a white pony and took a tour of the kibbutz well beyond the fence of the nursery. She spent special days with him, and even her mother was in a better mood, smiling more readily and more broadly.[47]

This was the last family parenthesis ("I remember the train moving away, the rain seeping in from outside and entering my heart"[48]) before the anabasis truly began. During the confusion in Port Said, with the logistics managers of the 745th struggling to check the containers being loaded onto the ship, the two musicians of the company, Moshe Zeiri and Reuven Kohen, are concerned only with the harmonium, ready to perform any kind of ruse to let it pass unnoticed.[49] In the euphoria of Bari, it is the most prominent Italian Jew of the 745th, Bruno Savaldi, who leads the dance, thanks to his obvious command of the language and his experience as a pioneer of Italian Zionism.[50] With Duvdevani and others, Savaldi sets up a refugee center to coordinate assistance to Jews in the part of Italy already liberated: Puglia, Campania, and Calabria.[51] Savaldi enlisted in the 745th on the advice of Enzo Sereni, the founder of Kibbutz Givat-Brenner. Now he is helping Sereni, who is waiting to be parachuted from Puglia beyond the front line, into Northern Italy, where he hopes to do something for his brother, Emilio, a communist partisan arrested by the Nazis.[52]

So many paths crossing in that early spring of 1944 among the docks of Taranto, the roads of the Tavoliere, the hairpin bends of Gargano. In turn, fresh from landing, the very well-fed Polish troops of General Anders pass through Lucera, engaged in a anabasis much longer and more picaresque than that of the 745th Company. They departed from the Soviet Union, passed through the Caspian Sea and Iran, and then stationed in Palestine and Egypt before reaching Puglia and marching in forced stages toward Monte Cassino, where they are preparing to fight in the longest and most epic battle of the Italian campaign. Among the tens of thousands of men under General Anders, at least one thousand are Polish Jews.[53] In contrast, the Jews of San Nicandro Garganico, whom Enzo Sereni visits as an emissary of the Zionist movement, can be counted on the fingers of a few hands: a handful of peasants converted to the religion of Moses by an illiterate villager, Donato Manduzio. With no scrolls, rabbis, kippah, or candlesticks, no phylacteries or talliths, Manduzio and his followers have been striving for years to respect the Jewish calendar, if not to correspond to all the ritual obligations of the Orthodox. Now, in the hustle and bustle of war and liberation, they dream

more than ever of realizing their life plan. They dream of making the aliyah, replacing the hills of the Gargano with those of Palestine.[54]

Unlike General Anders's Polish Jews, at the beginning of April 1944, the Jews enrolled in the 745th Company did not have to go to the Monte Cassino slaughterhouse. From Lucera, they move to a bombed-out Benevento, where they set up a rear camp for the Fourth Indian Infantry Division of the British Army, that of the Nepalese Gurkhas: thirty-seven Nissen huts, a mile and a half of water pipes, kitchens, latrines, and access ramps. In May they reach Nola from Benevento, and in June they settle in the immediate surroundings of Naples, between Ottaviano and Torre del Greco.[55] Movements are evident from Moshe's letters to Yehudit, albeit with the discretion military secrecy imposes. The movements were also evident in Menachem Shemi's paintings, which illustrate, in this case, the Palestinian volunteers in southern Italy. Mowers. Tilling the vineyard. A street in Naples. The shoemaker family. The windows of an apartment building in Naples. Neapolitan view. Neapolitan prostitutes. Sailors and ladies.[56]

"Springtime blossoming in the South of Italy, the almond and olive trees. The pleasant villages, first impressions that made you forget home. Then the move to the Benevento camp with its enchanting surroundings, and then the Nola camp, with the walnut gardens and the endless scrolls that I wrote to you from there. Then the transfer to Naples, the period of the small school with fifteen to twenty pupils. The Company parties, the singing lessons, the visit to the Opera." Moshe recounts all this in a letter to Yehudit a year and a half later, containing the alpha and omega of his experience as a Jewish soldier in liberated southern Italy.[57] The 745th tarbutnik has by no means lost his enthusiasm to organize company parties, based on biblical readings and Hasidic melodies.[58] The lessons are those that Moshe receives in Naples from a singing teacher who thrills him when he teaches him the baritone romances of *Rigoletto* and embarrasses him when he asks him to practice with his daughters, two quick and voluptuous girls.[59] The visit to the opera is for a performance of *Tosca*, at the San Carlo Theater, which Moshe finds "indescribable" for its beauty.[60] And the small school with fifteen to twenty pupils is the one that Palestinian volunteers manage to start at the headquarters of the Jewish community, in Via Cappella Vecchia, in the heart of historic Naples.[61]

After the children of Benghazi, Moshe's new children are in Naples. They are nearly all Italian children belonging to the small local Jewish community, which is recovering from the traumas of the war.[62] For them, the Jewish school means, above all, relatively large meals compared to those offered in one of the makeshift refuges before the liberation. But the Jewish school also means that during the summer and autumn of 1944, they could finally go swimming in the sea, at the Torregaveta beach, beyond Pozzuoli, which could be reached by train on the Cumana railway or even, with a little luck, in one of the British Army vans. Less popular, at least with older pupils, are Mr. Zeiri's Hebrew lessons—not so much for the commitment itself, which required having to deal with new sounds and alphabet, but rather for having to learn nursery rhymes like *Hashafan Hakatan*, "the little rabbit," meant for kindergarten children. Even at parties organized on Shabbat, the older kids would cringe at the announcement (as if were the best news possible): "And now, children, it's time for sing-along!"[63]

In Naples, there are also foreign children among Moshe's. They belong to Jewish families from Central and Eastern Europe who had found a precarious refuge in Italy in the late 1930s, except for being treated—after Italy's entry into the war on June 10, 1940—as stateless or as citizens originating from various enemy states and as such subject to a variety of restrictive measures, from confinement to internment.[64] For these Polish, Hungarian, German, Austrian, Bohemian, Serbian, Croatian families, it was a gift of fate to be in some province of the South already free the day after September 8, 1943, when the Germans occupied a large part of the peninsula, and all the more after November 30, when Police Order no. 5 called for the arrest and deportation to concentration camps of all Jews present on the territory of the Italian Social Republic.[65] In the tragedy of the war and the Holocaust, these were the families of the lucky Jewish children.

Can a child like Isaak Weintraub, a student of Moshe's at the Jewish school in Naples, be called lucky? In any case, he is representative of a destiny shared by many Jewish children who lived precariously as refugees in Italy with their families, even before the outbreak of the war. Born in Leipzig in 1936 and the eldest son of a furrier separated from his wife, Isaak had to leave his mother and younger sister, Helga, in advance of September 8, 1943. He joined his father, a forced resident of Guardiagrele, a village in Abruzzo. During the period of the German occupation, both hid for months in country houses thanks to the help of a couple of local farmers who would be recognized, half a century later, as Righteous Among the Nations. (In the meantime, Helga and her mother managed to flee to Switzerland on the initiative of a Lombard couple who would also be recognized as Righteous Among the Nations.)[66] After the liberation of Abruzzo by the Allies, Isaak Weintraub followed his father to Bari and Calabria before settling with him in a rented room in the Vomero district of Naples—still unaware of the fate of his mother and sister, whether or not they had been saved too.[67]

As in Benghazi in the autumn of 1943, so in Naples in the autumn of 1944, Moshe Zeiri is confronted with a city raped by the war, where street children in particular live only by their wits. One October day, Moshe crosses the poorest streets of the historic center to reach the Villa Comunale, on the Riviera di Chiaia, and visit its gardens. The Spanish Quarter of Naples reminds the Kopychyntsi native of the Jewish villages throughout Galicia, except that poverty in the shtetl was for everyone, and they found company in a common misery, whereas in Naples the poor are condemned to live side by side with the rich, exposed to the abundance of others on a daily basis. There are scenes right out of Rossellini's *Paisan* or Malaparte's *The Skin*. Totally ignoring the wonders of the villa, starting with the stone and marble statues scattered in the gardens ("When will we ever have similar ones in Palestine?" Moshe asks in a letter to Yehudit), a band of street urchins throw stones at the leaves of the hazelnut trees, to gather the fallen hazelnuts by hand.[68]

In the gardens of the Villa Comunale, the street urchins also harass the Neapolitan girls who go out with the Allied soldiers, publicly punishing them by slipping off their underpants.[69] Naples in 1944 is a city where the women attract many of soldiers of the 745th like flies, and Moshe tries hard to keep away from them, despite all his need for a feminine embrace.[70] Heinz Rebhun, the German Jew of the company, the one with an enviable camera, has fallen in love with a good girl, Luciana Gallichi, and is preparing to marry her.[71] Others of Moshe's fellow soldiers have had less luck and need to be treated for venereal diseases. For different reasons, luck came scarce to one Palestinian soldier of the British

Army who was connected to Moshe by family: his brother-in-law, Yosef Nuriel. Rivka's husband is an Iraqi Jew whom the kindergarten teacher at the Ayelet Hashachar kibbutz met and married before the war.[72] Yosef is a communist, and he can't seem to hide the fact. When this reaches the ears of the British, they see fit to remove him from the company in which he served. Now he is depressed, Moshe writes to Yehudit in a letter dated November 5, 1944. Yosef has asked to be integrated into a fighting unit, or an auxiliary unit formed by Arabs.[73]

A few weeks later, it's Moshe's turn to receive a letter from his sister. Rivka writes to him from Palestine to discuss the delicate situation in which Yosef found himself in Italy. But Rivka also writes to her brother to share the agony of a discovery: the annihilation of their shtetl.

KAPUTT

In 1944 Naples—or, more precisely, on Capri, in a villa straight out of an architecture magazine—there was one man who had known it for some time. Curzio Malaparte had known the truth since the winter of 1941–42 and had almost let it be understood in his war correspondence published (and censored) by *Corriere della Sera*.[74] Malaparte had visited the Polish Governorate in person, in the midst of the Final Solution. In Warsaw, the captain-writer of the Fifth Alpine Regiment sat at the table with the lawyer Hans Frank, governor-general of occupied Poland. Together with Frank, Malaparte had even taken a sort of guided tour of the Warsaw ghetto.[75] The journalist-officer had also had a firsthand view of the Galician ghettos, even though he had left before their liquidation.[76] These are the visits and viewings that Malaparte chooses to deliver, in October 1944, in the tragic sentimentality of *Kaputt*, the most self-indulgent (and, in many ways, the least reliable) of any real-time reports on the extermination of Europe's Jews.[77]

In one Polish ghetto after another, during the winter of 1941–42, "the dead lay stretched out in the snow between extinguished menorahs." Other dead "lay on the floor in the halls of houses, on the landings, in the corridors, or on the beds in rooms thronged with pale and silent people. Their beards were sodden with mud and slush.... They were stiff and hard, they looked like wooden statues. Just like the dead Jews in a Chagall canvas." As for the living in the ghettos, they were barely alive, and for only a little while longer. "The faces of the women and children seemed made of paper. In every face there was already the bluish shadow of death. The eyes, in those faces the color of gray paper or white chalk, seemed like weird insects busily rummaging with their hairy little legs in the pits of the sockets and sucking what little light still shone in the hollow of the orbits. As I approached, those loathsome insects became restless, they broke away from their prey for moment, came out from those sockets as if from a lair, gazing at me in fear.... The eyes of the women were courageously steady; they held my glance with insolent contempt.... But the eyes of the children were terrible, I could not look at them."[78] If Moshe Zeiri had already mastered the Italian language well enough to knock on the door of the Casella bookshop, at the Dogana del Sale, and if he had bought a freshly printed copy of *Kaputt* and read it—despite the annoyance of a piety that was as narcissistic as it was expressionistic—many things would have been clear even without the arrival of his sister's letter from Palestine.

Rivka discovered the truth about Kopychyntsi from an article in *Davar* on November 29, 1944, under the title "Letters from the Valley of Death: From Kopyczynce." After the liberation of Galicia by the Red Army, a timber merchant wrote to a friend from Tel Aviv, himself a native of Kopychyntsi, to tell him the essentials about the annihilation of the shtetl. The mass graves, massacres, and deportations to the Belzec extermination camp took place from March to December 1942 in Kopychyntsi as in the other Jewish towns and villages of eastern Galicia: Lviv,

Chortkiv, Probizhna, Husyatyn, Skalat, Terebovlia.[79] If liquidated in mass graves, the women had to strip naked on the edge before being shot in the back of the head. As for the children, it was preferable that they be killed by hitting their heads against walls or rocks, in order to save ammunition. The timber merchant had lost all his relatives this way: his father-in-law and daughter in the first *Aktion*, his sister-in-law in the third, and the rest of the family in the eighth. After the liberation, he calculated that there were no more than sixty survivors in Kopychyntsi, out of the thousands of Jews who had inhabited the shtetl in the 1930s.[80]

Rivka reads this in *Davar* on November 29, and she reports it the same day, in her tortured letter to Moshe. He then passes the news on to Yehudit, and he would like to write to her about something else. He would like to tell her about the Neapolitan preparations for the Hanukkah festival, which involve both the Palestinian volunteers of the British Army and the children of the Jewish school in Via Cappella Vecchia. He would like to tell her more about what he's planning to do at the show: singing solo, one of Simone's arias from Handel's *Judas Maccabaeus* oratorio (he tried it again and again with his singing teacher, and he feels he can pull it off). But how could he write about anything else, after receiving Rivka's letter? "Images of slaughtered children chased me all night, I couldn't sleep. So, to ease the desperation, I sat down to write to you."[81]

Moshe writes again and again to his wife in the winter of 1944–45. He has always written since he left voluntarily, at the rate of a couple of missives per week. He tells her about his teaching job; he describes the students of the Hebrew course, the children as well as the adults. And he reacts to the letters received, to Yehudit's tales and stories about life in Kvutzat-Shiller. Joyful tales about Nitza's growth, about her tiniest everyday gestures. Sad or even painful stories, because the kibbutz experience wears on one—it tires the body, clutters the mind, dries up the heart. One can be crushed under the weight of forced coexistence, lack of intimacy, and systematic gossip. Even the distribution of mail is a community ritual on the kibbutz: the arrival of the red van in the midafternoon, honking its horn at the small crowd waiting at the clearing in front of the offices and calling out the names of the recipients. Even the frequency of letters sent by soldiers to wives can be scrutinized by everyone, fueling the rumor mill. Beyond this, what emerges from Yehudit's letters is the loneliness felt by an involuntarily single mother, which borders on a wife's resentment toward her husband for having voluntarily left for war.[82]

Moshe's letters, in turn, reflect conflicting moods. The military bulletins are obviously encouraging. On the Western Front, they report the advance of the Allies in Lorraine, the invasion of Germany, and the Rhine campaign. On the Eastern Front, they report the advance of the Red Army into Poland, the Vistula and Oder campaigns, and the liberation of Warsaw, Kraków, and Łódź. And on the Italian front, despite the military stalemate of the winter, there is an extraordinary piece of news: the integration of auxiliary units of the Royal Engineers with combat units of "Palestinians" that the British have finally agreed to form and that, after training in Egypt, landed in Taranto as the Jewish Infantry Brigade Group. Although the men of the 745th are not part of the Jewish Brigade, they are proud that Jews have finally been recognized as worthy of fighting the war in every sense. But all this is not enough to erase, in Moshe's letters, the empty passages, the discouragement, and the crises; his nostalgia for home life, for Yehudit's body, and Nitza's smile; and the awareness of how much, after the victory, would be irreparable in defeat. "Each country is now busy determining borders and quantifying the damage, no country is concerned with our destiny":[83] the destruction of the Jews of Europe, and the end of their world of yesterday.

One day in March 1945, Moshe decides to take a trip to Capri. He then jokes about it, writing to Yehudit that he had to go there, otherwise how could he have justified himself, with Nitza, for having lived near one of the most beautiful places on Earth without ever giving himself the time to set foot there?[84] Moshe wanders around Capri and probably ignores the fact that he is just a few steps from Villa Malaparte. Moshe is perhaps unaware of the existence of the author who, a few months earlier, in *Kaputt*'s introduction, was keen to emphasize, "But I prefer this Kaputt Europe to yesterday's Europe—of twenty or thirty years ago. I prefer starting anew, rather than accepting everything as an immutable legacy."[85] Moshe Zeiri, the Galician Jew, can hardly know anything about the arch-Italian Curzio Malaparte. Yet from his point of view, he has to deal with that very outcome. The ruin of what was yesterday's Europe, including the immutable legacy of Eastern European Jewry. The need to redo everything, by building a new life for the surviving Jews.

UNCLE ALFRED

When the American soldiers entered Aachen, the first city in Nazi Germany to be liberated, they encountered very few surviving Jews—to be exact, only one. On October 21, 1944, when the GIs had managed, after three weeks of fierce fighting,[86] to conquer the city that was a bastion on the Siegfried Line, the only Jew they found to welcome them was a sixty-four-year-old widower who, after the suicide of his wife, had been hidden in the house by a young Christian woman he would eventually wind up marrying.[87] This Jew's name was Alfred Löwendahl. He was the brother of Wilhelmina Meyer—Yehudit's uncle. A German Jew like the others, but luckier than many others, including his brothers and sisters. Luckier than Uncle Benno, the Jew from Cologne, who fell on the field of honor in 1916. Luckier than Aunt Henrietta, a Jew from Hamburg, deported to Theresienstadt and gassed in Treblinka.[88]

The Rhine campaign went more slowly than expected for the Allies. The Siegfried Line held even after the fall of Aachen, and the Western Front experienced another winter of war. The

Americans did not enter Cologne—just eighty kilometers to the east—until March 6, 1945. Similarly, on the Italian front, the Gothic Line held even after the breakthrough of the British Eighth Army along the Adriatic, in the autumn of 1944. If Cesena had been liberated on October 20, 1944, Bologna—just ninety kilometers to the west—would have had to wait until April 21, 1945. This would occur after the battle of the Senio River, which began on April 9 and saw the soldiers of the Jewish Brigade— Palestinians with the blue star, Jews fighting under the shield of David[89]—engaged alongside the Indian and New Zealand divisions of the British Army, as well as the Polish troops of General Anders.

During the battle of the Senio River, the soldiers of the 745th Company remained in the rear, in Naples, receiving a prestigious visit from Moshe Sharett, the head of the political department of the Jewish Agency. Moshe Zeiri was deeply impressed. "He spoke like an actor, refined in language and perfect in diction," the former student of the Tel Aviv school of dramaturgy writes to Yehudit. "He did nothing to give us false hope, nor did he promise us anything."[90] He explained how uncertain the political prospects of the Jewish settlement remained in Palestine. Above all, he discussed the news that Zionist emissaries were communicating from the liberated territories of Hitler's former empire, east as well as west. There was the consoling presence of surviving Jews, who biblically considered themselves the saved who save, but also the material difficulty of gathering these surviving redeemers, of assisting them, healing them—indeed, in the case of children, the difficulty of identifying them, hidden as they had been under a false name. The little ones may even have forgotten their original names. And there was the difficulty of receiving them from the families and institutions that had protected and saved them. From Christian parents who had grown fond of the Jewish children, and who felt they had adopted them. From Catholic congregations who had provided baptism to them and used the argument of baptism as a good reason not to return them to the embrace of relatives still alive.[91]

During those same days in April 1945, Moshe Zeiri promotes another important meeting for the soldiers of the 745th. With the collaboration of Menachem Shemi, the artist of the company, he brings Esther Lurie from Rome to Naples. A Lithuanian Jewish artist herself and the winner of the Dizengoff Prize in 1938, Lurie had been locked up in the Kaunas ghetto from 1941 to 1944, then in the concentration camp of Stutthof, until the arrival of the Red Army in January 1945. Within two months, Esther Lurie managed to reach Italy, taking with her some sketches she had drawn in captivity. At the Jewish Soldiers' Club in Rome, Shemi immediately found a way to set up an exhibition of these drawings.[92] At the Naples encampment, Zeiri organizes a conference with the young artist. She is the first person escaped from the Final Solution whom the soldiers of the 745th have the opportunity to meet. By gathering around Esther Lurie, the Palestinian volunteers experience firsthand what to expect in the immediate future. Welcoming the surviving Jews, be they few or numerous. Listening to their words, more or less disjointed by the enormity of the trauma. Finding something to say, if ever possible, to alleviate the suffering, to somehow transform their individual salvation into collective redemption.[93]

VIA UNIONE

"Italian patriots executed Benito Mussolini... The brains which took Fascist Italy into the war ooze onto the filth of a dirt plot in the center of Milan. Along with Mussolini, the patriots killed his mistress, Claretta Petacci... Blood stains showed crimson on the dainty white blouse with lace ruffles, which miraculously had escaped most of the muck and filth which covered the bodies of Mussolini and the others." Thanks to an article by James Roper, war correspondent of the United Press, even the readers of *The Palestine Post* discovered the gory details in the story that appeared on the morning of May 1, 1945.[94] The details quickly make a tour of Jerusalem and reach a child in the Kerem Avraham neighborhood, who is particularly rich in imagination. Amos Oz is six years old when he hears about the public display in an Italian piazza of Benito Mussolini and Claretta Petacci's bodies hanging upside down, and he struggles to understand how it could have happened. He does an experiment: he tries to hang himself too, feet up and head down, from the pipe running along the wall of the house. He soon faints and then feels pity even for a villain like Mussolini and his floozy lover. But he can't get that Italian scene out of his mind. In fact, he begins to collect little shutter-holders, "*mentschelekhs*, I mean the little men who held the shutters open during the day, those little metal figures: when you wanted to close the shutters, you swiveled them around so that all night long they hung head down. The way they hung Mussolini and his mistress Claretta Petacci at the end of the World War."[95]

As already happened after July 25, 1943, when Italians took out their rage on an effigy of the Duce, they do so again on April 25, 1945, only this time on his lifeless body. Unsatisfied even after hanging the corpses in Piazzale Loreto, Milanese anti-fascists still want to overthrow the cult of Benito Mussolini, which for too long had held the Italian people under its sway. In Via Unione 5—in the center of the city—partisans of the Matteotti Brigades take out their revenge against a bust of the Duce that dominated the premises of Palazzo Odescalchi, the seat of the Amatore Sciesa regional club (for twenty years, the most prestigious in Milan among fascists).[96] They hurl the bust down the marble staircase, damaging some steps.[97] These partisans from the Matteotti Brigades gain in strength the more they believe that they have been protagonists in the battle for the liberation of the city. During the days of the insurrection, they were the ones who occupied the prefecture and the town hall, as well as army barracks, police stations, public offices, and newspaper offices. They also occupied the various Fascist Party district offices known as Case del Fascio, including the one a few steps from Via Unione, at Piazza San Sepolcro, where everything had begun in 1919.[98]

At the age of fifty, Colonel "Vittorio" is one of the leaders of the Matteotti Brigades: commander of the Ninth Naviglio Division, deputy commander for the entire province of Milan.[99] He has a long military past as a former Bersaglieri officer in the trenches of the Great War. He has a dignified political past as an anti-fascist exile in France during the 1930s. He has a tragic family past: his brother, Fausto, an antique dealer in Via Sant'Andrea, was one of the first Milanese Jews captured on the street after September 8, 1943, briefly detained in the San Vittore prison, and forced to board a train from platform 21 of Central Station—destination Auschwitz.[100] Colonel Vittorio is a Jew; his name is Davide Mario Levi at the registry office. Perhaps also for this reason—in the free, feverish, merciless Milan of late April and early May 1945—he works hard for other Jews. As far as some of the partisans are concerned, he even works too hard.

The local Jewish community is trying to get back on its feet.[101] The most energetic of its leaders, Raffaele Cantoni, rushes from Switzerland to Milan in those days of the insurrection.[102] Cantoni has close relations with the socialist leaders of the Resistance and easily identifies Levi as a man useful to the Jewish aid machine. On April 26 (when there is still fighting in the streets of Milan, and the Duce and his mistress are still hoping to get away), Colonel Vittorio orders that the Jewish community be supplied with a "large cooking pot" and a "big fish pond." He then opens a Jewish Refugee Assistance Committee in the same location as his partisan command, in Piazza Carnaro 4, collecting clothes and objects to be immediately distributed to the Jews. And in the very first days of May, it is Colonel Vittorio who takes over the Palazzo Odescalchi in Via Unione. As deputy provincial commander of the Matteotti Brigades, he helps allocate the former Amatore Sciesa regional club to the Milanese Jewish community (the premises in Via Guastalla were unavailable because they were destroyed in an aerial bombing raid in 1943).[103] Colonel Vittorio does so much for the Jews that he provokes a complaint to the Piazza Command in Milan by a group of partisans from the Magenta Collection Center Command. "On May 15, 1945 some wagons unloaded about 23 boxes of cutlery, 6 packages of blankets, a box for table services, and about 400 pairs of shoes" in front of the Naviglio Grande unified command. "That office saw a to-and-fro of people recognized as Jews who went out, some with shoes, some with blankets, and some with material." So the signatories "merely ask for an inspection in order to establish the extent and legality of these goods. They are Partisans, many of them old conspirators and former political prisoners. They fought and still fight for freedom, for justice, which is linked to honesty."[104]

Anti-fascist or antisemitic, this denunciation of Colonel Vittorio's trafficking goes up the partisan bureaucratic ladder as very different forms of assistance are being organized for the Jews. Later in May—with the arrival in Milan of the Palestinian companies of the British Army—the building in Via Unione 5 becomes the headquarters of a military mobilization destined to be transformed by the summer into a mobilization at once material and spiritual, legal and illegal. Dodge trucks with the Star of David drawn on the doors load or unload a wide variety of materials at Via Unione 5: equipment abandoned by fleeing Germans, spoils of war recovered in railway yards, weapons and ammunition stolen from the British Army. Pronounced with a Polish, Russian, Hungarian, German, Yiddish, or Hebrew accent, or simply in Italian, Via Unione becomes the magic formula to mean many things, among them resumption of a communal everyday life for the Milanese Jews, with offices, a synagogue, and ritual spaces. It is the first reception center for Italian and foreign Jews returning alive from the bloodlands, and a base of operations for Zionist emissaries, declared or disguised, working toward the emigration of surviving Jews to the Promised Land.[105]

Moshe Zeiri arrived in Via Unione around May 15–16. I don't know the exact day, and the historical diary of the 745th doesn't help; by that date, the Solel Boneh Company was almost dismantled. It matters little; that was more or less the moment, and Zeiri's letters testify to it (even taking military secrets in account). Everything went quickly after that. In the euphoria of a May Day of freedom, Moshe told Yehudit what he knew about the capture of Mussolini and his display at Piazzale Loreto.[106] On May 5, what remained of the 745th was ordered to move north from Naples. Four hours by train, then a seven-day stop at the Laterina camp, in the province of Arezzo. On May 8, the news of the German surrender left Palestinian volunteers in a state of astonishment, relief mixed with fatigue, joy with doubt. Like a good sabra, Reuven Donath had himself portrayed smiling in the center of a group of fellow soldiers holding up a copy of *Union Jack*, the British Army newspaper with the announcement of victory.[107] But the smiles of his companions are more tentative than his own. Now that the war was won, what would become of them? Would Ben-Gurion really accept the British Command soon demobilizing the Palestinian companies without reacting? And would the Jewish volunteers really be happy to return home, turning their backs on the surviving Jews, not caring about their future?

The company didn't even have time to ask questions before it was ordered to proceed northward again. The Po Valley, although devastated by the war, amazed Moshe: a spectacle of fertile land "which I have never seen, not at home in Palestine, or in Poland, or Egypt or Libya." But Moshe is at least equally impressed by the spectacle of Milan in the aftermath of the liberation: a city covered in red, paved with the insignia and symbols of the partisan brigades. These partisans had unleashed the insurrection before the arrival of the Allied troops, had eliminated Mussolini and the Fascist hierarchs in advance of having to hand them over to the Allies, and now went around Milan with long hair and scarves

blowing in the wind not just as winners but as revolutionaries—and executioners. They unleashed the hunt for fascists and their collaborators, trying to eliminate as many as possible before being called by the Allied Military Government to inevitably hand over their weapons.[108]

On May 17, Moshe describes his initial impact with Via Unione to Yehudit. The first Jews arriving from the bloodlands, who incredulously recognize other Jews as soldiers of the British Army, with the Star of David sewn on their uniforms. The first tales of the survivors, endless stories of pain and horror, singular stories of remorse and relief. The rumors, more or less plausible, about the drowned and the saved. Like when Moshe is informed of the presence, in the Palazzo Odescalchi, of a Jewish woman originally from Kopychyntsi. But he tries in vain to identify her among the gaunt profiles of the refugees queuing at the refectory, or lying on the beds in the chaos of the dormitories. He tries in vain to embrace something more full-bodied than a ghost from his shtetl.[109]

FIVE

THE DROWNED AND THE SAVED

THE PARTISAN AVREMALE

For some reason, on May 10, 1942, the Germans in the Reichskommissariat Ostland gave up on completing the liquidation of the Raduń ghetto. The adult males who had been digging mass graves in the cemetery for slaughtered Jews since the dawn of that Sunday were left alive. In the evening, backtracking along the road to Grodno, the excavators were escorted back into the confines of the ghetto. And the next morning, instead of starting the massacre again, the Germans organized the distribution of work permits, because there was no lack of work to be done. The surviving Jews had to first of all bury the dead scattered along the road: those who had not even reached the cemetery, who had been killed on the way by SS soldiers or Polish or Lithuanian auxiliaries. And then at the cemetery, the surviving Jews had to spread earth over the mass graves that had swallowed the corpses of their parents, brothers, and children.[1] They had to fix a landscape that was contaminated forever.[2]

Pinchas and Avraham Lipkunski returned to the Raduń ghetto. On Sunday evening, they found themselves in the apartment on Lida Street from which they had been uprooted a few hours earlier, but they were without their little brother, and without their parents. They were convinced that their father, Moshe David, had also been killed in the cemetery, that his naked body had joined the naked bodies of Sara Mina and Yekutiel and the Koralniks and all the other Jews shot dead on the ridge. Pinchas and Avraham cried until they ran out of tears. Then on Monday morning, they presented themselves to the Germans to register for work. "We're both blacksmiths, two good blacksmiths." But already that evening, the Lipkunski brothers collected, among the ceiling beams, their most precious possession: the last pieces of silverware, the cases of phylacteries. The following evening, they knocked on the doors of other homes in the ghetto, where other survivors of the massacre were holed up. They asked Jakob Moshe, the soda maker, for advice; they asked Haim Pik, the carpenter, as well. On the third day, they decided to escape to Dugalishok, with the idea of hiding out in the pine forest. It was the enchanted forest where, when they were children, their father had taught them to recognize every tree and every clearing.[3]

Pinchas and Avraham also knew the way from Raduń to Dugalishok like the backs of their hands. They had covered it many times, coming home from the yeshiva for family vacations. On the night of May 13, 1942, they stayed away from the road. Rather than risk misadventure, they preferred to move across the fields, in the mud of a thaw by now complete. Once they arrived in Dugalishok, after waiting for first light, they went to a Christian farmer—a trusted client of Moshe David the farrier—and heard the most extraordinary news: Their father was alive! On the Sunday of the massacre, in the cemetery, he had taken advantage of a diggers' revolt and managed to escape. He was now hiding in the forest, but periodically he came back to one of his old clients, who in spite of the risks supplied him with bread and milk fresh from the cow. There were a few more days spent among the peasants' stables, respecting every possible measure of prudence, before the fateful moment came. On a morning in late May, Pinchas and Adam hugged their father, whom they thought had been lost.[4]

The two brothers suffered all the more when Moshe David explained to them that they would have to separate again (except to meet every now and then, in agreed-upon places) for security reasons, to have a better chance of surviving. But before saying goodbye, the father reminded the children of the forest's secrets. The birds' voices, which they had to listen for and distinguish in order to predict rain or unwelcome presences, ferocious animals or men. The bounty of the undergrowth, especially during the summer, with blueberries, raspberries, and strawberries. The meaning of the tracks left on the ground, near or far, natural or mechanical, human or feral. The respective advantages and disadvantages of trees, bushes, and meadows. Thanks to all this, once they were separated from their father, Pinchas and Avraham quickly turned into two wild boys. They approached the farmhouses only if they were sure to be inhabited by devout Christians. And they stayed away from the shepherds, who were as ubiquitous as they were treacherous.[5]

The summer of 1942 passed like this, in the strangest and most precarious conditions of freedom imaginable, until the two Lipkunski brothers began to prepare for winter. At the beginning of September, they gathered the logs needed to build a bunker: a den to live in underground, for when the snow would reign supreme outside. Pinchas and Avraham had already begun to live in the bunker when they first got wind of the partisans in the forests—mainly Soviet soldiers, left behind a year earlier after the catastrophic retreat of the Red Army. But there were also Jews from the area among them, as well as Poles, Lithuanians, and Belarusians, who in some daring way escaped the liquidation of the ghettos and grouped together in loosely organized, ragtag gangs.[6] They were in the great Rudniki forest, between Vilnius and Eišiškės, and in the huge forest of Nača, a few kilometers from the small forest of Dugalishok. Not far from them.[7]

That was the disaster. A double disaster: the feeling of security of living in the bunker, the exciting rumors about the presence of partisan gangs in the surroundings. It was just enough to make Pinchas and Avraham less cautious and too self-confident. One October night in 1942, the two brothers decided to return to the shtetl—back home, to Dugalishok. They went with the hopeful idea that there they would be able to make first contact with the partisans. They didn't imagine, however, that in the meantime a Lithuanian family had settled into the Lipkunski house, and that precisely this family, struck in turn (for opposite reasons) by the rumors of partisan bands in the surroundings, had requested that very night the intervention of a patrol of armed men. A cleanup operation—good riddance—so they could finally stay there in peace for a while. Shortly thereafter, a patrol of Polish policemen arrived in Dugalishok, at the service of the Germans.

It all happened very quickly, without even time to realize what was going on. When the two brothers reached the entrance to the shtetl and approached what had been their home, someone shouted, "Halt, who goes there?" and immediately shots rang out. Pinchas and Avraham started running. Pinchas ran faster, but a moment later Avraham heard Pinchas's voice saying, "They shot me!" And for the rest of his life, he would never forget it. The memory of the scene would haunt him forever. "Pinchas's last scream, I'll remember it until my dying days, it will accompany me to the grave. I saw him fall to the ground, I saw his body crashing down on the opposite side of the rock we used to climb up as a game when we were children, on our way to Papa's foundry. And I was running, I was running away, I didn't even stop to hold him, hug him, caress him. It was as if an invisible hand was pushing me away, farther and farther."[8]

Avraham managed to escape, and within half an hour, he reached a Christian's farm where he knew his father had found refuge. In the middle of the night, he had to tell him the horrible truth: Pinchas was dead. After that, when the day was over,

Moshe David and Avraham learned from their protector what was rumored about the firefight that had taken place in Dugalishok. One Jewish bandit killed, another on the run. The one killed was buried in a hurry by the Lithuanian man living in the Lipkunski house, on the edge of farmland that had also belonged to the Lipkunskis. The fleeing Jew was actively being sought by the auxiliary police. Then Moshe David and Avraham, the only ones in the family still alive, swore that they would never be separated again. And they fulfilled their commitment at least for a few months, the remainder of autumn and the whole winter of 1942–43, during which the Christian farmer who protected them agreed to hide both of them on the farm. They lived in a sort of cell created in the barn, where the father and son tried, quite simply, to survive—with no other food than the monotonous but regular fare procured by their guardian angel, with no other consolation than the morning prayers recited with the phylacteries inside their tiny hideout.[9]

In April 1943, however, with the thaw at an advanced stage, Avraham decided to join the partisans in the Nača forest. In vain he tried to persuade his father to do the same. But at forty-five, Moshe David didn't feel he had it in him to follow his son.[10] He preferred to stay back and count on the protection of his former clients. It often happened that Jews determined to join a guerrilla band had to separate from family members—from a parent, wife, or child—who remained alive. Young or old, male or female, the partisans of the forest found a new family among their comrades, and through the new family they were reborn into a new life, one no less dangerous than before, no less fraught with the risk of dying—and yet intoxicating in an altogether different way. They were no longer living like sacrificial victims, lambs destined for slaughter. It was the life of a free fighter, a Jew from the Bible, capable of striking and eager for revenge.[11]

In the Nača forest, Avraham's meeting with the band of Elke Ariovitz ("Todras") regenerates him. Because Todras, a decade older than him, is not just a former schoolmate of his at the small yeshiva in Raduń, nor is he merely a former apprentice blacksmith well-known in the past at the Lipkunski foundry in Dugalishok. Todras is a natural leader. He has always been, ever since he marched through the streets of Raduń wearing the black Betar uniform. Now, he dresses like a Cossack and moves on horseback, in the forest, like a charismatic avenger of wrongs. He is respected and appreciated—not only by the seventy individuals who make up his Jewish band but also by numerous Christians living in the surrounding area. Because in their brusque, partisan way, Todras and his men are accommodating people. They give a hand in the fields at harvest time. They help make illegal vodka. Indeed, they protect the Polish farmhouses with arms from the raids of the Germans in search of food.[12]

For a few weeks after his arrival in the gang, Avraham has to be content with being part of the "family group": women, children, and the elderly who in close quarters share the armed men's rhythms of life, but who have nothing of the fighting Jew. Avraham thus finds himself regretting both his fourteen-year-old immaturity and his small size, which does not make him look older. But already in May, with his own nom de guerre, "Avremale," Moshe David Lipkunski's second son is authorized to carry a weapon. And he participates in his first actions: sabotaging bridges and railway lines; destroying the granaries requisitioned by the Germans; and attacking food warehouses, fuel tanks, and whatever else is needed for the enemy's logistics.[13] These are operations marginal to the huge war that the Wehrmacht and the Red Army are fighting on the Eastern Front—nothing more than local guerrilla activity. Yet it is an activity sufficiently important, in the eyes of the Soviets, to get the Todras gang incorporated among the auxiliary units of the Red Army, under the name of Leninski Komsomol Brigade.[14]

The epos of the Jewish gangs of Eastern Europe would sooner or later strike the imagination of novelists, including Primo Levi in his only novel, *If Not Now, When?* And it would move the pen of another writer who passed nearby: a child who also survived the ghetto and the forest, like Avraham Lipkunski, and was then picked up by the Red Army marching west.[15] Aharon Appelfeld would write *The Partisan Edmond*. More than a novel, it is the parable of a band of Eastern Jews as a community of redeeming survivors, of the saved who save. "We have seen a lot of sadness in this world, more than in previous generations, it is not surprising that it has not cleansed us more. Such great pain darkens rather than enlightens, but fortunately the Lord has brought us to these wonderful mountains that have straightened our posture and connected us together. Now each of you is a messenger of the Lord in this world."[16] From the forest of Nača, in 1943, the partisan Avremale cannot know the pages of an Israeli book that would be published seventy years later. But Avremale might feel like a messenger of the Lord when, straightening his posture (and challenging the judgment of his most skeptical companions), he decides to always carry with him, tucked into the pockets of his partisan's jacket, the phylacteries his mother had given him on the day of his bar mitzvah.[17]

Everything else in that spring of 1943 just adds to the tragedy. His father, Moshe David, is killed by antisemitic thugs from Armia Krajowa, the Polish interior army, during a manhunt against the last remaining Jews in the Dugalishok district.[18] Then comes the death of his leader, Todras, who is arrested on the initiative of Soviet emissaries infiltrating the Leninski Komsomol Brigade. He is tried in public before the peasants of a village on the edge of the forest and accused of having committed embezzlement and reprisals. He is sentenced to death and shot in the head—not because he was really guilty, but because he is resistant to the political order imposed by the Red Army's advance guard.[19] It is the same Red Army undertaking the historical task of saving those among the Jews of Eastern Europe who remain alive, the army of a totalitarian and brutal state such as Stalin's Soviet Union, without whose advance westward no Jew from the East will survived the Final Solution.[20]

In mid-June, the Wehrmacht launches a massive operation against the partisans of the Nača forest. It is a successful operation that causes the death of many and forces the others to disperse in the woods to the north or south, toward Vilnius or Grodno.[21] From the summer of 1943 to the spring of 1944, the Jewish gangs active on the border between Poland, Lithuania, and Belarus lose all military effectiveness. Having escaped the roundup with a few companions, Avraham Lipkunski survives the winter by moving from one den to another, sinking into the bunkers under the snow of the woods. Only in April, after the thaw, does contact with Red Army scouts allow his group to reintegrate with the partisans. The Soviets entrust Avraham and his comrades, all locals, with intelligence missions. However, the progress of the Red Army makes the action of Armia Krajowa all the more virulent in the area: the Polish resisters from the interior fight with renewed energy against both the Germans and the Soviets, who are perceived as invaders rather than liberators. And they openly fight against the Jews, accusing them of communism.[22]

In May 1944, Avraham experiences the most tragic period of the two years after Raduń's massacre and since the beginning of his life in the forests: six companions of his group are ambushed by "White Poles" and killed. They are all locals, born and raised among the pines of Dugalishok, the synagogues of Eišiškės, and the Jewish schools of Raduń. They are Haim and Itchele Asner, Etka Gures, her cousin Sara, Liebke Hefetz, and Aharke Berkovitz. Carnage.[23] This time, however, the partisan Avremale and five others of the group are able to react. They know the name of the Polish peasant who was the informant, and they remember that the God of the Bible is also an avenging God. The sun sets late at the end of May, around Grodno. The six Jews reach the village at dusk. Three of them remain on guard along the road, the other three proceed toward the spy's house. Avremale keeps watch, and Yankl Asner and Niomke Rogovski break down the door. The peasant jumps out of the window to escape into the fields, but Niomke chases him and kills him right away.[24]

A few weeks later, the Red Army arrives. The soldiers of the Werhmacht surrender by the thousands. The SS also give up, at least those who are allowed to flock to the prisoners' pens, those who are not summarily executed. As for the partisan Avremale, between June and July 1944, he is affiliated with the Soviet political police and plays his part as a local guide, to settle scores with the Poles suspected of collaborating with the Nazis. Like other Soviet-recruited Jews on the Eastern Front, fifteen-year-old Avraham Lipkunski wanders like a nemesis among the ruins of his shtetl and surrounding townships.[25] "They gave me a Red Army uniform, and I found myself riding a horse with a platoon of soldiers. I had to escort them to the villages in areas we knew were infested with White Poles. I had to indicate the best way to surround these villages, to guard their entrances, to control their exits." The Soviets took care of the rest: raids, searches, interrogations. Anyone who resisted was shot on the spot.[26]

One day in August 1944, early in the morning, Avraham Lipkunski sets off from Raduń toward Dugalishok armed with a rifle. He is alone, and he has a very clear idea of how much he wants to achieve that day. He knocks on the door of a random peasant. He tells him he is an agent of the Soviet political police and orders him to prepare a horse, a cart, and two spades. They have to go to Dugalishok to exhume the corpse of a partisan, whom they will take back to Raduń. At the shtetl, they go straight to what used to be the Lipkunskis' home. The Lithuanian who has taken possession of the house is terrified when they arrive. Avraham explains that he only wants one thing: to be shown where he buried Pinchas's body. When a skeleton emerges from the earth, Avraham wonders if it really is his brother. He quickly finds proof: phylactery straps are wrapped around the bones. He then has the peasant load the body onto the cart and has it transported to Raduń. At the cemetery, he gathers the ten men needed for a Jewish funeral. By evening, the remains of Pinchas are buried next to the mass grave that on May 10, 1942, had collected the bodies of Sara Mina, Yekutiel, and the other thousand Jews machine-gunned on the edge.[27]

FIT TO MARCH

For the entire duration of the Warsaw ghetto uprising, from mid-April to mid-May 1943, Henoch Wexler had hardly taken off his headphones. From Mr. Lubinski's apartment in the Łódź ghetto, day after day the shochet of Janowo listened to radio SWIT, the underground station of the Polish Resistance. His heart palpitated with each new broadcast, with hope or despair, depending on the news of the day. "He seemed absorbed in an endless prayer," his son Adam would recall half a century later. After all, Henoch had managed to convince the members of the group to pray with him: his son, Shaya; his brother, Yankl; and others who frequented the secret gatherings at Niecała Street and joined their voice to that of the ritual slaughterer. Tea and psalms never hurt anyone, goes a Hasidic adage.[28]

The psalms were not enough to redeem the fate of the Warsaw ghetto rebels. Nor did the other news gathered through the clandestine radio station have anything to cheer up the brave people of the Łódź ghetto—at least not for a few more months. Even after the German capitulation at Stalingrad, the Red Army's advance along the Eastern Front was terribly slow. By the end of 1943, the front line was still in Belarus and Ukraine, hundreds of kilometers east of the prewar border of the Republic of Poland. Only from the beginning of 1944, without waiting for the thaw, did the Soviet troops break through the German defenses in the direction of the Carpathians, cutting the Lviv–Odessa railway line and invading eastern Galicia. Then Shaya Wexler, from the clandestine listening post on Niecała Street, was finally able to smile,[29] all the more so as the radio frequencies of the Polish Resistance foreshadowed formidable news on the Western Front as well, suggesting the concrete and imminent possibility of an Allied landing on French soil.

Adam refused to pray. At thirteen—and after three and a half years in the ghetto—he simply couldn't see the point. In general,

he proved increasingly resistant to paternal authority. He was working now. He had a salary, he received food stamps, and he was tempted by high self-esteem. He responded with a bad attitude to Henoch until a well-delivered smack reminded him of the sound principles an old-fashioned upbringing afforded. Thanks to the family's entry into Rumkowski's Judenrat (and thanks to a false ID, according to which Adam was born in 1928 instead of 1930), all the Wexlers had official jobs. So they cultivated the reasonable hope of avoiding the deportation trains to Chełmno, which were less frequent between 1943 and 1944.[30]

Mindel mended carpets. In theory, her husband, Henoch, was employed in a mattress factory; in practice, he circulated among his coworkers by spreading the news gathered on the radio. Dov had always worked in the nail factory on Zgierska Street. As for Adam, he had been hired in a shoe shop on Brzezińska Street, which produced straw-filled boots for German soldiers mobilized on the Eastern Front.[31]

The center of Adam's life, however, remained Niecała Street, the clandestine listening post. In the parlance of the secret club, the radio had been called "Sefer Torah," the Pentateuch scroll. And the adepts looked at Shaya Wexler at once as the scribe of the Book and as the reader of the Sabbath. Surviving the Shoah of Things was the diary of an Austrian writer imprisoned in the ghetto, Oskar Rosenfeld, who was not directly part of the Niecała Street group but who benefited, along with other reclusive intellectuals, from Shaya's spiritual generosity. Sunday, April 29, 1944: "Nice, quiet atmosphere over good coffee and *lejkach* [gingerbread]. . . . Shayek, who again and again was giving us the voice of the caller in the oasis (not in the desert), bringing consolation and misery, and sowing hope." Saturday June 3, 1944: "Shayek came with a golden heart and sang something for me." At first Shaya seemed to be bringing Rosenfeld mere words. Beautiful, moving, but ethereal, almost anesthetic: out there is a world that exists in its humanity, and which is ready to help us. Only recently had Rosenfeld sensed an otherwise profound tone, a rhythm. Only recently had he measured, through Shaya's words, "the real situation of the Getto-habitants [sic]." Even if the troops of the Red Army were about to arrive, even if the "redemption" of the surviving Jews was imminent, "now I know what we have lost."[32]

In the following page of the diary, on Tuesday June 6, the writer notes, "Shayek appears at eight-thirty [in the morning], something has happened."[33] With due discretion, Rosenfeld evidently records what Shaya Wexler was able to communicate to him in real time: D-Day, the Allied landing in Normandy. This is the last occurrence of Shaya's name in Rosenfeld's diary. Because the next day, Wednesday, June 7, 1944, decrees the end of the brave Niecała Street rebels. At six in the evening, Adam is returning from work in the shoe shop. He is headed for the clandestine listening post and follows the usual route. He goes up Łagiewnicka Street, crosses the market square, and resumes Łagiewnicka Street, preparing to turn right. That is when he is overtaken by a Kripo car. In the Łódź ghetto, vehicles were rare enough to be recognized by everyone: "Rumkowski's carriage was invariably pulled by a gray horse," the "fatal black cars" belonged to the German Criminal Police. The car moved slowly, followed by a carriage that also belonged to the Kripo. When Adam sees them turn right into Niecała Street, his heart sinks. He starts running. "When I arrived in front of the house, I saw my father, my brother Shaya, my uncle Yankl and Yitzhak Lubinski lined up on the sidewalk, with their heads down." Beside them is a German with a gun in his hand. In the blink of an eye, the four are put into the Kripo vehicles and vanish around the corner. "I never saw them again."[34]

On that day and in the following days, the *Tageschronik*—the daily news review of the Łódź ghetto, authorized by the Germans, of which Oskar Rosenfeld was the editor in chief—provides information on the fall of the group. Acting on the tip of an informant, the Kripo had first arrested a certain Altszuler, at 38 Wolborska Street. Then, at 9 Młynarska Street, they arrested Moshe Topel, the synagogue cantor who spoke foreign languages. After that, it was the turn of the three Wexlers and Lubinski in Niecała Street, and another Wexler (Uncle David) at 61 Łagiewnicka Street. The roundup had been completed on Lutomierska Street, at the Tatarka barber shop. Even the transcripts of the radio bulletins had been seized, a sort of clandestine newspaper: enough to capture numerous customers of the salon. In all, there were twenty-one arrests. Chaim Widawski, the leader of the group, had preferred to commit suicide rather than be taken alive in the clutches of the Kripo. "The entire ghetto is extremely agitated, since most of the arrested are well known, quite apart from their function as transmitters of news.... The ghetto has always been filled with all sorts of rumors. Now it turns out that a few persons were daring enough to listen to the news right in the ghetto, and to pass on what they heard.... The event is discussed in whispers everywhere, and fear for the lives of these people has a stranglehold on everyone who knew them."[35]

On Niecała Street, Henoch Wexler is quick to conceal the radio set just before the police arrive. By the time Adam climbs up to Uncle Yankl's apartment, Aunt Zosha can at least reassure him about this: Kripo agents rummaged left and right, both at Lubinski's and there, without finding anything compromising. Most important, they did not find the radio. And luckily Shimek and Karol, the two sons of Yankl and Zosha, are outside, safe. But all this does not relieve Adam of the task that awaits him: to return home to Łagiewnicka Street and inform his mother and brother. He tells Mindel and Dov everything. "I walked like a sleepwalker, like an uninhabited body." The thirteen-year-old—who an hour earlier was heading to Niecała Street, eager to learn more about the fantastic news of the day before, the Anglo-American landing in Normandy—no longer exists. He is left on the sidewalk with the four men lined up, and no new boy will come in to replace him. On the way home, Adam meets Dov. It is better this way; he is the older brother. It is up to Dov to find the right words to tell their mother.[36]

Are there any right words for such things? Mindel collapses to the ground and seems to disappear, in space as well as in time. "She was lying on the floor, tiny, like a little child. She no longer recognized us. She was talking to Henoch, her husband, about distant episodes with him, twenty years ago and more. She hummed melodies from her childhood." Dov and Adam thus realize that they are now the men of the house. Typhus had taken Yosef away at the beginning of life in the ghetto, and the Kripo took Henoch and Shaya away when life in the ghetto promised to come to an end. Now it's up to them to take care of Mindel. "For a long time we stood beside her, motionless, as if paralyzed. Then we took her in our arms, we soothed her, we whispered sweet words to her." But even this is not enough, the trials of the day are not over. Adam still has to cross the landing to tell Uncle David and his wife, Rosa—only to discover that in the meantime Uncle David has also been arrested. He had nothing to do with the Niecała Street group; his only fault was that of being a Wexler.[37]

Dov and Adam have to think about the radio too. They have to make it disappear. Renia Kagan organizes the operation in the following days; she is the girlfriend of their cousin Karol. The plan is for Dov to retrieve the hidden device in the Niecała Street apartment and for Adam to transport it, hidden in a basket of vegetables, to a new hiding place in Ciesielska Street. The greatest danger comes from the need to get through the unavoidable Zgierska Street, where armed German guards stand watch at the wooden bridge connecting the two distinct sectors of the ghetto—guards who reserve the right, of course, to search any Jews in transit. "I wasn't checked,"[38] Adam will recall dryly many decades later, when the Wexler radio is in Israel, an object on display at the Ghetto Fighters' House in Western Galilee, the first museum in the world dedicated to the Shoah and the Jewish resistance.[39]

Meanwhile, by order of the German authorities, the liquidation of the Łódź ghetto has begun. Through mid-July, the sealed wagons make their way to Chełmno's gas trucks; starting from the beginning of August, they head for the gas chambers of Auschwitz-Birkenau. Of the 76,701 inhabitants of the ghetto that Oskar Rosenfeld, the editor of *Tageschronik*, recorded as alive on June 1, 1944, 65,000 are forced to move to one or the other destination. Rosenfeld himself is deported to Auschwitz and gassed upon arrival. The same fate falls to Haim Rumkowski, who for four years had presided over the administration of the ghetto as "king of the Jews."⁴⁰ Mindel Wexler is also part of the August transports; she is deported to Auschwitz along with her two remaining children. But in Birkenau, as soon as they get off the train, the men are separated from the women. Dov and Adam lose sight of their mother on the landing ramp, and they will never see her again.⁴¹

Mindel is also gassed on arrival. The majority of Jews don't get past the first "selection," the one made along the railway platform when they get off the train. In theory, Dov and Adam's mother could have been among the women running naked to the gas chambers, visible in one of the only four extant photographs of the mass extermination carried out in Birkenau, photos taken secretly by Sonderkommando inmates, in August 1944, to document the reality of the Final Solution to the world. Or Mindel's body could have been among those of the Jews already killed with gas and cremated in the open, as shown by two of the four photographs, against the backdrop of the birch forest to which Birkenau owes its name. There were tens of thousands of women gassed and cremated during August 1944, but "to know you have to imagine for yourself." Today as yesterday, the photographs of the Sonderkommando in Birkenau serve to reject the temptation to treat everything as unimaginable.⁴² As for Henoch and Shaya and Yankl and David Wexler, it is not clear whether they were deported and gassed in Chełmno or Auschwitz, or whether they were already killed on the spot in Łódź, within the walls of the ghetto's Rote Haus, the red brick house on Kościelna Street that served as an operational base for the Kripo, where they would carry out investigations and torture.⁴³

Oddly enough, Adam is not selected on the Birkenau ramp to be among the Jews sent immediately to be gassed. According to the Final Solution's age criteria, a thirteen-year-old should have gone there upon arrival. Instead, some Charon in the uniform of an SS medical officer points him to the group on the right instead of the left. This is the group of adult males destined for internment in the barracks, rather than the group of elderly or infirm males destined to join most of the women and children already queuing up for bogus showers. And it's Dov's group as well. "In Auschwitz, I literally lived in the shadow of my brother. I felt lost as soon as he moved away from me." Together Dov and Adam undergo the initiation rituals: lice treatment, the striped shirt, a number tattooed on the arm. Together they get to sleep in the same bunk of the same barracks. And together (almost incredibly) they get transferred from the Birkenau camp to the Auschwitz camp proper and assigned to the Kommando Union.[44]

The members of the Kommando Union—a thousand men and women—are so designated because they work during the day at a nearby munitions factory, the Weichsel Union Metalwerke. They are considered skilled workers and therefore enjoy various advantages: more abundant food rations than the average, relations with German civilians, various possibilities to "organize," and access to the goods and services of the black market. With one brother in the tools department and the other in the locks department, Dov and Adam are two privileged people in the extermination camp. They can converse during work breaks, and at the factory they even run into old acquaintances. So on one autumn day in 1944, Adam runs into Beyle, the big sister of Shayke, a childhood friend of his in Janowo. She's the daughter of Volf Rotsztejn, the shtetl butcher. Unfortunately, when Adam asks about Shayke, Beyle bursts into tears. Shayke was selected for the Sonderkommando, and from that kind of work in the camp, carrying people to the gas chambers and crematory ovens, there was no chance of returning alive.[45]

On another autumn day, dozens of SS men break into the union, guns in hand. Terrified, Dov and Adam and the other slaves at the munitions factory imagine that the end has come. Then after interrogations and beatings, they reconstruct what happened. On the initiative of some workers, explosives taken from the union were used to fuel a revolt of Birkenau's Sonderkommando on

October 7, 1944.[46] Four Kommando Union workers are arrested on October 10, repeatedly tortured, and eventually hanged in the roll call square on January 6, 1945. During the following days, the entire concentration camp system of Auschwitz-Birkenau is demobilized by the Germans before the arrival of the Soviets. Prisoners who are *marschunfähig*, "unable to march," are left behind (presumably to die) in the infirmary barracks. All the others set out in a column toward the west. With fifty thousand companions in misfortune, Dov and Adam Wexler march together along the roads of Silesia. They march through the snow for tens of kilometers—a death march.[47]

And yet they stay alive like thousands of others, in spite of everything. They are able to march to some unknown Polish village, where they are loaded onto a freight train that transports them south. There are two days of very slow travel through Czechoslovakia and then Austria, with more and more space available in the sealed wagon as passengers die of starvation and are thrown out. "A hellish journey, punctuated by frequent and bloody confusion, especially at night, in the anonymity of the dark. I really believe that Dov's fists saved our lives several times." A few days follow in the Mauthausen concentration camp, where the Wexler brothers openly enjoy the protection of a fellow prisoner they met at Auschwitz, a German Christian—a German Communist—by the name of Gotthard. Then there is another march under guard, down to the Danube valley, toward the Gusen camp, where terrifying violence reigns sovereign, and death mows down the last surviving prisoners, be they Jews or Gentiles.[48]

Crossing the Gusen camp, accompanied by a gypsy to whom Gotthard has entrusted him, Adam passes by the hospital and remains petrified. Ahead of him is a small mountain, a couple of meters high, of skeletal corpses wedged into each other. "The gypsy tried to reassure me: don't be afraid, they were Jews." In Gusen, Dov and Adam don't work at all. The German administration of the camp, now reduced in terms of numbers and efficiency, made Gotthard the secretary of barracks 17, and he managed to pass the brothers off for two Polish Christians and get them exempted from work. The Wexler brothers sit on their plank all day, trying to be forgotten. Forgotten by the Jews who know them, who have come from Auschwitz like them, some even from the Łódź ghetto. Forgotten by the real Polish Christians detained in the camp, who could easily unmask them as Jews. From the window of the shack, Adam sees the clearing in front of the camp hospital, and he sees the corpses stacked on top of each other in the pile, higher and higher. "We were in March 1945, it was cold. The bodies froze, they looked like pieces of wood."[49]

The Americans arrive on May 5. First a white car with three or four civilians, then two tanks and three armored vehicles. The last German guards surrender without putting up any resistance. At that point, the inmates who are strong enough—Germans or Poles, French or Italians, Ukrainians or Russians—devote themselves to looting, feasting, and settling scores. "Many *kapo* disappeared like this." Dov and Adam—less hungry than other prisoners, and less ruthless—avoid both deadly indigestion and summary executions. When Gotthard leaves the camp, he invites Adam to come with him. Adam can't say no, and he follows him at night to a nearby village. But already the next day, he returns in regret to Gusen's barracks 17. He goes back to Dov.[50]

TOO YOUNG

Suti Weisz had come down the Birkenau ramp two full months before Dov and Adam Wexler. The three trains from Nagyszőlős had left on May 20, May 27, and June 3: three of the 147 freight trains used by the Germans, between spring and summer 1944, to transport 450,000 "pieces" from Hungary to Auschwitz.[51] The Birkenau ramp itself—the new one, which entered directly into the extermination camp, reaching almost to the entrance of the gas chambers—had been built precisely to speed up the liquidation of the Hungarian Jews (which also proves useful in August for dispatching the last deportees from the Łódź ghetto). Whole families are together, precisely because family units guarantee the executioners maximum collaboration on the part of the victims, since the strongest adults, those most able to resist, would not jeopardize the lives of their weakest family members, the elderly and children.[52]

It doesn't take much effort to imagine the Weisz family coming to Birkenau. There is a photographic album made by two Nazi officials of the camp, *The Auschwitz Album*, that documents in detail the reception of a convoy identical to theirs: the first of the two trains departing from Berehove (fifteen kilometers from Nagyszőlős) between May 24 and 29. When the Weisz family arrived, everything looked exactly like in this album: the early morning lights, the fresh concrete quay along the camp's Haupstrasse, the SS officers in charge of selection, the prisoners in striped shirts assigned to cleaning up the ramp and transporting the luggage of the new arrivals to the Kanada warehouses, the chimneys of the crematoria. The photographs in *The Auschwitz Album* portray the Jews of Berehove, but the experience lived by the Jews of Nagyszőlős is for all intents and purposes the same. The arrival of the freight train at the platform. The selection, on the ramp, between "able to work" and "unable to work." The path of the unable—men, women, elderly, children—toward the "shower" buildings. The assignment of the able-bodied to forced labor, women on the one hand, men on the other. The last moments of life for the unable just before entering the gas chambers.[53]

Five members of the Weisz family descended onto the platform. Vilmos, the head of the family, and four of his children: the two older girls, Aliz and Hedi, fourteen-year-old Suti, and twelve-year-old Icuka. Bandi, the eldest son, avoided deportation by escaping from a Hungarian brigade of forced laborers. Mother Terez died of cancer a few months earlier, marking the end of Suti's wonderful childhood: the little house among the vineyards on the slopes of the Black Mountain, father's distillery near the castle of the Perényi barons, swimming in the river and racing sleighs, collecting stamps and feasting on raspberries. After mother's death in January, things fell apart. Under the pressure of an ever closer alliance between Admiral Miklós Horthy and the German Führer, Hungary ceased to be the last safe island for Eastern European Jews. In March, the Weisz boys had to stop going to school. Starting in April, they had to crowd with their father—and hundreds of other families—into the four streets of the Nagyszőlős ghetto. And one day between May 20 and June 3, the five of them had to go to the open area in front of the train station. Three or four tables on the sidewalk, three or four typewriters, three or four improvised typists, forced by the Germans to draw up the lists of Jews leaving. The typist who recorded the Weisz family data (without even looking up from the paper, and wiping a tear after finishing) is Victor Ortutay, Suti's private tutor.[54]

In Birkenau, on the ramp, Suti holds Icuka's hand tightly. His father told him over and over again: When we arrive, you take care of Icuka. But there's a lot of confusion around, the weakest need help getting out of the sealed wagons, the Germans in uniform have the air of wanting to do things quickly, and with the prisoners in striped shirts, communication is difficult because they speak more Yiddish than Hungarian. There is not even time to look around as the five Weiszes are already queuing along the platform, like all the others, scrutinized by an SS doctor. There is just enough time to collect someone's advice on the fly—say you're sixteen—and Suti has already lost Icuka's hand. He turns around to look for her. Then the elderly Mrs. Rosenberg, a neighbor from Nagyszőlős, recognizes Suti and reassures him: Don't worry, I'll take care of her. Now she's the one holding Icuka's hand. He joins his father in a line of men and sees Aliz and Hedi in a line of women. In Suti's memory, the last image of his little sister Icuka will remain that of her on the ramp, in a blue dress with suspenders, holding Mrs. Rosenberg's hand—half an hour before both, like most newcomers, are told to undress for a Zyklon B shower.[55]

Decades later, Suti Weisz—or Yitzhak Livnat, his new identity assumed in Israel—will decide to talk about his Auschwitz experience at length. The immediate separation from his father, the assignment to the Kinderblock, the block for children. The smell emanating all around, that "terrible smell" of Birkenau which "came from the burning body of my little sister." The loss of any faith in the God of the Bible. Surviving various selections during that summer of 1944. Working in a brigade at the Kommando Kanada, emptying the trains that arrived in Birkenau of all their contents, cleaning and disinfecting them for the next trip. The protection of his kapo, an illiterate Polish Jew who saves Suti from selection in September by literally buying his life, paying five cans of sardines and twenty American dollars to have him excluded from a group of children about to be sent to the gas chamber. The general demobilization of the camp in January 1945, with the death march westward, and at a certain point, after about twenty kilometers, exhaustion, no strength left and the decision to stop right there, in the snow.[56]

Decades later, Suti Weisz will also recount his rescue thanks to a good German (if it makes sense to put it that way). "I sat in the snow. And I started to feel really good. I couldn't care less. And I heard the German who was following us to make sure no one stayed alive, the one who gave everyone the coup de grace. I knew he was coming, but I couldn't care less. It was the lowest point in my story. And I felt great, I felt like I was in a dream. This SS man arrives, looks at me, and barks at me: *'Du bist zu jung!'* You're too young! And he kicks me. He kicks me. And I jump up, and I start running." Suti runs toward the rest of the Jews lined up in the snow. He runs toward all that is awesome and terrible awaiting him. The train to Mauthausen, in open wagons, with the Soviet air force targeting the convoy and a traveling companion killed this way, by impossibly friendly fire. And then—in one of the Mauthausen barracks—the most incredible of surprises. He runs into Vilmos. He realizes that his father is still alive.[57]

Decades later, Suti Weisz will also talk about the flipside of that realization. Because Vilmos was "the leftover of a father," and "we had to switch roles." "Instead of him taking care of me, I had to take care of him. And this was... it was a terrible situation for me. Because what I had found was my father's body, but without the soul anymore.... We were together since that day in January... end of January '45, to May '45. And it was the most terrible time I ever lived through. My father couldn't... he just couldn't be a father anymore. He was spiritually drained." They are transferred together, father and son and a few thousand surviving Hungarian Jews, to the Gunskirchen subcamp. There, Suti turns fifteen before falling ill with typhus, like Vilmos. Both of them are dying on May 5, when the concentration camp is liberated by the American soldiers of the Seventy-First Infantry Division. After being transported and treated in a US Army field hospital, Suti discovers upon leaving that his father did not make it. Along with hundreds of other Jews who have died after the liberation, Vilmos Weisz is buried in a mass grave near the US base.[58]

VOLUNTEERS IN THE REICH

That October evening, everything was ready for escape. Meir and Feige Liberman had insisted that Inda go to bed early; they needed to be rested the next day, and she was the youngest. The man said he would come and pick them up at dawn. He had reassured them the plan would be respected to the letter: a passage through the barbed wire of the ghetto followed by crossing the border into Romania, then by ship to neutral Turkey and from there quietly to Palestine. Meir had paid a lot for this, all that was left from the plentiful days of the pharmacy in Rivne. But at dawn, the man didn't show up. The Libermans were wondering what to do when they heard the sound of gunfire—indeed, of real explosions. Then Feige woke Inda and in a trembling voice told her and Adela that the two of them had to leave immediately. The two daughters had to escape because the *aktzia* had begun. You two go. Father and I will join you as soon as possible.[59]

At the liquidation of a ghetto, it was the young people who tried everything possible, especially the boys but also some girls. Compared to their parents (not to mention their grandparents) the young people had more energy, more hunger for life.[60] The same was the case at dawn on October 13, 1942, in the Volhynian town of Zdolbuniv. In a flash, Adela and Inda got dressed, jumped out the window—the house had only a ground floor—and joined a handful of boys who were determined to flee at any cost. There were Meir Rozenboym, his brother Liebish, and a few others. One of them had a hammer, which he used to knock down a piece of the first ghetto fence, then another and another, until they were in an open space and realized they were outside. At home, Inda hadn't had time to put on her shoes, so she held them in her hand as she ran away. She injured her calf on the barbed-wire fence. Still, she ran as fast as she could after Adela and behind the boys. She had strong legs; all those years spent at the ballet school in Rivne had finally proved useful.[61]

The fugitives looked back before dispersing into the countryside around Zdolbuniv, and they saw a column of smoke rising from the ghetto houses. But there was no time to ask too many questions; they had to keep running away toward the fields. After all, it was better to remain in doubt about what would become of Meir and Feige Liberman, or the parents, brothers, cousins, and uncles of Meir and Liebish Rozenboym, or the 422 Jews that the Third Reich bureaucrats register as captured in Zdolbuniv on October 13, 1942.[62] Among the photographs documenting the Final Solution achieved through the mass executions, those taken on October 14 and 15 on a cliff near the village of Mizoch—three or four kilometers from Zdolbuniv—are perhaps the most explicit of all. It is not clear to me whether these photos show only Jews from the Mizoch ghetto, liquidated in the same days, or some Jews from the Zdolbuniv ghetto as well—in which case there could also be Feige, the mother of Adela and Inda, in the queue of children and naked women waiting for the shot to the back of the head.[63]

After getting separated from the boys, the two sisters wander the fields in search of help. The quality of their education in Rivne helps them, in that they are fluent in Polish, Ukrainian, and Russian. Linguistically they can blend in easily, but not for the rest, starting with clothing. The daughters of Volhynian peasants do not dress like Adela and Inda Liberman. No one would ever have a coat like theirs, in shaved wool with a fur collar. So as soon as the Ukrainian peasant woman in the cottage answers the knock on the door, she immediately recognizes them as Jewish. But the peasant woman is Christian enough not to report them to anyone, and she provides them with more suitable clothes. She keeps the two wool coats with fur collar for herself and dresses them from head to toe in long skirts, coarse wool coats, scarves, and kerchiefs. They now look like two Ukrainian peasant girls. She encourages them to look for work nearby. Labor is needed, the sugar beets have to be harvested before it snows.[64]

For a few days in the fall of 1942, the teenage daughters of two Polish Jewish pharmacists wander from cottage to cottage in the countryside around Rivne, pretending to be Ukrainians, picking vegetables for scant pay, arranging to spend the night sleeping on the haystacks in the stables, and wondering about their parents' fate, about the smoke they had seen rising from the houses of the Zdolbuniv ghetto, about their mother's reassurance at the moment of the escape: You two go. Father and I will join you as soon as possible. Adela and Inda remember what their father had always recommended: If for any reason you have to part with us, go to Ksenia Alexandrovna. She was a young friend of Meir Liberman's, his classmate in Kyiv, a long time ago.[65] Wrapped up like peasants, the two sisters then return to the Rivne of their childhood. At first they search in vain for Ksenia Alexandrovna at the address of Spółdzielcza Street, where the Libermans themselves had lived before the war. Then, on the recommendation of a neighbor of hers, they find her in a house on 13-ej Dywizji Street. It is a few steps from the building of their old school, the Jewish high school, now uninhabited, and a short distance from the ruins of the Rivne ghetto, which German soldiers and Ukrainian militiamen liquidated the previous July.[66]

When she recognizes the girls, Ksenia Alexandrovna is moved to tears. She decides she can keep them, at least for a while. They go to the attic, where the clothes hang out to dry. Adela and Inda will have to hide behind a pile of old furniture, taking care not to give any sign of life in case other tenants in the building go upstairs, back and forth with the laundry. Ksenia will bring them food and empty the bucket for their toilet needs under cover of the night. But a few days later, in the late afternoon, the two sisters hear German voices coming from the stairs. Immediately they think the worst: a tip, a search; this is the end. But why isn't anyone going up to the attic? Why isn't anyone coming to pick them up and take them away? Still the German voices continue to resound up the stairwell throughout the evening and most of the night. The next morning, Ksenia explains the truth to them in a whisper. Her son works for the Gestapo. The German voices they heard are those of the Nazi thugs getting together with him for a Sunday drinking session. She can't go on like this, she can't hide them anymore. Adela and Inda have to go.[67]

But go where? At first, Ksenia Alexandrovna's advice sounds so incredible that it seems like a cruel joke: Go to Germany! Right into the wolf's mouth! But upon reflection, that advice makes sense. Why not take advantage of the wave of migration that has been going on for months, since the beginning of 1942, and has pushed hundreds of thousands of Ukrainians to volunteer for work in the Third Reich? Many of these migrants were women.

Mostly they are young rural women, attracted by the prospect of a good salary in German marks.[68] Yes, Adela and Inda would show up—of their own free will—at a police station of the Reichskommissariat Ukraine. They would give a false name, make everyone believe they were Polish peasants, and say they had gotten off at the Rivne station to drink some water and then missed the train on which they were traveling to Germany with identity documents and all the rest. Among the policemen, who could have imagined that Janina Słowińska and Halina Kluczyńska might be two Jewish girls? Since the German invasion, had two young Jewesses ever been seen knocking on the door of a police station? No sooner said than done: believing their story, Ukrainian militiamen escort the two girls to the Rivne station.[69]

Accompanied by gallant collaborators, Adela and Inda Liberman, aged sixteen and fourteen, respectively, board a civilian transport bound for the Third Reich. They are surrounded by teenagers like themselves, mostly country girls, who cross the Reichskommissariat Ukraine from east to west, all the way to the General Government. But because of a complaint by a traveling companion (something isn't right with those two; maybe they're Jewish?), the sisters have to face the hardest test. At the Lublin station, they are taken off for police checks. They are led nearby to a sort of barracks surrounded by barbed wire. They are interrogated separately by a German armed with a truncheon, and each of them must find the strength to cling to her story: I am Janina Słowińska. I am Halina Kluczyńska. A new interrogation follows with the additional presence of two dogs, two German shepherds. There is half a day like this before a brusque young man from who knows where comes and frees them both without much explanation. He takes them back to the train station, revealing the name on the barbed-wire barracks: Majdanek.[70]

Adela and Inda arrive in Germany in November 1942. For the next two and a half years, until April 1945, they work as volunteers in the Third Reich. They work as dishwashers in a hotel in Torgau, fifty kilometers east of Leipzig. They are in good company: historians estimate fifty thousand female servants were employed in Germany at the time as "workers from the East."[71] Except that the two dishwashers of the *Friedrich der Große* hotel in Torgau were two young Jews. Now, I look at the vintage postcards of Friedrich Platz on the computer screen, I look on Google Maps at the imposing profile of the hotel at the corner of the square (it still exists, even if it has changed its name), and I wonder how lucky those two and a half years were for Janina Słowińska and Halina Kluczyńska. So much luckier than that of three million other Polish Jews. Lucky enough to guarantee them a roof and a table, clean sheets and regular meals. But every day they needed to be scrupulous about not betraying themselves and not letting even half a compromising sentence escape. They lived with the constant nightmare of being unmasked, denounced, and deported. And they kept remembering the sentence pronounced by their mother, in the Zdolbuniv ghetto, at dawn on October 13, 1942: You two go. Father and I will join you as soon as possible.

On April 20, 1945, the owners of the *Friedrich der Große* inform the staff, now reduced to half a dozen people, that the hotel is about to close and that they are about to leave. Better to flee west as soon as possible, better the American occupation zone than the Soviet one. The owners offer the employees the opportunity to escape with them. The three German cooks—Charlotte, Inge, and Hildegard—accept. Alphonse, the French waiter, also accepts, as does Wanda, the Polish waitress. Polish dishwashers Janina and Halina—the Liberman sisters—refuse. They remain alone in the large hotel on Friedrich Platz and take refuge in the cellars during the following days: the days of the Soviet attack beyond the Oder-Neisse line, what is known as the Torgau Offensive, with the historic meeting between the soldiers of the Red Army and those of the US Army.[72] And it is right there in Torgau, on April 26, that the famous "handshake" on the Elbe River is staged.[73]

The day before, when Soviet soldiers broke into the hotel lobby, they initially thought there was no one there. It fell to Adela and Inda to come up from the cellars, to welcome them by speaking Russian, to embrace them as liberators. And starting April 25, it is the men of the Red Army who take charge of the Liberman sisters. They transport them by boat to the other side of the Elbe. They accompany them from military truck to military truck, along the endless bumpy roads of the Eastern Front. It takes ten days to reach Poznan, then a night on the train and arrival in Łódź on May 8, 1945—the day of the German surrender, the day of victory.[74] It's a strange victory for two Jewish girls of nineteen and seventeen with no family, no home, and no country. Yet in its own way, Łódź presents itself as the right place from which to start again, if not exactly as a place to be reborn. Compared to other large Polish cities, it is less devastated, almost intact. Freed in January by the troops of Marshal Zhukov, Łódź is vibrant with industrial, trade union, political, and cultural activity. With Warsaw razed to the ground, it is the de facto capital of the new Poland. It is also the capital for surviving Polish Jews.[75]

There are about twenty thousand Jews in Łódź during the summer of 1945. Half of them lived in the city before the war; they escaped the years in the ghetto, deportation to concentration camps, selections, and death marches. The other half are Jews like Adela and Inda Liberman, refugees from some other Polish city or shtetl, who escaped a variety of circumstances that extermination entailed, such as hiding, internment, and survival in the forests. Now, both the Jewish aid organizations and the Zionist movements are looking after them—above all, the orphans. Beyond the southern edge of the old ghetto, in 20 Zachodnia Street, there is a shelter that is a bit like a larger version of Via Unione 5 in Milan: a land port for the saved Jews. The port is equipped with dormitories and kitchens, game rooms and study rooms, functional spaces and ritual spaces, where young or mature Jews lodge: a mix of locals and foreigners, secular and Orthodox, those impatient to leave and those determined to stay.[76]

Housed in Zachodnia Street, the Liberman sisters plan to continue their journey east. They want to follow the route they had taken by train almost three years earlier as volunteer workers in the opposite direction: Lublin, Kovel, Lutsk, all the way to Rivne. They want to go and see. They are not resigned to the fact that their father and mother have vanished into thin air.[77] But the leader of their youth group, a Gordonia executive named Yeshayahu Flamholtz—who has survived a little bit of everything: the camps, the forest, fighting in the ranks of the Red Army—prevents the two girls from venturing along the roads to Volhynia. Even after the end of World War II, Poland remains an unsafe place for Jews.[78] Adela and Inda's stay in Łódź thus extends from spring to summer and from summer to autumn, while Flamholtz and the other militants of Gordonia speak the language of Zionism to them, waving the geographical map of the Promised Land, a map so much more glittering now that nothing remains in Poland of the Jewish world of the past. With dozens of other orphans in Zachodnia Street, the Liberman sisters are preparing to "ascend" to Palestine.

But before they leave the bloodlands forever, Adela and Inda have something important to do. A Jewish Historical Commission operating in Łódź in 1945 has set itself the task of collecting every possible document on the extermination of the Jews during the German occupation. Teachers, writers, and historians work there, particularly committed to collecting the testimonies of survivors, and they are determined to pass on its content to the magistrates who are conducting, in Łódź itself, the trials of various war criminals.[79] In December, the deposition of a fifteen-year-old who escaped the ghetto and gas trucks, Szymon Srebnik, is the highlight in the trial against Rudolf Krampf, the former Polish printer of German origin sentenced to death as "executioner of Chełmno."[80] A few weeks earlier, Adela and Inda Liberman submitted their version of the events in the Sosenki forest to the Jewish Historical Commission: the massacre that in November 1941 had inaugurated the extermination of the Jews of Rivne.[81] The two sisters' version is not very credible, particularly because it is explicitly based on hearsay. Nor does their complaint against the civil commander of the Zdolbuniv district at the time of the German occupation sound more persuasive; they speak of a certain Keller, when in fact it was Georg Marschall.[82] But one could hardly have expected perfectly accurate historical reconstructions from Adela and Inda—or any of the other witnesses who escaped the Final Solution.[83] Their priority was another. During their depositions before the Jewish Commission, the two sisters first of all kept in mind the biblical commandment regarding Amalek: Do not forget.

Another orphan of the same age, Nina Boniówka, who is also housed in Zachodnia Street, wants to obey that commandment. Nina is a young Jewish girl from Warsaw who, on July 18, 1942, at age thirteen, experienced with her elder sister Izabela one of the most memorable days in the entire history of the ghetto: when a theatrical performance, *The Post Office* by Rabindranath Tagore, was staged at Janusz Korczak's Orphan House, recited by the children of the institute in Sienna Street.[84] The extraordinary day was only three weeks before the Pan Doktor and his two hundred orphans were escorted by the Germans to the Umschlagplatz, the assembly point, and from there to the gas chambers of Treblinka. Those soon-to-die Jews had experienced an afternoon of spiritual distraction, or even just of movements and colors, of excitement and applause. It turned out to be their last movements and colors, because on that same July 18, the head of the SS, Heinrich Himmler, ordered the liquidation of the ghetto. Nina Boniówka would be destined to survive (along with her sister Izabela), unlike her father, mother, another sister, and her brother, all drowned in the Final Solution. Nina was daringly saved right there on Umschlagplatz, in the last days of the ghetto uprising, and then saved again later, extracted from Warsaw thanks to a network of Christians who would be recognized as Righteous Among the Nations. Nina would be entrusted after her release to a provincial orphanage, and then she would wind up in Łódź, in the reception house in 20 Zachodnia Street.[85]

At the Jewish Historical Commission on Nazi Crimes, Nina tells her version of the circumstances in which the Boniówka family was exterminated.[86] But Nina's voice will not remain confined within the archives of the Historical Commission. Her story will become the chapter of a book of denunciation, *Children Accuse*, published in Kraków in 1947 and based on the testimonies of seventy very young survivors.[87] The book will openly pose the problem of antisemitism not only in Nazi-occupied Poland but also in Poland liberated by the Soviets: the eternal problem of antisemitism in Poland that not even the Final Solution was enough to placate.

SIX

THE HOUSE OF MUSSOLINI

VIA EUPILI

"Don't be shy, open the gate and come in. Go up three steps, and you'll be in the school corridor. On the right, there's a yellow glass door with a sign, DIREZIONE, in Italian and Hebrew. Knock on the door, you'll get an answer in Italian or in Hebrew, 'come in!' *bevakasha*! Don't be afraid if it's a familiar voice, surprisingly similar to mine. It won't just be similar. It will be *my* voice. Because that's where you'll find me, sitting on a couch near the wall. On the opposite side is Lea, the new secretary. And unless someone calls her on the phone or she's busy elsewhere, there will be the director, Matilde (Rachel since my arrival). She'll welcome you warmly. She looks like she's thirty years old, but she's only twenty-two."[1]

Saturday, June 2, 1945: "Shabbat Shalom, my dear," Moshe writes under the date of his letter to Yehudit. It's Saturday, but he has a lot of work to do. "There's nobody in the house. Rachel and the children went to pray. All quiet, only the echo of the bricklayers, not loud enough to disturb me. And around me a pile of paperwork: students, teachers, kitchen, store room, wardrobe."[2] It's Saturday, but work at the Jewish school in Via Eupili has been going on for more than a week, since right after Zeiri's arrival in Milan as a soldier with the 745th Solel Boneh Company. And if Matilde (or Rachel, as he keeps calling her, insisting she take the biblical name) is the director, Moshe is the operational manager. It's up to him to actually get the Jewish school up and running in Milan, to raise it from the ashes of war, persecutions, and deportations, without waiting for a too-distant autumn. It is in the urgency, relief, and pain of that late spring of freedom.[3]

Why it's up to him becomes clear quickly. In Via Unione 5—at Palazzo Odescalchi, the center of Jewish life in Milan, be they Italian or foreign Jews, locals or refugees, civilian or military, ex–internally displaced or ex-deportee—Moshe Zeiri has met the right people at the right time: the two most immediately effective protagonists of Milan's Jewish spring. First of all is Davide Mario Levi, the provincial deputy commander of the Matteotti Brigades, known as Colonel Vittorio. Zeiri tends to exaggerate, though, his exploits as a leader of the Resistance with the "Palestinian" soldiers of the British Army. Writing to Yehudit, Moshe builds Colonel Vittorio into the primary architect of the April 25 insurrection and all that followed, including the hanging of Mussolini at Piazzale Loreto. "He was the head of the Partisan army in Milan. He freed the city, and in the early days he acted as governor. He was the one who gave the order to capture the former dictator of the country, and to hang him." As Moshe allusively explains to Yehudit with an ellipsis, "Vittorio took part in a few unofficial meetings with us..."[4] The colonel also took part in just as many official meetings. He was working together with Bruno Savaldi of the 745th Company, the strongman of a nascent Zionist group from Milan.[5]

In Via Unione, Moshe also meets Raffaele Cantoni. He is a man with a very different type of strength, a longtime antifascist and Zionist whom Riccardo Lombardi, the acting prefect of the liberated Milan, elevated to the position of special commissioner of the local Jewish community. Full of energy and resourcefulness, he is a force of nature.[6] Cantoni and Zeiri hit it off immediately. They could almost be father and son: Cantoni is about fifty, and Zeiri is thirty. Despite the age difference, the two look alike and understand each other from the start (also because Cantoni is among the rare Italian Jews who knows some Yiddish, and Zeiri's Italian keeps getting better and better). "From the outside, he looks like a shuffling laborer. Poorly dressed, dirty clothes, absent-minded. But actually he's one of the most worthy characters in Northern Italy. A fantastic man." Moshe doesn't skimp on adjectives when describing Cantoni to Yehudit. With Cantoni too, he exaggerates, or misrepresents, his role as a political and military leader, calling him a central figure in Italian socialism, a high-ranking officer of the Garibaldi Brigades. But Moshe is not mistaken in recognizing the elective affinities that bind him to Cantoni and vice versa. "From the first moment, we had a magnetic agreement."[7]

There is a need for capable people in Via Eupili. They have to urgently renovate the two villas that the Jewish community owns in the Sempione area, facing along the railway tracks: the two elegant buildings that on the eve of the war—after the racial laws of 1938—had become, through schools of every kind and grade, the heart of Jewish life in the city before falling into the hands of the German occupiers on September 8, 1943.[8] Nor is it just a matter of organizing a few didactic or recreational activities as summer sets in. Food and accommodation must be guaranteed for the children of families more or less marked by the war, families left homeless and unemployed, or worse, left without news, unaware of the fate of any number of their relatives, or crushed by the certainty of loss. In addition to rearranging the school, a refectory and a dormitory must be operative, and there is a limited amount of material available. "There are desks in the classrooms, but we have to move them back and forth to use them elsewhere as dining tables. On the other hand, there are no chairs and no benches. The Germans took them all

away."[9] So Moshe goes out of his way with that formidable ability to work that has always set him apart. And Cantoni appreciates it so much that he always points him out as an example. "When he saw me dirty and sweaty, he greeted me enthusiastically," Moshe writes. "He says to everyone: 'look at Zeiri, who does everything himself.'" Zeiri who moves the benches, coordinates the teachers, looks after the children, repairs the plumbing, and takes care of the cleaning.[10]

Zeiri and Matilde were like one person. He clicked immediately with the young woman whom Cantoni—the bachelor—trusted most in the world: Matilde Cassin. As a girl in prewar Florence, she was already active in the Zionist movement in which her boyfriend, the anti-fascist Max Varadi,[11] was an activist. She had been involved since the outbreak of the World War, in a relief organization for foreign Jewish children, refugees in Italy with their respective families.[12] She was not only an active girl but also reckless in German-occupied Florence, where Matilde flanked Cantoni in a network of clandestine Jewish assistance until she ran up against Nazi-Fascist repression.[13] She managed to escape to Switzerland and found Cantoni, who had fled in his turn, and she worked as an animator at a school for Italian refugee children near Lucerne.[14] But she hadn't given up on her dream of the Promised Land, which Cantoni himself kept proposing. "You now have one task: prepare yourself to be able to go with Max to Palestine," he said. "Let me tell you, the steamship is your only solution!"[15]

Right after the Liberation of Italy on April 25, 1945, both Matilde Cassin and Raffaele Cantoni rushed to Milan. In no time Matilde found herself managing the most trivial daily needs at the school in Via Eupili, able to count on Davide Mario Levi—Colonel Vittorio—as well as her steadfast suppliers. One day in May, the school administration sent the deputy commander of the Matteotti Brigades a receipt for five shirts, ten pairs of trousers, ten dozen knives, ten dozen spoons, five dozen forks, three bags and a box of rice, a coat, thirty-five blankets of wool, ten boxes of milk powder, a pack of candles, and an unspecified number of canned tomatoes.[16] On another day in May, "I would ask you to give these Palestinian soldiers what you have kindly promised us," Matilde wrote to Colonel Vittorio, specifying that she expected the delivery of "one sewing machine" and "one gramophone."[17] But in doing so she risked fueling the prejudice certain partisans had that the Jews were greedy.

Initially, Moshe Zeiri arrived in Via Eupili as a Hebrew teacher. Education aside, Moshe soon got involved in logistics. He was a good carpenter and sawed the legs of chairs and desks to adapt them to the needs of children, both in the classroom and in the refectory; he also turned some of the office furniture into a cupboard for dishes. Like an engineer, he organized a dishwashing area in the dining room to keep the traffic from a distant kitchen to a minimum. In short, he tried to solve problems, especially problems related to the shortage of material resources. What to do, for example, with a bolt of rough fabric they managed to get somehow? Curtains for windows or clothes for children? And where to find at least some toys? So Moshe went from being a Hebrew teacher to the rector of a boarding school,[18] sitting there on the sofa near the wall on the ground floor of Via Eupili 6, surrounded by files and shouting "come in!" or *bevakasha!* to whoever was knocking on the glass door of the director's office.

When he writes to Yehudit, Moshe does nothing to hide his intense collaboration not only with Raffaele Cantoni but also with Matilde Cassin. "I work shoulder to shoulder with a particularly endearing man, and with a woman whom nature has endowed with extraordinary talents."[19] The husband is transparent with his wife and speaks to her about Matilde (or Rachel) with ease and admiration. "Her work is quiet, inspired, systematic."[20] It seems as if Moshe doesn't realize that receiving those letters from Milan—over there in Palestine, in the open area in front of the Kvutzat-Shiller offices, after the red mail van arrives blowing its horn and the names of the recipients are called out in front of everyone—is a young woman the same age as Matilde, a young wife who hasn't seen him for a year and a half. Moshe doesn't seem to take into account how the shadow of his partnership with Matilde is destined to lengthen the distance of his relationship with Yehudit. This is exacerbated by the return on leave of other volunteers mobilized in Italy with the British Army, and the gossip that reigns supreme in every kibbutz only make things worse.

At the end of June, the Milanese Jewish community will count eighteen children hosted in the boarding school in Via Eupili and fifty-one children enrolled as external students.[21] But Moshe Zeiri does not wait for the end of the month to look ahead and beyond—beyond Via Eupili, beyond Milan, beyond Italy. Weeks go by after May 8, after the end of the war on the Old Continent, and it becomes clear that the destruction of the Jews of Europe has not been complete, a rather high number has survived—in concentration camps, or hidden by merciful Christians, or re-emerging from bunkers in the forests. As the Joint and the United Nations Relief and Rehabilitation Administration (UNRRA), the rescue agency of the newly formed United Nations, take care of the Jews gathered in the refugee camps of Europe;[22] as the emissaries sent from Palestine are getting organized to identify in Germany, Poland, Czechoslovakia, and Hungary the healthiest and liveliest survivors, those most eager to reach Italy as a dock from where they can embark on a ship to the Promised Land; as all this matures (and matures quickly in the feverish heat of the first few weeks of freedom),[23] Moshe Zeiri works on a project he had shared with his wife even before arriving in Milan with the British Army's 745th Company of Royal Engineers.

On May 12, from the Laterina camp in Tuscany, Moshe had written a letter to Yehudit that contained an overall balance sheet with regard to his life and projects. It took into account his kibbutz years before he left for the war, and it was basically negative. Moshe evoked a very frank conversation he had had on the subject with Aarontchik, his partner in Kvutzat-Shiller, one of the few to whom he had confessed the pains of his work as a tarbutnik, or cultural attaché, in a community that appeared to believe in it only to a certain extent. Moshe's pain was that of someone who now felt limited by the narrow horizon of the kibbutz, and by the categorical imperative that governed its morality: to sacrifice oneself for the collective interest. "I no longer want to be a burden to an apparently democratic community whose members don't understand me. Or if they do understand me, then where my own ambitions are incompatible with the criteria for building the community itself," Moshe wrote to Yehudit.[24]

The life project moved from this feeling of being stalled to transforming it into a desire to reinvent himself. Moshe confided that he could inject something positive into his kibbutznik identity if only two things were allowed after his demobilization by the army and return to Palestine. On the one hand, the possibility of resuming studies in the fields of music or education. On the other hand, the possibility of a large-scale absorption of Shoah orphans into the kibbutz—those same children and youngsters who between spring and summer of 1945 started exploring if not Via Eupili (where almost all the pupils are Italian), then at least Via Unione. The very first arrived in Milan among the young survivors of the Final Solution. Six Katz brothers and sisters from Hungary, as well as four Gruenwalds and two Taubs, along with Josef Krausman and Bernard Rosner; Szaya Dembinski and Pinkus Goldhammer, Poles from Łódź, and a handful of other Hungarian, Polish, and Romanian Jews whom the Jewish community of Milan then registered as "orphans from Auschwitz and Mauthausen," via Modena.[25]

In his letter of May 12, Moshe Zeiri thought of them—without having met them yet. He wrote to Yehudit that he was planting the seeds for a clear and distinct project for the future: to work with orphans, in the future Kvutzat-Shiller. "To return to these young people at least something of what was stolen from them by our cruel generation."[26]

LOOKING FOR HOME

One problem at a time. Kvutzat-Shiller is tomorrow, and the kibbutzim of Palestine will reserve for tomorrow the question of how to welcome the survivors of the Shoah. Today there is Milan, today there is Via Eupili and a spring of freedom already spilling over into summer and calling for quick action.

Today there is the need to organize a summer camp for Jewish children and young people in Milan, Italian or foreign, orphaned or with parents. Because keeping them in the city—in the plains and the heat—from July through August and into September is unthinkable. After all they have been through in the past few years, who more than them is entitled to a vacation? Who deserves the fresh mountain air, outdoor games, and walks in the woods more than they do? So on June 12, 1945, Moshe Zeiri and Matilde Cassin leave by car (with whom else is unknown, although most likely they are accompanied by a leader of the Milanese Jewish community) for Selvino, a holiday resort in the Bergamo area, a thousand meters above sea level on a plateau above the Val Seriana. At twenty-two kilometers from Bergamo and seventy kilometers from Milan, it isn't just any resort; it's the seat of the local Amatore Sciesa Club's alpine resorts, the poshest club in fascist Milan, the same as the one at the Odescalchi Palazzo in Via Unione 5. In fact, during the fascist period, the Selvino resort was called Sciesopoli.

Moshe and Matilde are enchanted by it. Selvino offers a lot to win them over. "The mountain people who live there call it 'the end of the world,' because that's where the road ends, near the border with Switzerland, and this makes it magic." (In reality the Swiss border is farther away, beyond the Bergamo Alps and Valtellina.) Moshe tells Yehudit that Selvino consists of snow-capped mountain peaks, streams that gurgle towards the plateau, and "God's peace."[27] But apart from the countryside, it's the resort that wins over Moshe and Matilde. Sciesopoli is a large building designed in rationalist forms by a renowned architect from Milan and inaugurated with great pomp in 1933, under the auspices of fascist leader Benito Mussolini himself.[28] The building is practically new. Surrounded by a fir and larch forest, it is

equipped with the most modern infrastructure: infirmary, laundry, ironing room, gym, indoor swimming pool, and cinema. "An ideal place. This is it, we've decided."[29] There is one small problem: Sciesopoli also tempts others. The legitimate owners have lost control of it since the fall of fascism, and the colony is occupied by the Opera Pia Fanciulli Gracili in Milan,[30] which takes care of minors and the aged. But it's also in the sights of partisans from Sesto San Giovanni, who would like to turn it into a convalescence center for former prisoners of war in Germany.[31]

Private Zeiri is not the type to retreat easily. On the day of his visit to Selvino, as soon as gets back to Milan, he goes to the office of Raffaele Cantoni, who not only works as a special commissioner of the Jewish community but also holds a top role in the National Liberation Committee of Northern Italy, as president of the Central Financial Commission. In addition to being a man of faith, Cantoni is a man of power. He is closely linked to the Socialist Party, and as president of the Financial Commission, he is responsible for tax police searches relating to the assets belonging to former fascists,[32] such as the Sciesopoli resort, owned by the very fascist Tonoli Melloni Foundation in Milan.[33] Nothing in this world should be wasted, Zeiri insists with Cantoni. "Here is a house built by the fascists that we can fill with new content. Cleaning it of their filth and giving it new life."[34] It might not be ready immediately, but it should by July or August, for the summer. Or it might take longer. In either case, Zeiri will not give up easily. Sciesopoli is exactly what's needed to welcome the orphans of the Shoah, eager to be reborn.

Indeed, that's what's needed. But will it be enough? The meeting with the first orphans who arrived in Milan—"leftovers from the concentration camps who have already been to the other side"—leaves an "indelible impression" on Moshe. And it immediately leaves him with a clear perception of his fundamental inadequacy: of the difficulty, or even the impossibility, in which he finds himself to really assist them. "I cannot personally help them," he confesses to Yehudit. Whether in Via Eupili or in Sciesopoli, Moshe is unable to put the orphans in a place that truly resembles a home: a familiar, maternal environment. Nor can he create an atmosphere around them capable of dispelling what inhabits them: "nostalgia, anguish, pain, anger, and especially harshness." Certainly not with the human resources at his disposal, with the old director of the Jewish school in Milan, Rabbi Yoseph Colombo, and with a teaching body of "seasoned spinsters" whom Moshe considers totally inadequate, all rife with authoritarian, if not reactionary, educational principles.[35]

Pedagogically speaking, Moshe's North Star lies elsewhere: it is the star of Janusz Korczak, the "Pan Doktor" who had founded the Orphan House in Warsaw, the children's republic of Krochmalna Street, on whom the ax of the Final Solution fell with his deportation and extermination in Treblinka.[36] Moshe speaks to Matilde Cassin about the Pan Doktor from the beginning. As he reads stories of the Orphan House and by Korczak to her, Moshe thinks aloud about the true objectives of their common educational commitment and tries to remedy the feeling of powerlessness coming over him as well. "What should the purpose of our work be? Give children the house that was torn from them. The warmth of a home. And this can only happen if they feel free, just as they would feel at home."[37]

The month of July 1945 keeps Moshe busy both in Milan, with the intense activity of the classes and boarding school in Via Eupili, and outside Milan. Every now and then, he has to return to the bases of the 745th Company, in the Bicocca or Taliedo neighborhoods, to answer to his superiors with regard to the proper use of his Royal Engineering Corps uniform. In addition, he needs to find a location for the children's summer camp. Ultimately the vacation would take place not in Selvino but in another mountain town in the Bergamo area: Piazzatorre, in the upper Brembana Valley. But in that month of July, Moshe's commitments revolve mainly around his new arrivals, who become the source of his unease. There is a steady stream of Shoah orphans entrusted to him by the Joint or the Jewish community as they reach Italy and Milan. The discomfort comes from the enormity of the suffering that each of them carries, as well as from the discovery of the historically unprecedented nature of the tragedy they have survived. Moshe writes about it to Yehudit and struggles not to be crushed by the weight of it all. He wants to believe that he can do something about it, but he is continually given to doubt.

"First of all, we have to treat the children's disease. We have to bring back the rhythm and warmth to their frozen hearts. Because there's no way here to express the meaning of the word 'mourning,' about which I have read many things, and which I have also heard pronounced by a man who has just returned from 'over there.' Suffice it to say that no children under the age of twelve have survived. Do you have any idea what these words meanly exactly? All of them have been exterminated, in the most horrible ways. It's hard to even imagine it. How is it possible that in the all of the various refugee camps in Germany, Austria, and

Bavaria, you can't find a single child of elementary school age? It's a terrifying discovery. I learned about it from a young man who was working on the relief effort, and I want everyone at Kvutzat-Shiller to know about it. They need to know that we didn't join the war just to defeat Hitler: we went to save the remains of our people. But only now do we have the opportunity to get a hands-on understanding of what a huge task lies ahead of us and how hard the rehabilitation work will be."[38]

Moshe's discomfort also stems from concern about the orphans' future in Eretz Israel. It comes from the surprisingly prophetic intuition of the difficulties awaiting them if they ever manage, after the Italian stage, to make it to one of the kibbutzim in Palestine. "From an educational point of view, the situation of the survivors is far from ideal. When young people like these arrive in a kibbutz or kvutza, we'll be likely to have forgotten the terrible stories in the newspapers told by some of the witnesses. When they are awkward in their work, or if they fail to integrate quickly, I'm sure they'll attract criticism. It's sad, but that's how it is. So there's no solution or remedy, people forget quickly. Life continues, as always."[39] Moshe Zeiri's unease is that of the Zionist militant who finds it natural to foresee a future in Palestine for the Shoah orphans, and to imagine it in the kibbutz movement. But he knows the environment too well not to worry about potential misunderstandings.

For now, the most flagrant misunderstandings are between Moshe and Yehudit, who is embittered by the prolonged separation, even after the war, and by her husband's renouncing a chance to return home on leave. Since his arrival in Milan and the beginning of the adventure in Via Eupili, Moshe hasn't managed to write as often as before, and his letters are thinner. For her part, Yehudit has no longer been able to write Moshe the kind of letters to which he had become accustomed over the years. Serene letters, despite her loneliness and the distance between them. Letters full of the ordinary everyday life at Kvutzat-Shiller: Nitza's progress in speaking and reading, Yehudit's work as a kindergarten teacher, all the mischief her schoolchildren got into, singing and Arabic lessons, and rehearsals with the choir. Letters also full of love and desire. "I'm thirsty for you, when will I be able to have you next to me?"[40] Or, "a cornucopia of torrid kisses, from the one who misses you terribly."[41] During July 1945, Yehudit sends Moshe letters full of intimately desolate nothing.

"What should I write to you about? Not even today do I know. The heat is always the same heat and the discomfort is always the same, and ever since you've started writing less, the feeling of loneliness has grown bigger and deeper. I won't hide from you that added to all this is a feeling of estrangement. Your letters interest me and fill me with joy, pride, even happiness. But I look in vain for that personal tone that I now need probably more than ever. You know how I get on hot summer days; but I've never felt such a state of depression."[42] Elsewhere, she describes it: "Do you know how I feel? It's as if I were talking to someone on the phone, and suddenly I realized that the line has dropped and the other person can't hear me anymore."[43]

HUMAN MATERIAL

Haim arrived at the Military Academy of Modena wearing the gray-green uniform of the Royal Italian Army. It was two or three sizes too big for his skeletal physique, but he would be fine anyway. An Italian soldier, a sergeant, had gotten it for him in Ebensee, Austria, at the Red Cross field hospital. Put this on and come with me to Italy, the sergeant had told him in the days of their convalescence, after the Americans had freed the concentration camp near Mauthausen and after the unbelievable news of the German surrender. Come to Italy, where there is also a Jewish Brigade, with Jews who fight. The Italian spoke some German, and Haim answered him in Yiddish. Come, I'll take you to them. So Haim Luftman, a Polish Jew from Poznan, left with the sergeant. They got rides from one military truck to another, in a landscape that in places was destroyed and in others wonderful. He had crossed Upper Austria, Salzburg, Tyrol, and from the Brenner Pass, he arrived in the Military Academy of Modena, in that gigantic old building that had been through so much.[44] Until a few weeks earlier, the German occupiers had dictated the law. Now it was crowded with the British of the Eighth Army, the Americans of the Fifth Army, and Italians half defeated and half victorious. There were also ex-deportees returning from concentration camps—hundreds, perhaps thousands, and especially soldiers and Jews.[45]

It was the last days of June 1945, and Haim Luftman had nothing left to lose. From 1939 onward, little by little he had lost everything: his childhood home in Żydowska Street (the "Street of the Jews"), when the Germans had come to Poznan immediately after the start of the war;[46] the apartment assigned to his family in the Łódź ghetto, inhabited for four years with his mother and sister (his father had been taken away by the Gestapo as early as 1940 and was never heard from again); and his work as slave labor in a shoe factory in Marysińska Street. He also lost his mother, selected on the Birkenau platform the very day of their arrival, a summer day in 1944. And his sister, who also went up the chimney. At just seventeen, Haim Luftman was totally alone in the world. In a sense, he was completely free. He could return to Poland, as some Jews around him said he wanted to do. But in Poland, where, and why? He could leave for the United States, as suggested to him by an American rabbi in the Red Cross hospital. No, he said to himself, better to leave for Italy. Better to reach the Jews who fight. Because who can be sure the Germans won't come back?[47]

The Dodge truck with the Star of David on the door was parked in the piazza in front of the military academy. Haim saw it, approached it, and tried to figure out why and how. In Yiddish, he spoke to the driver—a Middle Eastern–looking man—who didn't understand and answered him rudely. But Haim didn't give up. He stayed within range of the truck, waited for someone else to arrive. And someone did arrive: an officer wearing a British Army uniform. He spoke Yiddish and explained everything to him: 1942, volunteers enrolled in the British Army, training camps in Egypt, working as engineers in Libya, the crossing from Port Said to Malta, landing in Taranto, liberated Italy and Italy yet to be freed, in the rear at Monte Cassino, Naples, the formation of the Jewish Brigade, the Battle of the Senio, the final march in the Po Valley. Then Haim told the officer about himself, about the Łódź ghetto, Birkenau, and Mauthausen—the essentials. After that, the officer invited Haim into the academy building. He introduced him to other Jews, who spoke to him about Milan, Via Unione 5, and Palestine. They provided him with a British uniform. They sent him to Milan with three or four boys his age. Haim camped out in Via Unione for a few days, and from there they took him to the outskirts, to Magenta.[48]

In Magenta, thanks as usual to Cantoni's good offices, emissaries from Palestine were organizing a cover activity.[49] In theory, it was an agricultural camp preparing youth for the aliyah, the "ascent" to Palestine. In practice, it was a secret depot of weapons and ammunition stolen from British military camps and hidden on a fake farm by the Solel Boneh engineers, who would learn better and better how to hide them inside the construction machinery. Indeed, Italy in the summer of 1945 was crawling with a growing number of secret agents from the Jewish settlements. They took advantage of both the incorporation of volunteers into the British Army and the diplomatically ambiguous status of Italy (a strategic ally of London, in view of the Cold War, or a defeated and militarily occupied former enemy?) to promote arms trafficking toward Palestine, in preparation for an imminent war of independence. They also worked on the so-called Aliyah Beth— that is, the illegal immigration of Jews to the Promised Land, in violation of the quotas prescribed by the 1939 White Paper.[50]

Between July and August 1945, Aliyah Beth agents lay the groundwork for the autumn operations. With the help of Italian Zionists, they identify discharged vessels in the ports of Liguria and Puglia that can be rearmed and utilized—in the heart of the seas—for the transport of illegal immigrants. With the collaboration of a person acting as a front, they buy the boats and finance the repairs. At the same time, they look for commanders and naval officers ready to take on the cargo. Then they organize the chain of command delegated to select the candidates for emigration, to convey them to special assembly centers and to bring them, on the eve of day X, to the port of departure and the ship bound for Palestine. It is the adventurous story that Ada Sereni,[51] a participant in those illegal operations, would tell many years later in *Clandestini del mare* (Illegals of the Sea). Ada was the widow of Enzo Sereni, a pioneer of Italian Zionism, whose parachuting behind the front lines in German-occupied Tuscany in 1944 resulted in his dramatic capture, deportation to Dachau, and execution by firing squad.[52]

From the Magenta farming camp, Haim Luftman sees little of this. The operational heart of Aliyah Beth is located in Milan, at the center in number 5 Via Cantù.[53] There, an apparently innocuous Jewish Soldiers' Club masks the headquarters of a secret service, with its radio sets, walkie-talkies, and the coming and going of agents like Shalhevet Freier, the twenty-five-year-old son of Recha Freier, the charismatic lady who founded Jugend-Alijah in Berlin in 1933.[54] In Magenta, Haim sees the falling roof of the fake farm, which Solel Boneh's men work to repair to keep the dormitory from flooding on rainy days. And Haim sees other boys like him arrive in Magenta: Shoah orphans, too old to be looked after as children, too young to be treated as adults.[55] With some of these children, Haim builds a close, exclusive relationship impervious to any disciplinary measures—as was often the case among teenagers in refugee camps all over Europe, creating serious problems for those responsible for the camps.[56]

To escape the Final Solution, it had almost always been necessary for Jews to be young, strong, and healthy.[57] The ones who were saved were mostly robust young people with strong constitutions (though not too young; as a general rule, little children didn't survive). So after the end of the war, the most numerous among the survivors were boys and girls on the threshold of adolescence in the years between 1941 and 1944.[58] Boys like Haim Luftman, or Shmuel Milchman, a sixteen-year-old who in turn escaped various death sentences: the Łódź ghetto, Birkenau, Mauthausen, and Ebensee.[59] He arrived in Magenta after meeting men from the Jewish Brigade in the streets of Innsbruck, Zionist officers and soldiers who, during the summer of 1945, had mobilized to collect the miserable remains of the Jewish people based at the Tarvisio Pass just across the border in Austria.[60]

Major Yissachar Haimowitz, the highest ranking officer of Moshe Zeiri's 745th Company, was then responsible for the connection between the Center for the Diaspora operating in Italy and Zionist emissaries operating beyond the Alps.[61] But a systematic organization of the Bricha movement, the general "flight" toward Palestine of the Jews who survived the Final Solution, would not be ready before autumn 1945.[62] In the summer months, Bricha is more spontaneous than coordinated.[63] It must also face the difficulties in which Zionist emissaries find themselves, for understandable reasons, in correctly assessing the number of Jews who survived and are potentially interested in emigration to Palestine. Their very first calculations estimate the total at five thousand.[64] In reality, the number of Jews gathered in the refugee camps of Western Europe was almost one hundred thousand, and the number of survivors in Poland alone was around sixty thousand.[65]

If the quantities remain unclear, the quality of "human material," as the Zionists tend to define it, appears poor to more than one emissary. Aharon Hoter-Yishai, a civil lawyer serving as Jewish Brigade officer in the military, was among those responsible for searching out surviving Jews in the refugee camps of Austria and Germany. He carried out the task zealously but had no illusions about the mental health of the survivors, nor about the effects of their mass transfer to Palestine. In the unfortunate hypothesis that all Jews still alive in Europe would wind up in the Promised Land, the Jewish settlement would become a "large psychiatric hospital."[66] He was echoed by Yechiel Duvdevani, the noncommissioned officer of the 745th Company whom Moshe Zeiri knew well. In refugee camps, the quality of human material left much to be desired.[67] The Shoah had selected the species of survivors not by privileging more suitable individuals in a Darwinian manner but rather by privileging, by chance, the luckiest individuals, or even by maliciously rewarding those most inclined to an accommodation with the executioners: the most physically and morally corrupt.[68]

In Palestine, many political leaders of the Jewish settlements took an equally disenchanted position on the issue of survivors as that of certain Zionist emissaries.[69] To this they added the habit of taking sides on an ideological basis, particularly within the kibbutz movement. The militants of Hashomer Hatzair, the leftist component, accused the emissaries in Europe of benefiting the candidates for emigration who had already affiliated themselves before leaving the refugee camps to an ideologically moderate component, such as Gordonia. Nor did the accusation lack political significance, because the historical leader of Gordonia was Pinchas Lubianiker, a very high-ranking leader of both the Mapai Party and the Histadrut Union. For his part, the most illustrious son of the Kopychyntsi shtetl did not hesitate to criticize the prospect of massive immigration to Palestine of the Jews who escaped the Final Solution. In which case, Lubianiker warned, a "terrible holocaust" threatened the life of the party and the union.[70]

But in the summer of 1945, the calculations and speeches of the politicians of Palestine had little effect on the concrete mobilization in Europe of the Jewish organizations engaged in the relief work, starting with the Joint, the American organization financing the bulk of the interventions in the many various countries. For their part, the volunteers of the Palestinian companies incorporated into the British Army, starting from the 745th Solel Boneh headquartered just outside Milan, prefer facts to numbers and words: they lavish attention and care on the survivors, all the more if they are young. So in the Magenta farm colony, which is also a secret weapons depot, a boy like Haim Luftman can spend his first summer of freedom not so much (or not only) preparing to go to Palestine but also just becoming a child again.

This, at least, is the memory Haim would retain of that summer over sixty years later while sharing his own story as a saved Jew with a Yad Vashem interviewer. "At that point, I went back to being a child. Because . . . let's put it this way: the boy who had been Haim Luftman was actually dead. Now a new child was born, with the same name. I was like reborn. In some respects, I went back in time . . . five years. I was no longer seventeen, I was twelve. From all points of view. It was as if the period of the ghetto and the camps was erased." In Magenta, Haim would explain in 2008, none of the soldiers or emissaries asked the Shoah orphans to evoke their past. "Nothing. No account. No story. They didn't ask us, and they were right. It was impossible to tell. There's no language that can tell that story, it didn't exist then and it doesn't exist now. How can you talk about it?"[71]

On the fake Magenta farm, Zionist emissaries "did many things." For example, "they brought people there who had collaborated with the Germans, and put them on trial." Clearly, it was not a suitable place for children. "I was still considered a child. I *was* still a child." So "they transferred us to a place exclusively dedicated to children. It was called Selvino. I don't know if you're familiar with Italy a little . . . Bergamo is north of Milan. From Bergamo you go up into the mountains, and at the top there was a place that had been a fascist youth camp. Mussolini had built it. There was a sign with Mussolini's name. The Jewish

Brigade had taken this house from the Italians ... they received it from the Italians. And that was where they gathered all the children."[72] That was Moshe's children's home.

FROM PIAZZATORRE TO SELVINO

Haim Luftman had forgotten about Piazzatorre. In 2008, responding to the Yad Vashem interviewer, he spoke of being sent directly from Magenta to Selvino, omitting an intermediate stage: the alpine resort in Val Brembana, where Moshe Zeiri, Matilde Cassin, and a handful of educators hosted nearly two hundred Jewish children in the month of August 1945.

About forty were children like Haim, orphans and foreigners. The others were either Italian children who still had their parents but had been entrusted to Moshe and Matilde for a vacation in Piazzatorre—a natural continuation of the welcome offered in Milan at the boarding school in Via Eupili—or foreign children who had found refuge in Italy with families already before 1939, and who in Italy (at the price of a thousand adventures) had managed to save themselves from the Final Solution. One of the latter was Isaak Weintraub, the son of a Leipzig furrier who had been Moshe Zeiri's pupil at the Jewish school in Naples in 1944. In Piazzatorre, Isaak found his sister Helga, from whom he hadn't had any news since the time of the German occupation.[73] Siegbert and Marina Loewi were also foreign Jews. Their father had been lost in the Shoah, but they had managed to save themselves, along with their mother, not far from Piazzatorre. It was in Gandino, a town in the Val Seriana, thanks to the help of four local peasants, an employee, an office worker, and a teacher, all of whom Yad Vashem would recognize as Righteous Among the Nations.[74]

In a group photo taken on Saturday August 11, 1945, the children of the Piazzatorre camp appear all together, without distinction between Italians or foreigners, orphans or not. Nevertheless,

as much as the alpine holiday could be healthy for all of them, between swings and playing capture the flag, walks in the woods and climbing trees,[75] the condition of some remained profoundly different from the condition of the others. It was one thing to know that at the end of the summer camp, there would be someone to return to. It was another thing altogether to know that there would be no one. Yet even if the orphans had no one to return to, they did have somewhere to go: they could ascend to Palestine.

The message that Moshe Zeiri was keen to convey to them went beyond the enchantment of days like August 11, the day of the group photo ("how nice it was for me now to be able to send the children to relax for a Sabbath rest after a three-hour hike in the mountains, through the woods, near the roaring waterfall. We talked, skipped, jumped like deer on the felled trees ready to be removed.... We came back tired, we ate with a huge appetite, then went out again to take a picture of all of us together").[76] And it is as a Zionist—with the prospect of the orphans' rebirth in Palestine—that Moshe reads Bialik's stories to them. First, the story of King David in the cave. The king of Israel, who hadn't really died but was asleep in a secret cave, waiting for someone to wake him up so he could return to the world stage and save the Chosen People. "I read Bialik, translating it for them from the original Hebrew into Yiddish. For three hours they wouldn't let me go, and they sat there and devoured the story."[77]

To help transform these individual salvations into a collective redemption the Moshe of Piazzatorre conjures up the Moshe of Tel Aviv—when he was a student at the Habima Theatre School—and animates Bialik's story as if he were a theater actor on stage. "I brought the characters to life again, and I was happy to see children in front of me whose childhood innocence and ability to get excited hadn't been killed by the years in the camps. There was no disbelief in their eyes when the river spoke to the boys who had gone to look for King David's cave, or when the dove showed them the way."[78] Moshe confirms the life plan he conceived three months earlier, in Laterina, on the road to Milan: Building a bridge between the Shoah orphans and the birth of the new Israel. Working with orphans, and for orphans. Opening up a future for them. Offering them, if not parents to embrace, then at least a home where they feel nearly at home, and a community of adults and peers they can recognize as an adoptive family.

The Piazzatorre experience allows Moshe Zeiri to better draw the contours of this life project. And it presents him with an opportunity to inaugurate it—even before reaching the Promised Land in Palestine. He can do it in Italy, between Milan and Bergamo, in the land where the Zionist emissaries were gathering many Shoah orphans from the bloodlands. So as a first step, Moshe writes a letter to the kibbutz. He writes "ten long pages" to the Kvutzat-Shiller community ("I know that many will not read them, but you certainly will," he comments to Yehudit[79]) in an effort to convince them of his willingness to stay in Italy even after the demobilization of the 745th Company, when his term as a volunteer in the British Army is finished. In addition, Moshe exchanges letters with Yosef Baratz, who is, as founder of Degania, not only a legendary figure of the kibbutz movement but also the head of Jewish military assistance in Italy.[80] Among the various emissaries often competing with each other, Moshe shows that he confides most of all with Baratz, an old ally of Pinchas Lubianiker and Gordonia.

At the end of August, when the Italian children leave Piazzatorre to return to their families, Moshe, Matilde, and the other educators remain in the mountains with only the foreign orphans, "forty mouths to feed." Forty mouths are still a lot, considering the lack of funds for the summer camp. But forty mouths are not enough in light of the "even bigger enterprise" that Moshe has started to imagine during the summer: the foundation—possibly in Selvino, in Mussolini's house—of a "Youth Aliyah House" for "two hundred children of Israel" ("I have established the number based on the site's reception capacity"). Indeed, Zeiri intends to model that house on the Korczak Orphan House, and already in Piazzatorre, he discusses it with those forty mouths, the Polish and Hungarian orphans. But it is a disorganized and desultory group: "too many different ages, and you can't keep the number of people so low."[81]

To achieve a project that lives up to his ambitions, Zeiri needs both Raffaele Cantoni and Yissachar Haimowitz. He needs Cantoni to get the former fascist colony of Selvino assigned to the Jews. He needs Haimowitz for the Diaspora Center to elect Sciesopoli as the main reception house for the Shoah orphan refugees in Italy. For his part, Cantoni—testifying to how strong the personal understanding with Zeiri is—goes up to Piazzatorre on September 6.[82] It is probably on this occasion that the special commissioner of the Milanese Jewish community (who is also the president of the Central Financial Commission) develops with Moshe the battle plan that will result in a dispatch from the Allied Military Government at their Milan headquarters, dated September 21, 1945: "The Allied Authorities have directed the Intendenza di Finanza to make the Sciesopoli Building at Selvino, Bergamo, available to the Comunità Israelitica di Milano."[83] The operation is accomplished thanks to the decisive intervention of Luigi Gorini, a biochemist from Pavia whom the men of the Resistance had appointed commissioner of the Tonoli Melloni Foundation, the legal owner of Sciesopoli.[84]

Two days after Cantoni's visit to Piazzatorre—September 8, 1945 according to the Christian calendar—the camp celebrates Rosh Hashanah, the Jewish New Year of 5706. The cook went out of her way for the occasion: fish, preserves, meat, and fruit; "a New Year the way God would have commanded," Moshe writes to Yehudit. But apart from the menu, what Moshe wants to share with his wife in Palestine is the spiritual atmosphere of that first day of celebration, in particular the climate at the time of the various blessings and prayers contemplated by the ritual tradition. "I saw that the children were intimidated, and I said to myself: well, I'll have to be the one to go before the Ark. And I decided to extract the memories of my youth from the archives of my mind." Moshe remembered the feasts of Rosh Hashanah at the shtetl, when the synagogue echoed melodies sung by his father, David Kleiner, and the ram's horn blown by Abraham Yaakov, Yehuda Yakar, and Avrami Peled. "Yes, I was praying without the melodies of the cantors, but with a wholly Jewish candor." After all, it had been years since those children—the Hungarian orphans, and especially the Polish orphans—had savored the taste of a holiday. Finally, the day of recompense has arrived.[85]

"In the evening everyone was dressed up, we wrote on the blackboard with colored chalk: 'One year ends with its curses, another begins with its blessings.' We lit the candles, and I prayed. Everyone came, from the largest to the smallest, and we felt so good. It was as warm as it used to be, like when the child was me, and in the children's faces I saw my face back then, when I was young. I prayed, and the children helped me with the traditional melody. At the end of the prayer I turned to wish them a happy new year, and here everyone was crying. They held out their hands, kissed each other and cried. 'Happy New Year.' They didn't cry loudly, but it was a heartbreaking cry. Even I was struggling to get through that moment, but knowing how contagious it was, I dressed up with joy and congratulated them out loud, 'Happy New Year,' and said that it was forbidden to cry on Rosh Hashanah. We must rejoice, as much as we can! May it be a beautiful and sweet year!"[86]

On the dinner tables, in the premises of the Opera Pia Bergamasca, which housed the Jewish colony, the white tablecloths were decorated with flowers and candles. "We blessed the wine, and sang a happy New Year song: but the song wasn't a song, because our hearts were crying." Certainly, Moshe assumes, every child would think back to their homes, their parents, and the holidays they had celebrated with them. "It's hard to sing when the heart is weeping." But slowly the melancholy dissipated. "By the end of the meal almost everyone was singing, and at the end of everything we started dancing." So despite the enormity of the pain, both personal and general, the feast of Rosh Hashanah 5706 was a true feast. And Moshe's pride comes through in his letter: "I felt I had done something great. Even if they were only forty children. Yes, my dear, I directed the prayer for forty orphans of Israel from whom our time had stolen the things they cherished most: home, parents, the sense of youth. And I, in part, have returned these three things to them."[87] For forty of Moshe's children, Rosh Hashanah in Piazzatorre can mean a truly new idea of themselves. A remediable solitude. A future life to live.

SEVEN

A REPUBLIC OF ORPHANS

NOTHING BUT THE CHILDREN

In Sciesopoli, the director's office is not large, but Moshe Zeiri finds it beautiful and elegant.[1] There is a safe in which to keep money and a table with a typewriter. A desk with a leather-covered top is perpetually in disorder: ink bottles and blotter, a hole puncher, letters, bills, and receipts. In a corner of the room, you can see a wall clock and a lamp with a decorated lampshade. On the other side are some shelves, a wardrobe, two leather armchairs—one for Moshe, the other for Matilde. A fan rests on the safe. The floor is covered with linoleum; it makes no noise when you walk on it. The curtains screen the windows for half their height.[2]

The Youth Aliyah House opened its doors in the last week of September 1945. Along with Moshe Zeiri and Matilde Cassin, the educators, employees, and forty foreign orphans remaining in the camp after the departure of the Italian children had all moved from Piazzatorre to Selvino—from Val Brembana to Val Seriana. But once in Sciesopoli, the numbers grow quickly. The Jewish community in Milan, the American operators of the Joint, and the Zionist emissaries of the Aliyah Beth direct a number of

orphans who have landed in Italy from the bloodlands to Selvino. Already at the beginning of October, there are more than one hundred. It was just what Zeiri hoped for when Janusz Korczak's Orphan House was proposed as a model: a numerically significant group of children that could be structured, formed, and given responsibilities by age group. At the same time, the director is experiencing the rapid growth of Sciesopoli with concern. It isn't the workload that frightens him—a thousand organizational tasks, which add to his daily hours of teaching Hebrew— it's the lack of teaching staff and their inexperience. The lack of educational and recreational material frightens him, as does the scarcity of health workers and medicines. There are not enough clothes, fuel, stoves, and food ("the small portions, hardly any fats, proteins and carbohydrates").[3] It all frightens him.

And the director is frightened by the conversations of the children who survived the Final Solution: "a whole world of experiences, sensations, visions and perceptions of life," which leave Moshe, as he confesses in his letters to Yehudit, with a feeling of inadequacy or even inferiority. "When I listen to the stories of these kids, I feel so small and insignificant. What is my strength compared to their life experience, and the wisdom they've acquired? If only I could review them one by one, write down the number tattooed on their arm, and transmit each of their worlds. Trace its external description and inner essence. The habits they had picked up 'over there,' indecent habits. And the extraordinary social discoveries of helping one another, the willingness to sacrifice for a friend, over and over. I wish I could stand aside, be invisible. Observe them for a long time, them and their lifestyle. It's better than books and newspapers. But for their good it's also necessary to know them and study them. Prepare in order to know how to give them back what's been stolen from them."[4]

Fortunately, Moshe Zeiri isn't alone in founding the house. Beside him are Matilde Cassin, Reuven Donath, and Noga Cohen. Reuven is the young volunteer of the 745th Company whom Moshe had initially distrusted, recognizing in him the ruthlessness and insensitivity typical of a sabra. But after having lived through the experience of the war and especially through his interactions with the orphans, Reuven reveals to Moshe his various qualities. "He was one of those boys who laugh at everything sacred and every ideal—cynical, consumed by bitterness, complaining about everything. He's changed so much that he is no longer recognizable." Smiling, lively, and sporty, Reuven enjoys the children as well as the work, and he couldn't care less about Bergamo, Milan, and everything else that the men in their third year of military life hope to find in the city.[5] Besides, Reuven Donath doesn't need to go far because Noga is nearby. Noga, born Eugenia Cohen, is a young Jewish woman from Milan (originally from Turkey) whom Zeiri and Donath met in Via Eupili in May. She followed them as a teacher, first to Piazzatorre and then to Selvino, and quickly became a pillar at Sciesopoli—as well as Reuven's girlfriend.[6]

Seventy years later, in a kibbutz near Ashkelon, on the border with the Gaza Strip, a former Selvino child—Yaakov Meriash, a Lithuanian Jew—would share with me his memory of the four founders of the orphanage. It was a mild June day, and we sat in the garden in the shade of the date and pomegranate trees (Sara, my daughter, was also there, as was Nitza, Moshe's daughter, with her brother, Avner, and sister, Tali, the lady of the house). Yaakov had brought me a copy of his memoir, *The Cut Tree and the New Tree*, as a gift. He flipped through it, stopping at the pages that contained photographs, and told me about the Kaunas ghetto and the Dachau concentration camp, the Modena Academy and his arrival in Selvino—where life had begun again, where the tree had been reborn. "For them, for Moshe, Matilde, Noga and Reuven, there was nothing but the children. Day and night, all they had on their minds were the children." And what was Matilde Cassin like? "In Hebrew, we would call her *nechama*: a soul. As I remember her, she was an angel."[7]

The day before—at the opposite end of Israel, in a Haifa nursing home on Mount Carmel—Sara and I had met Noga Donath. More than ninety years old, her Italian was still fluent, and she was charged with a humanity that seemed inexhaustible. I asked her in what language she spoke with the Sciesopoli children. Noga explained to me that back then, she didn't know a single word of Hebrew, Yiddish, Polish, Hungarian, or any of the orphans' mother tongues. Moreover, "they didn't talk about the past, but at night they woke up, screaming, crying.... We had no words in common, only gestures, washing them, dressing them, only love ... I didn't say anything. I only spoke with my hands, with caresses and kisses."[8] After offering us tea and the lemon cake that she had prepared for us, Noga pulled out a crumpled notebook, her Selvino notebook, and opened it to the page that was most dear to her: "For my dear little mom, a memory of your Liliana. Selvino 30-10-45."[9] Seventy years later, Noga still didn't know that child's surname. I was the one who was able to tell her, there in Haifa, by opening my Excel file in front of her with the names and surnames of all the children of Selvino: Liliana Friedrich, born in Fiume (today Rijeka, Croatia) on December 12, 1936.[10]

In the autumn of 1945, in addition to the four founders, the management team of Sciesopoli is made up of a doctor and two teachers. The doctor is Dr. Pesia Kissin, who lives in the Youth Aliyah House with her nine-year-old daughter, Avivit. Both escaped the Final Solution by fleeing the Kaunas ghetto in Lithuania and surviving thanks to the help of a Catholic priest who would be recognized as Righteous Among the Nations.[11] The doctor's husband, Avraham Kissin, who was the principal of the Jewish school in Kaunas and a protagonist of cultural life in the ghetto,[12] didn't manage to save himself. One of the two teachers is Arieh Soleh, a young historian from Munkács (today Mukachevo), in Transcarpathia: a "nice boy," "open and awake," whom Moshe Zeiri liked from the first moment.[13] In the prewar Munkács, Soleh was a teacher at the Jewish high school, as well as an active Zionist militant. He was saved together with his wife and daughter, who are in Switzerland, preparing to join him in the Bergamo area.[14] Moshe entrusts him with the advanced Hebrew language course.[15]

The other teacher is Zippora Hager. Aged twenty-four, Zippora is a qualified teacher and speaks four or five languages.[16] Originally from a Hasidic family in Transylvania, she escaped both the hell of the Oradea ghetto and the liquidation of the Hungarian Jews in the summer of 1944. Moshe Zeiri finds her "very wise" but "more sensitive than others." She is certainly a young woman besieged by memories. On the Birkenau platform, when her mother had taken the path to the gas chambers, Zippora ran after her, but she had been beaten back three times until she fell to the ground unconscious. When she came to, "her mother was already an ash heap," Moshe writes to Yehudit. "Yesterday, during a conversation, she was looking at a distant point in the emptiness, bewildered: 'Why did they take me out of the oven? I could have burned together with my mother, what would I have missed? The world is so repulsive, and I have no one.'" He adds, "I understood how far I am from knowing all the people here. This Zippora always laughs cheerfully... but actually she laughs a lot less lately. And that's how much pessimism hides behind her laughter."[17]

Then there's Moshe Unger, whom everyone calls "Fetter Moshe," which means Uncle Moshe in Yiddish, the lingua franca at Sciesopoli. The Russian-Jewish Fetter Moshe doesn't live in Selvino; he goes back and forth as the driver of the truck used to transport both the orphans gradually entrusted to the colony and the food necessary for its operation. Fetter Moshe is an expert driver, and he takes advantage of his driving experience with the British Engineers to face the hairpin turns of the vertiginous dirt road connecting the Selvino plateau to the village of Nembro, in the Val Seriana below.[18] Fetter Moshe, with his contagious humanity, left his wife, Leah, and two young daughters behind in Palestine so he could volunteer with the 745th Company. Now he's adored by the children of Sciesopoli, some of whom, having grown up, will not hesitate to call him (with the Hebrew word, this time) a *tzadik*: a righteous one, if not a saint.[19]

DEPARTURES

Over the winter, when Moshe Unger was preparing to leave Italy to sail to Palestine, Moshe Zeiri wrote to Yehudit in heartfelt terms. "His absence will be very evident, he was the father of the house. You saw it every time 'Fetter Moshe' came in. At a distance of twenty to thirty meters from the entrance, he honks his horn to announce his arrival. Then the children race out from all over the house. They hang on him from all sides with a cascade of kisses raining on him. He positions the truck, seats everyone around him, and enters like a winner through the camp gate. Clearly, there is no greater happiness for him than this. He unloads the things he's brought for 'his kids,' arranges them to

be put in their place, then takes out the box of candies and distributes them, one for each. You won't find many like him. He's one of a kind."[20]

Even before the departure of Moshe Unger deprives the children of a father, Matilde Cassin's departure on October 12, 1945, almost immediately after the opening of the house, deprives them of their most maternal reference figure. "She is the mother and soul of the institute," the director of Sciesopoli wrote of her just a few days before in a long letter to his wife—a wonderfully candid letter, entirely dedicated (as Moshe explained to Yehudit) to "your questions about Rachel." Once more, nothing was kept silent about the understanding that Moshe felt he had had with Matilde from the first moment of their relationship. And much was said about the relationship between Matilde and her fiancé,

Max Varadi, a pioneer of Italian Zionism. Varadi was ten years older than Matilde, and they had been separated during all the years of the war. He was impatient to rejoin her and marry her as soon as possible.[21]

Matilde's departure leaves Moshe in a state of withdrawal. He tells Yehudit about it with his usual frankness. "My darling, three days have passed since Rachel left, and I walk around as if stunned, I don't know where to start. In theory, she promised to come back, but I'm sure he won't let her. Nor do I want to judge him; I don't know what I would have done in his place."[22] For her part, Matilde begins to write a series of letters to Moshe, tormented letters, at times desperate. The tasks concerning Sciesopoli that the young woman manages from Florence—the purchase of toys, preparing furs for the winter, printing letterheads on paper for the Youth Aliyah House—are nowhere near enough. They can appease neither her nostalgia for Selvino's children nor the desire to support Moshe again in the running of the orphanage.[23]

Matilde's nostalgia and desire crash against a barrier of obstacles, first of all against the jealousy that Max Varadi shows with regard to Moshe Zeiri. Unmotivated jealousy, judging from Matilde's letters to Moshe: the relationship between the two having remained well within the limits of a fraternal friendship. Moreover, Matilde's feelings hit the obstacle of ideology: against the irreconcilable diversity of views with regard to religion in educational work with the Shoah orphans. Varadi challenges the secular character of the Zionist education that Zeiri plans to offer Selvino's children. "Observance of the sabbath, the tefillot, kosher diet, a little study of Torah": these, in Matilde's words, are the conditions set by Max to allow for the prospect of his fiancée's return to Sciesopoli—conditions rejected by Moshe, either halfheartedly or in no uncertain terms. Finally, Matilde's feelings shatter against the opposition of Raffaele Cantoni, who is critical of any compromise between Zeiri's secular Zionism and Varadi's religious Zionism.[24]

Not even a week after Matilde's departure, the first fifteen children destined for Palestine leave Sciesopoli. In their case, this is a fully legal emigration. The Union of Italian Jewish Communities and the Zionist emissaries of the Center for the Diaspora have compiled a list of four hundred names, to be counted among the annual quota of fifteen thousand immigration certificates that the British Palestine authorities have committed to issue. Priority is given to orphans under the age of fourteen, pregnant women, and the parents of "Palestinian" soldiers who enlisted in the British Army.[25] On this basis, fifteen of the four hundred Jews included in the Italian lists of autumn 1945 are Selvino children. For the most part, they are orphans who had already been to Piazzatorre, so seeing them go away is—for the teachers—all the more burdensome. "I knew that one day it would happen, but I didn't imagine so quickly, and above all that I would have to separate from them without the 'mother,' without Rachel," Moshe writes to Yehudit in a letter of October 17.[26]

That same letter contains a loving review of Moshe's fifteen children about to leave. The youngest of all, Batia, two years old, arrived in Piazzatorre and didn't even know how to walk. Within three months, she had "turned into a real person." She ate alone, mumbled a bit of Hebrew, sang, and played ("if you saw her big eyes, like two cherries, black as coal"). Batia's naughty brother, Yosef, when scolded, would put on a face as serious as it was innocent. Esther was calm and scrupulous, with an unfailingly sad expression. Her sister, Jaffa, was the exact opposite, impulsive and tempestuous. Sara had her hair cut like a boy's because of a skin disease; "what tenderness her bent figure arouses, almost curved like a grandmother." She was sixteen years old with her incredible maturity, like a mother for her younger sisters, Erszébet, Edith, Rosi, and Irén. Pinchas, whom everyone calls "Stupid" ("he really is stupid, but he's dear to me, too, like every child to a parent"). Israeliko, with the same "mute soul" in the beginning as Yehudit, who was picked up from a convent in Italy and "remained as she had come—quiet, timid and reserved; she doesn't complain, doesn't question, doesn't demand what she can't receive," like the antihero of the famous Yiddish story by I. L. Peretz, "Bontsha the Silent."[27]

Who else? "Yitzhak and Zarach, the twins, will forgive me. They've always stayed in the shadows, too, that's why I forgot to list them. Not particularly awake or developed, it seems that the dose of talent normally bestowed by nature to a single individual has been divided between them. But maybe that has something to do with the scientific experiments in the camps, the blood samples taken from the twins to get to the secret of the phenomenon, injecting their blood into gypsies to see what influence it would have. Maybe, together with the blood, they extracted the essence of the twins' vigor. For a long time I'll remember the day when Zarach tried to escape from the previous camp. When I ran into him while he was leaving, his painful little figure got even more compressed, so that I wouldn't see it. How ridiculous and tragic his appearance was, with a sack tied to a rope on his shoulders. There was something about him that symbolized our time. A Jewish boy who wanders aimlessly. 'Where are you going, Zarach?' I asked. 'I don't want to be here, I'm hungry.'"[28]

Overcoming his own emotions, the director had to communicate to all the orphans of the institute that fifteen of them were leaving for Palestine—not an easy announcement. Moshe decided to make it in the evening, in the square in front of the main building, on the occasion of Sciesopoli's daily twilight ceremony: the flag-furling—the flag, of course, being the blue and white banner with the star by David—accompanied by the choral singing of "Hatikvah," the Zionist national anthem. But "the moods were tense," Moshe had to admit. Although the director tried to reassure children and young people, explaining to them how the departure bell for the Promised Land would soon ring for everyone, there were many who did not believe his words. Nor was Moshe's decision to have the dining room prepared as for Shabbat, with white tablecloths and flowers on the tables, enough to raise their spirits.[29]

There was no need to beat around the bush. From those days of mid-October 1945, the problem of selecting candidates for departure hovered like a ghost over the Youth Aliyah House, and over the authority of Moshe Zeiri as head of the institute. All the more so as the lists of those departing became secret lists: lists of Jews transported clandestinely by Zionist emissaries to the ports of Liguria or Puglia, and stealthily embarked on ships sailing for Eretz Israel. Who among the orphans of Selvino would be able to leave at the first opportunity, albeit at the risk of having to face the opposition of the British authorities in the heart of the seas? And who would have to resign themselves to staying in Italy indefinitely? According to what criteria would Zeiri and the managers of the Joint or Aliyah Beth include some names on the lists and exclude others? For the moment, it was understood that the youngest children were leaving. But later, how would things work? Would the children who had a relative in Palestine, and therefore the prospect of some family life, have priority? Or would the children alone in the world, and therefore destined for a kvutza or a kibbutz, go first? Would brothers and sisters have the right to leave together, or would they be separated? Would males and females leave equally, or would one gender have preference over the other? And to leave earlier, what did one have to do? Stay calm and good, curry Moshe's favor? Or come across as restless, polemic, and rebellious, garnering hostility to be included among the kids needing to leave as soon as possible? Also, would the first arrivals in Selvino be the first to leave? Or not? Wouldn't seniority be a defining criterion? In which case, what about the new arrivals? In the ears of every Sciesopoli orphan, the throttle of Fetter Moshe's truck must have been charged with a meaning as painful as it was festive, because the arrival of new orphans might entail a delay in the departure of those who had been in Selvino for some time.

All these questions inevitably drifted through the minds of Moshe's children as the orphanage grew in numbers until it exceeded 150 by the last days of October. It was clearly only a drop in the sea of twenty thousand refugees who escaped the Final Solution and ended up in Italy: half of them were housed in about seventy Jewish farm camps, while the other half were set up in the seventeen camps (including that of Selvino) financed by the Joint and UNRRA.[30] But beyond the numbers, which nevertheless remained significant, Sciesopoli was particularly pressing to the Zionist emissaries operating in Italy, if only for the symbolic significance that derived from the Aliyah Youth House being a camp specialized in the reception of orphans: the saved Jews who had the right to a second life in the land of Israel more than anyone else. Hence the particular attention that Zionist leaders such as Haimowitz and Duvdevani gave to Zeiri's institute, which they visited several times during that autumn 1945.[31]

The multiplying arrivals in Selvino also corresponded to renegade departures: real escapes—individual or collective—of orphans who couldn't handle the rules at Sciesopoli. The problem of escapes had already arisen in Piazzatorre in August. A few days after their arrival in Val Brembana, Haim Luftman and four of his companions had fled to the plain. Between marches and hitchhiking, they returned to the fake Magenta farm, except they were told that they couldn't stay there and then wound up in Selvino, monitored and watched, known as the "Magenta gang."[32] In October, at least three escapes were recorded in Sciesopoli: a boy who ran away after stealing from his neighbor in the dormitory, two brothers who disappeared into thin air, and two Orthodox boys who fled the house because when they prayed, they were ridiculed by their companions. "Our conditions in terms of human material are not easy," was how Moshe reported it to Yehudit.[33] In fact, behind the problem of escapes, there was a wider and more serious problem: the difficulty of building a relationship between the Shoah orphans and those who wanted to revive them.

Much later—more than sixty years later—Haim Luftman, the fugitive from Magenta, would talk to the Yad Vashem interviewer about it. He would evoke the Hebrew courses of Moshe Zeiri ("I liked them very much") and generally define the conditions of life in Selvino as "good." But "not good enough," he would say, because they were undermined by a pervasive lack of communication. "They didn't know how to treat us. We weren't just orphans. We were orphans from another planet."[34]

ARRIVALS

Avraham Lipkunski did a lot since that day in August 1944 when—armed with a rifle, and more or less recognizable as an agent of the Soviet political police—he presented himself at the door of his old house in Dugalishok, forcing the Lithuanian who was occupying it to show him where Pinchas's body was buried. He recognized his older brother's remains by the phylacteries coiled around the skeleton, and he transported them to Raduń, where he buried them near the mass grave that contained the bodies of their mother, Sara Mina, and their little brother, Yekutiel, lying with a thousand other Jews of the shtetl. In October, in Grodno, the fifteen-year-old ex-partisan, nom de guerre Avremale, sat down among the benches of a Red Army military school for cadets. But after a few weeks of courses, he preferred to get away—as far as possible from Poland, from the nothing that remained of his previous life. In November he was in Vilnius, the city where he had taken refuge with Pinchas in 1940. He waited in Lithuania for the end of the war, the German surrender of May 1945. After that, with no money in his pocket and living by his wits, he headed for the only goal that seemed plausible to him: the Promised Land.[35]

At first, Avraham tried the Black Sea route. Through Białystok, Lublin, and the Carpathians, he reached Oradea, Romania, with the idea of sailing from Constanța to Istanbul and the

Mediterranean. He was held back, though, by the rumor that the Soviet occupation authorities were arresting Jews who tried to embark for Turkey. So to go east, he had to turn to the west. One stage after the other, partly by truck, partly by train, he crossed Hungary to Graz, Austria. There, he fell ill with typhoid fever in a refugee center but, while still recovering, left for Belgrade. In the Yugoslav capital, the leaders of the local Jewish community issued him falsified documents to be used as credentials in Italy, with which he could emigrate to Palestine. Then trains again. In Trieste, Avraham saw the sea for the first time in his life. Then Venice, Milan, and Via Unione 5. Then more buses and finally, in the beginning of November 1945, his arrival in Selvino. He was alone, like a stray dog, a fur hat on his head, boots on his feet, and a jacket lined for the Russian winter.[36]

His encounter with Moshe Zeiri is not easy—far from it. The director of Sciesopoli wants to get rid of this loose cannon and send him back to Via Unione. Whatever Avraham Lipkunski's Yugoslav documents may indicate, Moshe considers him too visibly adult to be at home with the other orphans of Selvino.[37] It's as if Avraham's physical aspect spoke for himself, as if the former student at Raduń's little yeshiva had etched into his body his story of being the only Jew saved from the massacre on the edge of a trench, the story of the very young partisan in the forests, the inflexible agent of the Soviet police.[38] Only after the young man's continual insistence does the director of Sciesopoli agree to host him for one night, on probation. And Moshe doesn't know that in doing so, he is welcoming someone destined to weigh on the internal balance of the house: a charismatic orphan.

Yaakov Meriash is among Avraham's first friends in Selvino. Maybe what draws them to each other is the fact that both are *Litvaks*, Lithuanian Jews, rather than *Galitsianer*, Galician Jews. Maybe it is because they share not only a language, northern Yiddish rather than southern Yiddish, but a common way of being: a direct rather than indirect approach to things, more rational than

sentimental.[39] Certainly, the fact that they both knew quite a bit of Hebrew before arriving in Selvino contributes to their mutual understanding. So together they attend the advanced language course, the one taught by Arieh Soleh. Insofar as the events of one Shoah orphan's life, in its utter uniqueness, can compare with another's, Avraham and Yaakov are also united by the analogies of their families' pasts. Yaakov was also the second of three sons. His mother had also been slaughtered in the liquidation of a ghetto, in Kaunas. And Yaakov too was completely alone in the world. His father and older brother had been worked to death in Dachau, whereas his younger brother had been deported to Auschwitz and was never heard from again.[40]

Avraham and Yaakov soon become inseparable, and with Shmulik Shulman, they form a fixed threesome. Like Avraham, Shmulik also came from an Orthodox Jewish family. His father was a beverage maker in Lutsk, Volhynia, and a stalwart Zionist.

The youngest of four brothers and sisters, Shmulik had grown up constantly hearing about Jabotinsky, Bialik, and immigration certificates to Palestine. Then World War II broke out, and after two years of Soviet occupation, the Germans arrived. At Lubart Castle, which towered over the city of Lutsk, Shmulik's father was the first to be killed. The rest of the Shulman family had been locked up in the ghetto. Shmulik's brothers and sister managed to escape. When the ghetto was liquidated, he was still interned together with his mother. But then Shmulik himself managed a daring escape, sadly abandoning his mother to her destiny: the Polonka mass grave, with seventeen thousand Jews exterminated in four days while singing *Shema Yisrael*, "Listen, O Israel."[41] For a year and a half, Shmulik had been in hiding in the surrounding countryside, helped by Bolak, his good Pole, a glazier who had worked at his father's beverage factory. When the Soviets arrived, the only other survivor of the Shulman family was Shmulik's sister. The two brothers had also been killed, one before Polonka, the other after; one by Germans, the other by Ukrainians.[42]

In Sciesopoli, the trio often becomes a quartet. The three inseparables—Avraham, Yaakov, and Shmulik—are joined by a boy who arrived at Selvino in Fetter Moshe's truck, the same way as Yaakov Meriash. The new arrival is a fifteen-year-old Polish native of the Janowo shtetl, on the border between Masuria and Mazovia: Adam Wexler. He traveled to Selvino together with his brother, Dov. They arrived at the beginning of October after months of wandering and adventures, first in Austria and then in Italy: from Ebensee to Linz, from Linz to Modena, from Modena to Rome, then back to Modena, and finally Milan's Via Unione. Dov and Adam saw it all: American soldiers, Austrian prostitutes, volunteers of the Jewish Brigade, survivors of the Sonderkommando, human traffickers, nurses, British officers, Italian railway workers, town mayors, UNRRA employees, Zionist emissaries.[43] Willingly or unwillingly, they crossed the world and underworld of postliberation, the wide variety of humanity revolving around

the countless wanderers of a devastated Europe.[44] And on the way, they learned how liberation from the Shoah was not an event but a process.[45] Nothing more than a truce? That's how it would be described by one Italian Jew, Primo Levi, who finally managed to get back to Turin from Auschwitz. In any case, it is something one lives through over time—with patience, as one would in a healing process.[46]

Dov Wexler's best friend is Haim Luftman. They hadn't met in their Łódź ghetto years, cramped in those four square kilometers of open-air prison with 150,000 forced residents. Rather, they meet in the mountains above Bergamo, at the Jewish orphanage of Selvino. They are about eighteen years old or less, and they hope to be chosen by Moshe Zeiri (perhaps for opposite reasons, inasmuch as Dov is calm while Haim is restless and eager) as candidates to be among the first to emigrate to Palestine. Adam Wexler, in contrast, confides with Avraham Lipkunski. When they're not with Yaakov and Shmulik, and when they're not absorbed by the intense routine of community life[47]—the morning reveille and gymnastics, the flag-raising, the hours of study, lunch at the refectory, the afternoon workshops, the reading sessions or singing rehearsals, the flag-furling, then dinner—Adam and Avraham are looking to talk to each other.

Both of them grew up in Hasidic families, and they feel the problem of God after the Final Solution more urgently than their other companions. Adam had refused to pray already in the ghetto, in Łódź, distinguishing himself in this from his father Henoch and brother Shaya, from the other brave ones of the radio station in Niecała Street. Avraham never stopped praying, not even underground or inside the bunkers of the Nača forest, and he had managed to carry the cases of phylacteries that his mother had given him on the day of his bar mitzvah all the way up to Selvino. In the Youth Aliyah House, the two boys spend the small hours discussing God—whether he really exists or never existed or no longer exists. Sometimes in the dormitory, they slip into the same bed to go under the covers and continue in a whisper, without disturbing their comrades in the dormitory and without being reproached by the educators.[48]

The dormitories are large, some with thirty beds and others with even sixty. Because new arrivals keep coming during the autumn of 1945, it's difficult to keep track of everyone. But on one November day, Villi Tessler, a fifteen-year-old Romanian orphan, sees from the large window of the dormitory a boy his age walking out in the Sciesopoli courtyard. He rushes down the stairs, runs out, and throws his arms around him: Suti has arrived! Suti Weisz, his fellow prisoner in Mauthausen and Gunskirchen! The very Suti who had lost his father, Vilmos, after his release, with the Americans now masters of Austria. Once Suti was cured of typhoid, he left for the Soviet occupation zone, toward Hungary, to return to Nagyszőlős. He wanted to understand whether someone from the Weisz family was still alive. Maybe his brother, Bandi, who had not been deported. Or as if by a miracle, Aliz

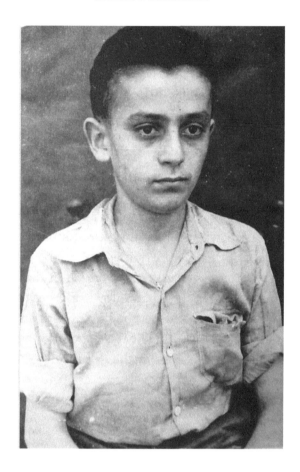

and Hedi, his two big sisters, whom Suti had glimpsed on the Birkenau ramp in a different group from that of his younger sister, Icuka, and Mrs. Rosenberg. The trip was fruitless. In Nagyszőlős, between the distillery and the Perényi Palace, the Weisz house was occupied by someone else; nor did Buksi, the dog, show any appreciation for Suti's return. In a photograph Suti had taken in Budapest in August 1945, he looks small and very delicate, a man's head on a child's body.[49]

In those same days of November, the Youth Aliyah House registers the arrival of a particularly large contingent of orphans: about thirty boys and girls who arrive together in the Bergamo

area after a trip that started in Łódź, Poland, and continued for several weeks through Czechoslovakia and Austria.[50] They are accompanied by an executive from Gordonia, Yeshayahu Flamholtz, and they form a lively and close-knit group, to the point of initially making Moshe Zeiri wary. "In this group there's a sort of artistic company of talented young people: singers, storytellers, etc. They crossed the cities of Poland with the idea of moving mountains and seas. They expected to do it here too, but they came across a different reality. Here they found a strict director who, aspiring to a unified framework, doesn't want to recognize them as a distinct body, but rather merge them into the overall team." Eventually, Moshe's wariness quickly gives way to satisfaction. "They progress in their studies, they're thirsty for knowledge. They listen to everything and never tire of it."[51]

Before leaving Poland, the boys and girls of the group lived for several months in a reception house located on the edge of the old Łódź ghetto, in Zachodnia Street 20. There, they studied Hebrew, listened to lectures on the history of the Zionist settlement in Palestine, and organized themselves to take part in various artistic activities: a theater company, a girls' choir, a dance class. So when leaving for the south with Eretz Israel as the ultimate destination, one girl from the group proudly packed the photo of herself in a dancer's pose, doing a split. To my knowledge, it's the oldest saved photo of Inda Liberman.[52]

TO BUILD AND BE BUILT

"The hour is late according to the mountain people's conception of time. After eleven the house is silent." At night, only Moshe Zeiri stays on in his office in Sciesopoli. He has to end the day's activities by transferring the accounts to the books. He has to anticipate the following day's emergencies, official correspondence, errands inside the camp, supplies, and new arrivals. And he must always ask the question: What can be improved, adjusted, added to the life of the community? As long as Matilde Cassin was at Selvino, Moshe's reflections were shared with her, keeping the experience of the Warsaw Orphan House as a North Star ("when Rachel was there, I used to read Korczak, which impressed her enormously"). After Matilde's departure, the responsibility for shaping the Youth Aliyah House falls entirely on Moshe's shoulders. He recognizes in Reuven Donath and Noga Cohen two worthy coworkers, but more for practical matters than for pedagogical choices.[53]

Modeled on the example of Korczak, the Sciesopoli system is based on the principle of self-management. Under the coordination of Zeiri and the other educators, it is the young people themselves—elected by their comrades in various commissions: work, culture, emigration—who direct and organize community life. The work commission establishes the rotation criteria for the tasks and appoints the managers of the kitchen, laundry, maintenance, cleaning, and gardening services. The culture commission prepares the Shabbat celebrations and other festivities, organizes the calendar of the film screenings, and plans the trips and sports competitions. The emigration commission has the delicate task of drawing up the lists of candidates ready for the ascent to Palestine. Obviously not everything goes smoothly from the start. But beginning in late autumn, the system shows signs of working, especially after the integration into the community of singularly mature and enterprising boys and girls, who can be found in abundance in the group from Łódź.[54] Among them are the two sisters from Rivne, Adela and Inda Liberman. There is an Ozorków orphan, Avraham Kutner, who survived the Łódź ghetto, the Auschwitz selections, and the death march. There is an orphan from Warsaw, Nina Boniówka, who lives in symbiosis with her best friend, Eva Ginat, herself an escapee from the Łódź ghetto and the Birkenau gas chambers.

"Building and being built," one of the most uplifting slogans of early Zionism,[55] finds its natural application at Selvino's Aliyah Youth House, a Zionist institution by definition. Even in Sciesopoli, as in the prewar aliyah training schools, young Jews are preparing to build the Israel of the future. In the handicraft workshops, they learn manual trades—carpentry, shoemaking, ironworking, sewing, embroidery—to be put to good use on the kibbutz once they reach the Promised Land. And the young people are preparing to be built, casting off their identity of Diaspora Jews—haggard, cerebral, ugly—and being reborn as tanned, muscular, combative Jews (in addition to track and field, Sciesopoli offers gymnastics and even boxing). Obviously the boys and girls study the history and legends of the pioneers: the intrepid ones who had defied malaria to work the marshy lands and discovered the secret to making the desert bloom. But compared to prewar Zionism, postwar Zionism has to deal with the immense historical and psychological rupture resulting from the Final Solution.

Up to and including Moshe Zeiri's generation, being born again as Jews in the land of Israel meant paying the price of becoming an orphan—but it was more symbolic than real. It was voluntary. Members of the next generation—Jews like Moshe's children—did not choose to deprive themselves of their parents. They saw them die of starvation in the ghettos, they saw them disappear in the clutches of the SS, they saw them slaughtered on the edges of mass graves, they lost sight of them on the access ramps to the death camps. There was nothing elective about their being orphans; they were subjected to it entirely. For Moshe's children, the prospect of being reborn as Jews in Palestine entails a surfeit of laceration, anguish, and even guilt. Because precisely their old identity, the one they are urged to throw behind them, is all that remains for those rescued from the world of the drowned: the world of parents and siblings, cousins and grandparents.

The Sciesopoli teaching staff is then enhanced by some teachers from Palestine, particularly from Kibbutz Degania. Yosef Baratz, as a Zionist emissary in Italy, helps Moshe Zeiri to achieve the goal, perhaps also in the name of a partnership with Pinchas Lubianiker, since the Zeiri institute is considered an affiliate of Gordonia in that context.[56] In any case, for Moshe, it's not just a matter of getting other expert teachers to work alongside Arieh Soleh, the teacher of advanced Hebrew. The presence in Selvino of men and women who came from the Promised Land is meant to counterbalance, so to speak, the presence of adults from the bloodlands, such as Soleh, Zippora Hager, Dr. Kissin, and several other employees of the house.[57] It allows the children and young people of Sciesopoli to be exposed to the direct influence of new Jews rather than ancient Jews—Jews already reborn, living incarnations of the pioneering myth that the director was passing on to his students in his history class on the Jewish settlement in Palestine.[58]

Not that it was easy to remedy the Sciesopoli orphans' educational deficit. Almost all of them had learned very little as children, at the home school of melamed, the old Hebrew teacher. And for three or four years, they hadn't attended any structured schools because their childhoods were razed by racial persecution, imprisonment in ghettos, and deportation to concentration camps. Their educational deficit was particularly serious in scientific subjects, arithmetic, geometry, biology—disciplines poorly cultivated in Sciesopoli, even after the arrival of teachers from Palestine. The director of the institute was aware of all this, but he certainly had no miracle cures. On the other hand, in the eyes of Moshe Zeiri—himself a lackluster student in his Galician childhood—extracurricular acculturation was even more important than the work done within the confines of a class.

Moshe had not forgotten his years as a tarbutnik, a cultural attaché at Kvutzat-Shiller. He simply could not betray his love of music. So among his many duties was the direction of the Sciesopoli choir, with a repertoire of songs in Yiddish but above all in Hebrew. Nor could Moshe betray his enduring love of theatrical acting, so reading aloud was frequent at the Youth Aliyah House, where children and young people were invited to discover the poems of Bialik or Alterman, and the tales of the "beautiful literature that revives the historical context." ("Yes, my dear, I am reliving the days of the past, when I was studying at Habima," a nostalgic Moshe explained to Yehudit.)[59] That didn't prevent the children and young people from reading on their own. If they wished, they could take advantage of a library that was gradually becoming better supplied and extended beyond the Zionist literary canon. For example, Baruch Rosner, a Hungarian boy who was among the first already in Piazzatorre, would never forget two books he read thanks to the house's library: a Vincent van Gogh biography by an American translated into Hebrew and Upton Sinclair's socially conscious novel *The Jungle*.[60]

Then there was the cinema. In the same wing of Sciesopoli that housed the indoor swimming pool, a room in the so-called Dux Pavilion was equipped for projections. On Saturday evening after Shabbat, or on Sunday morning, a handmade screen was placed against the back wall (where a fresco by a fascist painter commemorated a heroic feat from 1922, the assault on the Milanese headquarters of the newspaper *Avanti!*, during which the young fascists Tonoli and Melloni were killed).[61] The cameraman, Amedeo Barbaglia, was living his moment of glory after having gone up to Bergamo expressly with the "Jewish truck."[62] As for the films shown, Moshe Zeiri avoided restricting the field to edifying cinematography coming from Jewish or Zionist propaganda. "Tonight I brought a new movie, a 'cowboy' movie with chases, horses and brawls. Although not so important or educational, the little ones had fun. They've been whole years without seeing anything," Moshe noted on a Sunday in October 1945.[63] Among the films shown by Signor Amedeo were the comedies of Laurel and Hardy.[64]

Also, the Sciesopoli orphans had gone whole years without a Shabbat, to the point where the prayers and rituals had been lost in their memory, or lacked sharpness: they were confused with other images of their shattered families and community life, torn apart by the war and the Final Solution. All the more reason, according to Zeiri, to interpret the Youth Aliyah House as a place dedicated to a rediscovery of Shabbat. A secular rediscovery, so to speak. Indeed, a renewed investment in the aura of civil religion that had already surrounded the founders of Zionism. And despite appearances, those founders had never stopped reading the Bible. They questioned it (and loved it) as "atheists of the Book," as venerable storytelling: the story of the Chosen People.[65] So on Friday night in Sciesopoli, Moshe celebrated Shabbat as he had learned from his father, David, in the shtetl, in the wooden cottage on the banks of the Nichlavka: white tablecloths, lighted candles, sabbath food and wine, blessings, songs. Everything except the fringed tallit and phylacteries. Everything except the synagogue, and faith in God.[66]

The highlight of the training given in the house was to come not only from Shabbat but especially from the holiday theater. The Jewish holidays that mattered most to the Zionist ethos— Hanukkah, Purim, Sukkot—were also staged in Selvino, according to the aesthetics of a civil religion already practiced intensely

in Palestine since the 1930s.[67] Exemplary, in this sense, is the Hanukkah celebration organized by Moshe Zeiri during his first autumn as director of Sciesopoli. The celebration was carefully prepared in advance, with everything necessary. He had the boys build a "huge Hanukkah menorah" thanks to the "wood of the forest." They hoisted it up to the roof of the main building and set up a system of electric lights behind it, which had been brought up from Bergamo. And again he held rehearsals with the entire community of orphans for a musical and choreographic contribution.

"The bell rings. Everyone gathers in the courtyard and arranges themselves by age in groups of three, the choir at the head, then the youngest ones follow, proceeding gradually, according to age. On both sides of the procession are the torchbearers. When the procession arrived in front of the sign saying FESTIVAL OF LIGHTS, it stopped. When ordered to stand at attention, the *Hannukia* was lit on the roof illuminating all of us gathered below. Excited, I welcomed the parade and gave a speech: It happened 2,110 years ago. Then a menorah was lit in the purified Temple, where sacrifices had been offered to the god Zeus. Now a menorah has been lit above a house in which a new Diaspora was created, and from which came the law to hate the Jews. At the point where our eight-branched candelabra stands, only a short time ago stood the fascist symbol that enslaved the soul. The wheel turns full circle. In the place where they taught the youth to hate us, we are the lords. It is the irony of fate. We hope that, just as we defeated the Greeks then and defeated the Antiochus of our day, Hitler, so we will also defeat the decrees below in the form of white papers that block our return to Zion."[68]

When Moshe Zeiri finished speaking, the singing of the "Hatikvah" hymn resounded loudly through the Selvino evening (according to the Christian calendar, it was November 30, 1945). The children and boys of the choir declaimed, "We carry the torches," after which Moshe took the floor again, addressing all his orphans: "You are the youth that is left, you are all that remains of a diaspora totally erased from the face of Europe. And you must be the bearers of light for the surviving adults." At that point, one would have tried in vain to find in Sciesopoli's snow-white courtyard the face of an adult or child that wasn't wet with tears.[69]

CONFLICTS

Life at Sciesopoli was also marked by states of tension, or even open conflicts. Generally, they were conflicts between the director and older children: those who already felt they were adults, either by birth date or experience. If the Łódź group had been quickly domesticated after arriving in Selvino, resulting in a fruitful collaboration between Moshe Zeiri and the new arrivals, Moshe was less able to manage the relationship with some of the orphans who resisted his authority or who explicitly argued with him. Among these were Haim Luftman, the natural leader of the "Magenta gang," and Adam Wexler, who tended to collide with the director more than his brother, Dov.

Moshe wrote in a letter to Yehudit in early November 1945, "I'm writing to you after a two-and-a-half-hour conversation with my cadets. A conversation not so much heated as tense. In its honor we failed to abide by the lights off at 10 pm policy. Since they wanted to talk, they expressed what worried them! I listened, even though many illogical and meaningless things were said. I've learned to deal with situations like these without reacting with irritation."[70] The matter of contention here was the money from the UNRRA. The United Nations relief agency financed each of the Sciesopoli orphans through the bureaucratic mediation of the Jewish community of Milan, in the amount of three thousand lira per month.[71] But some of the boys had managed to get funding, as Jewish refugees, even before being admitted to the Selvino institute. This was the case of the Wexler brothers, who for this purpose had traveled from the Academy of Modena to the Rome offices of the UNRRA. Together with other comrades in the same situation, Adam and Dov claimed their right to keep the three thousand lira per month that the United Nations agency paid on their behalf. Zeiri, in contrast, demanded that they deposit that money into a common fund. Moreover, Adam refused to give the money that the Wexler brothers had received from a relative who had been mobilized in Italy with the Polish Army of General Anders. Zeiri placed the renunciation of personal money (the Wexlers' as much as anyone else's) as a necessary condition for remaining in Sciesopoli, under penalty of exclusion.[72]

The result of the tug-of-war was a victory for the director and defeat for the cadets. "In two days 16 checks were brought to the secretariat for the common fund, and the sum was by no means a pittance," Moshe exulted in his letter to Yehudit. Moshe was the first to grasp what was at stake: the recognition of Sciesopoli as a space of equality, where the dynamic of the collective interest had to overshadow the existential contingencies of each orphan. "It's a huge achievement. Young people, greedy for anything 'personal' were able to overcome their instincts and hand over the money to fulfill their wish to remain in the institution." Except that Moshe probably underestimated those young people's need to return to existing on an individual basis, as single people as well as guests of the institute. Moshe did not imagine that they could want to own anything of their own, like "cameras and watches." And Moshe rejected the very idea that they could be impatient to go down the road from the Sciesopoli gate, which led to the tiny center of Selvino, to go shopping for whatever: "With this step the excursions to the town's shops have ended. Who would have thought I could have done it so easily!"[73]

Money matters aside, the very nature of Sciesopoli was at the origin of a latent conflict. Indeed, the Youth Aliyah House was based on the principle of a communal life to be lived within a limited space. That is, it was based on the same principle that the orphans of the Shoah had forcibly experienced for years as inhabitants of a ghetto or interned in a concentration camp (of course, with the fundamental difference that the constitutive principle of the ghetto and concentration camp was communal death within a limited space rather than communal life). The logic of the house's functioning provided exclusively for community rhythms and rituals. In the dormitory as in the refectory, in the classroom as in the laboratory, in the cinema as in the swimming pool, children and young people were treated as members of a community rather than as individuals. And the institution's

Zionist culture urged them, moreover, to perpetuate this condition even after the aliyah, to the extent that it pushed them to opt, once they arrived in Palestine, for the kibbutz social model. Thus, almost inevitably, life at Sciesopoli also produced protests and protesters.

The most delicate matter (and the one that widened the front of the conflict) was the question of meals: the lack of food rations served in the refectory. In short, as Yaakov Meriash would describe it to me decades later in the shade of the fruit trees on a kibbutz near the Gaza Strip, it was the problem of hunger. He explained how Moshe Zeiri had hung on to the "kibbutznik mentality," the spirit of Kvutzat-Shiller. "He thought that one should be content with little. And the children, after four years of hunger, did not understand, 'Why just one sandwich?' . . . Food was Moshe's real weakness. He didn't understand that ours was a special hunger. It was a hunger that stayed with us all day and all night, every single minute. . . . I tried to tell him: 'Moshe, you've never felt this hunger!' It was no use. He didn't understand. . . . Even Fetter Moshe tried to convince Moshe. He was a mature man who understood. And with the truck he brought everything, fruit, meat, vegetables." Nothing doing. As soon as the truck was unloaded, the Sciesopoli manager had the stockpiles put in storage.[74]

For the orphans of Selvino, Moshe Zeiri's severity in the matter of food would become a stain—often the only stain—on a memory of him otherwise bathed in admiration and gratitude. "He wanted us to starve," one of those orphans, Alexander Czoban, would say. He was joking but not entirely: "He said we had to live with very little to get used to the hardships that awaited us in Palestine."[75] As for Avraham Lipkunski, he would recall the episode of Zviek, a more delicate child than average, who had not resisted the temptation to remove a tin of canned meat from the kitchen. Unfortunately, the tin was already open, and its contents, dripping in his pockets, had soon stained poor Zviek's trousers with a suspect color.[76] Persecuted by hunger and obsessed with food, the Sciesopoli youth did not hesitate to steal bread or anything else edible, which they then hid under the mattress in the hope of going unnoticed. Or to obtain the right to more abundant rations, they practiced collective forms of protest. They all left the refectory together or symbolically besieged the director's office.[77]

The strictness of the rules for meals did not concern only the quantity of food; it extended to its quality. The guests of the institute were forced to eat whatever was served to them. Anyone who rejected a dish had to leave a note with his name next to the plate, so that the same dish could be served to him, without alternatives, at the next meal. Once, at lunch, Sara Goldman's neighbor, a fifteen-year-old Polish girl, refused the food but without signing a note. An educator asked Sara to reveal the identity of the culprit. Sara refused, saying she was ready to suffer any punishment rather than be a spy. She would never betray anyone, she said, and repeated it after leaving the refectory in tears and deserting the afternoon activities. She thus lived up to her sister Lea's example: in the Lublin ghetto, in order not to betray a friend, Lea had preferred to be arrested by the Germans and, at the age of sixteen, had been tortured to death.[78]

All this does not mean that the atmosphere of Sciesopoli was heavy, that the tension in the air could be cut with a knife. On the contrary, the photographs taken at the Youth Aliyah House testify to a relaxed or even serene atmosphere. The air was electrified by the orphans' privileges, rather than by their complaints. For example, the privilege of being able to ride in a real Jeep thanks to the director's membership in the British Army. Right there, in the courtyard of Sciesopoli. They were like real soldiers, imagining themselves already mobilized in a war of independence for Eretz Israel. The privilege was proudly shared by even the most vocal

protesters of Moshe Zeiri's authority, like Haim Luftman. In a photo dating back to the autumn of 1945, Haim is sitting behind the wheel of the Jeep, with a scowl worthy of the role. Sitting on the hood, his friend Dov Wexler seems to want to keep him at bay with his quiet strength. As for Yaakov Meriash, recognizable on the left edge of the photograph, he is already raising the two fingers of his hand in a sign of victory.[79]

EIGHT

LIFE AFTER DEATH

IN THE VILLAGE

Dov Zugman never lost his passion for stamps, even though that passion had cost him dearly in the ghetto. In Sokal, Galicia, when the commander of the German occupation forces, himself an avid philatelist, had heard of a local Jew's stamp collection, he ordered the Judenrat officials to bring the Jewish collector to his office. When he found a twelve-year-old boy in front of him saying that he hadn't brought the collection with him to the ghetto, the German commander was furious. He smacked him repeatedly and had him locked up for three days in a security cell. Yet Dov Zugman remained a stamp enthusiast. So in the Jewish colony of Selvino, he became the postman. Each day, he walked the distance that separated the Youth Aliyah House from the village post office—ten minutes at a brisk pace. He collected the correspondence, brought it to Sciesopoli, and distributed it to the adults and children. In return, he hoped to receive as many used stamps from them as possible.[1]

With the exception of Dov the postman, the guests of the house did not frequent the village of Selvino very much. They had no right to, because Moshe Zeiri had forbidden it. Deliveries in and out were tightly controlled. They could only go to town once a week, no more, and only the older kids. Clearly, the orphans suffered as a result. Some criticized the director, rejecting the idea of being confined to Sciesopoli as they had already been—granted, in situations that were much more dramatic—behind the walls of a ghetto or the barbed wire of a concentration camp.[2] Yet Zeiri felt all the responsibility of leading an institution where both children and young people, for various reasons, had to be preserved from an excess of promiscuity with the locals. Relations with the outside world were therefore limited to the essentials, not just for going out but also for visits from outside. In Sciesopoli, the only two local employees were the caretaker and the cook. In addition, the baker, the milkman, and the barber often entered. Occasionally someone else could come in: the butcher, Flaminio Grigis, who was also the mayor of the town, or Amedeo Barbaglia, the cameraman from Bergamo. Otherwise, the gates of the house were opened only for Jews. Better if military and foreign, like Fetter Moshe. The gates were especially open to drivers of vehicles who unloaded food supplies.

Ah, the kitchens of the Jewish colony! For the local inhabitants of Selvino, the time of the Jews would be fixed in their memory as the time of others' abundance. The Selvino locals had nothing to put on their plates—they were starving. The Jews had everything, they were inundated with food.[3] Yet they contributed only marginally to the local economy. Apart from bread, milk, and gas canisters, they bought everything from the outside, in the plains, keeping their goods in modern refrigerators. "Why were they getting their food, all their stuff... like sheeps, goats... from down below? because they ordered everything... those fridges there, still original... They had it all." Besides, what did local production offer if not a few chestnuts and hazelnuts in the autumn? Like almost all mountain villages in postwar Italy, Selvino was very poor. "We lived on grass here. Because you went to the gardens ... 'I'm going!' 'No no, I'm going!'" That is, to the villa gardens

of the noble families, the Reggiani, the Turani, of the bourgeois families of Bergamo or Milan, who in the 1930s ambitiously built second homes. "We went to cut the grass for free . . . just to take away the cut grass and give it to the cows."[4]

Elena Gianini Belotti would also talk about it; she was the daughter of the elementary school teacher who came from the city, the stranger who became an educator herself, even before being a writer. Selvino's children were not just dirty, uncouth, and ignorant. They were also hungry. Apart from the *passo* season, the too brief period of birds (siskins, robins, thrushes) which they hunted among the rocks, that golden season of *polenta e osei*, all they ate was a gruel made of boiled milk and leftover polenta.[5] So while the Jews were there, the Selvino locals would station themselves at the Sciesopoli gate. The kids did it hoping to get something out of it. "Maybe you just stand there by the pole . . .

waiting for them to give us a sandwich ... maybe with a piece of chocolate, or fruit juice.... That's why we used to come here ... you just had to stand right there ... and you saw all the Jews, what they were doing there all day ... We were there grazing the cows. Every now and then you looked ... every now and then someone came and gave you a sandwich."[6] Even the adults went, some of the less inhibited housewives. Lidovina, for example. "I saw her with my own eyes ... every day." She came in the evening and waited at the entrance to Sciesopoli for the Jews to finish eating, and then she collected the leftovers and took them away, walking with her clogs in hand to get home faster.[7]

The barber, Andrea Cortinovis, was one of the few people from Selvino authorized to regularly enter the Jewish citadel. "I used to go there every Friday ... to cut their hair.... They were very kind. And ... they started their holy day ... you know better than me maybe ... at five on Friday evening. The holiday began ... and I was there, even late, to cut all that hair.... Then they celebrated there ... They put out two candelabras in the hall ... with two glasses of wine ... but they didn't drink it ... at least, that's what they said."[8] Otherwise, for the boys of the town, the best opportunity to enter Sciesopoli came from soccer matches. "Because just as you entered on the left, there was a ball field." They would play on Saturday afternoons, after the end of Shabbat and during the good season, from spring onward. "We used to go there to play soccer with the boys. But we understood that ... because even in '45–'46 there was nothing to eat ... we understood that if we won, they didn't give us anything, but if we lost ... and so we always lost! Because they kept them there like ... they had everything. Like relics, they kept them."[9] If the young Selvino boys had the foresight to be beaten, they would get some refreshments from the Jews.

"We also had stone fights in the woods," in the fir and larch forest that surrounded Sciesopoli. But even stones were child's play—innocent games, without prejudice. "We never let anybody say ... because they're Jewish ... there was none of that."

If anything, the locals regretted that the rich weren't more generous with the poor. "That's how they saw us . . . they could've . . . not who knows what, but a small tip . . . nothing doing." On top of the regret, the local Selvino boys were bewildered by the orphans' behavior, which they considered rude—even though they themselves were rough mountain people. "I mean practically they . . . they went outside, they just squatted down . . . coming up from the street . . . there weren't many houses . . . or even up there towards the meadow . . . in ten or twelve, all to . . . to take care of their needs . . . Which, between us, seems like . . . You could see them, they went down the road, fifteen, even sixteen years old . . . they spread their legs and they did it right there, on the road . . . no respect, none at all." But nothing more serious, no burglaries or the like. "No, no, they didn't touch anything! . . . No, they weren't bad people."[10]

In Selvino, the Bazar Banella is in the center of the village. It's been there since 1929, as the sign above the shop entrance proudly claims. It is a vast assortment of household items, hardware, gift ideas, gardening supplies, appliances, home furnishings, heating and gas canister service, today's website assures. It was there, at the Bazar Banella, that on an October day in 2014, I met Giovanni Grigis, the owner. He wore his eighty-four years well and had vivid memories of the Sciesopoli Jews. In particular, he remembered one young orphan whose name he couldn't tell me. Nor am I able to reconstruct it here years later, after rewinding the recordings of my dialogue with him, after rereading the notes and scrolling through the Excel file with names, surnames, and personal data of the Jews hosted in Sciesopoli from 1945 to 1948. It matters little. Signor Giovanni's memory is equally valid, and it retains its power intact apart from the historical inconsistencies, or perhaps precisely because of them.

"And me one evening, I was fifteen, with a girl... yeah... or no ... they arrived later... '45–'46... fifteen or sixteen... that's when you start looking... no?" He laughs. "A young girl, we walked a ways together... and I said stupidly... but I didn't know anything about what had happened . . . I said, 'What about your father?' And she didn't even . . . She just went like this." He makes the gesture of someone who puts his hands forward to push something. "She said 'I took him with the wagon to the crematorium oven'... I was just like... She... she didn't even cry, you could see she'd seen it all, right? 'What about your father?' Just like this, she went..." He repeats the gesture. "'I took him with the wagon to the crematorium oven,' she said.... She said it... but I didn't understand... still, I understood what a crematorium oven was... eh... but not what that moron over there who wiped out so many did." What language did he and the girl speak? "Bah, now I don't . . . But I know that she said those words to me in Italian. And they just... Even though... I don't know how long I'll be in the world, but it always comes to mind, here. That girl there... eh... and I remember... even if I'm still in the world for some... for sure... Because afterwards, the crematorium oven, on the radio, the TV, they talked about everything... everything they'd done to them over there.... Afterwards I went up there to see the place ... I took my Volkswagen ... took my family." Where did he go? "To Austria, the one ..." To Auschwitz, Poland? "Auschitz."... "That's it, we went up, and I went to see the crematorium ovens... because..." He gets emotional. "Eh..."[11]

In mountain villages, the surnames are always the same. The town of Selvino is the land of the Grigis. At the time of the Jewish colony, Emilio Grigis—known as "Ciusca"—was the owner of the tobacco and salt shop. He sold postcards as well and had equipped himself for photographs. It wasn't a real photo studio but something similar. If you wanted to have a picture taken without going down to Nembro, you had to go to Ciusca, in the piazza, near Bazar Banella. Provided, of course, that you weren't so wealthy as to have your own camera. At the Youth Aliyah House, Reuven Donath had one. He had brought it from Palestine and carried it with him for the entire duration of the war. He certainly did not stop using it in free Italy. Who knows how many of the snapshots from the early days of Sciesopoli were taken by him? Even some of the orphans possessed a camera, those who still had someone left from the Shoah, some American relative rich and generous enough to give them one—much to the dismay of Moshe Zeiri, who was always hostile to anything that could arouse envy among the boys and girls, as well as opportunities for theft. But in Selvino, you basically had to go to Ciusca for photos.

Many Sciesopoli orphans had not managed to save anything from the Shoah, not even a single photograph of their parents, not a photo of themselves as children. Only after the end of the war, through perhaps fortunate circumstances, would some of them manage to get hold of a copy of a prewar photo: mostly the typical family portrait, all together in their best clothes taken by the shtetl photographer on a papier-mâché background and sent with best wishes for Hanukkah to relatives who had already emigrated to Palestine or Canada, the United States or Brazil. But

this would have been a subsequent story. In Selvino, the photos of Ciusca represent, for many of the Sciesopoli orphans, the first photos of their life after death. And they take on a much greater value in their eyes, because the Final Solution had been the annihilation of bodies as well as of souls. So looking at each other in a photo by Ciusca was nearly equivalent to handling the proof of one's resurrection.[12]

Decades later—in Israel, flipping through old photo albums—former Sciesopoli orphans would search for words to express all this. Ruth Rotenburg: "Our house was isolated on the hill, the entrance and exit both closed to us, and to strangers. But once a week, we could go to the village. And more than anything else, we went to take pictures of ourselves. Because we had no photos, and the memories were important." Chana Garfinkel: "The photo was important. It was a special thing in life. So we could remember our childhood. Because we had nothing, and this was the age of diversity. You wanted to see yourself, to have a different relationship with yourself, and it was the photographer who could give it to you. When we went to town, we dressed up." Lea Ratmanski: "We wanted to look beautiful, with long hair, especially since we had been bald for years... and this was very exciting.... We were all posing, so that the socks and shoes could be seen."[13]

BODIES AND SOULS

Young children in Selvino's Youth Aliyah House were rare. The reason is that young children who survived the Final Solution in the bloodlands were rare. Most of the Sciesopoli guests were born between the late 1920s and early 1930s, with a peak in the two-year period 1929–30: they were between the ages of fifteen and eighteen. Few were born between 1935 and 1939, almost none after the outbreak of the Second World War. In fact, not all of the youngest Sciesopoli children were orphans. On the contrary, they were more easily saved if at least one of their parents had remained alive. They were children like Avraham Auerbach, a Jew from Galicia, eight years old in 1945. Initially he was in Selvino with his sister, Bronka, five years older, but then they were joined by both parents: the mother in charge of the house's kitchens, the father in charge of shoemaking. They were children like Yehudit, the tiny daughter of Arieh Soleh, who taught advanced Hebrew. They were children like Batia, five years old in 1945, who was in Selvino with her mother, Zippora Gurman.[14]

Twenty-seven-year-old Zippora taught arithmetic (in Yiddish) to the Sciesopoli orphans. A Polish Jew from the Lublin province, she had lost her husband in the liquidation of the Kovel ghetto. "The story of her life is short, simple and unsettling because of its tragedy," as Moshe Zeiri summarized it in a letter to Yehudit. "When the great deportation of the children of the ghetto began, she was afraid that they would take her one-and-a-half-year-old daughter from her, and she couldn't imagine letting her die. So she tied a small cross around her neck and attached a letter. She left the girl by the door of a childless Christian family. Three years passed, the girl grew up and developed, she called her foster parents mom and dad, she settled into the new conditions the way a small child settles in. When the real mother came back to get the baby, the goyim didn't want to return her. She is truly beautiful, dark-haired like a gypsy, with beautiful eyes and a dimple on her cheek, intelligent and wise. Her name is Batia, and she speaks only Polish."[15]

There's a photo of Batia in the arms of Moshe (the other child is Yehudit Soleh), holding a little dog who belonged to the Sciesopoli guard.[16] "It's an artistic thing, like a movie,"[17] Moshe will say about this photo. The little ones lent themselves to being portrayed in photographs that clearly also served propaganda purposes: to raise awareness of the international public about the fate of the children who survived the Final Solution, and also to document the quality of the welcome offered by the Youth Aliyah House, fueling the Joint fundraising campaigns.[18] "Soon I will be able to send you some photographs in which I am immortalized with the Joint superiors," Moshe wrote to Yehudit

on January 9, 1946. He was referring to a visit that the leaders of the American assistance organization had made to Selvino a few weeks earlier with the emissaries of the Center for the Diaspora, which had given rise to a photo shoot: many shots, "perhaps a hundred," of adults as well as Sciesopoli children. "They send them to America for propaganda purposes," Moshe specified in his letter to his wife.[19]

A few weeks later, Moshe explained to Yehudit that he had learned from an emissary how "all the photographs of the meeting of the Center for the Diaspora here with us, in which your husband appears among all the greats of the Joint and the Center" had been sent even to Palestine, to Kvutzat-Shiller.[20] But the Sciesopoli director, self-effacingly proud of himself, didn't mention a controversy that had broken out in Sciesopoli regarding the public use of those photographs. At the origins of the dispute was the usual suspect: Adam Wexler. He, like the others in the photos, had been asked to sign a letter of thanks that the management of the institute reserved to forward, on behalf of each orphan, to recipients from overseas. Suspecting that there was money behind the circulation of the photos, Adam refused to sign and encouraged his companions to follow suit.[21]

Moshe Zeiri was aware of the narrative potential (if you can call it that) which sprang from the Sciesopoli community. "If I had the talent for writing, how much material I could put on paper from here!" he exclaimed in a letter to Yehudit. So he resigned himself to his limits: "My language is poor, and my style is poor."[22] Were Moshe's language and style really that poor? Not if one were to go by his correspondence. However, it is true that by welcoming a growing number of young people saved from the Shoah in Selvino, gradually discovering the kind of experiences each of them lived through, and simply measuring himself against the enormous amount of pain accumulated within the confines of Sciesopoli, the director saw his feeling of inadequacy, if not of impotence, grow. Both Zeiri and the other educators lacked any specific training that prepared them to treat the wounds of orphans, especially these orphans, from whom the Shoah had stolen goods too precious for any wounds to heal completely. "The theft of youth is an irreparable laceration," Aharon Appelfeld concludes half a century later—with the conscience of someone who had lived through it, and the language skills and style of a professional writer.[23]

Yehudit would eventually insert a text by Janusz Korczak into the envelope of one of her letters to Moshe and even go as far as writing the inscription: "That you may penetrate the souls of your students like this great educator."[24] Yet Moshe had to deal with more than ordinary pupils. Their souls would have been difficult for even the most experienced educator to penetrate. The soul, for example, of a Polish boy who arrived in Selvino from a refugee camp near Rome and who had a reputation for being rebellious. "The moment I entered him in the institute's register, when I asked for his mother's name, he told me that he'd burned his mother himself when he was in the camp. His job was in the crematoria, and he slipped his mother into the oven with his own hands. Yes, my darling, I was deeply shaken when he told me this, and he said it with a sort of stoic calm."[25] The survivor of a Sonderkommando among the guests of Sciesopoli? It could very well be. Maybe more than one. From another of Moshe's letters: "Downstairs I hear the sound of the stoker. I've given permission to turn on the heating. They're two professional 'stokers,' they dealt with this in the camps. There, of course, they prepared the fire for the bodies of our brothers, while here they work to prepare for them the warmth of the dormitories."[26]

Moshe's children bore the whole range of tragedies from the Final Solution. Not just the tragedies of extermination—the liquidation of the ghettos, the selection for the gas chambers, and the death marches—but also the tragedies of survival: life as a stray in the forests, forced conversion in convents or Christian families, or the violation of their bodies subjected to slavery. All without mentioning the sense of guilt that the survivor feels daily when confronted with questions as to why he or she was saved and the others drowned. In the face of all this, could Moshe Zeiri always find the right words, gestures, and behavior? "How difficult it is from time to time, wanting to fix things and imperfections, without hurting them. I can't. I wind up getting the opposite result."[27] This son of a Galician shtetl, the carpenter apprentice from Lviv, the Zionist militant of Gordonia, the kibbutz's cultural attaché, the laborer in the citrus groves of the coastal plain, the longshoreman in the port of Jaffa, the drama school student, the volunteer soldier and sapper, the Hebrew teacher in Benghazi and Naples, the summer animator at Piazzatorre, the director of Sciesopoli—despite all this experience, Moshe Zeiri knew that he did not have the means to cure his children of their incurable wounds.

Reuven Kohen probably had a few more tools to work with. A Bohemian Jew of solidly bourgeois origins and culture, he had been Moshe's colleague in the 745th Company of the Royal

Engineers and helped him at Port Said to embark the harmonium in the container of the ship bound for Taranto. In the winter of 1945–46, Kohen reaches Sciesopoli to work as a teacher. He can teach everything from Hebrew to mathematics, or even music and the mandolin. But above all, according to Moshe, he's an exceptional person for his listening and relationship skills. "The arrival of Reuven is a blessing for the institute. He has such precious qualities! That good heart, that boundless patience in any situation."[28] Later, in Israel, Reuven Kohen-Raz will become an illustrious university professor, a world authority in the psychopathologies of the developmental years.[29] No doubt those months in Selvino, as the interlocutor for Moshe's children, presented him with his first research experience in the field.

"A thousand children, a thousand complexes": immediately after the liberation of Italy, the Zionist emissaries visiting the refugee camps had issued categorical judgments on the multiple traumas suffered by the youngest survivors of the Final Solution.[30] In this sense, one could perhaps estimate, with regard to Sciesopoli from 1945 to 1948: seven hundred children, seven hundred complexes. Wounds of the body and mind. Wounds of the spirit too—as with the orphans, especially the girls, who had saved themselves among the Catholics by converting to Christianity. As such, they felt bound to their new confession. Polish Jews like Aviva Czoban or Rivka Polak silently kneeled beside their bed in Sciesopoli at night, praying under an imaginary crucifix hanging on the wall of the dormitory.[31] Then there were the orphans who remained faithful to their ancestors' religion, but they themselves were uncomfortable if they wanted to pray. This was because apart from Moshe Zeiri's Shabbat rituals, the Youth Aliyah House was an entirely secular environment, and because the hunger for life in the aftermath of the Shoah was stronger and more dominant than the hunger for God.[32] So those who prayed in broad daylight were mocked even when they prayed to the God of Moses.

Seventy years later, I would also speak to Avraham Lipkunski about this in his Tel Aviv home one June afternoon in 2014. Avraham and Ayala offered Sara, Nitza, and me a takeaway pizza. Avraham guaranteed us, very convinced, that we hadn't tasted anything like it. Not even in Naples! Then we started looking at the photographs, the only two left of his life before death. The portrait in the Raduń workshop, Sara Mina with her three children, Pinchas and Avraham in Talmudic student shirts and Yekutiel in a sailor suit. The photo of Moshe David on the deck of the *Andes* ocean liner, traveling to Argentina with the other third-class passengers. At that point, Avraham got up. "Wait a moment," he said. When he returned to the living room, he held the two phylactery cases in his hand. They were the ones his mother had given him on the day of his bar mitzvah, with which he had prayed both in the barn of the Dugalishok farmer and inside the bunker in the Nača forest. I asked him, "Did you pray with these in Selvino, too?" And he confirmed to me: In the beginning, yes, but then no more, because everyone made fun of me.[33]

Sciesopoli's other big taboo was sex. This was normal in a community of presumably inhibited and certainly supervised teenagers, some (or many) of whom may have been sexually abused at one time or another during their persecution. But keeping silent about sex obviously didn't mean that boys and girls didn't think about it. This comes through in an incident from the autumn of 1945 that leaves an impression on Moshe Zeiri and gives him cause for self-criticism. During a Hebrew course, the students read a love poem by Bialik, after which they are encouraged to take part in a game about memories—the memories of a Saturday afternoon from their childhood. The game is called "exquisite corpse": on a folded sheet that passes from hand to hand, "each student writes a line about this theme, and the next continues without seeing what his companion has written." Moshe reports the result to Yehudit: "70 percent wrote pornography." What in Bialik's poetry is a dream of pure and delicate love becomes a complete and explicit sexual act on the Sciesopoli orphans' sheet of paper.[34]

"One wrote: 'on Saturday afternoon, a boy and a girl went out of town and went to bed together.' A second wrote that they did it inside the house. 'A third wrote: a boy and a girl lie down together to procreate.'" And so on, independently of each other. "When I read this, I was shocked," Moshe admits. "I was able to gauge how far I still am from knowing them, how many areas I haven't yet breached about them, contenting myself with a superficial vision. I tried to delude myself that there were no sexual problems, but I was naive. On the first occasion when they were able to write what they had in their hearts, everything surfaced." In contrast, Moshe considers impractical any approach other than silence to the question of sex. "We can't organize discussions on the topic, because it would intrigue and attract them even more. In our conditions, there are no solutions."[35]

A scabies epidemic that bursts out in Sciesopoli during the fall of 1945 causes two significant incidents. First of all, there is a kind of rupture between Moshe Zeiri and Adam Wexler, who is also one of those patients infested with scabies. He feels betrayed and abandoned by Moshe when the director of the institute, in agreement with Dr. Kissin, orders a hospitalization in Milan for Adam and the other more serious cases. Too bad that in Milan, in the chaos of Via Unione 5, with so many coming and going, no one takes care to actually hospitalize them. So after a night in Central Station, Adam and the other sick boys return to Selvino on their own, to be treated in the Sciesopoli infirmary. By now the damage is done. In the decades to come, Adam Wexler will continue to consider the scabies affair as the best proof of Moshe Zeiri's inability to empathize.[36] Yet Zeiri was concerned above all with containing the infection. And when the boys returned from Milan, "on foot, hungry, weak and tired," he had been "ashamed to look them in the eyes," as he confessed to Yehudit.[37]

The other incident caused by the scabies epidemic concerns two thirteen-year-old girls, Bronka Auerbach and Malka Shafrir, both affected by the infestation and therefore obliged to apply a black ichthyol-based ointment on their skin. One day, when they are assigned to laundry room service, the two teenagers decide to cleanse themselves as thoroughly as possible (their wounds as well as the ointment) by jumping naked into the laundry tub. With the hot water, soap, and foam, Bronka and Malka have a great time.... But they don't notice that an increasingly large group of boys has gathered on the roof of the laundry room, where from a skylight they can enjoy the show.[38] It's a scandal with accusations, tears, and punishments. It's hard for everyone to learn how to live life after death through the body. "In Selvino, after years of hunger, we started growing again," Bronka will remember forty years later. "Our bodies took shape, breasts sprouted. We thought that big breasts were a kind of deformation, an unnatural growth, and we tried to flatten them by wearing very tight bras that we sewed by ourselves to hide them."[39]

Yet the apprenticeship of the body in the second life at Selvino was not only a matter of containment, transgression, and repression. Thanks to the work of the educators, it was just as much about stimulus, discovery, and liberation. Reuven Donath in particular was very good both in leading the sports competitions within Sciesopoli and in organizing the excursions away from the base: in the woods and through the surrounding mountains, where the orphans, big and small, were guided as soon as the season was mild enough to allow for it. If instead there was snow (and there often was in those postwar winters), the gentle hills of the village offered boys and girls the thrill of a ski slope. Then even Adam Wexler, the contrarian, could forget the scabies and everything else, to smile happily in front of the photographer's lens.[40]

THE PRICE OF REBIRTH

The Shoah orphans represented only a small percentage of the total number of children that World War II had left without parents, without a home, without a homeland. They were incarnations

par excellence of both the victim and the refugee. It was not clear who had the right to protect these placeless children, whose lives hung suspended, disputed: The extended family after the death of their parents? Their country of origin, which in many cases changed at the end of the war? The new international humanitarian organizations concerned with the children's best interests? They were everybody's children and nobody's. And in the postwar world, depending on the case, they could be the source of problems or interest. They created problems as undernourished, traumatized, marginal children, or they created interest as reborn, transplantable, convertible ones.[41]

In the case of the youth who survived the Shoah in the bloodlands, their language, their mother tongue, was among the losses—the loss of Yiddish was added to the loss of their parents, homes, and a more or less stepmotherland. The repository idiom of an entire civilization, which in just four years of the Final Solution, had been transformed from a living language into a dead language. Yiddish had come to summarize all the languages of the thousand-year-old Jewish Diaspora, and in 1945 it had become, in spite of itself, the language of the victims and a victim in its own right: eight million speakers on the eve of World War II, two million at the end.[42] What was more, Yiddish was also targeted by the Zionists themselves. It was the language of the shtetl, of the Jews who lost, because they were landless Jews. Whereas Hebrew, the Zionists promised, was the language of the future, the language of victory to come, thanks to its intrinsic and necessary link with the land of Israel.[43]

For Moshe's children, the loss of Yiddish takes place in Selvino. All the rest was gone before—community, family, home—but the language is lost within the confines of Sciesopoli. And it is Moshe who wills it, it is Moshe who sends it away, though not overnight, of course. For months and months after their arrival at the Youth Aliyah House, children and teenagers of various backgrounds—Lithuanian or Galician Jews, Bohemians or Hungarians, Russians or Romanians—continue to communicate with each other (and with most educators) in the only language common to them, although pronounced differently according to regional inflections. But it's only a moratorium, a truce. In Sciesopoli as in all refugee camps placed under the authority of Zionist emissaries, unwritten rules of engagement provide for the abandonment of Yiddish in favor of Hebrew. The deafening resistance opposed by several survivors amounts to little, whereas the collaboration openly provided to educators by some orphans who knew Hebrew even before arriving in Selvino, and who become its best ambassadors within the new community of belonging, proves to be a great value.

One of these ambassadors is Avraham Lipkunski. Thanks to Arieh Soleh's courses, he quickly perfects the Hebrew he'd learned during his studious childhood, following Pinchas at the Talmudic schools of Raduń. Two other ambassadors are the Liberman sisters, Adela and Inda, equipped with what they learned, as girls of a good family, at the Tarbut and the Jewish school of Rivne—far better than the rudimentary Hebrew many Selvino youth had listlessly overheard as children from their village melamed. Showing off an increasingly fluent Hebrew already worthy of a kvutza on the coastal plain or a kibbutz in Galilee, youngsters like Avraham, Adela, and Inda become models in the eyes of their companions, offering the possibility of rebirth at Sciesopoli—albeit a rebirth that entails, among its prices, the atrophy of their mother tongue. An atrophy all the more painful for orphans as it would seem to them, ultimately, a betrayal of their lost mother. That is, to say it again in the language and style of Aharon Appelfeld, the annihilation of memory and the flattening of the soul.[44]

If it were up to Moshe Zeiri, there would be an additional price that all the Sciesopoli orphans must pay to be reborn: a name change—all except those, of course, who already have a Hebrew name. So enough, for example, with the overly Polish names of the Liberman sisters; they should give way to more Jewish names, if not actual biblical names. Adela would become Adina, and Inda would become Ayala. And the Hungarian Sándor Weisz, or Suti? He would become Yitzhak. Yes, new names to guarantee new identities. Hadn't S. Y. Agnon, one of the greats of modern Hebrew literature, written as much? Hadn't he remembered the saying of his ancestors, "Whoever changes his name changes his destiny"?[45] Therefore the Youth Aliyah House will give new names to the reborn. It will be Arieh instead of Lonek, Yaakov instead of Yanek, Yitzhak instead of Ijo, Zippora instead of Kazia.[46] And who cares if certain orphans don't want to, who cares if they stubbornly cling to the name that their parents had chosen for them—although an exception will be made for the recalcitrant, because one cannot force them if they don't want to.

To be born again, one must also pay the price of silence. Moshe Zeiri imposes on the orphans of the house the order of keeping silent about the past. They must never evoke—neither among

themselves, nor with the educators—their life before death. "Not a word," the director of Sciesopoli tells them.[47] Not a word about their childhood days, when their parents, siblings, cousins, and grandparents were still there; and when they could still take a stroll after school through the streets of the city or down the lanes of the shtetl; and they still celebrated Shabbat and on Saturdays in the winter afternoons, they played with sticks or snowballs; and then in the good season, they chased each other along the river or in the park while the parents chatted comfortably on the grass. Not a word about the time of the war, when the Germans arrived and locked everyone into the ghetto; and people were dying of hunger, of cold, of madness or typhoid fever; and at some point the *aktzias* started, and Jewish policemen helped the German soldiers or the Polish, Ukrainian, Lithuanian, or Belarusian auxiliaries to gather all the Jews near the cemetery or at the station square to shoot them with a machine gun or deport them in the sealed wagons; and those who were still alive after the trip would arrive in the concentration camp, even though the day of arrival was for many their last day.

Not a word about all of this, Moshe insists, believing he is doing them good. Because lingering on the past is of no use; it will not return anything or anyone to the orphans. One has to live in the present if one wants to invest in the future. "Let's not sing about blood and battles, let's sing about life and creation," says the slogan on the fixed cloth of the curtain that frames the singers of the Sciesopoli choir.[48]

THEIR WORD

Sciesopoli has its own newspaper; today, we would call it a newsletter. Its name was *Nivenu*, which in Hebrew means "our word." Issue number one came out on Saturday, October 27, 1945, and Moshe Zeiri wrote to Yehudit already that evening or that night, after the Youth Aliyah House greeted the launch with a party, singing, dancing, reading all the articles aloud. "There was a great joy between the listener and the speaker and among the editors, although the happiest of all was me. This is the first expression of community." True, only a few are involved in the newspaper. Mainly Yaakov Meriash and Shmulik Shulman, inseparable here too, helped not just by their friend Avraham Lipkunski but especially by Baruch Rosner and the Liberman sisters. Those few, however, work with a momentum that impresses Moshe. And they remind him of his earlier days, in Kopychyntsi and Lviv: "I saw myself again from fifteen years back. I was enthusiastic and excited in the same way, when in the summer I moved from our town to the big city. Even though I was more developed than them, because I hadn't spent four years in the camps, bunkers and ghettos."[49]

In theory, *Nivenu* is published in Hebrew. In practice, most of the texts are written in Yiddish or Polish because not many of the Sciesopoli orphans can actually write in Hebrew. Most of the time, it's the director of the institute himself, Moshe, who translates the originals at night.[50] Other times, the texts remain in Yiddish (but not in Polish or Hungarian; the pages of *Nivenu* always use Hebrew characters). It comes out fortnightly, the pages oscillating between four and eight in number. The newspaper is handwritten, so it's produced in an extremely limited number of copies, perhaps even in a single copy. With the exception of the editorial that opens each issue, and which can be anonymous, the articles are signed. These are mostly prose texts, but poems are not uncommon. Here and there, rarely, a drawing appears.[51]

In the first issues especially, *Nivenu* sounds very much like a propaganda newspaper, a Zionist bulletin from a postwar refugee camp.[52] Although Moshe claims he has kept out of the editorial process, letting the editors do everything,[53] the voices of the Sciesopoli orphans initially sound like students echoing their teacher's cue. The same with the Yiddish verses of Shmulik Shulman, who survived the Lutsk ghetto. They are as saturated with the role of the helpless victim as with the desire to become—in the Promised Land—a Jew capable of fighting back:

> Enough have we suffered in exile, brothers!
> Enough has our spilled blood stained.
> Enough have we bowed our heads,
> Enough we have been put in chains.[54]

The first issues of *Nivenu* abound with precepts about the need to eradicate the "bad habits of the diaspora," replacing them with habits suited to a new life in Eretz Israel, even in the "deserted expanses of the Negev. . . . There we will be able to demonstrate that the Jews were not made to be turned into soap, but that they are capable of working the land, of building and defending themselves," Aharon Steinberg guarantees in a Yiddish editorial entitled "Our Word."[55]

In their contributions to the Sciesopoli newspaper, Mordechai Stern, Yaakov Hollander, Dvora Goldstein also favored the future over the past. They looked forward rather than backward, with a resolve that Zeiri would certainly appreciate. As would an article by Avraham Hasman, a sixteen-year-old orphan from Łódź, published under the title "My First Letter to My Uncles and Aunts in Tel Aviv." The nephew reassured his relatives in Palestine, "I won't sadden you by reporting all the details that have touched me and my family since the war broke out." No details, not a word about the Łódź ghetto where—as Avraham Hasman will testify ten years later, for the Yad Vashem archive[56]—he lost his mother, Adela, and two of his sisters, Dvora and Cesia. No details, not a word, about the fatal Birkenau selections that led to the death of his father, Mordechai; his brother, Yehoshua; and his sister Sara. "Here, I've exchanged my family for another. My father will be my strength of action, through which I will form and defend myself in spite of any obstacle. My mother: Eretz Israel, to whom I will devote all my energy and talent. My brother and sister: the friends who are with me and who will help me achieve the goal."[57]

Not a word about the past, Moshe Zeiri insisted. And he meant the recent past, what the Sciesopoli orphans had experienced on their own skin. Whereas if someone wanted to indulge in the heights of the distant past, perhaps going back to the decisive hour in the history of the people of Israel—the gift on Mount Sinai of the tablets of the law to Moses—then it was not a problem to talk about it, not at all. Better still if in verse, as Shalom Finkelstein, a sixteen-year-old Polish Jew from Łomża, was inclined to do. In the pages of *Nivenu*, his voice has a particular timbre, resounding with a metaphysical depth:

> And suddenly the voice of God is heard,
> a voice that flashes and destroys the mountains.
> The words come out His mouth with fury
> and pierce the hearts of the people:
> "If you give your ear and listen to my precepts
> you will see the land of your fathers,
> but if you refuse to listen to your hearts
> your burial will be right here!"[58]

Not a word about the recent past? Easy to say; less easy to do. From one issue to another of *Nivenu*, some of the orphans of Sciesopoli use the opportunity to write for the newspaper to process the grief and express their loss. Adela Liberman (signing her name now as Adina) certainly thinks of her own past, of her escape together with Inda (now Ayala) from the ghetto of Zdolbuniv, after the *aktzia* had started and their own mother had pushed them: You two go on. Your father and I will join you as soon as possible. Adela certainly thinks of this when she dedicates a poem to the "lonely abandoned" orphans, before sublimating the pain in the form of a vow for the future: "We will chase away the shadows of the ashes, / we will break the storm of darkness. / We will reach the shores of our homeland, / and then spring will bloom and flourish."[59] Other voices in *Nivenu* sound less supervised, more direct. They speak openly with the language of remembrance, regret, tears. Among these is the voice of Suti Weisz.

Suti (now Yitzhak) writes more than once in the Sciesopoli newspaper. He doesn't write to just grieve or weep. He also writes in amazement at Selvino's quiet evenings, "when a serene peace covers everything, and the last bat of the valley curls up into sleep."[60] The fifteen-year-old Nagyszőlős orphan has a poetic soul, and he is not ashamed to show it. In a letter dated January 15, 1946—written in Hungarian, and translated into Hebrew by a willing editor[61]—Suti addresses his mother, Terez, after "two long years" since she died of cancer. The illness precipitated the end of the Weisz children's wonderful childhood but spared their mother the rest: the four streets of the Nagyszőlős ghetto, Ortutay the teacher transformed by the Nazis into the accountant of death, Icuka's blue dress on the Birkenau ramp, Aliz and Hedi disappeared who knows where, and then the selections again, the death marches, *"Du bist zu jung!"*, and Father Vilmos in Mauthausen and Gunskirchen—a father who is no longer a father, dried up before succumbing to typhoid fever.

"You have certainly met Papa in the kingdom of heaven. He also left us and followed you, the one my soul loved—loved to death. Did you find Icuka among the six million innocent victims? If not, look for her, so that my poor little sister won't be alone," Suti writes. "Mama! Your little son Yitzhak has grown up, he will soon be sixteen and is a tall boy. Just like with you, books are everything for him too. . . . Again the years of happiness flow in my memory. We were all so pleasantly together in our family's small house. That house is no longer there, the puppies Medi and Buksi no longer sit in front of the house, the cat Futi no longer climbs on the roof, and even the maid Menzi has stopped entering the kitchen to ask for a piece of bread so as to produce more milk to breastfeed Fimta... Everything has been lost forever. The family home is still alive only in my memories.... I will include three that must not be forgotten, the memories... home ... parents... brother and sister... playing in the garden among the bees... the swing on the mulberry tree... a fight, whoever catches little Icuka will kiss her... leaving my room to polish the bicycle."[62]

Avraham Lipkunski is also ready to disregard Moshe Zeiri's injunction about "not a word." The past knocks too hard inside his head to be able to silence him by thinking only of the future. But with his Selvino companions, the former pupil of Raduń's minor yeshiva needs not only to share images of destruction, defeat, and mourning. Of course, when he tells of his arrival in the uniform of the Red Army—two years after escaping from the trench that became a mass grave—to the cemetery of Raduń where his mother and brother and a thousand other defenseless Jews had been shot, Avraham must admit that he was stunned. The mass graves were no longer distinguishable, the landscape contaminated by the dead of the people of Israel had already found time to reorganize, erasing traces and defying memory.[63] And yet from that landscape, Avraham had been able to hear the cry of Yekutiel, the cry of innocent blood.

Thus the former partisan Avremale of the Leninski Komsomol Brigade can also evoke images of struggle and vengeance by writing in *Nivenu*. "The cry of the unfortunate children and infants' blood, spilled like water, came from that tract of land. So, in my heart, I said to myself: Why has liberation come for me? Why abandon the direction in which I found life? I don't want an end to the war. I won't be able to live without war. I want to see the murderers' blood under the blood of those unfortunate infants. And then, at the order of our commander, we chased the collaborators, who had sought refuge in the tangle of the forest."[64]

NINE

KIBBUTZ SELVINO?

THE HAIFA ORANGE

The first clandestine ship above a certain tonnage sailed from Vado Ligure, near Savona, Italy, on December 14, 1945. The Zionists called her *Hannah Szenes*, in homage to a "Palestinian" heroine of the war against the Germans. She was a young Jewish woman of Hungarian origin who, after being parachuted by the Royal Air Force behind enemy lines in Yugoslavia in 1944, had been captured, tortured, and killed.[1] The *Hannah Szenes* carried 250 passengers and was added to smaller ships that the Aliyah Beth emissaries had previously managed to set sail from the piers of Puglia or Lucania, from Bari, Taranto, and Metaponto.[2] In fact, the Zionist agents benefited from the Italian authorities' politically ambiguous attitude. In theory, the authorities were determined to obstruct any illegal transport to British Palestine. In practice, they were not always sorry to cause a variety of political and diplomatic problems for the London government by turning a blind eye to the boats carrying Jews.[3] Out of sixty-four armed Aliyah Beth ships between the summer of 1945 and the spring of 1948—that is, between the end of World War II and the proclamation of the State of Israel—thirty-three would have left from

Italy, for a total of over twenty thousand migrants clandestinely boarded from ports on the peninsula.[4]

Upon having reached the waters of Nahariya, at the northernmost tip of Palestine, the *Hannah Szenes* evaded the control of the Royal Navy patrols guarding the coast.[5] The arrival of those 250 Jews in the Promised Land on December 25, 1945, ushered in a particularly vital myth in the following years: the myth of Holocaust survivors brave enough, after all they had suffered during the Nazi persecution, to openly challenge the new oppressors, His Majesty's navy. Brave enough to settle down, huddled together, in the hold of derelict boats made seaworthy again. Brave enough to face days and days of navigation, in the heart of the seas, chastised by emissaries forced to speak loudly to contain the hunger, the nausea, the indiscipline of the passengers. Brave enough to hoist the blue and white flag with the Shield of David once in sight of Palestine. And brave enough to engage in fistfights if blocked by coast guards to have their right to live free in the land of Israel recognized.

With a poem published in the newspaper *Davar* on January 15, 1946, it was again Nathan Alterman's turn to exalt an event—the lucky journey of the *Hannah Szenes*—to the heights of the Zionist epic. "In Response to an Italian Captain" honored not only the Jewish passengers but also the goy commander of the merchant ship that had challenged the British navy:

> No Lloyds would insure your little one,
>   secret vessel,
> Nor the perilous battle it fights,
> But even if no document
>   is kept in the logbook,
> We will report it in the annals of history.[6]

During the short interval between the arrival of the *Hannah Szenes* in Nahariya and the publication of Alterman's poem in *Davar*, a second boat—much larger than the first, and much more loaded with passengers—sailed from Vado Ligure to Palestine. The Zionists also wanted to give this ship the name of a Palestinian hero who had been killed during the war: an Italian Jew who was parachuted beyond enemy lines in 1944 and was then captured, deported, and killed by the Germans. Thirty-seven meters long and with a capacity of 410 tons, the *Enzo Sereni* had been purchased and rearmed thanks to the decisive contribution of Ada, the hero's widow. It raised anchor from Vado at dawn on January 7, 1946.[7] With an impressive show of strength, the Aliyah Beth emissaries managed to get more than nine hundred illegal immigrants from the sea onto the ship.[8] Among them were about thirty orphans from the Youth Aliyah House in Selvino—about thirty of Moshe's children.

In Sciesopoli, it had been difficult to agree on who should leave. Since November, the serenity of the house had been troubled by disputes about the criteria for selecting the first illegal migrants. In particular, a group of orphans (about twenty-five, between males and females) had proposed to Moshe Zeiri to adopt a criterion that Moshe himself, writing to Yehudit, defined as "extremist." According to them, the very first group of illegal immigrants departing from Selvino should be made up exclusively of orphans totally alone in the world: without any relative, not even remotely, who had been saved or lived in Palestine. They said this criterion was meant to be sure that the group would remain united even afterward, that it would not be dispersed upon arrival in Eretz Israel. Moshe appreciated the proponents' Zionist fervor ("they were just as enthusiastic as we were in Galicia, and they drank up everything they could about the 'land of Israel'"), but he rejected the proposal. The lists of first to go would be formed not on the basis of group affinity but by identifying the most suitable candidates one by one: those physically and psychologically ready.[9]

Among those chosen to board the *Enzo Sereni* were Haim Luftman and Dov Wexler. Adam Wexler was left out. His big brother was leaving, but not him. After having lived through

all the tragedies of an early life together, from the Łódź ghetto to the Birkenau ramp, from the death march to the Gusen barracks, the two surviving sons of Mindel the seamstress and Henoch the shochet had to endure the trauma of separation in Selvino. They had to resign themselves to experiencing separately the high point of their second life, the ascent to the Promised Land. The trio made up of Avraham Lipkunski, Yaakov Meriash, and Shmulik Shulman, who had been among those who had asked Zeiri to select the totally alone orphans in the first group, were also left out.[10] As for the rest, the thirty or so boys and girls who were leaving had behind them a series of dramas common to Moshe's children. At least one other boy had made it out alive, like Haim Luftman and Dov Wexler, from the Łódź ghetto: his name was Julek Reich, and he had survived a bit of everything—Birkenau, the death march, Mauthausen, and Ebensee.[11] Yeshayahu Lichtenstein himself escaped Auschwitz, Mauthausen, and Ebensee. And several girls of the group had known the Birkenau barracks, among them Malka Shafrir, who in Selvino contended with her friend Bronka Auerbach for the reputation of "beauty" of the house.[12]

The Sciesopoli orphans to be embarked in Liguria had left Selvino a few days before the scheduled departure of the *Enzo Sereni*. Driven by Fetter Moshe, an Aliyah Beth truck transported them to Magenta, the fake agricultural colony, and at the last moment, the night between Sunday, January 6, and Monday, January 7, 1946, from Magenta to Vado Ligure. That night, theirs was only one of the dozens of tarpaulin-covered trucks that had brought over nine hundred illegal migrants to the scene. The operation director, Shalhevet Freier, took advantage of his British Army uniform to lead the column in a Jeep. The laborious boarding operations followed in the dark and cold. In the hold, the wooden berths had been previously replaced by canvas berths to gain additional space. But it was also necessary to find a place for food, tanks of drinking water, and the fuel needed for the entire journey. As secret as it was illegal, the *Enzo Sereni*'s route could not include intermediate stopovers.[13]

In an autobiographical novel, *The Boy Who Wanted to Sleep*, Aharon Appelfeld would offer Israeli literature a depiction of the trauma of his clandestine journey from Italy to Palestine in that same year of 1946—sixty years after having experienced it. He would describe the nausea, the vomiting, the abuse of adult refugees against young and defenseless passengers.[14] More benign, by comparison, is Haim Luftman's own memory of his journey. Still, it is explicit with regard to the harsh experience shared by the thirty Sciesopoli orphans on the *Enzo Sereni*. "Like sardines. I'm not exaggerating, we were like sardines." They lay against each other because "the boat was really small." To relieve themselves, they had to queue outside scarce and fetid latrines. In general, moving from one point of the hold to another was almost impossible. "Let me be clear, it's all relative. After what we had experienced between Birkenau and Ebensee, this was child's play. Being squeezed like sardines wasn't... the

problem was that during the day we had to stay below deck. Only at night could we go out, breathe fresh air." They spent ten days that way because the Zionist emissaries feared being spotted by British reconnaissance planes. Toward the end, there was almost no more water, hardly any food, and women giving birth on board.[15]

The *Enzo Sereni* reached the waters of Haifa at dawn on Thursday, January 17, 1946. But she was intercepted by a unit of the Royal Navy, which began to escort her toward the port. The nine hundred passengers then witnessed, from the bridge, the spectacle that Zionist propaganda loved to represent as the quintessence of landing in the Promised Land: they saw the soft profile of Mount Carmel appearing on the horizon.[16] Haim Luftman said in his 2008 interview, "I see Haifa and Carmel. Well, there is no language to tell this either." In addition, there was a small group of people on the Haifa pier to welcome the illegal immigrants from the sea, even though it was very early in the morning.[17] People were shouting at the new arrivals, in Yiddish and in Hebrew. "Kind

things. 'Welcome!' Things like that." Oranges too. "When we got out, they threw oranges at us. One hit me in the head. I picked it up, it was the first orange I ate in Israel. And this too would need a special language to be told. In our language, there are no words to describe the taste of this orange. It was a golden orange."[18]

But not all that glitters is gold. On the morning of their arrival, Haim Luftman, Dov Wexler, Yeshayahu Lichtenstein, Julek Reich, Malka Shafrir, Rivka Polak, Shmuel Boim, Alter Katz, Gershon Klein, Avraham Landau, Aharon Rakotz, Lea Laiberg, Miriam Fisher, and the other Selvino orphans, along with all or almost all the Jews disembarked from the *Enzo Sereni*, are transferred by the British to the Atlit detention camp. It is not far away—ten or twelve miles south of Haifa along the coast. A concentration camp? Not really, but almost. It is a detention camp for illegal immigrants, with its watchtowers, barbed wire, separate barracks for men and women, and the showers where you have to undress before disinfestation. "Atlit reminded me of Auschwitz," Haim Luftman summed up sixty years later.[19]

Fortunately, Atlit was not Auschwitz. So Haim, Dov, Malka, and the boys and girls of Selvino who descended on the Haifa pier from the *Enzo Sereni* bridge have to wait only a few weeks—a short quarantine—before they are allowed to walk freely on the soil of the Promised Land.

POLONIA PALACE HOTEL

The Liberman sisters, Nina Boniówka, Avraham Kutner, and the thirty other Polish orphans indoctrinated by the Gordonia Zionist movement, who had reached Selvino from Łódź in November 1945, made up less than one-thousandth of the Jews—about thirty-three thousand—who left Poland in May and December 1945. Another fifteen thousand would follow them in the first half of 1946.[20] The Polish Jews passed directly from the nightmare of extermination to the disenchantment of a liberation that first translated into a mockery, then into a threat. The mockery was that of a homeless homecoming: Jewish houses occupied by Polish, Ukrainian, Belarusian, or Lithuanian Christians, and almost never returned to their legitimate owners, with the indifference or complicity of the state administration. Moreover, it was a mockery for those saved children or young people whose return to school often had to be carried out in anonymity: keeping the false names and surnames assumed during the Nazi persecution, to avoid hostility in Poland. The threat, all too concrete, was that of physical aggression, as in Rzeszów, Kraków, and Nowy Sącz.[21]

If Jews left Poland by the tens of thousands, some went in the other direction, back to Poland. Previously emigrated, they returned to their country of origin with various intentions. This was the case with the Zionist emissaries engaged with the Bricha, the organized flight to Palestine.[22] This was also the case with Jacob Pat, a Bundist intellectual who had left Poland for the United States in 1938 and had become a union leader in New York.[23] In the first winter of peace, he crossed the Atlantic in the opposite direction. He got to Warsaw in January 1946 and embarked on a sort of documentary pilgrimage among the smoking ruins of Jewish Poland. The cities, from Warsaw to Łódź, from Białystok to Wrocław, from Katowice to Kraków. The villages of Galicia. The extermination camps. *Ashes and Fire* will be the title of the report published by Pat after his return to New York, to suggest how much fire still smoldered under the ashes of the ruins. The fire of Jewish life, but also the fire of Polish antisemitism.[24]

"I have seen thousands of Jews, and every one of them is a miracle of survival." Jacob Pat met men, women, and children who fled the liquidation of ghettos and death marches, escaped by sinking into the forests, were hidden by compassionate Christians. He saw just as many Jews in liberated Poland who were seething with a "migratory fever," eager to leave. So they were preparing for the aliyah, attending some agricultural schools, some technical schools set up by the Zionists. They could no longer stand the "brutal anti-Semitism" of postwar Poland. "I have seen Jewish children, and every one of them is a relic of a buried civilization." Those children were exasperated by the climate around them, like the orphan Pat met at an institution in Otwock, "a ghetto leftover, with no father or mother." He was able, during the Nazi occupation, to survive the woods with the partisans. He was unable to stand the abuse of his Christian peers after the war. "He said he wanted to hang himself. 'I can't take any more of this life.'"[25]

For some Jewish survivors, marriage is also a possible escape route. The same goes for the "petite and graceful" young woman who questions Jacob Pat in the atrium of Polonia Palace, the only luxury hotel opened in Warsaw at the end of the war, the temporary seat of numerous diplomatic delegations. The woman is elegantly dressed and sweetly scented, and Pat recognizes her as the daughter of a friend of his in Poland during the twenties and thirties: Alter Kacyzne, the intellectual, one of the most talented writers about Yiddish culture, as well as the photojournalist from Poland for the New York–based newspaper *The Forward*. Unlike

her father, murdered near Ternopil in the summer of 1941, and unlike her mother, deported from Lviv to the Belzec extermination camp in the summer of 1942, Shulamit Kacyzne had managed to save herself. She did whatever she needed to do to save herself—real documents and false documents, commitments and escapes, loves and betrayals.[26] And now Shulamit is about to get married within a few days. In fact, she asks Pat, her father's old friend, if he can be one of the witnesses. The husband? An Italian, and a highly esteemed one at that. None other than the ambassador of the Kingdom of Italy in Warsaw.[27]

With her femme fatale air, Shulamit Kacyzne bewitched an experienced politician (and a consummate Don Juan) such as

Eugenio Reale, a high-ranking member of the Italian Communist Party wanted by the general secretary himself, Palmiro Togliatti, as diplomatic representative of the new Italy at such a delicate posting as 1945 Warsaw.[28] And perhaps his marriage to twenty-two-year-old Shulamit, celebrated in a secular rite on a "snowy February evening,"[29] contributed to making the royal ambassador more sensitive than others to the plight of the Jews. Of course, on matters concerning the conflict between the Polish government in exile in London and the Soviet-protected Lublin Committee, Reale moves to Warsaw as a Communist of the Third International, a faithful ally of Moscow. Nevertheless, his attention to the Jewish cause has something singular compared to the positions then widespread among the Western chancelleries.[30] During the entire course of the year 1946, of all the diplomats to settle under the Belle Époque vaults of the Polonia Palace, the Italian ambassador proved to be the Polish Jews' best foreign friend.[31]

And not just the Polish Jews. Around the time of his wedding, Eugenio Reale informs Alcide De Gasperi, Italy's prime minister as well acting as foreign minister, of the mission he has entrusted to an official of the Italian embassy: an inspection at "the internment camps of Oświęcim and Birkenau." It was the first ever visit by an Italian public official to the Auschwitz concentration complex. This visit was carried out together with a delegation of former political deportees, and it was made all the more significant by the opportunity to leaf through "some voluminous registers" of the deceased inmates, "in which our delegates found many Italian surnames, especially Jewish, as well as various foreign surnames common among Italian Jews." Taking advantage of the occasion, the members of the delegation copied some of the Italian surnames taken at random. With a more systematic approach, the ambassador recommends that all the Auschwitz registers be subjected to an accurate examination, in such a way as to reveal "the mystery that still exists regarding the fate of so many Italians arrested by the Germans, and which still feeds so many useless hopes among their families."[32]

In a dispatch dated February 20, 1946, Reale refers explicitly to Jacob Pat, who arrived in Warsaw from New York "to investigate the living conditions of Jews in Poland." Yet the ambassador refrains from making any explicit link between the country's antisemitic mood and the migratory movements of the surviving Jews.[33] In reality, the two dynamics are closely related. Italy in 1946 is a sought-after goal for several thousand Polish Jews because those Jews have decided to abandon Poland, where, as survivors of the Shoah, they deem it impossible to survive. It is also because the ports of Italy offer especially propitious docks for the Aliyah Beth ships to set sail for Palestine. For the same reason, the Youth Aliyah House in Selvino continues to register new arrivals, in 1946 no fewer than in 1945. Because among the Polish Jews who decide to leave, there are also young or very young orphans—generally, children and young people coming from within Zionist associations, mostly Gordonia or Hashomer Hatzair.

Moshe Zeiri sees himself less and less as the director of an institute affiliated with Gordonia. While maintaining regular exchanges with the leaders of the Lubianiker movement in Palestine, he tries to free his house from the ideological tensions within the kibbutz movement.[34] Moreover, in the beginning of 1946, Moshe also tries to free himself from the condition of a volunteer soldier in an auxiliary company of the British Army. Coinciding with the final demobilization of the 745th Solel Boneh, he tries to get an official secondment to UNRRA, the United Nations agency, or to the Joint, the Jewish assistance organization. The attempt fails due to a series of bureaucratic obstacles. In any event, even though Moshe must continue to wear the uniform in the winter of 1945–46, he remains above all devoted to his mission as director of Sciesopoli. The men of the 745th return to Palestine, whereas he stays. "The major has already left, the captain has been home for some time. Within two weeks the others will also leave." Moshe can't leave; he has to think about his orphans. They need him, and he needs them. "Even now, if I go away from home for a day, it feels like a year has gone by. A week ago I went to town for two days, and on my return the boys ran to meet me, cheering. They lifted me up on their arms and carried me in triumph. I didn't think they missed me that much."[35]

For Yehudit, everything is more complicated. From Kvutzat-Shiller, it is more difficult than in Selvino to resign oneself to a physical distance that tends to become—with the passage of time—psychological distance. As in the previous July, so from November 1945 to February 1946 is the correspondence between Yehudit and Moshe often obscured by the shadow of misunderstanding. "Most of the time, I don't even want to pick up a pen. Indeed, why should I make your clear sky overcast?" she writes. Or, "Nostalgia is growing day by day, becoming unbearable. If we don't see each other soon, I just don't know what's going to happen."[36] Yehudit's voice is that of a twenty-five-year-old woman who hasn't seen her husband for two years, and who alone raised a little girl, while her husband seemed to have nothing on his mind but the children of others. As for Moshe, he recognizes misunderstanding as the effect of "secret gossip," the dull work of a malice typical of the kibbutz. "I know that stories have spread about me in Palestine, maybe they even reached your ears. That I'm cheating on you, and that's why I don't want to leave. There are those who enjoy spreading rumors."[37] The correspondence between Yehudit and Moshe is also conditioned by the shadow of Matilde Cassin.

But there is a solution. If Moshe can't imagine going back and abandoning the orphans of Sciesopoli, and if Yehudit can no longer bear the distance from her husband and the father of her daughter, there can be only one solution: to welcome Yehudit and Nitza to Sciesopoli. This is the project that Moshe begins working on during the winter of 1945–46, taking into account from the outset that the leaders of Kvutzat-Shiller would present a thousand difficulties, that the kibbutz community would put forward a host of arguments to prove that Yehudit and Nitza's departure for Italy was inappropriate. "They will amass proof upon proof that this is illogical and unthinkable," he writes. "They are all good at reckoning for someone else, but who cares about your suffering, or that of the child and my own?"[38] No, it was not going to be easy. But what had ever been easy in the lives of Moshe Kleiner and Trude Meyer?

SCIESOPOLI IN ARMS

In Selvino, the day's mail was eagerly awaited. In the Youth Aliyah House, the director as well as the orphans wondered every day what happened to the boys and girls who had embarked on the *Enzo Sereni* to Palestine. And the arrival of news was more pressing than ever for those who had seen a brother or sister leave; this was the case of Adam Wexler, forcibly separated from Dov. But the craving for knowledge had infected everyone a bit, and it was burdened with anxiety over the possibility that the migrants of Sciesopoli were going to encounter dispersion—that once they arrived in Eretz Israel, instead of staying together, they would be sorted into different kibbutzim. Because that was the point, Moshe Zeiri focused on this more and more over the course of the winter. It was not only a question of creating the conditions for all the guests of the house to reach the Promised Land; it was also a question of getting them assigned to the same kibbutz. The goal, in short, was to create something similar to a Selvino kibbutz in Palestine.

Since the days of the liberation, Zeiri had imagined building on the kibbutz ideal in such a manner. He wanted to open to the Shoah orphans the prospect of being reborn in a community of equals, which might help compensate for their loss of family. After that, the success of Sciesopoli could only confirm the validity of the idea. "How happy I am to have been able to build the institute, brick by brick, and to feel that it is a project. And I'm not the only one who feels this way, so do the boys and the whole team," Moshe wrote to Yehudit on January 17, 1946. In a letter that began with "Good evening, love of my soul," he added, "How beautiful and wonderful it would be if you came to me, and if we finished this period of work together, making the aliyah with the last transport of our children. I'm sure they'd love you, and you'd bond with them as I have bonded. Perhaps we should think about our own kvutza: the 'Selvino kvutza.'"[39]

With the need to stagger the departures of the orphans, Zeiri initially thought of Kvutzat-Shiller as the natural place for their first settlement in Palestine. He then probed the leaders of his kibbutz of origin only to discover both their perplexities and reluctance.[40] Zeiri also had to deal with the ideological disagreements within the kibbutz movement. Because Sciesopoli was renowned as an institute affiliated to Gordonia, the competing parties tried to put up a headwind and prevent the boys and girls stepping off the *Enzo Sereni* from winding up together in a single kibbutz. "Hashomer Hatzair members spread rumors that our group had been dispersed, and there was nothing left of it." But the opponents' maneuvers were not very effective. On a beautiful day in March, the Youth Aliyah House received exciting news by telegram. The Sciesopoli orphans remained united even after the quarantine in the Atlit camp: they were all sent together to the legendary Kibbutz Hanita, in Western Galilee—the same one celebrated by the verses of Alterman in "Song of the Platoons." "The telegram arrived at dinner time," unleashing in the refectory "an applause like we haven't heard for some time." On the border with Lebanon, gathered under the Selvino Youth Association sign, Moshe's first children to arrive in Palestine were now helping to stand guard at its watchtowers and palisades.[41]

Already in Selvino, the boys of the house were subjected to paramilitary training. Alberto Cortinovis, the son of a farmer from Selvino, would tell me about it in his own words one autumn afternoon in 2014. He was about twelve years old in 1946 and delivered the containers of fresh milk in the morning for the institute's kitchens, transporting them from a nearby cow stable. "Between you and me, they were training, and there was one of them giving orders... kept them on their toes, woke them up at night... They were ready to go... to defend themselves, because they put them in kibbuses [kibbutzim] there, right?"[42] Shie Zoltak, a Polish Jew who was fifteen in 1946, would never forget his vigils along the walkway over the gate at Sciesopoli. He stood for two-hour night shifts, fighting the cold and sleep and making sure that no one came near the gate. "As far as I can remember, there had never been a living soul. But it was a way to make us feel ready to defend a settlement in Palestine."[43] There is at least one photograph of Sciesopoli in arms, saved by a Lithuanian Jew, Simcha Frumkin, who was then sixteen. In a break from day training, six or seven boys take pride in carrying real, though unloaded, rifles—.22 calibers, with a bayonet attached.[44]

Moshe Zeiri's Zionist motivation was so strong that if one of his children at the institute was planning a future for himself anywhere other than in Palestine, Zeiri changed his attitude toward him. Worse, he changed his nature: from the father that he was, he became a stepfather. In addition to the guard duty along the Sciesopoli walkway, Shie Zoltak would never forget when the director, discovering the boy's intention to join his maternal relatives in Canada, had ordered him to leave Selvino on the spot.[45] The case of Dov Zugman, the postman of Sciesopoli, a sixteen-year-old Galician Jew, was similar. He wanted to go to America, to an uncle, instead of going up with his companions to the land of Israel. Zeiri had him packing his bags as soon as possible. "One bad apple spoils the whole bunch."[46] In the winter of 1945–46, Zeiri learned that Baruch Rosner, a Hungarian orphan already in Piazzatorre, had almost been adopted by a rich American soldier,

who had met him at the Military Academy of Modena and was now preparing to welcome and support him in the United States. Disappointed, Zeiri let the rumor spread through the Youth Aliyah House that the boy was forced by the self-styled protector, once in America, to become a Catholic priest.[47]

Stepchildren aside, for the director of Sciesopoli, the months from January to March 1946 are filled with intense diplomatic work. On the Italian front, Zeiri seeks to increase his decision-making autonomy both with respect to the Jewish community of Milan and the Center for the Diaspora. He is supported in this by a living legend of Zionism: Yosef Baratz, who at the end of January also finds time to climb the Val Seriana road with its hairpin bends to Selvino. "How many times had the visit been postponed, and how much disappointment had I passed on to the children, after all they had heard from me about Degania and Baratz!" Impressed by Sciesopoli, Baratz becomes Zeiri's best advocate in the slippery environment of Zionist emissaries in Italy.[48] On the Palestinian front, Zeiri corresponds with the head of the Histadrut himself, Pinchas Lubianiker (his sister Rivka's great friend from the time of Kopychyntsi and the theatrical tours on improvised stages in Galicia), to receive advice about Yehudit's situation, what arguments to use with the heads of Kvutzat-Shiller, and how to get her and little Nitza to join him in the mountains of Bergamo.[49]

At the end of March, Moshe changes his bedroom. After six months spent on the institute's mezzanine, he moves to the fourth and top floor—in the room that the architect from Sciesopoli himself had designed as the director's room.[50] "My darling, in the last few days I've moved into Mussolini's room," Moshe tells Yehudit. "Up until now it was closed, I only gave it to passing guests." Clearly, Zeiri also believes the legend—how and by whom it was spread is unknown—according to which a room reserved for Il Duce had existed in Sciesopoli. "There is a very large double bed in the room, apparently he and his wife were very fat." In reality, Benito Mussolini had never set foot in Selvino; he had limited himself to taking part, as the first member, in the fundraiser opened in Milan for the construction of the Amatore Sciesa alpine camp.[51] Be that as it may, Zeiri moves to the fourth floor precisely because the director's bedroom has a double bed. He hopes for his wife to arrive soon. "When I walked in, my colleagues said, 'Moshe, how nice it would be if your Yehudit were already here.'"[52]

As April approaches, Nitza's birthday is also approaching. She will soon be four, and her father hasn't seen her for over two years. It's something that needs to be explained to her, and that's what Moshe begs Yehudit to take charge of. "My darling, I ask you something. On the baby's birthday, take her on your lap, indoors or out, and tell her how much dad loves her. How much he would like to be close to her already, and celebrate her birthday with her. Playing with her, going around with her, always being with her. Just tell her, in your own fitting language, why this can't happen yet. Tell her what I'm doing here for the children who that evil Hitler has hurt. They have no mom or dad, no house or kvutza. They have nowhere to stay. They want to come to Israel terribly, but they still can't, they are still not allowed. And I, her father, gathered them together and made a house for them, and they live here, where they study, play, and forget what they've been through."[53] Thus by saying the right words to her at the right time, Nitza would understand her father, the reasons for his distance. More than that, Moshe's little girl would begin to love Moshe's other children.

ON THE LA SPEZIA DOCK

Nitza was born in 1942, on the third day of Passover. In 1946, the date coincides with April 18 on the Christian calendar. But precisely in those days, a sort of political and diplomatic crisis forces Moshe Zeiri to hastily leave Selvino, perhaps relegating the thought of his daughter's birthday to the background.

On Friday, April 12, a telegram orders Zeiri the soldier to travel as soon as possible to Naples, where what remains of the British Royal Engineer Corps stationed in Italy is based. What is it that awaits him? Perhaps a discharge from the British Army? Or the move to a new company? Or a move to the Joint? "I didn't know what the reason for the trip was." Yet Zeiri believes he knows what's behind it: subtle maneuvers of Zionists hostile to Gordonia. "Hashomer Hatzair people 'attack' us. They want to infiltrate us, they are jealous of my influence on the children." While traveling from Val Seriana to Milan and from there to Rome, Moshe suspects that the summons to Naples prefigures the order to resume active service in the British Army. And abandon Sciesopoli? "It can't be possible, after having dedicated half of my soul to the home and to the children. I've neglected any possibility of study or specialization, I've founded a home and I'm the father of 300 children—I cannot return to the Company," Moshe vents with Yehudit from Rome, on April 16.[54]

In those very days, a much more serious political and diplomatic crisis was added to Zeiri's personal one. It was the crisis of the *Fede* and the *Fenice*, two steamers that Aliyah Beth agents had secretly rearmed in the port of La Spezia. On the night of April 3, they tried to pick up illegal migrants from central Italy, directed toward Palestine. Shalhevet Freier was the logistics manager of the operation, just as he had been for the boarding of illegal immigrants onto the *Enzo Sereni* in Vado Ligure.[55] But this time the Italian police tried to prevent it. Along the road from Sarzana, the police intercepted a column of cars made up of a British military Jeep and (in the words of the prefect of La Spezia) "37 other vehicles, loaded with about 1,000 people of the Jewish race," men, women, and children without any identification documents and driven by drivers in allied military uniform, "also of the Jewish race."[56] The prefect ordered the blockade of the two ships, the arrest of the four men in the Jeep, and the arrest of the thousand illegal immigrants. But within a few days, the local incident took on international dimensions.[57]

In protest, the prefect of La Spezia announced on April 8, with an encrypted telegram to the Interior Ministry, "The Jews have started a hunger strike this morning." And from British Palestine, some leaders of the Jewish Agency (including the most charismatic of the Histadrut executives, Golda Meyerson, later Golda Meir) saw fit to imitate them. Faced with a prolonged and widening crisis, Raffaele Cantoni, the new president of the Union of Italian Jewish communities, asked for an audience with Prime Minister Alcide De Gasperi. Although the hearing was granted, it was inconclusive. De Gasperi was personally in favor of a departure of the refugees to Palestine, but the Italian statesman remained subject to the directives of the Allied military command.[58] "You may also have heard that an Aliyah Beth ship was stopped before setting sail with a thousand on board, and that they are being held under armed surveillance," Moshe writes to Yehudit in his April 16 letter. "We still hope that they will be authorized to leave, since the most enlightened components of the Italian government are lined up on our side."[59]

The La Spezia incident marks a stage in the history of those saved from the Shoah. It exposes in full light the ethical and political problem of the fate to be reserved for the survivors of the Final Solution fleeing postwar Europe. And it openly raises the issue of what right they had to land, en masse—despite the quotas imposed by the British administration—on the shores of the Promised Land. From April 4, 1946, onward, the stranded refugees make headlines. They are talked about in the pages of the major Italian newspapers and even (in passing) in those of the *New York Times*.[60] A number of journalists converge on the Ligurian port. And not all of them are dyed-in-wool antisemites, like the anonymous envoy of Genoa's *Secolo liberale*, who describes the "strange herd" gathered in La Spezia on the Pagliari pier as "ragged people" with an "incomprehensible language," "grumpy and mute with strangers," but eager to congregate together, below deck, to take advantage of the "varied assortment" of provisions accumulated in the holds of the two ships, "from chocolate to chewing gum."[61] Other, more open-minded journalists also converge on La Spezia, such as the correspondent for *Corriere della Sera*, Milziade Torelli.

"You climb aboard the *Fede*. Here are the women, the ones on deck are all very young. They are beautiful, these Jewish girls: solid and slender, with dark skin and very big black eyes. So silent and reserved, they must be very beautiful when they smile. But when will they smile?" In his reports from La Spezia, the Livorno-born Torelli still speaks like a Latin male. And like an Aryan ethnologist: "At the pier the elders stand dressed in black. . . . Figures that seem embossed in bronze with their haughty bearing, those curly beards, the vigorous features of their noses, chins and cheekbones." The postwar Italian press can't magically get rid of their old stereotypes.[62] However, the prolonged meeting with the thousand Jews of La Spezia calls for a new openness of spirit in journalists like Torelli. And when, during the eight days of Passover, the Jewish refugees—who have agreed to stop their hunger strike—are forced to celebrate Passover rituals with whatever is available, the reporter is almost moved by the psalms sung by the elders on the quay, by the unleavened bread, by the dances hinted at in the moonlight. On April 19, "Passover on the La Spezia Pier" is the front-page headline of *Corriere della Sera*'s afternoon edition.[63]

Up and down the *Fede*, Milziade Torelli strikes up "friendships" (so he writes) with "three Jewish girls of Grodno": Gisia, Joha, and Lola.[64] Another girl stuck in La Spezia was originally from Warsaw. In April 1946, Nina Boniówka was not yet sixteen. She had been a spectator four years earlier of Tagore's *The Post Office*, performed by Dr. Korczak's children at the Orphan's House in Sienna Street. She had been saved, on Umschlagplatz, in the last days of the ghetto uprising. After the war, she had arrived in Italy with a group of orphans from Łódź and had been briefly hosted at the Youth Aliyah House in Selvino. From Sciesopoli, she had left for a refugee camp in Ostia with her best friend, Eva Ginat: a girl too old to stay in Selvino, a twenty-year-old survivor of the Łódź ghetto and the Birkenau selections.[65] Who knows whether Torelli had also met Nina and Eva on the La Spezia dock, waiting for weeks with the other thousand for the conclusion of the political and diplomatic dispute, and threatening the resumption of a hunger strike all the more difficult to sustain after having suffered from hunger for years. All to garner the solidarity of La Spezia's inhabitants, Christians as well as secular, mobilized in favor of Jewish migrants, until the long-awaited day when the *Fede* and *Fenice* would raise anchor and sail the Mediterranean in the direction of Eretz Israel.[66]

The effects of the La Spezia crisis also weigh on Moshe Zeiri's personal crisis as he is urgently summoned to Naples by the British military engineers. There is no one to ask, Moshe laments in a letter to Yehudit; from Milan to Rome, the Zionist emissaries are all busy with the question of the *Fede* and *Fenice*. So the Sciesopoli director, before arriving in Naples, cannot figure out the connection between his call to report and Hashomer Hatzair's anti-Gordonia plots.[67] One even wonders whether a link really existed, or whether the attack against Zeiri may have come rather from the circles of religious Zionism, from the emissaries—between the Center for the Diaspora in Rome and the refugee camps scattered throughout Italy—who operated so that the work of caring for the very young respected the minimum requirements of an Orthodox education. Surely voices must have been raised by the emissaries about the "terrible situation" in which the orphans from observant families found themselves in Sciesopoli. That is, (according to the calculations of the critics) about 80 percent of the total—all raised in Selvino's Youth Aliyah House without even a shred of respect for the precepts of tradition.[68]

In the kitchens of Sciesopoli, the critics reported, after a necessary inspection, the dishes for meat and those for dairy products were systematically confused. And the food served to children and teens wasn't even remotely kosher. Not to mention the prayer room: a real "disaster." However, when would the guests of the Youth Aliyah House ever have the time to pray properly? In the morning—after making their beds, raising the flag, and then gymnastics—the prayer was skipped completely. And even the beginning of Shabbat, late Friday afternoon, was not observed with respect for the exact time of sunset: candles were invariably lit at eight in the evening. So even though the most zealous emissaries had taken advantage of their inspection in the Bergamo area both to honor the house with a Torah scroll and deliver phylacteries to the male boys who requested it, the prospects for a religious education remained very bleak in Selvino.[69]

On this basis, Zeiri's opponents did not hesitate to ask for his "removal," even hoping that this would prove "timely." Nor did they hesitate to envisage a forced separation of Moshe's children. They imagined leaving the Selvino House after entrusting it to a new director, with the vast majority of orphans being those who wished to receive a spiritually Orthodox education. And they would get rid of the small minority of orphans "who have become truly anti-religious" by handing them over to a refugee camp along the lines of the secular Hashomer Hatzair.[70] No surprise, therefore, if Moshe started talking—in letters to Yehudit—of a "war" waged against him to rob him of Sciesopoli only to claim, a few days later, that he had come away with "full victory." Whatever the case may have been, at the end of the crisis, two things are clear. First, that Zeiri the sapper has been transferred to another Royal Engineers company, the 524th Field Service Coy. The second, that Zeiri has been reauthorized to run the Selvino orphanage as director.[71]

Moshe leaves Rome and Naples, and he arrives in Milan on March 23, 1946, two days after Easter: the very same evening that a group of neofascist militants broke into the Musocco cemetery looking for the body of Benito Mussolini in the hopes of symbolically resurrecting him.[72] On that Tuesday afternoon, the director of Sciesopoli travels by car from Milan to Selvino. Once on the high plateau, he has the satisfaction of discovering how the entire Jewish colony has prepared to celebrate his return. At lunch, many of the kids do not eat; they scatter around to collect wildflowers. Others are allowed to go beyond the gate, toward the center of the village, to meet the director's car. "I told the driver to stop, and even though it was a small Jeep, I took them all." Upon arrival in the Sciesopoli courtyard, the older boys carry him in triumph. But "the most moving thing was the chant of adults as well as kids, 'Moshe, Moshe' was all they could find to express what they had in their hearts."[73]

The orphans of Sciesopoli don't even have time to enjoy Moshe's return before having to mobilize for the May Day celebration: readings, songs, and a crowded procession along the streets of Selvino.[74] May Day—Labor Day—is an important holiday in kibbutz culture. In fact, from the Kibbutz Hanita, Moshe's children who have already ascended to Palestine write about it. They left brothers sisters and friends in the mountains of Bergamo, and now they maintain regular contact with Sciesopoli through open letters or private letters. Shmuel Boim tells of their first May Day in the land of Israel. Early in the morning, they left Hanita for Haifa. And in the city, they joined the immense procession, "all the workers from all movements" on the slopes of Mount Carmel; "there were 16,000 people" ("even a few Arab workers participated as well, but very few"). After all, explains Haim Luftman in another letter sent to Sciesopoli, from the heights of Hanita in the evening, you can make out the lights of Haifa and its port with the ships at anchor in the distance. A wonderful show. You'd think you were at the cinema.[75]

A week after May Day, Sciesopoli gets a visit (or inspection) from Gershon Gelbart, an American educator seconded to Europe as an official of the Joint who had gained experience in the most important Jewish refugee camp in Germany, the Feldafing camp, near Munich.[76] Together with UNRRA, the Joint is the main financier of the Selvino Youth Aliyah House. The American organization therefore reserves the right to verify the quality of the services provided. However, the Joint has a reputation for not being very sensitive to the ideological values of Zionism, so in theory the inspection might lead the director of Sciesopoli to worry. In reality, Zeiri cannot know, but Gelbart's report on Selvino is largely positive, almost enthusiastic. The "rehabilitation of children," writes the Joint official, is pursued in Sciesopoli "with intelligence, devotion, and effectiveness." Based on the pedagogical model of self-help, on the kibbutz criterion of integrated education as a way of life, and on the "firm leadership" of Moshe Zeiri, "the institute is one of the most brilliant achievements of our entire program in Italy."[77]

A competent educator, Gershon Gelbart was also a refined intellectual. Before the war, he had defended a doctoral thesis in Philadelphia on Marrano literature in Renaissance Italy. In particular, he had studied a Portuguese work published in 1553 in Ferrara, Samuel Usque's *Consolation of the Tribulations of Israel*.[78] The day after Gelbart's visit to Selvino on May 8, 1946, the tribulations of the thousand descendants of the Chosen People who had been blocked for over a month on the Pagliari pier in the port of La Spezia come to an end. The standoff between Zionist militants, Italian authorities, and British authorities concludes with a victory for the Jews. That day, following the London government's capitulation, both Aliyah Beth ships, the *Fede* and *Fenice*, take off from La Spezia and set sail for Haifa. And in their case, it is no longer a matter of illegal immigration. The thousand passengers have received formal authorization from London to move to Palestine.

Nina Boniówka brought a black leather notebook with her on board the *Fede*, where she could write down her emotions as a Shoah orphan finally within reach of the finish line, ever closer to the Promised Land. The humble memento is preserved today—like the Wexler radio—at the Ghetto Fighters' House Museum, in Western Galilee. A page of that notebook contains a few lines, written in Polish, which I imagine Nina addressed to Eva Ginat, her grown-up friend, whom she followed step by step from Łódź to Selvino and then from Ostia to La Spezia. As sparse as they are tender, Nina's words form something like a poem:

> Roses above
> Lemons below
> Let's go to Palestine together.
> Your friend from the orphanage
> Nina Boniówka.[79]

CHILDREN IN THE PROCESSION

In the land of Israel, Nina Boniówka would find more than roses and lemons. From the spring to the summer of 1946, the landscapes of Palestine were becoming less and less fragrant. In civilian life, relations between Arabs and Jews were tense. In political life, David Ben-Gurion and the other heads of the Jewish Agency were in an uncomfortable position. For a year after the end of the war, they had worked together with the leaders of Zionism's extremist wing, starting with Menachem Begin and the paramilitary organizations controlled directly by the Agency—the Mossad secret services, the underground units of the Haganah, and the Palmach's elite corps—that had contributed to the bombings as much as the Irgun terrorists. But on June 29, 1946, the evidence of close collaboration between the different factions of the Jewish resistance movement pushed the British authorities to conduct a police operation that went down in the history of Zionism as "Black Saturday." It entailed curfews, searches, and roundups in Jerusalem, Tel Aviv, Haifa, the kibbutzim of Galilee. Thousands were arrested, including Moshe Sharett, Ben-Gurion's right-hand man.[80]

In response to Black Saturday, Begin orders Irgun militants to strike at the King David Hotel in Jerusalem, headquarters of the British Mandate administration. On July 22, a high-potency bomb explodes, killing ninety-one people. It is a watershed date, after which breaking with Begin becomes imperative for Ben-Gurion if he wants to keep an open channel of dialogue with the British authorities. From then on, in terms of illegal operations, the Jewish Agency decides to invest exclusively in Aliyah Beth. It is also for the purpose of image, because it would send a message to international public opinion. The name of the Jewish Agency would no longer be linked to photographs of attacks, rubble, corpses on the cobblestones, and Zionists in handcuffs.[81] If anything, it had to be linked to the photographs of survivors of the Final Solution: men, women, and children piled on the decks of ships bound for the Promised Land. The happy ending of the *Fede* and *Fenice* crisis at the pier of La Spezia had taught Ben-Gurion and company a lesson: the Zionist cause had less to gain from the terrorists than from the victims. To achieve a future of glory, the Jews of Palestine first had to leverage the tragedy of their past.[82]

And not just their past but their present as well. On July 4, a centuries-old script of accusations, legends, and nightmares is replayed in the Polish city of Kielce. A Christian child goes missing, and there are rumors of a ritual murder. The headquarters of the Jewish Committee is invaded by the crowd, policemen start shooting, and stones are thrown at the helpless. In the end, forty-two Jews are killed, including women and children.[83] It is another watershed date, after which most of the Jews who escaped the Final Solution decide to leave Poland permanently (in the time interval between July 1946 and July 1947, there will be over one hundred thousand departures).[84] The mass exodus is so big that it makes the question unavoidable for Western chancelleries.[85] In the dispatches they send to their respective capitals, foreign ambassadors gathered in Warsaw under the vaults of the Polonia Palace can no longer minimize the situation, especially because the Polish government has authorized Jews to emigrate without a visa, without any bureaucratic formalities. Yet during the summer of 1946 itself, the King David Hotel massacre alienated any residual British benevolence from the Zionist cause. So not only does the London government keep the quotas of legal immigration to Palestine unchanged, at a maximum limit of 1,500 certificates per month, but on August 12, London orders all illegal migrants to be henceforth concentrated in internment camps specifically set up in Cyprus.[86]

The echo of the events in Palestine and Poland is also felt in Italy. Four days after Black Saturday, a procession of "several hundred people"—this is the estimate given by *Corriere della Sera* under the headline "Demonstration of Jews for Immigration to Palestine"—crosses Milan from the Northern Railway Station, through Foro Bonaparte and Via Dante, and down to Via Unione 5. "A large group of children, for the most part blond, led the parade," the Milanese daily explains.[87] They were Moshe's children. In protest against both the police repression in Palestine and the quota policy stubbornly practiced by the

British government, they were not content with joining a hunger strike proclaimed by the Zionists or participating as an institution in a donation for the Jewish National Fund. Accompanied by the director, more than one hundred orphans from Sciesopoli had traveled from Selvino to Milan to publicly assert the cause of the Jews in the streets.[88]

"It was an extraordinary occasion," Moshe told Yehudit a few days later. "How much participatory solidarity was felt on the part of the Italians who watched the procession! Photographers and journalists went along with it, and of course so did the police. The children returned home enriched by a profound experience. There were also the little ones. At our direction, they led the procession. Most of them wore white shirts and shorts, and walked in an orderly way, so they won the hearts of the spectators." Moreover—beyond the positive impact of the Milanese demonstration—Moshe tells Yehudit about the "dark reverberation" aroused in Selvino by the events in Palestine. He talks about the fear, amplified by the distance, that the situation over there could precipitate. And he talks about expecting reliable news amid the uncontrolled rumors about the destruction of kibbutzim, the torture inflicted on the arrested, and so on. "We Jews are not lacking in imagination."[89]

Later in July, Moshe's letters to his wife also contained an echo of the Kielce pogrom, and a forecast of the mass exodus to follow. The exodus's final goal would be the land of Israel, but it would inevitably include Italy as an intermediate stage, because it was impossible to immediately welcome all the Jews fleeing from Poland in Palestine: "For them, as soon as they start killing them there, it becomes necessary to pass through here." And among the refugees, there would inevitably be children and orphans. "So, my darling, don't listen to the advice of those who are convinced that the matter will be resolved quickly." On the contrary, Moshe advised his wife to get busy, knocking on the doors of all the right offices without being ashamed of bothering people. And knocking no longer in Kvutzat-Shiller, but directly in Tel Aviv. To finally get her passport. To finally reach the community of Sciesopoli in Italy. "I need you, the work needs you, and vice versa."[90]

Ten years after Trude Meyer's voyage on the Lloyd Triestino steamship *Jerusalem*, Yehudit too—as had already happened to Zeiri, a volunteer sapper in the Royal Engineers—had to "return to the diaspora."[91] History also imposed an anabasis on Yehudit.

TEN

IN ISRAEL'S WATERS

EXPLOSIVE SHOES

For a long time, Adam had been waiting for a letter from his cousins Karol, Shimek, and Ruth—Uncle Yankl and Aunt Zosha's three children. Like Adam and Dov, they had escaped the Łódź ghetto. They had evaded the roundup of Niecala Street, which proved fatal for Yankl, Henoch, and Shaya Wexler, the brave clandestine radio station operators. Finally, Adam received that letter—from Palestine. It was early July 1946, the same days that the children and youth of Sciesopoli demonstrated in the square in Milan against the quotas imposed by the British on the immigration of Jews. Adam was quick to answer in Polish, from Selvino. On July 8, Adam wrote to his "dear family," to the three cousins who had also escaped and landed in Palestine—like Dov—thanks to the operations of Aliyah Beth. Three siblings saved. But once they reached their goal, they were forced to count the relatives who hadn't made it. In addition to their father, Yankl, there was their mother, Zosha, who was worked to death in the Ravensbrück concentration camp. Grandma Gitel, who starved in the Łódź ghetto. Aunt Mindel and cousin Yosef. Uncle David and Aunt Rosa. Two other uncles, Shmuel and Arieh. Uncle Yitzhak, Aunt Shendil, Cousin Feje. The Final Solution of the Wexler family.

It was "difficult to express" the emotion Adam felt when receiving the letter from his cousins, "but reading, I understood with great pain that there's no longer any hope of life for the rest of the family. . . . Until now I was hoping that maybe, despite everything, it might be possible to find survivors. Today I've lost all hope. Even though you don't talk about it, it seems obvious to me." By now, it makes more sense to speak only of the present, and of the future. Of the Selvino Youth Aliyah House, for example. Situated in a "wonderful place," in the middle of the Italian Alps. "The view is splendid, but since I'm neither sentimental nor romantic... We study Hebrew, and I can already read many books. I'm the most advanced in my class, as I was in the ghetto too." Adam also reads German ("there aren't any books in Polish here, it's a shame") and studies English on his own, from an English–Polish dictionary that was given to him by a friend. Three hundred orphans trained in Selvino for the "future life," a collective existence to be lived in Palestine. "We look forward to the aliyah impatiently. Me even more than the others, since Dov is already there and we will finally be able to meet again. . . . Dov gave me his address, I'll write it down: Dov Wexler, Hanita, C.P. Nahariya, Palestine."[1]

Adam isn't the only one champing at the bit during those midsummer days when Moshe Zeiri is putting together a second group of secret migrants to sail across the sea. After the winter group aboard the *Enzo Sereni*, a summer group is to be embarked on an Aliyah Beth ship and sent to Eretz Israel. On July 15, accompanied by the educator Zippora Hager, forty-six boys and girls leave Selvino for the Jewish refugee camp of Bogliasco, near Genoa. Among all the orphans of Sciesopoli, they are "the best," Zeiri explains to the secretariat of the kibbutz movement in Palestine. They are the most prepared, in terms of their linguistic competence in Hebrew and their ability to adapt to the

Palestinian environment.[2] Among them are the three inseparable friends, Avraham Lipkunski, Yaakov Meriash, and Shmulik Shulman. There are the two Liberman sisters, Adina and Ayala. There are Alexander Czoban, Yaakov Hollander, Romek Shichor, Zippora Balam, and Anita Teitelbaum. They are some of the most exceptional orphans in the house, so seeing them go away is traumatic for the Sciesopoli director. "It's as if one of my limbs had been removed," he wrote to Yosef Baratz after their departure from Selvino.[3]

Few of the students in the advanced Hebrew course are excluded. Adam Wexler is one of them. Another is Lea Spivak, a sixteen-year-old Jewish girl from Volhynia who had saved herself from the Shoah by fleeing east to Uzbekistan and who, once she arrived in Sciesopoli, had made friends above all with the Liberman sisters, who came from the same land. A letter of hers has been preserved, addressed to Adina and Ayala when the two sisters from Rivne were still in Bogliasco, waiting in secret with the other kids from the second group to reach an illegal Aliyah Beth steamer destined for Palestine. "The question is: when will it be our turn to be in your place? This is what worries me, I can't wait any longer," Lea wrote to the two sisters before remembering the moment of farewell, just five days before. With several companions, Lea remained outside the Sciesopoli gate for a while: "We only went back inside when the truck could no longer be seen," after it disappeared on the horizon of the plateau.[4]

A week later, on July 27, 1946, the chief of staff of the Ministry of the Navy in Rome feels it his duty to communicate to the interior minister and the prime minister, who was also acting foreign minister, that suspicious movements were recorded in Bocca di Magra, in the province of La Spezia, the same province where "last April a contingent of Jews who tried to emigrate clandestinely aboard the *Fede* and *Fenice* provoked the intervention of the Italian and allied police authorities." Now, "about 500 Jews ... intend to leave the country with two steamships currently in service."

The admiral commanding the department of La Spezia then asks the navy minister for guidance. He wants to know how to react, also because he has heard of "unofficial instructions" that the interior minister sent to the prefect of La Spezia. In turn, the navy minister wishes to know whether the Italian government intends to notify the allied authorities. Basically, he wants to understand whether he should proceed again as in April, blocking the illegal expatriation of Jews but at the risk of sparking international criticism, or turn a blind eye and let the Jewish migrants sail to Palestine on their scarcely seaworthy ships.[5]

The unofficial instructions given by Rome apparently call for turning a blind eye, so between July 31 and August 2, both ships carrying Jews are able to set sail. Aliyah Beth emissaries called them *Katriel Jaffe* and *Ventitré* as homage to twenty-three Zionist martyrs who died at sea. On one they managed to load about six hundred migrants, on the other about eight hundred (much more than the five hundred reported in the ministerial information). Upon arriving from Bogliasco to Bocca di Magra, almost all the Sciesopoli orphans boarded the *Katriel Jaffe*, where they found a situation no better than what the orphans embarked on the *Enzo Sereni* had experienced: overcrowding, hunger, nausea, indiscipline, violence. On August 11, in the afternoon, while still offshore in the eastern Mediterranean, the *Katriel Jaffe* is intercepted by the British navy. At dawn on August 13, the ship enters Palestinian territorial waters. But the extreme joy of migrants when they recognize from afar the lights of the port of Haifa and the silhouette of Mount Carmel conflicts with the sad reality of Royal Marines escorting the refugees as if they were prisoners.

Precisely from that day on, in fact, the British administration of Palestine applied the new policy on illegal immigration of Jews established by the London government: immediate deportation to the island of Cyprus. The first two ships to undergo the treatment are the *Henrietta Szold* and the *Yagur*, which arrived in Haifa the night before from France and Greece, respectively. Their 1,200 passengers are forcibly transferred to the *Empire Rival* and the *Empire Heywood*, two cargo boats that the British refer to as "liberty ships," but which the Jews describe as "deportation ships." Because what awaits the refugees three miles north of Famagusta, in Cyprus, is nothing more than an internment camp. The British are hastily setting it up with military tents, guard towers, and barbed wire. The Cypriot correspondent for the *Palestine Post* describes the Karaolos camp as an open-air prison. Nor does the Jewish population of Haifa have the opportunity to express their support for the deportees, because the city has been preventively placed under curfew.[6]

Such is the situation on Tuesday, August 13, 1946, when about forty of Moshe's children approach the shore of Israel, just a few meters away, only to discover it is unreachable. But once the *Katriel Jaffe* anchors in the waters off the port of Haifa, some Zionist emissaries—as well as some infiltrators from the Palmach, the elite corps of the underground Jewish army—organize a resistance: the "desperate resistance" that the *Palestine Post* would report on extensively in the following days, which would also make headlines in the international press. The refugees do more than just call for a hunger strike. Both on Friday, August 16 and Saturday, August 17, six hundred of the *Katriel Jaffe* passengers (as well as the eight hundred of the *Ventitré*, which arrived in the meantime) physically resist two attempts by the British military to transfer them by force to the *Empire Rival* and *Empire Heywood*, back in Haifa after having deported the passengers of the *Yagur* and *Henrietta Szold* to Cyprus.[7]

So on the morning of Sunday, August 18, "the second act of the sordid tragedy of deportation," in the words of the *Palestine Post*, is staged. And this time, the soldiers of the Royal Engineers have prepared things to perfection. They have arranged a system of rafts between the two Jewish boats and the two cargo ships, forming a bridge of boats: rafts surrounded by barbed wire, to discourage any escape by water. At one end of the raft system, British engineers have built a turret from which to access the decks of the barges more easily. Equipped with such preventive measures, the Indian Pioneers of the British Army are called on Sunday morning to little more than child's play. They go into action with fire hydrants, forcing refugees from the *Katriel Jaffe* and *Ventitré* to abandon their blankets and take refuge in the holds. They continue with the tear gas fired below decks, which serves to weaken any will to resist further.[8] After emerging from the holds, "people started running along the deck, blindly, to escape the choking fumes." Then, on the rafts prepared by the Royal Engineers, the survivors of the Shoah, men, women, elderly, children, are "searched, disinfected and identified" before being pushed— without being able to set foot on the ground—toward the decks of the *Empire Rival* and *Empire Heywood*.

This is the welcome in Israel's waters that the British administration of Palestine reserves for Avraham Lipkunski, a Polish Jew from Dugalishok; Yaakov Meriash, a Lithuanian Jew from Kaunas; the Liberman sisters, Polish Jews from Rivne; Shmulik Shulman, a Polish Jew from Lutsk; Anita Teitelbaum, a Polish Jew from Lviv; Pinchas Ringer, a Polish Jew from Bielsko. All of them are orphaned Jews, along with dozens of other Sciesopoli orphans. Such is the welcome reserved for 1,400 other survivors of the Final Solution. The next morning, the *Palestine Post* headline on the front page reads, "Tear Gas Overcomes Deportees' Desperate Resistance." Farther down, in the special report from Haifa: "Numerous articles of clothing and other personal effects, with photographs, letters, paper clippings, were found this morning on the bottom of the rafts. As well as a prayer shawl and a couple of phylacteries."[9]

On Monday, August 19, the *Palestine Post* has one more story to tell, announced by the headline on the front page: "Cyprus Ship Forced Back to Haifa by Bomb Blasts." It seemed as if the British military operation was to end around 5:30 on Sunday morning,

with the departure of the two cargoes in the direction of Famagusta, but half an hour later there is a twist: two explosions aboard the *Empire Heywood* cause the ship's commander to return to the port of Haifa. "The explosion were caused by the detonation of two small electric torches containing gelignite. They were introduced into the hold through the hatchway with the object, it is believed, of blowing a hole in the ship's side."[10] The result of the double explosion is to damage the hull seriously enough to force the *Empire Heywood* to turn back—with hundreds of Holocaust survivors detained again for several more days in the waters of the port of Haifa, guarded by Royal Navy units, and barred from ground communication. And yet more important, they are illuminated by the spotlight of the local and international press—starting with the front page of the *New York Times*.[11]

A few years later, after the founding of the State of Israel, Palmach circles will allow the background of the sabotage operation to filter through. The blasting gelatin had already been introduced aboard the *Katriel Jaffe* in the days of the hunger strike by

Zalman Perach, an officer who was an expert in explosives. Three young female refugees (females were preferred to males, in the hope of arousing less suspicion) had accepted the risk of hiding the explosive in the heels of their shoes. The three girls were two sisters originally from Rivne and a friend of theirs originally from Lviv: Adina and Ayala Liberman, and Anita Teitelbaum. They had avoided body searches carried out on the rafts, so the explosive had been transferred from the *Katriel Jaffe* to the *Empire Heywood* thanks to the intrepid efforts of these three Selvino orphans. Once aboard the freighter, they returned the explosives to Zalman Perach, who, pretending to be a refugee, prepared the flashlights to detonate in the holds.[12]

This is how State of Israel will also be born. Thanks to anonymous soldiers[13] like those three Selvino girls, Moshe's children, seemingly above suspicion. In biblical terms: thanks to the saved who save, survivors who redeem.[14]

AVIEL

Eleven months after the "sordid tragedy" of the *Katriel Jaffe*, the so-called Exodus affair would transform the problem of the Shoah survivors rejected by the British at the port of Haifa into a political and diplomatic scandal of international proportions.[15] But the case of the *Exodus* would not have suddenly broken out had there not been a prehistory. This prehistory began in Italy, in the spring of 1946, with the case in La Spezia involving the *Fede* and *Fenice*. It continued in Palestine, with incidents such as that of the *Katriel Jaffe* and various others that followed. Above all, the case of the *Exodus* would involve the problem—the scandal—of the deportation to Cyprus of refugees who arrived in Israel's waters after having escaped the Final Solution of the Jewish problem in Europe. In total, from the summer of 1946 to the winter of 1948–49, there would be over fifty thousand Jews interned in Karaolos, the camp near Famagusta, and in another camp near Larnaca.

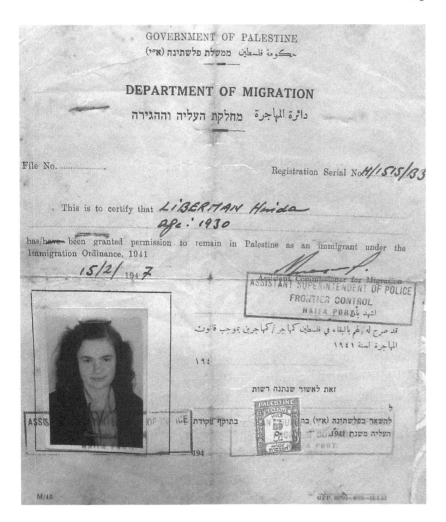

Among them, eight thousand were very young deportees, between twelve and eighteen—six thousand of them orphans.[16]

The forty orphans of Sciesopoli who had crossed the Mediterranean on the *Katriel Jaffe* reached Cyprus on August 27, 1946. They did so from the port of Haifa, aboard an *Empire Heywood* suitably repaired after the sabotage and duly escorted by a British destroyer. According to the *Palestine Post*, during the voyage, none of the passengers had been allowed to go on deck, "except for the use of the toilets, where they were accompanied two by

two." In Famagusta, the six hundred deportees agreed to carry out the disembarkation operations in an orderly fashion, simply singing the "Hatikvah" hymn and shouting, "Eretz Israel!"[17] The Sciesopoli orphans were then taken to Karaolos, where the guardians sorted them into the white tents that constituted (and covered) the landscape of the camp—a barren, desolate, almost lunar landscape, which Avraham Lipkunski and his companions had to get used to, and which Avraham would bring to Israel through a souvenir photo.[18]

In this group portrait, the seventeen-year-old former Talmudist from Raduń showed the straight back and haughty gaze he'd always had. After all, unlike many other Sciesopoli orphans, Cyprus was his first taste of an internment camp. You might as well make the best of a bad situation and take on the role of leader, or at least guide, among the Selvino alumni, at least initially until reuniting with Zippora Hager, the Hebrew teacher who in Bocca di Magra, Italy, had embarked on the *Ventitré* instead of the *Katriel Jaffe* and wound up in a different Cyprus subcamp than that of Moshe's children. So Avraham goes to great lengths, moving from one tent to another in his subcamp. He is now teaching the advanced Hebrew course, and he's the one who gives life to the first study groups—mathematics and poetry. Again, it is Avraham—along with the usual suspects, Yaakov Meriash and Shmulik Shulman—who prepares a new edition of the Sciesopoli newspaper, *Nivenu*, "Our Word." In Cyprus, it would be called *Nivenu Baderech*, "Our Voyaging Word," with a sinister, hand-drawn profile of watchtowers and barbed wire on the title page.[19]

Ever since Zippora Hager reunited with her boys, she is primarily the one who makes sure that Moshe's children maintain some internal cohesion—a team spirit, the Selvino team—in the vast and dispersed Youth Village where the British military administration has meanwhile transferred them. "Everywhere in the camp we were known as the *Kinderlach fon Selvino*," Alexander Czoban would recall a year later, "and it was a really good name. Also because, despite calling us that, the older ones did not treat us as kids at all."[20] The concentration camp regime makes it impossible in Cyprus to preserve the characteristics of the Sciesopoli community, which Moshe Zeiri had modeled on Korczak's Orphan House, as well as on the model of any good kibbutz training school, with self-management and alternating tasks. But with the help of Avraham Lipkunski, of the Liberman sisters, of Romek Shicor—that is, of the kids recognized by their classmates as being especially authoritative—Zippora Hager is ever more insistent on increasing their responsibilities. In Karaolos, the Selvino orphans study a lot, and not just Hebrew, to be ready for the day a British freighter takes them back from Haifa and Famagusta to reach not just the waters of Israel but also its well-deserved land.[21]

In Karaolos, there are also protests both against the London government, for its political decision to deport the Jewish refugees, and the British military administration in Cyprus, for the material conditions of internment. When a delegation of foreign journalists is allowed to visit the camp near Famagusta, the inmates—adults and children—take the opportunity to stage a demonstration in front of photo and film cameras. Marching in a procession against a background of barbed wire, those saved from the Shoah raise controversial banners. "LABOR GOVERNMENT, WHAT ARE YOU DOING?" is written on one of these. "FROM AUSCHWITZ TO PALESTINE VIA CYPRUS" is written on another. In particular, the inmates denounce the lack of infrastructure in the Karaolos camp. The scarcity of soap. Insufficient lighting (eighteen kerosene lamps for forty-two tents). Lack of privacy for married couples. And they categorically exclude the possibility of living with the German POWs from the Afrika Korps, who are also being detained in Cyprus and slated to be settled in a Karaolos subcamp.[22]

In Karaolos, they make love too. Or at least they fall in love. With the novelist's freedom of expression, the Israeli writer Yoram Kaniuk will describe the "unprecedented erotic mania" that "seized everyone" in the Cypriot camp. He will argue that the interned Jews only wanted one thing: to have children. "To perpetuate their race, in spite of those who wanted to wipe it off the face of the earth."[23] These are excessive formulations, but not overly. The forced coexistence of several thousand young men and young women—free to meet within the confines of the camp, if not to seclude themselves somewhere intimate—was quite favorable to the formation of couples. During the two and a half years of the forced internment policy in Cyprus, Jewish marriages celebrated in the two British detention camps amount to over eight hundred, and newborns on the island will exceed two thousand.[24] And even if the erotic craving was limited to the courtship phase, it is also true that the time in Cyprus coincided, for many saved young people, with that of a new availability toward peers of the opposite sex. Having learned to live after death, one could perhaps cautiously try to learn to love.

All the more so because relatively early in the autumn of 1946, at the beginning of November, rumors are circulating about an imminent release of the first contingents of deportees. Of the 1,500 certificates per month that the British administration of Palestine grants for the immigration of Jews, it is said half will be reserved each month for inmates in the two Cypriot camps. So the deed is done for the most part. The arrival of refugees in the Promised Land is no longer in question; it is simply a matter of time. Jerusalem is close, even if in that autumn, the *Empire Rival* and the *Empire Heywood* won't stop their shuttling between Haifa and Famagusta. Several times a month, British freighters deport illegal migrants to Cyprus, whom Aliyah Beth continues to push toward the land of Israel, though the Royal Marines will only allow them to appreciate the waters. But most of the work is done; it's a matter of time. And if Jerusalem is close, then one can start looking around to decide in whose company one wants to get there.

As they look around at the Youth Village of Karaolos, several Sciesopoli orphans look at each other. Yaakov has eyes only for Jaffa. Shmulik always goes to Bronka. Leike listens to Mundek's poems over and over. Anita is sensitive to Romek's charms.[25] What in Italy, within the Alpine landscape of the Bergamo area, was a bond of brotherhood between survivors of the Final Solution, in the Levantine landscape of Cyprus, it can and does become—in more than one case—a lovers' bond between Jews reborn. During the following years, other such bonds will be forged, if not in the Cypriot internment camp then in some kibbutz in Eretz Israel. Other Sciesopoli orphans will look into each other's eyes and realize that they want to take the road to Jerusalem together. Dov Wexler and Sara Goldman. Avraham Kutner and Zippora Balam. Yaakov Bander and Miriam Leiter. Moshe's newlyweds.

Avraham Lipkunski and Ayala Liberman will realize as much too. In the Karaolos camp, between a Hebrew course and a meeting for the newspaper, they began looking at each other differently

than before. And six years later, when they get married on June 9, 1952, in a small street in Tel Aviv at the office of a rabbi—too penniless to afford a ceremony in the synagogue[26]—they will decide to give themselves a new surname. No longer Lipkunski or Liberman, but Aviel: a surname that joins together the Hebrew consonants of their names, Avraham and Ayala. It shows to what extent the son of the blacksmith and seamstress from Dugalishok and the daughter of the pharmacists from Rivne felt that they had become one by being reborn.

EVERYONE'S DAD

For Moshe Zeiri, the departure from Selvino of the second group of illegal immigrants by sea was, on July 15, 1946, as traumatic as the amputation of a limb. But the Sciesopoli director was not a man to feel sorry for himself. Nor could he afford to, with all the work he had. There was the daily management of the institute. Correspondence with Zionist emissaries in Italy and with the kibbutz movement in Palestine. The organization of trips for children and teenagers in that first summer in the mountains of Selvino—organization made more demanding by the departure of Reuven Donath, the hiking specialist, who returned to Israel after his marriage to Noga. And Moshe couldn't neglect the Sciesopoli orphans' musical education—indispensable for a music lover like himself—which inspired him, in the beginning of September, to accompany dozens of the kids to Milan to see Bizet's *Carmen*, staged by the Teatro alla Scala (albeit a postwar Scala, still housed in the Palazzo dello Sport).[27]

Zeiri must also take care of external relations. Indeed, between pogroms in Poland, ships in the Mediterranean and attacks in Palestine, the fate of the European Jews who escaped the Final Solution has become a matter of general interest even in an Italy preoccupied with postwar reconstruction, the birth of the Republic, and the works of the Constituent Assembly. Shoah survivors make the news, and it is important, for the purposes of Zionism, that Italian public opinion feel involved in their vicissitudes. So it must have been considered a media score for Zeiri when, a few weeks after the Milan trip to see *Carmen*, a long article was published by the afternoon edition of *Corriere della Sera* with the headline "Poor Little Orphans, the Jews of Selvino."[28]

Signed by Ferruccio Lanfranchi, the article is based on a diligent inspection in Sciesopoli, but also (probably) on appropriate suggestions by Moshe Zeiri, who by now spoke Italian well. After having summarized the circumstances of the settlement of foreign Jews at the "summit of Selvino," in "that corner of earthly paradise" where the model resort of Milan's fascists was founded at the time, the reporter lists the first groups of orphans departing for Palestine. He emphasizes the existence of a link between the "racial hatred" still widespread in Poland and the new waves of refugees to be expected in Italy. He announces a diplomatic commitment from the De Gasperi government, which "has recently given transit permission for about ten thousand Jews" from Central European camps. He specifies that "among these there will be 500 young boys and girls, 200 of whom will be welcomed at the 'Sciesopoli' of Selvino." And he adheres to the "mirage" of the "last survivors of a biblical massacre of millions": the landing in the "promised land of the ancestors." Except that to reach Palestine, one must "deal with the Arabs and, above all, with the British."[29]

From the title to the conclusion, Lanfranchi's reportage is cloyingly sentimental. The poor orphans of Selvino "are as insensitive to joy as they are to sadness: indifferent to everything. All sensitivity has atrophied in them. They look with tired, absent eyes at the green of the meadows, the blue of the sky; they eat greedily, as if to make up for long, exhausting fasts.... There is no light of joy in their eyes, no mirth in their movements.... Most don't even remember their parents' faces.... 'Mom! Mom!,' these little ones seem to be saying. But for most of them, their mothers are gone forever." In Lanfranchi's depiction, the children of Sciesopoli become nothing more than painful sugar paste figurines straight out of the novel *Heart* by Edmondo De Amicis. And yet it felt good, for me, to see Moshe Zeiri's name written so clearly in *Corriere della Sera*. One might even say that it was right. In any case, it was significant to find, in the columns of the major Italian newspaper, both a compendium of Moshe's anabasis and a definition of his project: the rebirth of Shoah orphans as kibbutzim founders in the new Israel.[30]

"The apostle of this creed is a teacher who came from Palestine, Moshe Zeiri, a soldier of the Royal Engineers who took part in the war as one of the Palestinian Volunteer Corps. Already in Cyrenaica he and his fellow soldiers gathered Jewish orphans and founded a Zionist school in Benghazi, with the help of their officers and secretly from the English. Moshe Zeiri came to Milan in the wake of the allies and immediately wanted to know if there was a Jewish school and what had happened. Indeed, there had been one in Via Eupili, but the building was occupied and looted by the Germans, who even removed the water pipes. Palestinian volunteers went fundraising to get the school back up and running. Then they went around looking for orphaned children. They collected about thirty of them, taking them away from the Catholic institutes where they had found refuge and salvation. Gradually the initiative developed. Hundreds of children without families flocked in with the tide of refugees who survived the horrors of the 'concentration camps.' It was necessary to give them hospitality and education.... They also try to instill in the young people a love for the land and the spirit of solidarity that prepares them for communal life: because in Palestine they will have to found new villages where nothing exists yet. In a certain sense, they are being prepared for a return to the tribe. And then other families will replace those destroyed."[31]

On Wednesday, September 25, 1946, Moshe waits at the arrivals hall of the Naples maritime station. Who knows whether he is holding a fresh copy of *Corriere della Sera* in his pocket when he runs to meet a brunette woman and a blonde girl who have disembarked from the steamer *Cairo*, when he is finally able to hug his wife and daughter? He hasn't seen them in more than two and a half years, since February 1944. But here, on the exact day of their arrival from Palestine, Moshe could show Yehudit and Nitza that page of the most authoritative newspaper in Italy. Here it is, black on white, the gist of the whole story. The distance from the apostle's home, which seems interminably long, has not been in vain. It had at least served the poor orphans of Selvino. And as the newspaper stated, the job is not yet finished. Other little orphans, hundreds of them, are said to be fleeing Poland. They are expected in Italy and in Sciesopoli. After all, hadn't Moshe explained it to Yehudit a few weeks earlier, in the aftermath of the Kielce pogrom? At that time, he could still speak to her, but only in writing, through yet another letter of an endless correspondence. "For them it is necessary to come through here, ever since they started killing them there." From now on, however, everything will be different. Because now, finally, all three of them are together. Now Yehudit and Nitza will also be in Selvino. And for the two parents, there is Mussolini's room.

At the Naples maritime station, Yehudit arrives at the customs with a British Palestinian passport issued in Jerusalem in early September. Born in Cologne in 1920, the "kindergarten teacher" resides in Kvutzat-Shiller, and she is five feet two inches tall with brown eyes and brown hair. Her currency assets declared to customs are a miserable sum of twenty Palestinian pounds.[32] But in Yehudit's suitcases, there must be at least something of what Moshe, during the summer, asked her to bring. "I don't need anything. The main thing for baggage is to take books.... I go back to saying: bring books, lots of books." Above all, a Bible. And then children's books: grammar, arithmetic, science. And books of literature, "Eretz-Israel's beautiful literature. About the lives of children, about life in the East." And then, in addition to books, material for the holidays, and musical instruments. Nothing particular with regard to Nitza's clothing, because it's easier to find what she needs in Italy. "We'll get her a little fur coat and other suitable clothing. I think the little sabra will have fun in the snow."[33]

The little sabra who has never seen snow in her life is sure to have fun as soon as autumn comes and the mountains of Selvino begin to turn white. In Sciesopoli, Nitza is part of the group of younger children, aged three to nine,[34] the very group that the director has entrusted to Yehudit. Fifteen pupils in all, and each with a different level of preparation, Yehudit recounts in

a letter to her friends in Kvutzat-Shiller. And that is apart from the linguistic Babel of the class: except for Yiddish, Italian is the most widely spoken language, to which are added Polish, Hungarian, and Russian. Too bad that Yehudit, the teacher, does not know any Italian, and the children understand very little Hebrew. "None of them, apart from two, can read or write in any language." Although uneven, it is still a good group. "The children are happy, healthy and in good physical condition, even if some of them look younger than their age because they're small." Yehudit is confident that she can work well with them.[35]

But a few weeks after her departure from Palestine and arrival in the Bergamo area, Yehudit suffers as a result of the tragic news that reaches her in Selvino: the death of her father, hit by a British military vehicle. It happened on October 15 in Ramat Gan, a suburb of Tel Aviv, near the police station. Heinrich Meyer was riding his bicycle, and for some reason, he didn't see the policeman's motorcycle coming.[36] In the family, the accident would be explained by the disability that the reservist of the Landsturm Infanterie carried with him since World War I: the loss of sight in one eye. Yehudit's father died at the age of sixty-six after doing everything to live his second life to the fullest—unlike his wife, Wilhelmina, and unlike so many other German Jews who fled Hitler's Germany at middle age, and who lived in the land of Israel like in a hotel, with their minds and hearts still in a world of the past, the morning paper, the stock exchange, the opera, the holidays.[37] That was not the case for Heinrich Meyer, who had had the strength to take action: Hebrew courses for adults, opening the butcher shop, non-kosher meat to sell to the nonbelievers in Tel Aviv, no matter what the rabbis of Jerusalem shouted. Until he came to a road crossing in Ramat Gan, and a motorcycle popped out from nowhere.

In Selvino, Yehudit also suffers because her daughter, Nitza, according to the rules of proper kibbutz education, must be separated from her parents. She was placed in the female dormitory, along with the other girls of group 6. Yet in Palestine, in Kvutzat-Shiller, Yehudit had taken on the responsibility of sleeping with Nitza. As Moshe's military service was prolonged, she challenged the sacrosanct principle of the children sleeping together, judging that in the absence of the father, the girl needed the close presence of her mother. Now, in Sciesopoli, Nitza sleeps far from both her mother and father, and she is visibly distressed. In general, Nitza suffers from being treated by Moshe—always impervious to any form of favoritism—like a child of Sciesopoli rather than his daughter. And she suffers, as one of Moshe's children, because of the love between her father and the other children. "My dad was everyone's dad," she would sum up nearly seventy years later.[38]

On the identity card issued to him that autumn by the municipality of Selvino, the father of all the Sciesopoli children appears

(oddly) as a citizen of Poland, and by profession he is a "professor." In the passport photo, he no longer has anything bohemian from the ID issued by the British authorities in Tel Aviv a decade earlier—the one with long hair blowing in the wind, dark shirt open at the neck, in which "Moshe Ze'iry" was a "labourer." His hair is now short and combed, a light-colored tie diligently knotted under the collar of his striped white shirt. But Moshe's eyes still have that magnetic, rapacious gaze of the shtetl son who felt like a revolutionary. And again Moshe's forehead, like ten years earlier, appears marked beyond measure compared to his age; it does not look like the forehead of a thirty-two-year-old man. Around his eyes, early wrinkles have gouged out deep furrows. The father of all the Sciesopoli children is an apostle who has always put his entire being into spreading the word.[39]

Fortunately, Moshe Zeiri can count on the now unconditional support of the Joint. It hadn't been like that from the start—far from it—both because the American assistance organization's intervention philosophy corresponded poorly to the Zionist ideal, and because the leaders of the Joint in Italy had struggled to recognize the exceptional nature of Sciesopoli: the extraordinary quality of the Shoah orphans' rehabilitation experience at the Youth Aliyah House in Selvino. An internal report dated November 29, 1946, admitted frankly: for too long the Joint had shown "confusion and indecision" regarding the Selvino institute, which was also a "spearhead" of the Italian program. "Its leader, Mr. Zeiri, who was only recently formally appointed director, retroactively with respect to his dismissal from the Armed Forces, had to contend with an attitude of petty jealousy, Prussian bureaucracy, hostile interference and unfulfilled promises." Only recently had the Joint "begun to honor its commitments with Selvino."[40] Better late than never. The full support of the Americans is all the more necessary for Zeiri, as the house is preparing to welcome a particularly large group of orphans.

For the moment, the "500 boys and girls, 200 of whom would be welcomed at 'Sciesopoli'"—about which the afternoon edition of *Corriere della Sera* had written in the report on the poor orphans of Selvino—owed less to the Joint than to the Italian ambassador in Warsaw, Eugenio Reale. In fact, as early as August, he had been the one to urge the De Gasperi government to send a signal of humanitarian availability to what remained of the Jewish community in Poland. After the Kielce pogrom, Belgium and France had declared themselves ready to receive 750 Polish Jewish orphans. The ambassador in Warsaw had insisted that the newborn Italian Republic also play its part. So despite a diplomatic picture of an incipient Cold War, Reale, the Communist leader—and husband of a twenty-three-year-old Jewish orphan, Shulamit Kacyzne—had ended up getting that precise commitment from Rome: five hundred boys and girls do arrive in Italy.[41]

On December 4, 1946, "97 children of various nationalities, meant to be concentrated in Selvino," entered the national territory through the Brenner Pass, according to what the prefect of Bergamo communicated to the interior minister (in fact, "a more limited number actually got there because in Milan some of them were directed elsewhere"). Jewish children, "already in the 'Sciesopoli' organization's building," are added to another hundred children like them, "almost all" coming "from the concentration camps of Germany, Poland, Russia, Austria, etc." But in the inevitably bureaucratic jargon of the prefect of Bergamo, Moshe's children are nothing more than unidentified foreigners, to be brought to the attention of the Directorate General of Public Security. "Presently there are about 200 people in the aforementioned Colony without identification documents, and we know of their stay only from the lists of names requested and transmitted by the Municipality of Selvino."[42]

Beyond the border, in Switzerland, the Shoah orphans are one of the hottest subjects of the Twenty-Second Zionist Congress in Basel, a congress held in December 1946, in which Moshe Zeiri participates along with hundreds of other delegates from all over the world. In Palestine or in the Diaspora, what education should be given to the children and youth whom the Final Solution had deprived of their parents? An Orthodox education, the delegates of religious Zionism insist at the congress: the same (they argue) that their parents would have given them if they had remained alive. Whereas the delegates of Labor Zionism argue for a secular education: the same that children and youth ended up choosing during the years of persecution and extermination. In Basel, the staunchest delegate in defending secular education is Pinchas Lubianiker, founder of Gordonia and leader of Mapai. He warns religious Zionists against "holding a contest around murdered parents.... They were the parents of all of us. We all grew up in traditional Jewish families, and none of us have a monopoly on the last wishes of our parents."[43]

In a corner of the room, Moshe—Rivka Kleiner's little brother and Lubianiker's fellow countryman from Galicia and Kopychyntsi—presumably nods, agreeing with him. A year earlier, precisely on the issue of secular education, Zeiri had clashed with Max Varadi, Matilde Cassin's boyfriend, and a few months earlier, between Rome and Naples, he had succeeded in repelling the offensive waged against him by the religious Zionists. Zeiri certainly takes advantage of the Basel Congress to seek useful resources for the development of Sciesopoli. In particular, he knocks on the door of the ORT, the Jewish organization for professional training—the same one that had guaranteed him an apprenticeship as a carpenter in the Lviv of the thirties. And the people in charge of the ORT are open to him. Within a few days after the end of the Zionist Congress, funds have already been allocated for two quarterly courses to be held in Selvino, one for carpenter apprentices and the other for electrician apprentices. By Christmas Eve, "the woodworking benches for this purpose have already been purchased," a scrupulous Swiss ORT official assures from Geneva.[44]

ILLEGALS OF THE SEA AND ILLEGALS OF THE AIR

It is a very special Hanukkah festival that Avraham and about twenty other Selvino children celebrate on a British cargo ship between the evening of Wednesday and the morning of Thursday, December 18–19, 1946. It is the Festival of Lights to commemorate the rededication of the Second Temple. But it is also the celebration of a new consecration, because it marks the date of their arrival in the Promised Land. On Thursday, at the port of Haifa, "the police supervised the landing operations in the presence of military units," the *Palestine Post* reported the next day. Police or not, five hundred survivors of the Final Solution, coming from the two internment camps in Cyprus and destined for the detention camp of Atlit, saw the recognition of their legal right to live their life after death in Eretz Israel.[45]

The hour of freedom strikes at eleven in the morning on Sunday, December 29. Avraham Lipkunski, Romek Shichor, and a handful of other Sciesopoli alumni leave the Atlit camp by bus for Kiryat Shmuel, a suburb of Haifa. They no longer have to respond to orders from British police; they must only respond to the hosting Zionist organizations. Yet once off the bus, Avraham is less radiant than he might have imagined. Perhaps he is thinking about his comrades left behind, among the tents of the Cyprus camp—Shmulik, Yaakov, Adina, Ayala. Or about the tears of Anita Teitelbaum, who at the moment of saying goodbye to Atlit refused to let him go. "I don't know why I feel so depressed," he confides in a journal page. "Maybe because of Anita's tears. Or because of the landscape's very Arabian aspect." From Atlit to Kiryat Shmuel, through Haifa, not a single sign is written in Hebrew—all are in Arabic. "We've traveled many miles, and have seen nothing but Arab houses or military camps. And barbed wire on top of barbed wire, as if a war were going on here. Who are we fighting against, and why?"[46]

Who were they fighting against, these the Jews of Palestine, including those—like Moshe's children—who survived the Europe of the Final Solution? In the waters of Israel, they fought against the British. But in the land of Israel, were they not preparing to fight against the Arabs? And no longer in terms of readiness and cunning, with towers and palisades, as before World War II, but on an open field of combat, with no quarter—us or them. If that was the case, then perhaps the day that Yosef Baratz, the pioneer of the kibbutz movement, had feared since 1933 was imminent: the day when the Jews of Palestine would lose the essential quality of Diaspora Judaism, the virtue of compassion. The day of excessive patriotic instincts was imminent, the day in which the generation of children who abandoned all the tenderness of their fathers would lose their humanity.

In any case, for the moment there was still a fight against the British in front of that port of Haifa, which Zionist propaganda had depicted for decades as an enchanted landing place, though lived history turned it into an accursed dock. There is the need to fight like the illegal immigrants of the steamship *Ulua* did in early March 1947, in one of the most epic battles in this epic story of illegal migration by sea when the ship was sighted offshore by a Royal Navy submarine. It arrived in Haifa, escorted by five destroyers. British commandos tried to board, and furious scuffles broke out on the bridge. The commandos had to use tear gas to board. The *Ulua*'s commander deliberately chose to guide the ship aground on the beach. About fifteen daring Jews attempted to escape by swimming but were immediately captured by the marines. The captain and the officers of the boat were all arrested. All the passengers were transferred with special closed lifeboats from the beached steamer to the docks of the port, where they boarded cargo ships and were deported to the Karaolos camp in Cyprus.[47]

Among the dozens of ships that Aliyah Beth emissaries illegally sent to the shores of Palestine, the *Ulua* was the one that made the longest route; it came from the port of Trelleborg, in Sweden, where it had loaded more than six hundred passengers. After weeks of navigation and stops, from Copenhagen to Le Havre and from Gibraltar to Algiers, she approached the beach of Metaponto, in the Gulf of Taranto, where she hectically boarded another seven hundred illegal immigrants. From there, the steamship left with its cargo of Final Solution survivors only to come up against the overwhelming forces of the Royal Navy in the waters of Haifa. In all this, the most paradoxical detail was the identity of the commander of the *Ulua*: Lova Eliav. He was the talented Russian Jew who had served as a gunner in the ranks of the British Army since 1940, eventually enlisting as a volunteer in the 745th Royal Engineers. Also, he was Moshe Zeiri's companion during the nights of his journey along the caravan routes of Egypt and Libya, the same one who, decades later, would use the words used by others for Berl Katznelson to describe Moshe: "A terrible soldier, but what a man!"[48]

At the beach of Metaponto, Commander Eliav embarked about fifty of Moshe's children onto the *Ulua*: the third group of illegals of the sea to leave from Sciesopoli. They left at the beginning of autumn and, like the *Katriel Jaffe* orphans, moved to the Jewish camp of Bogliasco, near Genoa. But they were then forced to wait there for months for Aliyah Beth to be able to organize a departure for them as well—no longer from the ports of Liguria, which were now too guarded, but from the shores of Lucania, embarking refugees directly at sea, without the illegal ships even docking. That was how Adam Wexler, among others, had left for the Promised Land. Lea Spivak too. And Shalom Finkelstein, Aviva Czoban, and dozens of others. But they found themselves deported to Cyprus, after the lopsided battle to which the afternoon edition of *Corriere della Sera* dedicated a photo report (under the title "Little Anglo-Semitic Naval Clash off the Coast of Caiaphas") on the same front page that announced, at the top: "First Place Bartali Increases Lead in the 38th Milan–San Remo."[49]

Was the battle of the *Ulua* a defeat? Not exactly. From Cyprus, when he takes up his pen to write to his brother Dov at Kibbutz Hanita, Adam Wexler still manages to think positively. "Even though I saw the homeland only from afar and for a moment, my heart was filled with a feeling of victory. I could see Mount Carmel, which reminded me of the stories I'd heard as a child, and to the north the hills of Galilee shrouded in mist, with the snow-capped peak of Mount Hermon beyond, and my eyes filled with tears. I tried to look inward as much as possible, and with my imagination I could see you galloping over the hills of Galilee. And I thought that, if only you had looked in my direction, you would have seen your brother on the deck of a ship surrounded on all sides by warships, and you would have been beside me in those moments of anguish."[50] For Adam, the battle of the *Ulua* is yet another labor destined to make the landing in the Promised Land more glorious.

Shalom Finkelstein feels likewise. The Polish Jew from Łomża— who in Selvino, when writing in the *Nivenu*, already preferred to express himself in poetry rather than prose—returns to verse in Karaolos, the internment camp near Famagusta and addresses the city of Haifa and the sacred soil of Eretz Israel directly, in a poem entitled "I Will Remember."

> I will remember how our gaze traveled
> the coast we had longed for,
> and we looked at the distant mountains
> barely hinted at in the golden light.
> I will remember how quietly
> our hearts blessed your rivers
> and the soil, fields and furrows
> where your children earn their bread with joy.
> I will remember how we walked into your port,
> hearing the waves breaking on the beach,
> and the throb and buzz of your city,
> and at night the lights that lit your face.
> Then I saw the shore go away,
> farewell to the peaks of your mountains.
> But I will return to you soon, my homeland.
> I will not forget you, I will always remember you.[51]

A few days after the deportation, those of Moshe's children who had traveled on the *Ulua* meet other Selvino orphans who were in Karaolos. They had boarded another illegal ship in Metaponto, which in turn was captured by the British after arriving in the waters of Haifa. Among these is Sándor Weisz. Suti also has to tread the earth of Cyprus before he can get to Eretz Israel.[52]

According to a report by the Joint, in the spring of 1947, there were about 1,800 Jews detained in the two Cypriot camps. Almost one thousand are orphans of both parents, while nearly five hundred have lost either mother or father. About three hundred, however, still have their parents, and one of the three hundred is Shalom Finkelstein, whom the circumstances of the war had separated from his father and mother, but who was preparing to find them in Palestine. There are seventy-two "Selvino

children"—which the Joint document distinguishes from the ninety-two minors affiliated with Gordonia—forty-six males and twenty-six females, all but one aged between thirteen and seventeen. By nationality of origin, about fifteen of them are Romanian Jews. Half a dozen are Hungarian Jews, and another half are Russian Jews. All the rest are Polish Jews.[53]

A theatrical performance is staged in Cyprus between the end of March and the beginning of April. On the initiative of the inmates themselves, under a white awning in Karaolos, they perform a drama that had premiered with enormous success six months earlier on Broadway, New York's flashy theater district: *A Flag Is Born* by Ben Hecht.[54] It was the first starring role for a twenty-two-year-old actor from Omaha, Nebraska, who performed in the Stanislavski mode, a relatively new style in America. In the limelight of the Alvin Theater on Fifty-Second Street, Marlon Brando was the young David, a Polish Jew who escaped Treblinka proudly waving the fledgling flag of the title—the flag with the Star of David. Still, he openly denounced the passivity of the Jews of the Diaspora at the time of the Final Solution: "we heard your silence in the gas chambers." And he mocked the postwar solution of the Western chancelleries, deporting those saved from the Shoah to a desolate Cyprus. He also embraced the logic of the most extreme Zionism, that of terrorism: "We battle the English, the sly and powerful English. We speak to them in a new Jewish language, the language of guns. We fling no more prayers or tears at the world. We fling bullets."[55]

The illegals of the sea won't stop arriving in Cyprus. They come by the thousands, deported by the Royal Navy after waging battles in front of the port of Haifa for honor rather than victory. In April, it's the turn of a ship that the Zionist emissaries, in homage to their prophet, have named the *Theodor Herzl*, with 2,600 passengers embarked in the south of France, but mostly from Belgium.[56] It's the usual story of the intercepted steamer, the asymmetrical fight against the marines (in this case, with a couple of deaths among the migrants), and forced transfer to Famagusta.[57] THE GERMANS HAVE DESTROYED OUR FAMILIES & HOMES—DON'T YOU DESTROY OUR HOPES, reads the banner affixed by the passengers of the *Theodor Herzl* to the deck's railing. Among them—who knows if she's one of the girls on the bridge, in the photo on the internet I'm looking at today—is a fifteen-year-old Belgian, Mathilde Szwarcman, who escaped the Final Solution thanks to a Catholic rescue network active in Brussels. Mathilde may not know it, but she is about to meet her future husband in the Karaolos camp: Adam Wexler.[58]

This is followed, in the summer of 1947, by the sensational story of the *Exodus*, the American ship refitted by the Aliyah Beth in Italy, in the Gulf of La Spezia,[59] which challenges the British government by transporting more than 4,500 illegal immigrants from France to Palestine. It is the largest load of Shoah survivors that the Zionists have pushed into the waters of Israel, and the captain's intention is to imitate what Lova Eliav chose to do with the *Ulua*: deliberately bring the ship aground on a beach, so as to attract maximum attention from international public opinion.[60] In this case, however, the Royal Navy heads them off. The British board the *Exodus* some twenty miles from the coast, take control of it, and sail it to the port of Haifa, where they transfer passengers onto three cargo ships, to deport them to Cyprus. But in the meantime, the "affair" flares up to the point where the Cyprus solution is politically impractical. The passengers of the *Exodus* then begin a backward journey on the Royal Navy freighters that will take them first to France and then even, to the bewilderment of the whole world, to Germany with its Nazi memories.[61]

After the case of the *Exodus*, one can no longer reasonably argue what a certain "Mrs. S."—Ada Sereni, Enzo's the indomitable widow—had declared in June to a journalist of *Corriere d'informazione* (the afternoon edition of *Corriere della Sera*): that Europe and America knew nothing of the treatment reserved by the British government for Jewish refugees arriving in Palestine.[62] After the *Exodus*, no one will be able to feign ignorance with regard to the drama of the ships full of Jews. These vessels, however, arrive in the waters of Haifa even after the passengers of the *Exodus* have been forced to return to Europe. Again, as if in a replay, the ships are boarded by the Royal Navy, and again they are relieved of their human cargo, with those saved from the Shoah to be interned in the Cypriot camps. So in that summer of 1947, the leaders of Aliyah Beth decide to experiment with a different modality of illegal migration: the illegals of the sea try to alternate with illegals of the air.

In code, it's referred to as Operation Michaelberg.[63] For a fee, a couple of American pilots lend themselves to transport a few dozen Jewish refugees on a military cargo plane to an improvised airstrip in a clearing in Galilee. After a first run in Iraq on August 20, the appointment is set for the evening of September 17, in Italy, near Salerno and the area of the renowned Paestum temples. At dusk, the local peasants watch in amazement as an airplane

without any insignia or number touches down on farmland, and with "engines running," the carabinieri of Agropoli would later report, embarks "forty-nine young Jews of both sexes" and then "with a very rapid and perfect maneuver" immediately takes off "for an unknown destination." Upon their arrival at the scene, the police must limit themselves to stopping a middle-aged Italian lady, who was "very excited and anxious," and her Polish driver at the wheel of an Alfa Romeo with license plate number MI 62585. The police search and interrogate the lady at the carabinieri station, and she turns out to be Ada Sereni, "sister-in-law of the former minister" (the Communist Emilio Sereni, Enzo's younger brother and minister of postwar assistance in the second De Gasperi government).[64]

In the interview at the end of June, "Mrs. S." had recommended that the journalist from *Corriere d'informazione* visit a very special Jewish refugee camp: the "children's school" in Selvino.[65] And here, on a September evening, about twenty of those children (teenagers, actually) run at breakneck speed through the Salerno countryside. They run toward an American twin-engine, climb aboard in the blink of an eye, and take off on the first flight of their lives, away from Italy with a southeast route, a technical stop in Athens, and then away again with the lights off through the Mediterranean night, as far as to the air above Israel and to its land. Of the fifty or so refugees that Aliyah Beth emissaries have selected for the second venture of the Michaelberg operation, almost half are Moshe's children because, as Ada Sereni will explain decades later, the boys and girls of the youth groups were especially likely to make it as illegal migrants from the air. "Agile, without the bulk of packages ... without even a bag over their shoulders," they could "jump up into the plane."[66]

In Paestum, Bronka Auerbach jumps up into the plane. She is the girl from the laundry, the one who, with her friend Malka, had caught the attention of the Sciesopoli boys by bathing naked in the laundry tub. Sara Goldman also jumps aboard—four years after another jump, from the sealed carriage, thanks to which she had escaped from the gas chambers of Treblinka at the age of twelve.[67] Sara flies to Palestine, leaving Italy, Europe, and the bloodlands where her entire family had been exterminated behind her. Her father, Yaakov, and her mother, Elka. Her brother Leibel, with her sister-in-law Ester and their little Yaakov. Her brother Mikhael. Her sister, Lea, who in the Lublin ghetto had been tortured to death for refusing to spy. Uncle Shiye and Aunt Luba. Uncle Yitzhak and Aunt Zippora, and her four cousins, Yosef, Shlomo, Khanale, and Pesia. Uncle Motel, Aunt Mania, and Cousin Lea. Everyone except her brother Hersh. Such is the Final Solution of the Goldman family. Sara flies on the American plane to Palestine, and to a life after death. There, in the land of Israel, she will find another of Moshe's children destined to become her husband: Dov Wexler.

ELEVEN

THE ROAD TO JERUSALEM

DREAM OR REALITY

No more letters. Moshe and Yehudit no longer needed to write to each other, or eagerly await the arrival of the mail, to then stack the numbered letters of their endless correspondence one on top of the other. They were now together, in Mussolini's house and in Mussolini's room. They had to separate only when Moshe was traveling: when the director of the Youth Aliyah House in Selvino was called to some mission or other, in Italy or outside (though at least once, Yehudit accompanied him: to the Basel Zionist Congress in December 1946).[1] Everything else was, if not married life, then a communal life within the Sciesopoli community.

Everything else was, at best, the intense routine of a school for training young people to "ascend" to Palestine, with study in the morning, manual work in the afternoon, meals in the refectory, and recreational and sports activities. Albeit with all the obvious differences that came to the Selvino institute from being, so to speak, a Shoah Orphan's House: from the parentless condition of most of its members and the enormity of the grief inflicted on them by the Final Solution. And with all the differences that came to the institute from being, so to speak, a House of the Clandestine Jew, dubbed as such from its implicit but structural link with the networks of illegal migration to Palestine. For Moshe, the rest was mainly accounting, personnel management, and public or confidential external relations. For Yehudit, the rest was teaching work with the little kids from group 6, Nitza's group. And during the course of 1947, it also entailed the commitment of a pregnancy. By the end of the year, she would give birth to her second child, a boy named Avner.

In a sense, Moshe's voice fades out in this story after Yehudit arrives in Selvino. There is no longer a way to gather the immediacy and intimacy of a correspondence with his wife. After Yehudit's anabasis, Moshe's voice becomes Zeiri's voice, a voice that is necessarily more distant, that of the Zionist official in correspondence with his various interlocutors, from both Palestine and the Diaspora: leaders of the kibbutz movement, representatives of international aid organizations, local or national Italian authorities. It is Zeiri's voice at work, always at work. And it is mobilized on two fronts. On the one hand, in Sciesopoli, to continue to welcome, care for, and inspire the Shoah orphans fleeing Europe and determined to reach Eretz Israel. On the other hand, to continue to follow, whether in Palestine or Cyprus, the Sciesopoli alumni who had already left as illegals of the sea or the air. Because Moshe hadn't given up on his project, or dream: to one day gather all of his children in the Promised Land into a single community made up of victims of the Final Solution, reborn as architects of the new Israel. The project, or dream, of a Kibbutz Selvino.

Almost two years after its foundation, the Youth Aliyah House was recognized as a model institution even outside Italy. In May 1947, an internal report by the Joint stressed that the Selvino orphanage had been "enthusiastically described by a group of Swiss pediatricians as 'a children's paradise,' one of the most beautiful children's homes in Europe." Sciesopoli then welcomed 180 of the 595 Jewish minors present in the children's homes managed by the Joint in Italy, and those 180 children, the author of the report explained, formed "a separate community." Almost all of them were orphans, or at least alone and stateless, and had "found a home" in Selvino, so much so that after meeting them, one was right to wonder "if the word 'family' is not a better definition for this group than the standard expression 'children's community.'" There were, however, serious limitations to be reported, with regard to both the cleanliness of the Sciesopoli premises and the children's misbehavior and lack of discipline. Though "very intelligent," Moshe Zeiri was perhaps not up to running such a demanding institution.[2]

The experts of the ORT, the Jewish organization specialized in vocational training, thought differently. They emphasized the merit of the workshops opened in Selvino for both males and females. Dozens and dozens of apprentices—learning to be electricians, carpenters, embroiderers, and dressmakers—grew up in the Youth Aliyah House, and with better results than in the training centers activated at the other Jewish refugee camps in Italy.[3] Evidently, Moshe Zeiri had not forgotten Moshe Kleiner in his attention to these courses. The Sciesopoli director had not forgotten about himself in Galicia, learning carpentry in a course organized by the ORT in Lviv in the early 1930s. Nor had he forgotten that fortunate Zionist slogan, "To build and be built." After the poetry of the pioneers who had inaugurated the redemption of the Promised Land by overcoming malaria, planting citrus groves, and making the desert bloom, they would need the prose of everyday technicians, humble craftsmen of the Jewish state to come.

More and more over the course of 1947, Zeiri had to take care of not only the children present in Sciesopoli but also the absent ones who had left for Palestine, whether they had made it and lived in a kibbutz by now or were still counting the days in the British internment camps in Cyprus (in the autumn, Moshe could tally 200 boys and girls in Selvino and 150 who had already made the aliyah). He didn't only have to write to various

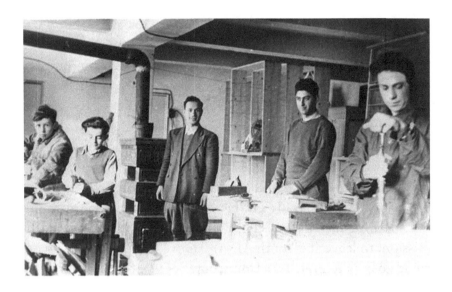

Zionist leaders—evoking the history of the Youth Aliyah House and inquiring about spots available in one of the kibbutzim—or pique the interest of Baratz, whose help could prove useful to the *Kinderlach fon Selvino*: now perceived, in Palestine as in Cyprus, as a separate group, autonomous from Gordonia, and therefore extraneous to the interests of the powerful Pinchas Lubianiker; he also had to correspond with the boys and girls from Sciesopoli themselves, far from sight but close to his heart.[4]

In a June 4 letter addressed to Avraham Lipkunski and Yaakov Meriash, Moshe urged them, in particular, to stay in touch with their Selvino comrades still stuck in Cyprus. He urged Avraham and Yaakov to remember how important it was for themselves, when they were still in Sciesopoli, to receive news from their comrades who had already left and arrived at the Kibbutz Hanita. He said that they should tell their comrades, in letters sent to the Karaolos camp, how beautiful or even exciting their experience was in the community that had welcomed them: the Kibbutz Mishmar Hasharon, along the coastal plain, near the city of Netanya. How they were training for real war with their first real weapons, which they had to hide from the inspections of the

British police by digging holes in the pine trees. About the May Day celebration in the streets of Netanya, waving both the red flag of socialism and the white and blue Zionist flag in procession. And about nights in which the three inseparable friends, Avraham, Yaakov, and Shmulik, would cram themselves into a pup tent to make room, in the dormitory, for Sciesopoli alumni who had just arrived at the kibbutz from the Atlit camp.[5]

This was what Moshe suggested to the apples of his eyes, Avraham and Yaakov. And he took the opportunity to share with them the plan he was working on. He wanted to organize things in Sciesopoli in such a way as to be able to go away for a prolonged mission, to leave the Youth Aliyah House in good hands, so he could go back to Eretz Israel for a couple of months. To go back—after three and a half years—to his world and his previous affections: the smell of the earth around Kvutzat-Shiller, the taste of Rehovot's oranges, the embrace of his mother, Zippora, and sister, Rivka. But also to embrace many of his children, who had already reached the Promised Land. And to discover with them whether the dream of a Selvino kibbutz could ever come true.

THE HANITA BELL

"For those who saw refugees integrate into the kibbutzim . . . during the last bit of the forties, it's as if they were faced with a preview of the resurrection of the dead." Having become a writer, one of those refugees, the orphan Aharon Appelfeld, would find the words to express in literature the exceptionality, the miracle, the beauty of this story, the stunned Shoah orphans resurrected as collective architects of the new Israel. But Appelfeld will also find the words to describe the fatigue, the price, the desperation.[6] Because even though integration in a kibbutz—that is, in a community of families—may have been the most straightforward way of being reborn into a life after the death of the community and family, this integration would nevertheless prove physically and psychologically burdensome. For many survivors, sooner or later it would become an unbearable burden.[7]

Freed from Atlit or Cyprus, Moshe's children were distributed by Zionist organizations, between 1946 and 1947, to a variety of kibbutzim either in Galilee, in the Jordan Valley, or on the coastal plain: not only Hanita and Mishmar Hasharon, also Merhavia, Ramat Yohanan, Avuka, and Kfar Ruppin. There, they experienced not only the vertigo of the weapons to be hidden among the pines, the thrill of carrying flags at the May Day processions, and the poetic nights spent in a tent under the moonlight but also, in spite of themselves, what Moshe himself had had the lucidity to foresee already in the summer of 1945, in a letter to Yehudit: "From an educational point of view, the situation of the survivors is far from ideal. When young people like these arrive in a kibbutz or kvutza, we'll be likely to have forgotten the terrible stories in the newspapers told by some of the witnesses. When they are awkward in their work, or if they fail to integrate quickly, I'm sure they'll attract criticism. It's sad, but that's how it is"[8]

Although the Sciesopoli director had tried to prepare his children for the impact with the harshness of life in Eretz Israel, he had not been able to prepare them, say, for the work of the stonecutter or that of the excavator. Moshe's children were not trained to break rocks on a new terrace of the kibbutz, as Erwin and his companions must do in Appelfeld's autobiographical novel, *The Man Who Never Stopped Sleeping*. Nor were they trained to transport wadi earth in rubber buckets to fill the pits beyond the retaining wall. They were not used to skinning their hands raw with a spade until they bled or numbing themselves with manual labor until they forgot everything else, including any semblance of intellectual life. "We sat down in the refectory, spread jam on a slice of bread and drank tea. We talked about the terraces and life without books."[9] In addition, the director of Sciesopoli was not able (nor did he wish, probably) to prepare his boys and girls for the impact of living with the sabra. The impact was already difficult in the 1930s, for the Zionist immigrants of Moshe's generation. But it was even more difficult after 1945, for those who escaped the Final Solution.

How, for instance, could they accept that hateful nickname, *sabon*? How could they accept that the Jews native to Palestine called the European Jews who had escaped the Holocaust "soap bars," on the basis of the legend that the executioners made soap out of their victims? Nothing expressed more clearly the contempt that certain young and strong sabras felt for some of their peers, gaunt and hungry leftovers of a people who had allowed themselves to be exterminated (this too was said) like a flock of sheep to the slaughter.[10] At the Kibbutz Mishmar Hasharon, Avraham, Shmulik, and Yaakov, along with the other former Sciesopoli members, considered themselves lucky because in the refectory, they were entitled to treatment identical to that of the sabra: same schedules, same dishes, same portions.[11] In other kibbutzim, the "soap bars" (or "numbered ones") had to eat at different times than the sabras, and they were seen to be offered more scarce dishes in both quality and quantity.[12] Not even the epic of a double war fought side by side—the victorious epic of the civil war and the Arab-Israeli war—would be enough to completely break down the wall that separated one from the other. "A wall of blood and silence, anguish and loneliness," as David Ben-Gurion will define it in 1949.[13]

Beyond the prejudices of the sabra, it was precisely the silence and anguish and loneliness that also made the Shoah survivors' integration in the kibbutz burdensome. It was the silence of the survivors, due to the difficulty of evoking what they had experienced. To talk about it among themselves as well as with others, with those who had not lived through it. And to speak about it in that new and obligatory language, Hebrew, a language of redemption because it is the language of the land and the language of arms. But it is also the language of betrayal, because it is an alternative to Yiddish, the language of their parents and the shtetl.[14] It was the anguish of the survivors, perpetually engaged in the effort to silence their memories, to fight the memory the way one fights an enemy.[15] And it was the loneliness of the survivors, fueled by their silence as well as by their anguish. The kibbutz model of life required exactly the opposite: it required them to come out of their own emaciated and tortured selves, to give themselves body and soul to a generous and victorious *we*.

Moshe's children tried. They tried persistently, with passion and courage. Already the first, those who arrived in Eretz Israel on the *Enzo Sereni* and were then welcomed into Kibbutz Hanita, had tried. That kibbutz was emblematic since its inception, founded in the midst of the Arab Revolt to secure somewhat of a foothold on the border with Lebanon for the future State of Israel. They tried, and they succeeded at least for some time, if only thanks to the climate of anti-Jewish hostility that surrounded them upon arrival, which immediately galvanized their determination. Sixty years later, Haim Luftman will tell a Yad Vashem interviewer about the welcome the *Enzo Sereni* boys had received from their new Arab neighbors, the villagers of al-Bassa. "They stoned us. Back then, the very day we got to Hanita. And I couldn't understand it. In Poznan, I told myself, they threw stones at me and yelled at me to go to Palestine. And here I was in Palestine, and they were still throwing stones at me and yelling at me ... where did they want me to go, back to Poland?"[16]

They tried. And they even succeeded when the emissaries of the Palmach (the elite corps of the underground Jewish army) recruited them and began to train them militarily, in the vicinity of one of the kibbutzim. Such was the case of Avraham Lipkunski and Alexander Czoban in Mishmar Hasharon, of Haim Luftman and Dov Wexler in Hanita. "I was an electrician," Haim will recall, "and I worked with a guy from the Palmach. We were part of the First Battalion. We started training with weapons. In secret, it was just '46. And for me to take up a rifle ... to feel that I could shoot ... They also taught us to use a machine gun. A Bren. Later,

I became a Bren specialist, I could take it apart and reassemble it with my eyes closed." And yet Haim Luftman himself, talking to the Yad Vashem interviewer, will elaborate on what made Moshe's children irremediably different from their sabra peers, as well as indecipherable to the gaze of even better-intentioned kibbutz leaders.

First of all, hunger. Try to explain how one fine day, while cleaning the male dormitory, whole loaves are discovered under the beds of the Sciesopoli alumni. Try to make them understand the all-consuming, never-ending hunger of the Birkenau survivors. Moshe didn't understand it in Italy, so how could those responsible for Hanita understand it in Palestine? "They complained that we wasted bread. And we couldn't explain why we hid it under the beds." But it wasn't just hunger. The irreducible difference with the orphans also stemmed from their other ghosts. "I'll give you an example. In Hanita they had this bell, which they used to wake everyone up at six in the morning. It was a metal tube hanging overhead, and they hit it to make it sound. So me and two others went to the kibbutz office and told them this bell reminded us of the concentration camp where we'd been locked up. Don't ring that bell, please. For us, it's terrible. 'Are you crazy?' they answered us. 'This is the bell, and you'll do as we say.' ... So what did we do? I organized a small group. And at night, we stole the bell. We pulled it off the pole and threw it down into crag towards Lebanon. The bell was gone."[17]

For Moshe Zeiri, as for many of his children, cultivating the dream of a Kibbutz Selvino meant hoping that Haim Luftman was an isolated case—just as he had already been in Sciesopoli for that matter, he and his three or four friends from the Magenta band were impervious to any established order. It meant hoping that the majority of Selvino's orphans would prove to be ready to recognize all the differences that separated Birkenau's siren call from Hanita's bell, and that they would prove to be all the more ready, as they are offered the chance to live in a special kibbutz—one with no sabra, or almost. A community of Jews born in Europe and resurrected in Palestine, defined by their condition as young people who escaped the Final Solution. Something different, therefore, from a kibbutz affiliated with any of the movements that animated Zionism (and tore it apart) according to whether they were secular or religious, right or left.[18] Neither a Gordonia kibbutz nor a Hashomer Hatzair kibbutz, nor a Betar kibbutz, nor an Agudath Israel kibbutz. A kibbutz of Moshe's children.

Except that Haim Luftman was not an isolated case. He shared with several other Sciesopoli alumni a growing suspicion of kibbutz philosophy: submitting the *I* to the *we*, sacrificing individual interest to the collective interest, renouncing personal ambition in the name of a togetherness theorized as revolutionary. Did the Shoah orphans really need this? How could they accept the idea of needing this when they were treated by the host kibbutzim almost as if they were aliens? And even though they were treated like human beings—who needed help to get involved in daily life, who could work with the sabras shoulder to shoulder (if they had the muscles for it), to whom the sabras could teach Hebrew, which most newcomers could barely manage—ultimately the orphans were human beings with whom the sabras did not want to identify. Broken people. Broken by life or by death, who knows. In any case, broken by history. Poor human material, too irremediably defective to really contribute to the redemption of the land and people of Israel.[19]

Suti Weisz would also remember this about the Kibbutz Merhavia, where he had asked to go ("I was a leftist then") after his liberation from the camp in Cyprus. There, he formed a deep friendship with a delicate boy from Bukovina, Dan Pagis ("when I think about it, I feel like crying . . . I'll never forget it"), who in the future would become the most important poetic voice of Israeli Shoah literature.[20] "They kept us separate, completely separate from the other kibbutz kids. Same age, but no soccer games together, no songs together, nothing together. And they pointed the finger at us, in public: Tell us, how did you survive? Basically, it was as if they were asking us: How many people did you have to kill to get by?"[21] Suti—who for decades now had gone by the name Yitzhak and had translated his surname into Hebrew, from Weisz to Livnat—recounted this in a lecture I attended myself, at the Ghetto Fighters' House, on January 7, 2016. Before that, I drove with him on a freezing rainy morning along the road from Tel Aviv to Western Galilee, and he told me the reasons for an initiative he had recently taken: to create and finance a master's program in contemporary history, for which he was preparing to hold the conference, the Weiss-Livnat International Program in Holocaust Studies of the University of Haifa.

Suti didn't last more than six months at Merhavia in 1946—six months of breaking stones, milking cows, picking cucumbers or tomatoes—before deciding that such a life was not for him. He left to go work, without much conviction, for a diamond cutter in Netanya. Then he joined the Haganah. He lied about his age, claiming to be eighteen when he was still a minor, just to be recruited into the underground Jewish army.[22] "The only thing I really wanted was to hold a weapon. I felt completely ... unprotected, I wanted to take up a weapon as soon as possible."[23] A Bren or a Sten or anything, as long as it was a proper weapon, a weapon with which to seriously protect oneself and with which to fight the enemy—the British, the Arabs, anyone who got in the way. And yet the young people saved from the Holocaust were at risk of humiliation even in the underground army, where they were also seen as different, strange, broken beings.

THE ENTHUSIASTS AND THE SKEPTICS

Moshe's children were among the first to leave the kibbutzim of Hanita, Merhavia, Mishmar Hasharon, and Kfar Ruppin. Females resisted even less than males in that closed environment, subjected to malicious gossip and rumors about why and how they managed to get by. Many of them looked around, asked for addresses, sent letters, knocked on the door of a near or distant relative, and dispersed through the districts of Palestine. Rivka, Lea, Miriam... a year and a half after the arrival of the *Enzo Sereni* group, only one girl still lived in Kibbutz Hanita, still keeping watch on the tower and palisade bordering with Lebanon. Out of a dozen who had been there, only Malka Shafrir still believed. And also for this reason—at the end of August 1947—Moshe Zeiri left Selvino and Italy. He left the Youth Aliyah House in good hands so he could travel to Palestine on a prolonged mission: to contain the dispersion of his children; to avert the danger of their aliyah in the land of Israel resulting in a Diaspora.[24]

He traveled by train from Milan to Prague. Judging by the stamps in his passport, he spent several weeks in Czechoslovakia (probably engaged in liaison activities with Zionist emissaries) before flying away. He landed at Lod airport on September 25.[25] His arrival in Palestine coincided with two bloody events attributed to the Irgun, the Zionist organization headed by Menachem Begin. On September 26, in Tel Aviv, an armed assault on the Allenby Street Barclays bank resulted in the death of four British policemen. On September 29, in Haifa, four other British police, four Arab policemen, and two Arab civilians were victims of a bomb attack against the police headquarters.[26] Writing about it to Selvino from Kvutzat-Shiller, Moshe says he is as horrified by the violence of the terrorists as he is struck by the attitude of the people: "It seems that by now it doesn't make an impression on anyone." At the time of the robbery and gunfights, he himself was in Tel Aviv, a short walk from Allenby Street. What had followed? A traffic block, a couple of streets cordoned off, nothing more. "They close a part of the road or roads that were damaged, and life goes on as if nothing had happened."[27]

After three and a half years away, Moshe moves far and wide through Eretz Israel. First he travels to northern Galilee, toward the Golan Heights. He goes to Kibbutz Ayelet Hashachar to hug his mother and sister again. Then he reaches the Kibbutz Hanita, where he reunites with Dov Wexler, Haim Luftman, and other Sciesopoli alumni (but Haim has his bags ready by now, and all he can think about is enrolling in the Haganah).[28] In Haifa, he reunites with Reuven Donath and other fellow soldiers of the 745th Solel Boneh Company. He crosses Galilee back to Lake Tiberias, stopping at Degania, the legendary kibbutz founded and animated by Yosef Baratz. A few days earlier, about twenty Selvino orphans had passed through Degania, recently released from Cyprus and headed for Kibbutz Avuka, farther south in the Jordan Valley: "Baratz told me they made a great impression."[29] Finally Moshe returns home to Kvutzat-Shiller. From there, he works to achieve the main goal of his mission: a summit with the delegates of the *Kinderlach fon Selvino*.

The meeting takes place on October 25, 1947, at Kibbutz Kfar Ruppin, in Lower Galilee, on the banks of the Jordan. On the one hand, there is something festive about it. It reunites Moshe Zeiri with some of his favorite children, and it reunites those children with some of the most memorable figures of the early days of Sciesopoli: the driver Moshe Unger, "Fetter Moshe"; Reuven Donath, the animator; and Arieh Soleh, the professor. On the other hand, there is something insidious about the Kfar Ruppin meeting. It becomes somewhat of a showdown among Moshe's children, which pits the enthusiasts against the skeptics: the more resolute orphans, determined to transform the dream of a Selvino kibbutz into reality, against the more cautious or even recalcitrant ones. Enthusiasts prevail among those who have arrived in the land of Israel most recently, those embarked on the *Katriel Jaffe* and *Ulua*, interned in Cyprus, and then gathered in various kibbutzim, but above all in Mishmar Hasharon and Kfar Ruppin. Skeptics prevail among the children who arrived with the first group, disembarked from the *Enzo Sereni*, and almost all gathered in Kibbutz Hanita.

Only one girl is on the record: Lea Spivak. Living in Kfar Ruppin (along with Adam Wexler, who had traveled with her on the *Ulua* and had been interned in Cyprus with her), Lea does the honors of the house. For the rest, the participants are males. Abek, Zeev, Emmanuel, Avraham, Shlomo, Alexander, Moshe, Shmulik, another Avraham, Menachem, and Aharon: at the summit, Moshe's children are Moshe's boys. Perhaps this is because the female Diaspora has been more pronounced than the male one. Or because in Hanita, Mishmar Hasharon, Avuka, Ramat Yohanan, an old unwritten rule of the kibbutz prevailed at the time of appointing the delegates: the ancient Zionist principle that men and women are equal in everything, except when it comes to deciding the important things. In any case, the most dramatic speech at Kfar Ruppin's meeting comes from Shmulik Shulman. During his stay in Selvino, this orphan from Volhynia, the son of a beverage manufacturer from Lutsk, discovered—thanks to the theatrical performances organized by Moshe Zeiri—a theatrical talent that would make him a professional actor when he grew up.

"Each of us," Shmulik reminds his fellow resurrected orphans, "was on his own, unhappily mulling over the recent past. Alone in the world, without even a piece of sky above his head. And with no purpose in life, except to reach Eretz Israel. Each of us was looking for a place where we could rest. We looked for such a place, and found it." That little corner of the world was Sciesopoli. More than a home, it was a family. When they arrived in Cyprus, "they called us the *Kinderlach fon Selvino* not because of our age, but because they considered us the children of a single family." For Shmulik, the real strength of those children had been their ability to see clearly. "We openly discussed the members of the group we considered unsuitable: 'Do we really want to be with these here, build a life with them?'" And even in Eretz Israel, it was necessary to face things without hypocrisy. To Hanita's delegate, Avraham Lindau, who proposes to postpone any choice regarding the foundation of a Selvino kibbutz ("there's no reason to rush decisions, to establish in twenty-four hours what we will be doing for the rest of our lives"), Shmulik Shulman replies with a visionary tone: "Reality is overcoming obstacles, and crowning dreams." And he urges all present: "Let's not break up the meeting without having decided for a yes or a no."[30]

Avraham Lipkunski intervenes in response to Shmulik, his dearest friend. It is useless to cry over spilled milk; "there are many reasons why many have gone, no use trying to blame anyone.... We had no experience, so we didn't always listen to each other and didn't always understand each other." But now they had to look ahead, and do it with the right amount of ambition. The Shoah orphans could and should show themselves as equal both to the Zionist pioneers who had preceded them in Palestine and to their sabra peers. "We must feel the strength of our youth. Despite all the horrors we have experienced, we must not give up on the idea of being able to behave like anyone else of our generation. Of course, the war has shorn us of all we hold dear, it has left us nothing but our spirit. So let's nourish it, this spirit, to walk with our head held high towards the future." If they really couldn't decide there, on the spot, about the creation of a Selvino kibbutz, then they could at least deliberate the establishment of a permanent committee to keep contact among the Sciesopoli alumni.[31]

Finally, the voice of Moshe Zeiri comes through in the minutes. After the Kibbutz Avuka delegate—a Polish orphan, Shlomo Krampf—has ruled for the establishment of a contact committee, the founder of Sciesopoli intervenes to smooth out the rough edges. "I don't want to see a Selvino Party," Moshe warns. No internecine wars between groups, Mishmar Hasharon against Hanita, or whatever. Rather, a work of mending and dialogue, a work of correspondence with the Shoah orphans who still hadn't ascended to the land of Israel. Those still hosted, by the hundreds, in the Selvino Youth Aliyah House, and those who left Italy but were still interned by the dozens in the Cyprus camps. Because the dream of a Selvino kibbutz remained viable, but it required a surplus of human resources. "We need fresh forces, especially girls."[32]

So on the afternoon of Saturday October 25, 1947, the meeting of Kfar Ruppin is adjourned on the basis of a compromise. The delegates of Mishmar Hasharon renounce the request of Shmulik Shulman, the immediate pronouncement for a yes or a no; they are content with a pledge to establish a liaison secretariat between the former members of Sciesopoli and their kibbutz—in the future. As for the delegates of Hanita and the other kibbutzim, they are committed to diligence in maintaining contact with the forthcoming secretariat of Mishmar Hasharon. Moreover, Moshe Zeiri gets all the delegates to sign a telegram of greeting and encouragement to their comrades from Selvino and from Cyprus. Within a fortnight, the director of Sciesopoli also manages to even go to Cyprus. He flies by plane from Haifa to Nicosia to visit the orphans interned in the Karaolos camp, near Famagusta. It is his last significant move before leaving for Selvino, by sea from Haifa, on November 21, 1947.[33]

Moshe returns to Italy just in time for the birth of his son, Avner, in Milan on the seventh day of the Hanukkah feast of the Jewish year 5708. The next day, December 14 on the Christian calendar, there is a second anniversary celebration organized in Selvino by the "Casa del Bambino" (as written in the bilingual invitation, in Hebrew and in Italian): a ceremony open to Milanese friends of Sciesopoli, which they can reach by bus from Piazza Castello at 2:30 p.m.[34] The following day, it is the prefecture of Bergamo that keeps the directorate general of public security updated in Rome: "We announce that the Jewish Foreigners' Colony of Selvino now numbers 246 members.... Since the establishment of this colony there have been no complaints from or incidents with the local population," the prefect specifies. As for the future, "it has not yet been possible to ascertain when the members of the Colony in question will be able to leave our

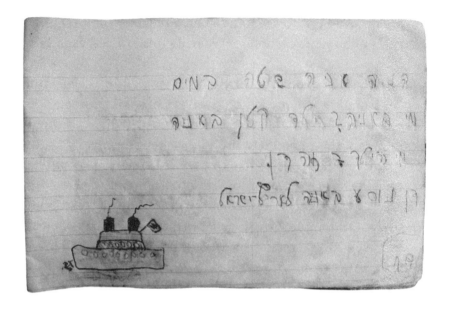

territory."[35] In other words, it is not clear when they will be rid of the Jews' disturbance.

The day of leave is also eagerly awaited by a little girl from Sciesopoli who, thanks to the lessons of her mother—Yehudit, the teacher—is learning how to write in Hebrew. Nitza was five years old then, and her notebook speaks clearly, both in the text and in the drawing. "Here is a boat sailing in the water. Who is on the boat? There is a child on the boat. Who is the child? It's Dan. Dan sails on the boat to the land of Israel."[36]

MOSHE'S SOLDIERS

The bus moved slowly. The driver of line 14 was wary, and the patrols of the British police who guarded the streets toward the center were not enough to reassure him. In Kiryat Haim, numerous passengers had boarded, although the civil war was also (or was above all, in Haifa and its surroundings) a bus war. The buses of the Jews, the buses of the Arabs; snipers against some, bombs against the others. That morning in mid-January 1948—it was only half past eight—two attacks had already occurred in the city, with at least one dead: the Arab passenger on a bus from line 5, attacked by Jews in Elijah Street. So the driver of line 14 proceeded slowly. From the start of the route, he peered right and left. He feared snipers were hiding behind the sandbags, at the windowsills of Arab houses. After bypassing the airport runway and skirting the railroad tracks, the bus passed the Shell bridge and drove down Nazareth Road to the Tel Amal roundabout. At that point, many passengers were preparing to get off, some to reach the docks of the port and some to the railway station, shops, craftsmen's ateliers, or the construction sites that tried to stay open that Thursday.

The crackle of automatic weapons suddenly burst out, and the windows of the bus shattered as the driver accelerated wildly, both to escape the Arab fire and to unload the dead and wounded at the nearby Rothschild Hospital, which was right there. The next morning, the *Palestine Post* reported two confirmed victims, a twenty-year-old Jew from Kiryat Haim and an unidentified middle-aged lady. Among the dozen hospitalized, it mentioned "Haim Rebhuhun," thirty, a "Palestine Foundation Fund employee," himself a resident of Kiryat Haim.[37] But in reality, he was included in the list of victims, having succumbed to the severity of his injuries. A Jew from Berlin, he was the Heinz Rebhun, who during the war had been a volunteer with the Royal Engineers of the 745th Solel Boneh Company; he was the owner of a camera, the Voigtlander to be envied, which from North Africa to South Italy had accompanied the movements of Moshe Zeiri and all the other "Palestinian" engineers. He got married in Naples to an Italian Jewess, Luciana Gallichi, who had given him a child, Miriam—orphaned since that day.[38]

Two days later—Sunday, January 18—the *Palestine Post* reported the official death count during the six weeks between November 30, 1947, and January 10, 1948. Since the United

Nations had approved the partition plan for Palestine, the Jews and Arabs had begun to fight each other in open warfare. Thirty British had fallen, including soldiers and policemen; 295 Arabs had died, almost all civilians;[39] 262 Jewish victims had perished, almost all civilians. In terms of casualties, the war remained balanced despite the fact that the Jewish community of Palestine was economically developed, ideologically motivated, and militarily organized thanks to the many thousands of Haganah soldiers who had come from the ranks of the British Army; whereas the Arab community was economically backward and torn by political, social, and religious conflicts.[40] However, in Haifa, as in Tel Aviv or Jerusalem, the two lived in mixed communities. Arabs and Jews lived within range of each other, literally, so they were targets for daily ambushes, like the one in which the electrician Heinz Rebhun lost his life—eleven years after he and his twin brother had chosen to ascend to Palestine, leaving behind, in Berlin, parents they would never see again, overwhelmed by the destruction of Europe's Jews.

In a port and industrial city such as Haifa, the drama of a civil war was experienced more acutely than elsewhere. There was also an internal war within the labor movement, a war of armed workers against each other. Pinchas Lubianiker, the historical leader of the Histadrut, pointed this out at the end of December 1947. Speaking to the Central Committee of Mapai, the founder of Gordonia had the courage to warn his fellow leaders of the Jewish settlement about the effects of their own upcoming victory. "There is a sediment of twenty years of education, and especially the last ten years, which has not inculcated in us the capacity for living together with the neighboring people. There is a primitive nationalism among the *tzabarim* [young Palestinian-born Jews, or sabra]. There is an historical instinct for revenge among the Oriental Jewish communities. There is a danger from the [Jewish] terrorist groups and the [right-wing Zionist] Revisionists and their nationalist megalomania." In the future state of

Israel, a restless Lubianiker wondered, would the Jewish majority ever have the will to treat the Arab minority as a community of equals?[41]

In Haifa, the street war would go on for months, until the second half of April, when the forces of the Haganah—taking advantage of an almost complete withdrawal of British troops—would take over. Meanwhile, the race for enlistments had begun in the kibbutzim of Galilee and the coastal plain. Among the recruits, there were many young Jews who had escaped the Final Solution. They may have exceeded 50 percent in the Palmach battalions.[42] A far cry from "soap bars." These muscular Jews, Shoah survivors, could contribute to the redemption of the Chosen People at least as much as their sabra peers. From Kibbutz Mishmar Hasharon, even the most inseparable of all the Sciesopoli alumni are recruited into the Palmach: Avraham Lipkunski, Yaakov Meriash, and Shmulik Shulman. Assigned to the Sixth Battalion, the first two are hastily trained as war nurses, and Shmulik is integrated into the combat units.[43]

Also a soldier in the first Palmach Battalion, Dov Wexler left Kibbutz Hanita in mid-April 1948 to fight in the plain of Esdraelon, at the fierce Battle of Mishmar Haemek. It's the first battle since the beginning of the civil war in which artillery is used. The volunteers of the Arab Liberation Army pound Kibbutz Mishmar Haemek, the historic training base of the Zionist militias, to take control of the Jenin-Haifa road. Dov fights shoulder to shoulder with the most elite soldiers of the Jewish army, 650 in all, against 2,500 Arab soldiers. Dov defends the palisades and trenches of the kibbutz as the buildings collapse and the animals die—until the men of the Palmach and Haganah find a way to go on a counteroffensive. After having dispersed the enemy troops, they obtained from the political leaders of Tel Aviv—from Ben-Gurion himself—the authorization to storm the surrounding villages of Ghubaiya-al-Tatha, Ghubaiya-al-Fauqa, and Khirbet-Beit-Ras. Dov works to evacuate Arab civilians from a large strip

of land around Mishmar Haemek. He works to terrorize them into escaping—men, women, elderly, and children—in the direction of Jenin and the hills of Samaria. He ransacks and burns their houses, razes entire villages to the ground.[44]

During the following weeks, as elements of the Haganah secure control of Haifa, the entire plain of Esdraelon, and much of the Jordan Valley, the civil war may appear to have ended to the advantage of the Jews. So much so that on May 14—coinciding with the end of the British Mandate in Palestine—David Ben-Gurion can proclaim, along with independence, the birth of the State of Israel. But that same day, another war erupts. This is a conventional war, which pits the newborn Jewish state against the military forces of Lebanon, Syria, Transjordan, Egypt, and Iraq. And that exposes the recent conquests of Israel to the threat of armies equipped with guns, armored vehicles, and even airplanes, compared with a Jewish army supplied at most with makeshift tanks.[45] Moreover, the soldiers of the Haganah have not managed, during the civil war, to ensure full control of the strategically decisive axis: the Tel Aviv–Jerusalem road. In the Holy City, tens of thousands of Jews are still held under siege by Arab militias, and supply convoys from the coastal plain struggle to reach them. Until the road to Jerusalem is secured, the War of Independence cannot really be said to be over.[46]

Operation Yiftach, Operation Erez, Operation Yitzhak, Operation Maccabi: these were some of the many milestones in the military epic of Israel's origins during that fatal month of May 1948. Or, according to Israel's detractors, some of the many stages of an incipient ethnic cleansing of Palestine.[47] In any case, Moshe's soldiers were presented with many opportunities to stand out. As part of the Yiftach Brigade, Dov Wexler fights against the Syrians in Upper Galilee until the liberation of Safed and the systematic evacuation of the surrounding Arab villages. Shlomo Krampf, who left Kibbutz Avuka to join the Golani Brigade, fights against the Iraqis on the slopes of Mount Gilboa, overlooking Samaria, where he is seriously injured. Shalom Finkelstein—the intense amateur poet of the *Nivenu* newspaper—is killed fighting with the Harel Brigade on Radar Hill, toward Jerusalem; he had recently found his father, Israel, and his mother, Chaia, in the citrus groves of Rehovot, both of whom had escaped the Final Solution. The three fellow soldiers of Mishmar Hasharon—Avraham Lipkunski, Yaakov Meriash, and Shmulik Shulman—are also part of the Harel Brigade. The former two as paramedics, the latter as an infantryman, they were mobilized on the Jenin front before reaching the salient of Latrun, in the Judean hills, along the road to Jerusalem.[48]

In July, the Yiftach and Harel Brigades both participate in Operation Dani. The Palmach Sixth Battalion—that of Avraham, Yaakov, and Shmulik—contributes from the rear, fighting on the heights of Latrun. The first battalion, Dov Wexler's, is directly involved in the plains, in the action that leads to the conquest of the city of Lod and the international airport. This is the very operation that an authoritative Israeli intellectual will, decades later, define as the "black box" of Zionism: the opaque place of its internal contradiction, or of its metamorphosis from an ideology of liberation to an ideology of oppression.[49] Terror is on the agenda from July 11, 1948, onward, when Lieutenant Colonel Moshe Dayan—a son of Kibbutz Degania, the second sabra born there, after Yosef Baratz's eldest son—leads his armored vehicles in a deadly raid through the streets of Lod. There are forty-seven minutes of strafing at close range, with Arab civilians gunned down by the dozens.[50] The next day, Palmach soldiers massacre civilians by the hundreds. In the following days, tens of thousands of Arabs either flee or are deported from Lod, marching toward a refugee life in the West Bank.[51]

"The names of Dayr-el-Hawa, Bayt-Nattif, Zakaria, Bayt-Nuba, Yalo, and other villages located in the war zone, would be forever inscribed in [my] memory," Avraham Lipkunski writes in his old age on the last page of an autobiographical book.[52] Conversely, for a long time the names of the Arab villages of Judea ravaged by the Harel Brigade in October 1948 would be absent from the collective memory of the Israelis—at least until a "new historiography" recalled them.[53] Today, looking at Google Maps, I try in vain to find any cartographic traces. None of those villages exist anymore. Depopulated of their inhabitants and plundered of their belongings, they were transformed into green areas, trees for Israel.[54] In contrast, a few clicks are enough to see a black-and-white photograph appear on the screen, taken at the end of the victorious campaign: soldiers of the Harel Brigade gazing smugly at the smoking ruins of Bayt-Nattif. I almost find it difficult to write, but today—zooming in on the photo—I'm afraid I might recognize in the faces of those soldiers the features of Avraham or Yaakov or Shmulik, the features of one of Moshe's children.

In other photographs taken then in Bayt-Nattif, men from the Harel Brigade methodically empty the homes of their inhabitants. Or they smile at the camera, showing the spoils of war: a basket of olives, a jar, three or four slaughtered hens. Other photos show piles of white stones—what remains of the houses in Bayt-Nattif that the Palmach soldiers blew up with dynamite. All throughout Palestine, the ruins of Arab villages were becoming a typical feature of the Israeli landscape, in particular the kibbutz landscape. Not surprisingly, they will recur in the pages of the most accomplished literary interpreter of the kibbutz experience, Amos Oz. The rubble of the mosque and minaret. Dried-up wells, clogged and fetid. Olive groves and orchards at the mercy of foxes and jackals. The dusty shards of earthenware jars, the millstones buried in the earth, the paths overgrowth with brambles. And no longer even the shadow of donkey drivers, people picking olives or pruning the sycamore figs.[55]

The end of the Exile corresponds with the beginning of an exile.[56] Tens of thousands of Jewish refugees—mostly Shoah survivors—find a homeland when hundreds of thousands of Arab refugees lose it.[57] In the countryside, Israel's first victorious war involves, above all, a land grab—millions of hectares of arable land. In the Arab neighborhoods of the cities, that victory is first and foremost the appropriation of things. Furniture, dishes, clothes—there is nothing that is not taken while waiting to legally expropriate the houses.[58] And at the cost of suggesting disturbing associations of ideas, as in the thoughts of a historical leader of Labor Zionism, Golda Meyerson (Meir), who visited Haifa in May 1948 and then spoke of a "dead city" from which the Arab children, women, and elderly tried only to escape: "I entered houses, there were houses where the coffee and pita bread were left on the table, and I could not avoid thinking that this, indeed, had been the picture in many Jewish towns."[59]

In the very days of the conquest of Bayt-Nattif and the other villages of Judea close to the road to Jerusalem, the army of the Jewish state launches Operation Yoav. The goal is the town of Beersheva, on the southern edge of historic Palestine, with everything beyond: the Negev Desert to the Red Sea. And among the mobilized units, there is still the first Palmach Battalion, Dov's battalion. The Egyptian army is the best equipped adversary among the Arab coalition. But the Israeli Defense Forces (the Haganah is now called Tzahal) nonetheless manage to win their first pitched battles.[60] Beersheva was conquered on October 21, and today I try to imagine the fatigue, the pride, the emotion of that Polish orphan, Dov Wexler, son of Henoch, who discovers for the first time—from the dusty bed of his truck—the biblical desert landscape. The dunes, the rocks, the crags. The surprise of a eucalyptus grove. The relief and danger of a descent toward the wadi. All that Promised Land to make blossom, to realize the redemption.[61]

TWO KIBBUTZIM

Very few men of the Harel Brigade fell in the hills of Judea during that triumphant campaign of October 1948. Among the few was a twenty-two-year-old officer, Aharon Shemi, known as Jimmy. He was the son of Menachem, the artist so admired by Moshe Zeiri at the time of their volunteer work in the 745th Solel Boneh Company. When his parents find out, they leave Galilee to reach the village of Abu Gosh, where the body of their son has been transferred. There, an eighteen-year-old soldier who will become a great writer, Yoram Kaniuk, sees them. "I remember that after they had taken Jimmy's body to a church, in Abu Gosh, his father, the painter Menachem Shemi, lifted the canvas covering him, and a young woman set up the body and removed the shroud hiding the face, and Shemi didn't utter a word, his expression was ice cold. Then he took out a sketch pad and a pencil and drew his dead son's face for a long time, without a single muscle moving on his own face. He was concentrated as if he had died instead of his handsome son."[62]

Over time, Jimmy Shemi would become a symbol: the most celebrated Palmachnik of all those who died in the War of Independence. He was the incarnation of the young sabra capable

of giving his life without thinking for a second, as long as Israel lived. Jimmy was buried in Kiryat Anavim, near Abu Gosh, in a shrine designed by his father.[63] In that same shrine were the remains of many young Jews who were not at all sabras: Jimmy's peers or even younger, who were born in Europe and had escaped the Final Solution, embarked on illegal Aliyah Beth ships. They had been patient in the tents of Cyprus and had barely set foot on the Promised Land before sacrificing themselves so Israel could live on. Shalom Finkelstein, the poet of the *Nivenu*, was also buried in Kiryat Anavim: one of the more than six hundred Shoah survivors who died in battle during the War of Independence, one-sixth of the total number of fallen Israeli soldiers.[64]

The events of the war were followed with passion on the Selvino plateau. In May, at the proclamation of the birth of the State of Israel, Moshe Zeiri and the orphans of Sciesopoli publicly celebrated, walking up the road from Val Seriana. "When they got their liberation, they came up from Nembro with the torchlight procession... They came up marching and singing, because they won, didn't they? It was like one of our Christian processions."[65] But in the autumn, the Sciesopoli experience was coming to an end. The Youth Aliyah House could now close, and it should, because the ascent to Palestine—the road to Jerusalem—was now open to all Jews. On October 19, the Joint warned the Jewish community in Milan, "The children's home in Selvino will close in the next few days."[66] And on October 30, in Rome, with a handwritten "very urgent" message by phone, the Foreign Ministry communicated to the Interior Ministry the imminent movement of "240 foreign refugees," from the Bergamo station to the port of Naples, "with three third class and two closed wagons."[67] Sciesopoli was leaving for Israel.

The police papers document the journey of the train, which in twenty-four hours, from 12:55 on November 2 to 12:50 on November 3, takes Moshe Zeiri; his wife, Yehudit; and all their children to the Naples maritime station.[68] The subsequent voyage by ship—a perfectly legal ship—then lasts five days and five nights. On November 8, 1948, the community of Sciesopoli disembarks at the port of Haifa.[69] A few days of quarantine follow in the Atlit camp, reorganized by the Israelis as a sorting center for immigrants arriving from Europe. After that, the Zeiri family returns home to the kibbutz in Kvutzat-Shiller, near Rehovot, where the idyll between a *Ostjude* and a *Westjude* had begun a dozen years earlier, between a young Galician Hebrew teacher and a very young Zionist from Cologne. According to Nitza's recollections, a group of orphans from Selvino also settles in Kvutzat-Shiller, but they struggle to settle down and will soon join the Sciesopoli alumni who have settled in the north, in Kibbutz Hanita.[70]

Like their fellow immigrants in 1946 and 1947, the latest arrivals to the land of Israel have to deal with the distrust, or even the contempt, that the sabras reserve for the surviving European Jews—for their broken Hebrew, their pathetic Yiddish, their obviously damaged lives after death.[71] The distrust and contempt of the sabra is not just limited to the more mature or older survivors: those like Amos Oz's Mr. Licht in *A Tale of Love and Darkness*, the neighbor in Jerusalem "whom the local kids called Million *Kinder*"; those of David Grossman in *See Under: Love*, with their incomprehensible babbling when on the bench they tell their stories about "Over There."[72] In the kibbutz, the distrust or contempt of the sabra extends to the young Jews of Europe, to the boys and girls who, Over There, had been saved who knows how. And if they had arrived last, when Palestine was now gloriously Israel, they couldn't even boast of badges earned for their efforts in the double war for independence.

In January 1949, a group of orphans from Selvino leave Kibbutz Hanita and move slightly farther west, still along the border with Lebanon but just off the Mediterranean coast. The distance is short (three or four miles as the crow flies) but very important. Unlike the land of Hanita, where the Selvino orphans had chosen to move, the land was not owned by Jews before the war. It is a land of conquest. And it is a land all the more charged with symbolic value because it governs access to the natural caves of Rosh Hanikra: since time immemorial, the northern frontier of historic Palestine. On that frontier, the army of the Jewish state decided to found the first of its "security settlements" planned for the postwar period. This is the Kibbutz Rosh Hanikra, whose founding fathers are veterans of the first Palmach Battalion from Hanita.[73]

One of them is Dov Wexler. He will soon get married in Kibbutz Rosh Hanikra to another orphan from Sciesopoli, Sara Goldman. Meanwhile Dov's brother, Adam, also helps found a security settlement, one of those kibbutzim that the Israeli army considers of strategic value because it is located on the borders or in the desert: military garrisons more than agricultural colonies.[74] With a platoon of the Nahal, the Fighting Pioneer Youth, Adam leaves Kibbutz Kfar Ruppin, on the banks of the Jordan, to go deep into the sands of the Negev Desert. Beyond the city of Beersheva, the younger Wexler works on rebuilding a military base that the Haganah had abandoned during the War of Independence as a kibbutz. There, at the entrance to the Sinai, Adam finds a group of Sciesopoli alumni coming from the coastal

plain, from Kibbutz Mishmar Hasharon. The founding fathers of Kibbutz Tze'elim are veterans of the Palmach's Harel Brigade, including the trio: Avraham Lipkunski, Yaakov Meriash, and Shmulik Shulman.[75]

THE WARDS OF THE SUN

At the turn of 1949,[76] the project of a Selvino kibbutz no longer had any raison d'être. Thanks to the War of Independence, in fact, two different elements of the same generation had ended up recognizing themselves as a single community with a common destiny. On the one hand, Jews born in Europe in the late 1920s or early 1930s and exposed as children to the horror of the Final Solution. On the other hand, the sabra born in Palestine during the same years, who reached the age of majority coinciding with the supreme test of the civil war and the Arab-Israeli war. Of course, for young immigrants from the bloodlands, full integration into Israeli society remained difficult even when they were welcomed into kibbutzim where the demand for willing labor was pressing[77]

because many sabras—too many—criticized (unfairly) the quality of the Final Solution survivors' performance in the battles of the War of Independence. But at least for a handful of these young survivors—for some of Moshe's children, and especially the Palmach veterans—the two security settlements at Rosh Hanikra and Tze'elim, in the far north and far south of historic Palestine, respectively, might well have seemed a reasonable and happy evolution to the dream of a Selvino kibbutz.[78]

The Shoah orphans had made it. They had not only reached the Promised Land but also fought for the birth of Israel. And now they took care to guard its borders, according to an interpretation of Zionism that Moshe Zeiri had transmitted to them, in Italy, through the principles of Gordonia: the conquest of work as a conquest of land, the Jewish state defined not by the class struggle but by the occupation of land. The problems would later arise less from politics than from life. During the 1950s, many of the Sciesopoli alumni—men and women—would come to feel suffocated by the atmosphere of the kibbutz. At work, they would cultivate more adventurous projects of personal fulfillment than those normally contemplated on a kibbutz. In the family, they would feel a strong need to have a house of their own, without having to submit to bureaucratic rules about the allocation of spaces or length of service. And they would prefer to raise their children without binding them to a horizon just a few hundred meters wide, the tower and the palisade, the pond and the sheepfold, the dovecote and the school, the refectory and the dormitory.

After all, they could continue to see each other—as Moshe's children—even after they left Rosh Hanikra or Tze'elim. They could meet outside the kibbutz, as Israelis free to fly over the "wards of the sun," like the bird in Bialik's poem "To the Bird." They could get together on holidays at one of their houses—at the Meriashes, for instance, in the city of Ashkelon, on the coast but close to the desert. They could get together in large numbers and pose in front of a camera, knowing how many things the Selvino orphans held in common even after some of them had become parents (eventually by marrying each other). And they would raise their children by telling stories of Sciesopoli too. Noga's wordless caresses. The horn of Fetter Moshe's truck. The flag-raising with the Star of David. Mountain tours organized by Reuven. The menorah on the roof for Hanukkah.

Today, I look at a photograph taken in Ashkelon around 1960,[79] and I recognize many of Moshe's children now grown up (Dalia Wexler, Adam's widow, helps me via email). There's Avraham Aviel, that is, Avraham Lipkunski, his hairline already receding. There's his wife, Ayala, who used to be Inda Liberman, with the sunglasses and the checked skirt. There's Yaakov Meriash, the only adult sportsman squatting. There's Adam Wexler smiling next to Dalia. Dalia herself helps me to recognize the others from Sciesopoli. That's Pinchas Ringer. Those two are Avraham Kutner and his wife, Zippora Balam. Among the little ones, Dalia points out Henoch and Uzi, the two children she had with Adam. Of the three inseparable friends—always together at Selvino in

Mussolini's house, then aboard the *Katriel Jaffe*, and then again at the Kibbutz Mishmar Hasharon and in the Harel Brigade of the Palmach—Shmulik Shulman is missing in the photograph. And he is missing for a very good reason: because he stayed in Tze'elim.

Shmulik never left the kibbutz in the Negev desert. At the meeting of Kfar Ruppin on October 25, 1947, he had declared, "Reality is overcoming obstacles, and crowning dreams." In the sands of Tze'elim, he saw the death of an orphan from Sciesopoli, the Russian Jewess Lila Nudelman, hit by a grenade during her watch. He recited the Kaddish for the orphan Shlomo Krampf, seriously wounded on Mount Gilboa only to take his own life in Tze'elim.[80] He continued to believe, Shmulik did. He got married on the kibbutz and raised his four children there. From Tze'elim, he went back and forth to study theater at Tel Aviv University. At the age of forty, he graduated in acting and directing. He worked in television and was known to the Israeli public as Shmuel Shilo. And he ended up making another of Moshe Zeiri's dreams come true. In the 1980s, Shmulik founded and directed the Negev Theater, a sort of traveling stage production, with actors taken from the various desert kibbutzim. It was the same kind of kibbutz theater company as the one that young Moshe had dreamed of founding half a century earlier as a student at the Habima drama school—when, between one crate and the other to be unloaded at the port of Jaffa, the son of the Galician shtetl had confessed to Yehudit that he felt like a revolutionary.[81]

IF YOU SURVIVE

TZE'ELIM, MARCH 31, 2016

I have never been to Tze'elim. Not even on March 31, 2016, when I had the best opportunity to go there for a meeting of the last Sciesopoli alumni still living. It was Nitza who first told me about it, announcing the presence, among others, of Yitzhak Livnat (Suti Weisz) and Yaakov Meriash. I would have liked to see them. I would have liked to discover there, in the Negev Desert, the white-haired boys and girls, other Moshe's children whom I had met through archival sources, though not personally. In particular, I would have been curious to meet Chana Garfinkel, a Jewess from Warsaw who I knew had been married in Israel to a Jew of Italian descent, Pesach Cerrone. Originally Pasquale, Cerrone was a convert from San Nicandro, Puglia. The boy with the beret on his head, smiling behind Enzo Sereni in the 1944 group portrait of those strange Jews from Puglia, with no rabbis and no scrolls, no menorahs and no kippahs, who were hoping to realize their dream, the "ascent" from the Gargano to Palestine.

But I didn't go to the Tze'elim gathering. A commitment kept me in Italy. I had to settle for Nitza's email reports before a video posted on YouTube gave me a chance to visualize things a bit.

Tze'elim, exterior, daylight: the verdant kibbutz like an oasis in the desert. Tze'elim, interior, still daylight: the conference room, the speeches of dignitaries such as the deputy mayor of Selvino and the ambassador of Italy to Israel. Yaakov and Yitzhak on stage, living witnesses. Noga Donath, still sparkling with energy and her quick reminiscence of Moshe Zeiri, words as simple as they are strong: "He wanted to convince the children that not everything in the world was evil and pain, that there was also hope for the future." The group photo of Moshe's last children, about fifteen: including Nitza, the eldest daughter of everyone's dad. Tze'elim, interior, night: music, singing, the dance of a lively Chana Garfinkel. And then the next day, again Tze'elim, exterior, daylight: the kibbutz children planting saplings, the laying of a Trees of Hope plaque, white doves released into the air as a sign of peace.[1]

Had I gone to Tze'elim, I would have specifically wanted to meet Avi Shilo, Shmulik's son. Because it is especially with regard to Shmulik that I regret having arrived too late and not picking up on the trail of the Sciesopoli Jews earlier. As a result, I missed every possible appointment with the inseparable friend of Yaakov and Avraham, with the third orphan of the trio. On March 31, 2016, I would have liked to reflect at least with Avi, his son, about the idea I had of his father as the most historically representative—if such an expression could ever make sense—of all Moshe's children.

I must try to explain here why Shmulik Shilo seems to me the most complete incarnation of a historical figure that is actually elusive and irreducible: "Moshe's child." Even though Shmulik's first life, in the bloodlands, had nothing more or less tragic than that of the other Selvino orphans, his second life, in the land of Israel, was fundamentally different from most of the other Sciesopoli alumni's precisely because Shmulik remained in the kibbutz for over sixty years: from the foundation of Tze'elim in 1949 until his death in 2011. Instead of getting bored over time,

he remained on that green island surrounded by the sands of the Negev. Instead of getting tired of milking cows or driving tractors, he exulted in the tasks, like in an old photo accessible on YouTube.[2] Instead of going off on his own way, with his wife and children, preferring family to community; instead of flying over the sunny wards as a free Israeli, like Bialik's bird, he stayed put.

Shmulik Shilo inherited from Moshe Zeiri his most striking and all-consuming passion: the theater. But this is not the point. The point is that Shmulik's existential path corresponds to the essence of Moshe's ideological lesson. It corresponds to the lesson of a fundamentalist Zionism down to its presuppositions, in the version espoused by Pinchas Lubianiker and Gordonia: the ascent to the Promised Land as the conquest of a land to be redeemed.[3] And It corresponds to the lesson of a Zionism made all the more fundamental, after the Final Solution, by the recognition of the enormity of the loss suffered by the youngest Shoah survivors, by those orphaned of everything. Others of Moshe's children, after fortunately landing in British Palestine and having fought valiantly in the War of Independence, gave up on interpreting their second life as a practical and perpetual reaffirmation of the Zionist ideal. Shmulik never buried his Palmachnik rifle, and it was for the same reason that he stayed on the kibbutz, in Tze'elim. He felt that precisely that kind of life, in the "security settlement" at the southernmost edge of historic Palestine, was the faithful application of what he had learned at sixteen, three thousand kilometers northwest, in the Alps near Bergamo.

In a Shoah commemoration speech at Yad Vashem in Jerusalem on May 1, 2008, Shmulik Shilo quickly evoked his story as a Jew from Volhynia who had escaped the Final Solution. The soda factory in Lutsk, the Lubart Castle, the mass grave of Polanka. Then Shmulik switched from *me* to *us*. He remembered the Youth Aliyah House of Selvino. He mentioned the director, Moshe Zeiri, "a member of Kvutzat-Shiller," and of Reuven Donath, "a sabra from Haifa." And he summed up—in his own way—a bit of this whole story. "We arrived there as serious kids, more mature than our age. A month later, we were playing soccer and courting girls. We worked, we studied, we prepared for immigration.... We knew that one day we would reach Eretz Israel. But we didn't want to get there as needy orphans. We wanted to give, not receive. We asked our teachers to tell us what the most important thing was that we could do for Israel. They replied: found settlements in the Negev and Galilee.... *We came to build and to be built* is more than a song, it's the essence of our lives."[4]

That May 2008 coincided with the sixtieth anniversary of the birth of the State of Israel. The anniversary was commemorated by an Arab counterpart—Al Jazeera, the Qatari television broadcaster—with an English-language documentary that had Shmulik Shilo as the main witness. The sprightly old man was filmed and interviewed in Tze'elim, on a bicycle, among the trees, in the refectory. Although his English was halting, he eloquently and imaginatively evoked the Aliyah Beth: "After the war we began, like birds, to fly toward Palestine." He was categorical in the idea that one could not expect the Jews who escaped the Final Solution to be moved by the plight of Palestinian refugees in 1948: "I understood that they were angry and that they fought. But

this is my life. There are seven Arab countries. Why they seven, and I nothing? It is like my brother has a big house and a lot of rooms, and I have to live on the street. We are brothers—give me a room." His firm conclusion: "I am ready to defend my country. I have a rifle, I have a tank, I have a pilot, and I can defend my children. My father didn't. And there's a very great difference—the difference of life."[5]

On March 31, 2016, I did not go to Tze'elim. I missed the gathering of Moshe's remaining children. But Avi Shilo and I ended up meeting anyway, at least virtually—one evening in June 2017, for a couple of hours of conversation via Skype. So six years after Shmulik's death—and thirty years after Moshe Zeiri's death—I was able to ask Avi how, as a son, he saw his father's relationship with Moshe. Their love for the theater. Their idea of Israel. He replied emphatically, emphasizing how "everything" or "almost everything" that Shmulik had achieved "as an adult" was "was taken from Moshe," starting from the desire to be "the cantor," "the one who tells the story." I then asked him about his father's relationship with Tzahal, the Israeli Defense Forces. "He loved the army," Avi said. A veteran of the War of Independence, Shmulik had been mobilized as a reservist for decades. "He used to say: 'I prefer to be stronger, and maybe play a little dirty, than being the Jewish victim.'" A sharpshooter, Shmulik Shilo had been primarily employed by Tzahal to train Fighting Pioneer Youth recruits.[6]

Throughout his entire existence, Shmulik embodied the strong version of the survivor. And he reiterated it—as if in a testament—through the title of a posthumous documentary film that features him. The film was produced in 2013 by the Hebrew University of Jerusalem, and the title, in English, was, *If You Survive: The Story of Shmulik Shilo*. If you survive: if fate can save you from the destruction of your family, your community, and your people, and whether such survival can truly be considered a salvation. But also, once you survive, whether you are ready or not to experience the history of the new Israel as that of a people perpetually threatened with extinction, and whether you are ready to recognize in the force of arms the only true form of life insurance. Whether you are just as ready as Shmulik Shilo who, at minute 62 of the documentary, addresses his son Avi: "When I was a night guard at Tze'elim, you children slept in the children's house. And quite a few times, over the course of several years, I sat on your bed, listened to you breathe, and thought to myself: 'My father couldn't protect me, but I will protect you.' And I kissed my rifle, because that rifle was the rifle of life."[7]

GLOSSARY

aliyah—"ascension," "ascent." In a figurative sense, the immigration of Jews from the Diaspora to Palestine.
Aliyah Beth—"ascent B." In the jargon of the Zionist emissaries, the illegal immigration of Jews from Europe to British Palestine.
bar mitzvah—the status of religious adulthood, which male Jews achieve at thirteen. By extension, the ceremony celebrating the rite of passage.
Betar—a youth movement of revisionist Zionism, founded by Vladimir Jabotinsky in 1923.
Bundist—a militant of the Bund, General Union of Jewish Workers of Lithuania, Poland, and Russia, a Jewish socialist movement born in the Russian Empire that developed particularly in Poland between the two world wars.
Habima—stage. The name of a Jewish theater company founded in the Russia of the Bolshevik Revolution, then moved to Tel Aviv in the second half of the 1920s.
Haganah—"defense." Zionist paramilitary organization, created in Palestine in the 1920s to protect kibbutzim and other Jewish settlements.
Hanukkah—Jewish holiday that falls on the twenty-fifth of the month of Kislev (between November and December), to commemorate the reopening and purification of the Temple of Jerusalem (165–164 BC).
Hechaluz—"pioneer." Movement of international Judaism organized for the training of young Jews of the Diaspora for the agricultural colonization of Palestine.

Histadrut—General Confederation of Workers in the Land of Israel, founded as a Zionist trade union in 1920 and developed to form the institutional infrastructure of the nascent Jewish state.
Irgun—"organization." Zionist paramilitary organization founded in 1931, by splitting from the Haganah, at the initiative of Menachem Begin.
Joint—American Joint Distribution Committee (AJDC), an American organization of international Jewish assistance.
kibbutz—"assembly," "meeting." Collective agricultural settlement of Zionist inspiration, widespread in Palestine since the foundation in 1909 of the kibbutz Degania.
kosher—"right," "suitable." Adhering to the rules of Jewish life established by tradition, in particular with regard to food.
kvutza—"group." Small collective agricultural settlement (gradually becoming almost indistinguishable from the kibbutz).
Mapai—Hebrew acronym for Eretz Israel Workers' Party. Political party born in 1930 from the merger of the two Zionist movements inspired by Aharon David Gordon and David Ben-Gurion; it became the main Jewish political force in British Palestine.
melamed—"teacher." In particular, the tutor of children learning the Hebrew alphabet and Jewish religious studies.
mezuzah—"doorjamb." By metonymy, a ritual object containing a parchment with biblical verses fixed to the doorjamb at the entrance of an Orthodox Jewish household.
ORT—Organization for Rehabilitation through Training, an international Jewish organization specializing in professional training.
Palmach—Hebrew acronym for "strike force." Elite Corps of the Haganah.
palmachnik—member of the Palmach, elite soldier of the Zionist armed forces.
Pesach—the Jewish Passover, which falls on the first full moon of spring and celebrates the exodus of the Jews from Egypt.
Purim—"the fate." Jewish holiday celebrated on the fourteenth and fifteenth of the month of Adar (between February and March), to commemorate the failed extermination of the Jews of Persia.
rabbi—"teacher." Title attributed to Jewish doctors of the law, considered spiritual leaders of the community.
Rosh Hashanah—Jewish religious New Year, which falls on the first day of the month of Tishri (between September and October).

GLOSSARY

sabra—"prickly pear." Slang denomination to designate a Jew born not in the Diaspora, but in the Palestine of the British Mandate (or, even earlier, in the Palestine of the Ottoman Empire).

Shabbat—the day of rest, the seventh of the Jewish week, which begins at sunset on Friday and continues until sunset on Saturday.

shtetl—"small town." Jewish village of Eastern Europe before the Shoah.

Solel Boneh—"excavation and construction." Name of the cooperative company of the Histadrut, specialized in public works.

Sukkot—"booth." Jewish feast of tabernacles, or booths, celebrated in the month of Tishri (between September and October), in the past on the occasion of the autumn harvest, then linked to the memory of migration to the desert.

Tarbut—"culture." Zionist cultural organization, founded in Warsaw in 1922, specializing in the teaching of Hebrew.

tarbutnik—member of the Tarbut. Jargon, cultural attaché (mostly in the negative connotation of an individual with bookish knowledge).

Tzahal—Hebrew acronym for Israeli Defense Forces. Name assumed by the Haganah in 1948, to designate the armed forces of the newborn Jewish state.

yeshiva—"session," "sitting." Jewish cultural institution, generally run by rabbis, specializing in the study of traditional religious texts.

Yiddish—language of the Germanic family, traditionally spoken by the Jewish communities of Central and Eastern Europe, written in Hebrew characters.

Yom Kippur—the Day of Atonement (at the twilight of the tenth day of Tishri, between September and October), the most important Jewish holiday to commemorate Kippur, "the Atonement," through fasting.

GUIDE TO ABBREVIATIONS

ITALY

ACDEC—Center of Contemporary Jewish Documentation Archive, Milan
ACS—Central State Archive, Rome
ACSe—Municipal Archive, Selvino
AFGRN—Gallichi Rebhun Family Archive, Naples
AIAMAM—Institute of Assistance to Minors and the Elderly Archive, Milan
AISEC—Institute for the History of Contemporary Age Archive, Sesto San Giovanni
ASMAE—Historical-Diplomatic Archive of the Ministry of Foreign Affairs, Rome
AUCEI—Union of Italian Jewish Communities, Rome

ISRAEL

ABLH—Beit Lotamei Haghetaot Archive, Western Galilee
AFATA—Aviel Family Archive (Lipkuński-Liberman), Tel Aviv
AFBSR—Family Archive Ben-Dov Spivak, Rehovot
AFDH—Donath Family Archive, Haifa
AFDR—Donath Family Archive, Ramat Ha-Sharon
AFLTA—Livnat Family Archive (Weisz), Tel Aviv
AFMA—Meriash Family Archive, Ashkelon

GUIDE TO ABBREVIATIONS

AFSTA—Sarid Family Archive (Luftman), Tel Aviv
AFVG—Varadi Family Archive, Jerusalem
AFWRL—Wexler Family Archive, Rishon LeZion
AFZE—Zeiri (Kleiner) Family Archive, Erez
AHTA—Haganah Archive, Tel Aviv
AJDCJ—Joint Distribution Committee Archive, Jerusalem
AJITA—Jabotinsky Institute Archive, Tel Aviv
AMITY—Massuah Institute Archive, Tel Yitzhak
AYVJ—Yad Vashem Archive, Jerusalem

UNITED STATES OF AMERICA

AJDCNY—Joint Distribution Committee Archive, New York
AUSCSF—University of Southern California Shoah Foundation Archive, San Diego
AUSHMM—United States Holocaust Memorial Museum Archive, Washington, DC
AYIVO—Yidisher Visnshaftlekher Institut (Yiddish Scientific Institute) Archive, New York

UNITED KINGDOM

AFZSL—Zeiri Sarner Family Archive, London
APISML—Polish Institute and Sichorsky Museum Archive, London
AWLL—Wiener Library Archive, London
TNA—The National Archives, London

FRANCE

ABMP—Bibliothèque Medem Archive, Paris

POLAND

AŻIHV—Archive Żydowski Instytut Historyczny (Jewish Historical Institute), Warsaw

NOTES

THE BLACK BOX

1. In 2016, the originals of the letters written by Moshe Zeiri to his wife, Yehudit (about 230 for the time interval between April 1943 and August 1946), were deposited by the heirs in the archive of Yad Vashem, in Jerusalem, with other letters (about 30) written by Moshe to Yehudit between the beginning of 1939 and the spring of 1943, and with various other original documents (photos, passports, etc.). The heirs also deposited the originals of the letters (more than 300) addressed by Yehudit to Moshe between 1943 and 1946 in the Yad Vashem archive. The Zeiri Collection is currently in the reorganization and inventory phase, and it is provisionally cataloged in the O.90 series, code 5263222. Simultaneously, at the initiative of the heirs, a wide selection of excerpts from Moshe's letters to Yehudit was published in Israel (with unscientific criteria) in an edition (in Hebrew) not for sale: *Wait for Me and I'll Be Back: The Letters of Moshe Zeiri*, edited by Y. Yaari, Erez, 2016.

2. The references to the correspondence here will always be understood as referring to the transcription of the manuscript (in Hebrew). They are preceded by the words "AYVJ, Zeiri Collection, correspondence," followed by the date (if any) affixed by the sender. The translation is always by Chiara Camarda.

3. With regard to the saved Jews as Jews who save, see S. Norich, "Choosing Life: 'Where Did They Find the Strength to Choose Life?'" *Jewish Frontier* 66, no. 6 (1999): 7ff.; Z. Mankowitz, "*She'erit Hapletah*. The Surviving Remnant: An Overview," in *Holocaust Survivors. Resettlement,*

Memories, Identities, ed. D. Ofer, F.S. Ouzan, and J. Tydor Baumel-Schwartz (New York: Berghahn, 2012), 10–15.

4. The photo of the black box is taken from the site Huntmans in the Holy Land (http://huntsmansintheholyland.blogspot.it/2011/11/yad-vashem-and-mount-herzel-11611.html, accessed July 2017).

5. The photo of the envelope of letters, taken at Kibbutz Erez in June 2014, is mine.

6. For references to Oz's books, see A. Oz, *La scatola nera* [The black box], trans. E. Loewenthal (1987; Milan: Feltrinelli, 2002); A. Oz and F. Oz-Salzberger, *Gli ebrei e le parole. Alle radici dell'identità ebraica* [Jews and words], trans. E. Loewenthal (2012; Milan: Feltrinelli, 2013), 12.

1. FAR FROM WHERE

1. For the photo of the Kleiner family, see AYVJ, series O.90, code 5263222, courtesy of AFZE.

2. AYVJ, Zeiri Collection, correspondence, November 23, 1943.

3. From the testimony of Moshe's sister, Rivka Kleiner (from a radio program broadcast in Israel in March 1988, in memory of Moshe Zeiri, who died in 1987), which was transcribed and translated in English by Moshe's daughter, Nitza Zeiri Sarner; see AFZSL, 1988 radio transcript.

4. See L. Wolff, *The Idea of Galicia. History and Fantasy in Habsburg Political Culture* (Redwood City, CA: Stanford University Press, 2012), 380ff.; M. Pollack, *Galizia. Viaggio nel cuore scomparso della Mitteleuropa* (2001; Rovereto: Keller, 2017). On literary myth, see C. Magris, *Lontano da dove. Joseph Roth e la tradizione ebraico-orientale* (Turin: Einaudi, 1971).

5. See I. Babel', *Il sangue e l'inchiostro. Racconti e altri scritti inediti* [Unpublished stories], trans. C. Di Paola (Milan: Garzanti, 1980), 107, 121; I. Babel', *L'armata a cavallo* [Red cavalry], trans. R. Poggioli (1926; Turin: Einaudi, 2009), 130.

6. See above all Y. Bauer, *The Death of the Shtetl* (New Haven, CT: Yale University Press, 2009), 24ff.; also see S. Redlich, *Together and Apart in Brzezany. Poles, Jews and Ukrainians, 1919–1945* (Bloomington: Indiana University Press, 2002), 38ff.

7. See in particular Y. S. Agnon, *Una storia comune* [A simple story], trans. A. L. Callow and C. Rosenzweig (1935; Milan: Adelphi, 2002); Y. S. Agnon, *Appena ieri* [Only yesterday], trans. E. Loewenthal (1945; Turin: Einaudi, 2010).

8. AYVJ, Zeiri Collection, correspondence, November 12, 1945.
9. Ibid., January 8, 1945.
10. See M. Web, "Introduction," in A. Kacyzne, *Poyln. Jewish Life in the Old Country* (New York: Metropolitan, 1999), 1–13. For reference to photos, see AYIVO, Kacyzne fund, photos, RG 1270 F51 and F53.
11. See AYVJ, Zeiri Collection, correspondence, November 23, 1943.
12. AYVJ, Zeiri Collection, correspondence, n.d. (but autumn 1943) and July 16, 1943.
13. See Y. Friedman, *The Rebbes of Chortkov* (New York: Mesorah, 2003), 64ff.
14. See J. Baumgarten, *La naissance du hassidisme. Mystique, rituel et société (XVIIIe–XIXe siècle)* (Paris: Albin Michel, 2006), 463ff.
15. On the Galician youth of Moshe (and Rivka), I used information from a memoir communicated to me via email in February 2015 by Rivka Kleiner's son, Avraham Nuriel. The document is henceforth indicated as A. Nuriel, "Personal Testimony."
16. See AFZSL, 1988 radio transcript.
17. See W. G. Sebald, *Austerlitz*, trans. A. Vigliani (2001; Milan: Adelphi, 2002), 197.
18. AYVJ, Rebeca Nuriel (née Rivka Kleiner) Collection, code 3035/8 (Probuzna class); AFZE, various documents (Moshe with some companions).
19. For the biography of Pinchas Lubianiker (who, after the creation of Israel, took the name Lavon and rose to the rank of defense minister), the study of reference (in Hebrew) is E. Kafkafi, *Pinchas Lavon. Anti-Messiah* (Tel Aviv: Am Oved, 1998).
20. AYVJ, Rebeca Nuriel (née Rivka Kleiner) Collection, code 3035/2 (the amateur theater company). For the Kacyzne photo, see AYIVO, Kacyzne fund, photos, RG 1270/yarg1270_0344 ial.
21. See N. Sandrow, *Vagabond Stars: A World History of Yiddish Theater* (Syracuse, NY: Syracuse University Press, 1996), 303ff.; B. Dalinger, "'L'unica soluzione': Ideologia sionista e teatro," in *Verso una terra "antica e nuova": Culture del sionismo (1895–1948)*, ed. G. Schiavoni and G. Massino (Rome: Carocci, 2011), 122ff.
22. See G. Massino, *Fuoco inestinguibile. Franz Kafka, Jizchak Löwy e il teatro yiddish polacco* (Rome: Bulzoni, 2002), 52ff.; S. Friedländer, *Kafka, poète de la honte* (Paris: Seuil, 2013), 73–74.
23. F. Kafka, *Lettere a Milena*, trans. E. Pocar (Milan: Mondadori, 1979), 192 (letter from Prague, early September 1920; translation modified).

24. AYIVO, Kacyzne Collection, photos, RG 1270/yarg1270_0344 ial.

25. See Bauer, *Death of the Shtetl*, 25; H. Minczeles, *Une histoire des Juifs de Pologne. Religion, culture, politique* (Paris: La Découverte, 2006), 266.

26. AFZE, various documents (Rivka in the Tarbut group).

27. Precious insights in A. Shavit, *My Promised Land: The Triumph and Crisis of Israel* (New York: Spiegel and Grau, 2013), 28.

28. See A. Shapira, *Israel: A History* (Waltham, MA: Brandeis University Press, 2012), 33–34.

29. I limit myself to evoking I. J. Singer, *Yoshe Kalb*, trans. B. Fonzi (1933; Milan: Adelphi, 2014); I. J. Singer, *I fratelli Ashkenazi* [The brothers Ashkenazi], trans. B. Fonzi (1937; Turin: Bollati Boringhieri, 2011); I. J. Singer, *La famiglia Karnowski* [The family Carnovsky], trans. A. L. Callow (1943; Milan: Adelphi, 2013); J. Roth, *Ebrei erranti* [The wandering Jews], trans. F. Bussotti (1927; Milan: Adelphi, 1985); J. Roth, *Viaggio ai confini dell'impero*, ed. V. Schweizer (1919–27; Florence: Passigli, 2017); B. Schulz, "*Le botteghe color cannella*" [Street of crocodiles], in *Tutti i racconti, i saggi e i disegni* [Complete stories, essays, and drawings], trans. A. Vivanti Salmon, V. Verdiani, and A. Zielinski (1934; Turin: Einaudi, 2008).

30. See M. Web, "Introduction," 1–13. For the relationship with *The Forward*, see S. Lipsky, *The Rise of Abraham Cahan* (New York: Schoken, 2013), 147ff. For the photographer Kacyzne, see C. Zemel, "Imaging the Shtetl. Diaspora Culture, Photography and Eastern European Jews," in *Diaspora and Visual Culture. Representing Africans and Jews*, ed. N. Mirzoeff (New York: Routledge, 2000), 193–206.

31. See R. Ertel, *Le Shtetl. La bourgade juive de Pologne* (Paris: Payot and Rivages, 2011), 228ff.

32. About Warsaw between the two world wars, see G. Dynner and F. Guesnet, eds., *Warsaw: The Jewish Metropolis* (Leiden: Brill, 2015).

33. About the decline of Lviv, see E. Yones, *Smoke in the Sands: The Jews of Lvov in the War Years, 1939–1944* (New York: Gefen, 2004), 26ff.

34. See AYVJ, Zeiri Collection, correspondence, September 1944.

35. See A. Nuriel, "Personal Testimony."

36. See Ertel, *Le Shtetl*, 282ff., 306ff.

37. See A. Elon, *Israeliani. Padri fondatori e figli* (1970; Pavia: Editoriale Viscontea, 1988), 121–22; G. Shimoni, *The Zionist Ideology* (Hanover, NH: Brandeis University Press, 1995), 209ff.; Z. Sternhell, *Nascita di Israele. Miti, storia, contraddizioni* (1996; Milan: Baldini and Castoldi, 1999), 80ff.

38. See H. Near, *The Kibbutz Movement. A History*, vol. 1, *Origins and Growth, 1909–1939* (Oxford: Oxford University Press, 1992), 122ff.

NOTES 357

39. See A. Marzano, *Storia dei sionismi. Lo Stato degli ebrei da Herzl a oggi* (Rome: Carocci, 2017), 71ff.
40. See A. Elon, *La rivolta degli ebrei* (1975; Milan: Rizzoli, 1979), 353.
41. Near, *The Kibbutz Movement*, 1:176ff.
42. Pollack, *Galizia*, 15ff.
43. For the photograph of Moshe in the agricultural colony, see AFZE, various documents. For the memories of Moshe on the shaking of the streets, see AYVJ, Zeiri Collection, correspondence, letters of June 3, 1946, and January 10, 1945.
44. AFZE, various documents.
45. See G. Bensoussan, *Atlas de la Shoah. La mise à mort des Juifs d'Europe, 1939–1945* (Paris: Éditions Autrement, 2014), 11.
46. Information about the Liberman sisters from A. Aviel, *Freedom and Loneliness* (Tel Aviv: Kotarim International, 2008), 134ff.
47. A. Oz, *Una storia di amore e di tenebra* [A tale of love and darkness], trans. E. Loewenthal (2002; Milan: Feltrinelli, 2003), 194.
48. See (in Hebrew) N. H. Bialik, *Il re David nella caverna* (Frankfurt-am-Main: Omanut, 1923).
49. Information relative to the childhood of Avraham Lipkunski comes mainly from the autobiographical book, published with the surname he took on from the 1950s: A. Aviel, *A Village Named Dowgalishok. The Massacre at Radun and Eishishok* (London: Vallentine Mitchell, 2006). Also from the monumental study by Y. Eliach, *There Once Was a World: A 900-Year Chronicle of the Shtetl of Eishishok* (Boston: Little, Brown, 1998), passim.
50. For a biography of Bialik and a selection of poems from his youth, see A. Holtzman, *Hayim Nachman Bialik: Poet of Hebrew* (New Haven, CT: Yale University Press, 2017), 29ff.
51. See Eliach, *There Once Was a World*, 167.
52. See AJDCNY, Polish remittances 1, 1915–1917.
53. See J. Fibel, "The Argentine Connection," *Dorot: The Journal of the Jewish Genealogical Society* 8, no. 4 (Summer 1987): 11.
54. See AFATA, various documents.
55. Ibid.
56. See Ertel, *Le Shtetl*, 140ff.
57. See Eliach, *There Once Was a World*, 290ff.
58. See Aviel, *A Village*, 41.
59. Ibid., 53.
60. See Minczeles, *Une histoire des Juifs de Pologne*, 215ff.

61. See E. Melzer, *No Way Out: The Politics of Polish Jewry, 1935–1939* (Cincinnati: Hebrew Union College Press, 1997), 130ff.

62. See Y. Shavit, *Jabotinsky and the Revisionist Movement, 1925–1948* (London: Frank Cass, 1988), 198ff.; D. K. Heller, *Jabotinsky's Children: Polish Jews and the Rise of Right-Wing Zionism* (Princeton, NJ: Princeton University Press, 2017), 68ff.

63. See Aviel, *A Village*, 52.

64. For the Wexler family photo, see AFWRL, various documents. Information relative to the childhood of Dov and Adam Wexler come in large part from an autobiographical book, published by the youngest brother in a private edition in Hebrew (A. Wexler, *My Point of View, 1930–1945*; Rishon Le-Zion, n.d., but 2000) and then in French translation: A. Wexler, *J'étais cet enfant juif polonais . . .* (Paris: L'Harmattan, 2004).

65. See O. Nagornaya, "United by Barbed Wire: Russian POWs in Germany, National Stereotypes, and International Relations, 1914–1922," in *Fascination and Enmity. Russia and Germany as Entangled Histories, 1914–1945*, ed. M. David-Fox, P. Holquist, and A. M. Martin (Pittsburgh: University of Pittsburgh Press, 2012), 39ff.

66. See I. J. Singer, *Acciaio contro acciaio* [Steel and iron], trans. A. L. Callow (1927; Milan: Adelphi, 2016).

67. Wexler, *J'étais cet enfant*, 36.

68. See AYIVO, Kacyzne fund, photos, RG 1270_0558. On the children of the shtetl in Kacyzne's photos, see Zemel, "Imaging the Shtetl," 194–95.

69. Wexler, *J'étais cet enfant*, 43.

70. See B. Wasserstein, *On the Eve: The Jews of Europe before the Second World War* (London: Profile, 2013), 134.

71. See Melzer, *No Way Out*, 81ff.

72. Wexler, *J'étais cet enfant*, 49.

73. See ibid., 55–58.

74. Ibid., 62.

75. See ibid., 121.

76. For the Hungarian path to the Final Solution, the reference studies remain those by C. A. Macartney, *October Fifteenth: A History of Modern Hungary, 1929–1944*, 2 vols. (Edinburgh: Edinburgh University Press, 1957); R. L. Braham, *The Destruction of Hungarian Jews: A Documentary Account*, 2 vols. (New York: World Federation of Hungarian Jews, 1963).

77. On the ambivalence of Hungary in the 1930s (and then through 1944), on the one hand an almost happy island of Jews, on the other hand a

context of deep antisemitism, see S. Marai, *Volevo tacere* (1949–1950; 2013), trans. L. Sgarioto (Milan: Adelphi, 2017), 44ff.

78. Information relative to the childhood of Suti Weisz is taken largely from the documentary trilingual volume of M. Nagy, ed., *Nagyszőlős, the Centre of the World* (Budapest: Aposztróf, 2009). Also, from various conferences held by (with his Israeli name, Yitzhak Livnat) at the University of Haifa in the years 2014–2016: see *infra*.

79. Oral memories of the Weisz family have been gathered (according to documentary and narrative criteria more than strictly historiographical) by S. M. Papp, *Outcasts: A Love Story* (Toronto: Dundurn, 2009). The volume even contains the reproduction of photos of the time, including the photo reproduced here.

80. For Suti's final citation on his "wonderful childhood," see L. Lachmanovich and L. Bar-Ilan, eds., "'Do You Remember That You Taught a Boy to Sing?': An Interview with Yitzhak Livnat and Chaim Raphael," available on the site of Yad Vashem, the International School for Holocaust Studies, Interviews (consulted in July 2017). The photos of the Weisz family from there.

81. See A. Nuriel, "Personal Testimony."

82. See A. Patek, *Jews on Route to Palestine, 1934–1944: Sketches from the History of Aliyah Bet—Clandestine Jewish Immigration* (Krakow: Jagellonian University Press, 2012), 41.

83. S. Y. Agnon, *Nel cuore dei mari* [In the heart of the seas], ed. A. Rathaus (1926; Milan: Adelphi, 2013), 18, 27. On the Jews' fear of the sea, see T. S. Presner, *Muscular Judaism: The Jewish Body and the Politics of Regeneration* (New York: Routledge, 2007), 155ff.

84. See A. Nuriel, "Personal Testimony."

85. See A. Shapira, *Ben-Gurion: Father of Modern Israel* (New Haven, CT: Yale University Press, 2014), 68ff.

86. See I. Pappe, *Storia della Palestina moderna: Una terra, due popoli* (2004; Turin: Einaudi, 2005), 119.

87. See Near, *The Kibbutz Movement*, 1:31ff.; D. Gavron, *The Kibbutz: Awakening from Utopia* (Plymouth: Rowman and Littlefield, 2000), 20ff.

88. See A. Nuriel, "Personal Testimony."

89. See A. Ben-Amos, *Israël: La fabrique de l'identité nationale* (Paris: Éditions du Cnrs, 2010), 72ff.

90. Quote from Korczak's letter (dated October 8, 1932) is from J. Korczak, *La Palestine. Notes de voyage et correspondance, 1927–1939*, ed. Z. Bobowicz (Montricher: Les éditions Noir sur Blanc, 2002), 90.

91. For Korczak's first voyage in Palestina, se B. J. Lifton, *The King of Children* (London: Pan, 1988), 201ff.
92. On the pedagogical model of Korczak's Orphan House in Warsaw, see T. Lewowicki, "Janusz Korczak (1878–1942)," *Prospects: The Quarterly Review of Comparative Education* 1, no. 2 (1994): 37–48.
93. AYVJ, Zeiri Collection, correspondence, n.d. (but February 1939).
94. See Patek, *Jews on Route to Palestine*, 81ff. On the antisemitic climate in the Sejm, see Melzer, *No Way Out*, 133ff.
95. See Melzer, *No Way Out*, 133ff.
96. For the Singer novel (in English, original date unsure), see I. B. Singer, *Il certificato* [The certificate], trans. M. Biondi (Milan: Longanesi, 1994).
97. Content of an email Nitza Zeiri Sarner sent me on May 30, 2016.
98. Ibid.
99. AFZE, various documents.
100. See Shavit, *My Promised Land*, 49ff.

2. YEHUDIT

1. AFZE, various documents. For all the information relative to the life of the Meyer family, I am indebted to an indirect testimony sent to me by Nitza Zeiri in April 2016, henceforth cited as N. Zeiri Sarner, "My German Family."
2. See S. Friedländer, *La Germania nazista e gli ebrei. Gli anni della persecuzione: 1933–1939* (1997; Milan: Garzanti, 2004), 45ff.; A. Confino, *A World without Jews: The Nazi Imagination from Persecution to Genocide* (New Haven, CT: Yale University Press, 2014), 50–51.
3. See B. Becker-Jakli, *Das Jüdische Köln: Geschichte und Gegenwart* (Cologne: Emons Verlag, 2012), passim.
4. See Zeiri Sarner, "My German Family."
5. About the patriotic mobilization of German Jews in World War I, see A. Elon, *Requiem tedesco. Storia degli ebrei in Germania, 1743–1933* (2002; Milan: Mondadori, 2005), 266ff. About the military contribution of German Jews, see T. Grady, *The German-Jewish Soldiers of the First World War in History and Memory* (Liverpool: Liverpool University Press, 2011), 23ff.
6. See AFZE, various documents.
7. Ibid.

8. See Elon, *Requiem tedesco*, 304.
9. See B. Löwendahl, *Der Zeitpunkt des Gefahrübergangs beim Kaufe mit Eigentumsvorbehalt* (Leipzig: Abel Verlag, 1914).
10. See *Die Jüdischen Gefallenen des Deutschen Heeres, der Deutschen Marine und der Deutschen Schutztruppen, 1914–1918. Ein Gedenkbuch* (Berlin: Reichsbund Jüdischer Frontsoldaten, 1932), 69.
11. See "Heldengedenkfeier. 'Die Enthüllung des Gefallenendenkmals in Köln,'" *Der Schild*, July 18, 1934.
12. See *Kriegsbriefe Gefallener Deutscher Juden* (Berlin: Vortrupp, 1935).
13. See Grady, *German-Jewish Soldiers*, 136–38.
14. See AFZE, various documents.
15. See Zeiri Sarner, "My German Family."
16. For the impact of antisemitic legislation on the lives of German Jews, see above all M. A. Kaplan, *Between Dignity and Despair: Jewish Life in Nazi Germany* (Oxford: Oxford University Press, 1998), 94ff.
17. See Zeiri Sarner, "My German Family."
18. See G. L. Mosse, *L'immagine dell'uomo. Lo stereotipo maschile nell'epoca moderna* (1996; Turin: Einaudi, 1998), 55ff.; M. Zimmermann, "Muscle Jews versus Nervous Jews," in *Emancipation through Muscles: Jews and Sports in Europe*, ed. M. Brenner and G. Reuveni (Lincoln: University of Nebraska Press, 2006), 13ff.; G. Pfister and T. Niewerth, "Jewish Women in Gymnastics and Sports in Germany, 1898–1938," *Journal of Sport History* 26, no. 2 (Summer 1999): 287–325.
19. See Kaplan, *Between Dignity and Despair*, 113–15.
20. See Zeiri Sarner, "My German Family."
21. With the title *The Oppenheims*.
22. L. Feuchwanger, *I fratelli Oppermann*, trans. E. Pocar (1933; Milan: Skira, 2014), 187.
23. See T. Segev, *The Seventh Million: The Israelis and the Holocaust* (New York: Hill and Wang, 1993), 17–18; G. Bensoussan, *Israele, un nome eterno. Lo Stato di Israele, il sionismo e lo sterminio degli ebrei d'Europa, 1933–2007* (2008; Turin: Utet, 2009), 19–20.
24. Segev, *The Seventh Million*, 18.
25. See D. Dwork and R. J. Van Pelt, *Flight from the Reich: Refugee Jews, 1933–1946* (New York: Norton, 2009), 25ff.
26. See Friedländer, *La Germania nazista*, 70–71.
27. See B. Amkraut, *Between Home and Homeland: Youth Aliyah from Nazi Germany* (Tuscaloosa: University of Alabama Press, 2006), in particular 32ff.

28. For references to the issues of *Jüdische Rundschau*, see in particular note 100 from December 15, 1933, and notes 31–32 from April 17, 1935 (from which comes the quote from Ch. Weizmann, *Der schnellste und bequemste Weg nach Palästina*, ibid., 28).

29. See Dwork and Van Pelt, *Flight from the Reich*, 41ff.

30. Amkraut, *Between Home and Homeland*, 55; Dwork and Van Pelt, *Flight from the Reich*, 47.

31. Cited in R. Bondy, *Enzo Sereni. L'emissario* (1973; Aosta: LeChâteau, 2012), 205–6.

32. H. Arendt, "Des jeunes s'en vont chez eux," *Le Journal Juif. Hebdomadaire illustré*, June 28, 1935, 3; taken up again and translated in H. Arendt, *The Jewish Writings*, ed. J. Kohn and R. H. Feldman (New York: Schocken, 2007), 34–37.

33. See D. Cesarani, *Becoming Eichmann: Rethinking the Life, Crimes, and Trial of a "Desk Murderer"* (London: Da Capo, 2007), 48ff.

34. See Wasserstein, *On the Eve*, 339ff.

35. See S. Heim, "Immigration Policy and Forced Emigration in Germany: The Situation of Jewish Children (1933–1945)," in *Children and the Holocaust: Symposium Presentations*, ed. P. A. Shapiro (Washington, DC: Center for Advanced Holocaust Studies, United States Holocaust Memorial Museum, 2004), 3–4.

36. See AFZE, various documents.

37. For the migration statistics in 1935 Germany, see G. Bensoussan, *Il sionismo. Una storia politica e intellettuale, 1860–1940* (2002; Turin: Einaudi, 2007), 1:543.

38. See E. Bloom, *Arthur Ruppin and the Production of Pre-Israeli Culture* (Leiden: Brill, 2011).

39. Cited in Amkraut, *Between Home and Homeland*, 74.

40. See Kaplan, *Between Dignity and Despair*, 117.

41. See S. Bon, ed., *Trieste. La porta di Sion. Storia dell'emigrazione ebraica verso la Terra di Israele, 1921–1940* (Florence: Alinari, 1998), passim.

42. APISML, A60 fund, fasc. 41.

43. See "Jaffa Roadsted," *The Palestine Post*, December 31, 1935.

44. Oz, *Una storia di amore e di tenebra*, 236. English edition: *A Tale of Love and Darkness*, trans. Nicholas de Lange (London: Harcourt, 2004), 188.

45. See E. Kafkafi, "The Psycho-Intellectual Aspects of Gender Inequality in Israel's Labor Movement," *Israel Studies* 4 no. 1 (1999), in particular 200ff.

46. See A. Elon, *Israeliani*, 158.

47. See Y. Bar-Gal, "The Blue Box and JNF Propaganda Maps, 1930–1947," *Israel Studies* 8, no. 1 (2003): 8–9.

48. With regard to Arabs in Zionist propaganda and iconology, see M. Berkowitz, *Western Jewry and the Zionist Project, 1914–1933* (Cambridge: Cambridge University Press, 1997), 91ff.; A. Marzano, "Visiting British Palestine: Zionist Travelers to Eretz Israel," *Quest. Issues in Contemporary Jewish History* 6 (2013), in particular 195ff. With regard to the perception of the Palestinian Arab population on the part of Jewish workers affiliated with the Histadrut, see Z. Lockman, *Comrades and Enemies: Arab and Jewish Workers in Palestine, 1906–1948* (Berkeley: University of California Press, 1996), 65ff., 179ff.

49. See Shavit, *My Promised Land*, 71ff.

50. Cited in Bensoussan, *Il sionismo*, 2:1131.

51. See ibid., 2:1131–37.

52. See A. La Guardia, *Terra santa, guerra profana. Israeliani e Palestinesi* (Rome: Fazi editore, 2002), 83–87.

53. See O. Almog, *The Sabra: The Creation of the New Jew* (Berkeley: University of California Press, 2000).

54. Cited in A. Shapira, *Land and Power: The Zionist Resort to Force, 1881–1948* (Redwood City, CA: Stanford University Press, 1999), 262–63.

55. J. Baratz, *The Story of Degania* (New York: Jewish National Fund Library, 1937), 66.

56. Cited in Shapira, *Land and Power*, 263.

57. About the division of labor in the citrus groves, see Shavit, *My Promised Land*, 52ff.

58. Regarding the fortunes of the kibbutz Givat-Brenner, see D. Gavron, *The Kibbutz: Awakening from Utopia* (Plymouth, MA: Rowman and Littlefield, 2000), 43ff. About the Hebrew teacher as social pioneer of Zionism, see A. Ben-Amos, *Israël. La fabrique de l'identité nationale* (Paris: Éditions du Cnrs, 2010), 72ff.

59. For Moshe Zeiri's memories about the origin of the idyll with Yehudit, see AYVJ, Zeiri Collection, correspondence, October 10, 1944, and September 10, 1945. On the role of Moshe in the choice of the name Yehudit, see Zeiri Sarner, "My German Family."

60. See Zeiri Sarner, "My German Family."

61. See Ertel, *Le Shtetl*, 286ff.

62. See Near, *The Kibbutz Movement*, 1:373–74. In general, for the importance of tradition in the Zionist epos, see Y. Zerubavel, *Recovered*

Roots: Collective Memory and the Making of Israeli National Tradition (Chicago: University of Chicago Press, 1995).

63. On the circumstances of Zippora Kleiner's departure from the shtetl, see Nuriel, "Personal Testimony."

64. On the investments of the Joint a Kopychyntsi, see the site Virtual Shtetl (www.sztetl.org.pl; consulted July 2017), entry Kopyczyńce.

65. For this photo and others in this section, see AFZE, various documents.

66. D. Grossman, *Vedi alla voce: amore*, trans. G. Sciloni (1986; Turin: Einaudi, 1999), 10–11.

67. See Zeiri Sarner, "My German Family."

68. See Nuriel, "Personal Testimony."

69. See D. Barak-Erez, *Outlawed Pigs. Law, Religion and Culture in Israel* (Madison: University of Wisconsin Press, 2007), 27ff.

70. See Zeiri Sarner, "My German Family."

71. See D. Yerushalmi, "Toward a Balanced History: 'Ohel,' the 'Workers Theatre of Eretz Yisrael' as a Cultural Alternative to Habima (1935–1946)," *Journal of Modern Jewish Studies* 13, no. 3 (2014): 340ff.

72. AYVJ, Zeiri Collection, correspondence, respectively letters of July 16, 1943, n.d. (but February 1939), March 31, 1946, n.d. (but November 1945).

73. Cited in Shapira, *Land and Power*, 253–55.

74. AYVJ, Zeiri Collection, correspondence, January 29, 1939.

75. See S. Rotbard, *White City, Black City: Architecture and War in Tel Aviv and Jaffa* (2005; Boston: MIT Press, 2015), especially 121ff.

76. AYVJ, Zeiri Collection, correspondence, February 27, 1939.

77. Ibid., February 22, 1939.

78. See A. Helman, *Young Tel Aviv: A Tale of Two Cities* (Waltham, MA: Brandeis University Press, 2010), 143–45.

79. See Shapira, *Israel*, 111.

80. AYVJ, Zeiri Collection, correspondence, July 31, 1945 (with a reminiscence relative to 1939).

81. Ibid., February 22, 1939.

82. See B. Hoffman, *Anonymous Soldiers: The Struggle for Israel, 1917–1947* (New York: Knopf, 2015), 90ff.

83. AYVJ, Zeiri Collection, correspondence, June 14, 1939.

84. Cited in Shapira, *Ben-Gurion*, 115–16.

85. See Z. Golan, *Free Jerusalem: Heroes, Heroines, and Rogues Who Created the State of Israel* (Tel Aviv: Devora, 2003), 166–67.

86. See A. Shapira, *Berl. A Biography of a Socialist Zionist* (Cambridge: Cambridge University Press, 1985), 281ff.
87. Cited in Shavit, *My Promised Land*, 90.

3. CLOSE TO WHERE

1. See Wexler, *J'étais cet enfant*, 79–80.
2. Ibid., 86–88.
3. Ibid., 102–3.
4. See G. J. Horwitz, *Ghettostadt: Lodz and the Making of a Nazi City* (Cambridge, MA: Belknap, 2008); R. J. Van Pelt, *Lodz and Getto Litzmannstadt: Promised Land and Croaking Hole of Europe* (Toronto: Art Gallery of Ontario, 2015).
5. See I. Gutman, "The Distinctiveness of the Lodz Ghetto," in *Lodz Ghetto: A History*, I. Trunk (1962; Bloomington: Indiana University Press, 2006), xxix–lvii.
6. See Horwitz, *Ghettostadt*, 78ff.
7. See Wexler, *J'étais cet enfant*, 146–47.
8. AWLL, Photo documents 1938–1940, RG-68.27.
9. See A. Adelson, ed., *Il diario di Dawid Sierakowiak. Cinque quaderni dal ghetto di Lodz*, Italian edition edited by F. Sessi (1996; Turin: Einaudi, 1997), 88.
10. See S. D. Kassow, "The Case of Lodz: New Research on the Last Ghetto," *Yad Vashem Studies* 35, no. 2 (2007): 245ff.
11. See Wexler, *J'étais cet enfant*, 159ff.
12. See Van Pelt, *Lodz and Getto Litzmannstadt*, 75ff.
13. See I. Gutman, "The Distinctiveness of the Lodz Ghetto," lvi. For the photo of the Wexlers' radio, see ABLH, Photo collection, code 7795.
14. See Trunk, *Lodz Ghetto*, 397–98.
15. See A. Wieviorka, *L'ère du témoin* (1998; Paris: Fayard/Pluriel, 2013), 30–31.
16. See Bauer, *Death of the Shtetl*, 33ff.
17. See J. T. Gross, *Revolution from Abroad: The Soviet Conquest of Poland's Western Ukraine and Western Belorussia* (1988; Princeton, NJ: Princeton University Press, 2002), 23.
18. See M. Shore, *Caviar and Ashes: A Warsaw Generation's Life and Death in Marxism, 1918–1968* (New Haven, CT: Yale University Press, 2006), 153–78.

19. See D. Levin, *Lesser of Two Evils: Eastern European Jewry Under Soviet Rule, 1939–1941* (Philadelphia: Jewish Publication Society, 1995), 233ff.

20. See J.-P. Himka, "The Lviv Pogrom of 1941: The Germans, Ukrainian Nationalists, and the Carnival Crowd," *Canadian Slavonica Papers/ Revue canadienne des slavistes* 8, no. 2–4 (2011): 209ff.; Yones, *Smoke in the Sands*, passim.

21. See Web, "Introduction," in Kacyzne, *Poyln*, 12.

22. With regard to how Shulamit was saved, her false documents, and more, see a memoir (in Hebrew) by Shulamit dating back to 1955 and deposited in AYVJ, series O.3. code 642; see, furthermore, the archival material gathered in ABMP, Sulamita Kacyzne Collection, various documents.

23. See Bauer, *Death of the Shtetl*, 125–26.

24. See J. Burds, *Holocaust in Rovno: The Massacre at Sosenki Forest, November 1941* (New York: Palgrave MacMillan, 2013), in particular 28ff.

25. See AŻIHV, 301 fund, doc. 872 (trans. Magdalena Bialas).

26. Oz, *Una storia di amore e di tenebra*, 268 [English edition, *A Tale of Love and Darkness*, 216].

27. See Burds, *Holocaust in Rovno*, 86ff.

28. See Eliach, *There Once Was a World*, 565ff.

29. AJDCNY, Vilna refugees, 1940, "List of refugees," 57.

30. See Aviel, *A Village*, 60ff.

31. See ibid., 93–94.

32. See ibid., 100ff.

33. See A. Wieviorka, *1961: Le procès Eichmann* (Bruxelles: Complexe, 1989), 56, 156; H. Yablonka, *The State of Israel vs. Adolf Eichmann* (2001; New York: Schocken, 2004), 88–90, 93–94; D. E. Lipstadt, *Il processo Eichmann* (2011; Turin: Einaudi, 2014), 45ff.

34. This and the following quote from Avraham's testimony at the Eichmann trial are taken from the Nizkor Project (www.nizkor.org, consulted July 2017), which contains, in English translation, the transcription of the entire hearing.

35. See Aviel, *A Village*, 109.

36. The image of Avraham's testimony is mine, taken from a YouTube video screenshot.

4. ANABASIS

1. See Shavit, *My Promised Land*, 80ff.

2. See ibid., 93ff.

3. See Segev, *The Seventh Million*, 73–74.

4. See I. Zertal, "Connaissance et culpabilité: les Juifs de Palestine face à l'extermination des Juifs en Europe," in *Annales. E.S.C.*, May–June 1993, 679–90.

5. See Bensoussan, *Israele, un nome eterno*, 50.

6. See D. Porat, *The Blue and the Yellow Stars of David: The Zionist Leadership in Palestine and the Holocaust, 1939–1945* (Cambridge, MA: Harvard University Press, 1990), in particular 34ff.; I. Zertal, *Israele e la Shoah. La nazione e il culto della tragedia* (2002; Turin: Einaudi, 2007), above all 20ff.

7. See Y. Gelber, "The Meeting between the Jewish Soldiers from Palestine Serving in the British Army and 'She'erit Hapletah,'" in *She'erit Hapletah: Rehabilitation and Political Struggle*, ed. I. Gutman and A. Saf (Jerusalem: Yav Vashem, 1990), 60–80.

8. See M. Tagliacozzo, "Attività dei soldati di Eretz Israel in Italia (1943–1946). Il corpo ausiliario dei soldati palestinesi nell'armata di liberazione inglese," *La Rassegna mensile di Israel* 69, no. 2 (May–August 2003): 575–92.

9. AYVJ, Zeiri Collection, correspondence, March 31, 1946.

10. See D. Gavron, *The Other Side of Despair: Jews and Arabs in the Promised Land* (Lanham, MD: Rowman and Littlefield, 2003), 59ff.; D. Gavron, *Holy Mosaic Land: Stories of Cooperation and Coexistence between Israelis and Palestinians* (Lanham, MD: Rowman and Littlefield, 2003), 96–97.

11. See AFZSL, 1988 radio transcript.

12. AYVJ, Zeiri Collection, July 1, 1943.

13. Ibid.

14. Ibid., August 20, 1943.

15. See Moshe's retrospective assessment; ibid., October 21, 1945.

16. AYVJ, Zeiri Collection, November 8, 1945.

17. See AFDR, various documents, December 9, 1943.

18. See M. Rebhun, *Ho inciampato e non mi sono fatta male. Haifa, Napoli, Berlino: una storia familiare* (Napoli: l'àncora del mediterraneo, 2011); M. Rebhun, *Due della Brigata. Heinz e Gughi dalla Germania nazista alla nascita di Israele* (Livorno: Belforte, 2015).

19. AYVJ, Zeiri Collection, correspondence, August 27, 1943. The photo of six rifles that make up the Shield of David comes from AFGRN, various documents (the photo was taken by Heinz Rebhun in 1942).

20. TNA, WO 169/10766, War Diary, July 1943.

21. AYVJ, Zeiri Collection, correspondence, July 12, 1943, and July 16, 1943.

22. See G. Rochat, *Le guerre italiane 1935–1943. Dall'impero d'Etiopia alla disfatta* (Turin: Einaudi, 2005), 354ff.

23. See S. M. Mitcham Jr., *Rommel's Desert War: The Life and Death of the Afrika Korps* (Mechaningsburg: Stackpole, 2007).

24. See AFZSL, 1988 radio transcript.

25. See E. Salerno, *Uccideteli tutti. Libia 1943: gli ebrei nel campo di concentramento fascista di Giado. Una storia italiana* (Milan: il Saggiatore, 2008).

26. See R. De Felice, *Ebrei in un paese arabo. Gli ebrei nella Libia contemporanea tra colonialismo, nazionalismo arabo e sionismo (1835–1970)* (Bologna: il Mulino, 1978), 285ff.; M. M. Roumani, *The Jews of Lybia: Coexistence, Persecution, Resettlement* (Brighton: Sussex Academic Press, 2009), 22–39.

27. AYVJ, Zeiri Collection, correspondence, August 28, 1943.

28. Ibid., July 16, 1943.

29. The photo of the teachers and employees at the Hebrew school in Bengazhi comes from the annexed material of the testimony of a Libyan Jew who emigrated to Palestine, Benjamin Doron, who counted among his teachers even Moshe Zeiri: interview by K. Berman, available on the Yad Vashem site, the International School for Holocaust Studies, "Interviews." (https://www.yadvashem.org/articles/interviews/doron.html, accessed September 25, 2022).

30. AYVJ, Zeiri Collection, correspondence, August 28, 1943.

31. See Roumani, *The Jews of Lybia*, 43–44.

32. For Moshe's leave in Palestine and Nitza's crying, I took up the retrospective testimony of Nitza Zeiri Sarner, from an email message she sent me on November 16, 2013.

33. AYVJ, Zeiri Collection, correspondence, November 16, 1943.

34. See Bensoussan, *Israele, un nome eterno*, 28.

35. AYVJ, Zeiri Collection, n.d. (but September 1943).

36. AYVJ, Zeiri Collection, n.d. (but end of October, beginning of November 1943).

37. See Roumani, *The Jews of Lybia*, 44.

38. AYVJ, Zeiri Collection, correspondence, November12, 1943.

39. See G. Tadmor and J. Shen-Dar, eds., *Menachem Shemi (Schmidt), 1897–1951: Permanent Display from the Collection of the Haifa Museum of Modern Art* (Haifa: Haifa Museum of Modern Art, 1978).

40. AYVJ, Zeiri Collection, correspondence, August 27, 1943.

41. Ibid. The painting *Black Washerwomen in Benghazi* (oil on canvas) belongs to the collection of the Haifa Museum of Art.

42. With regard to Menachem Shemi's artistic work from 1943 to 1944, see the site dedicated to him by his heirs, www.menachemshemi.org.

43. AYVJ, Zeiri Collection, correspondence, December 20, 1943.
44. Ibid., n.d. (but end of October-early November 1943).
45. Ibid.
46. See TNA, WO 169/16447, War Diary, January 1944.
47. AFZE, various documents.
48. For this reminiscence, see AYVJ, Zeiri Collection, correspondence, January 29, 1946.
49. Ibid., April 12, 1944.
50. See A. Marzano, *Una terra per rinascere. Gli ebrei italiani e l'emigrazione in Palestina prima della guerra (1920–1940)* (Genoa: Marietti, 2003).
51. See Tagliacozzo, "Attività dei soldati di Eretz Israel in Italia," 579–80; E. Pfanzelter, "Between Brenner and Bari: Jewish Refugees in Italy from 1945 to 1948," *Journal of Israeli History: Politics, Society, Culture* 19, no. 3 (1998): 83–104.
52. See Bondy, *Enzo Sereni*, 411ff.
53. See N. Davies, *Trail of Hope: The Anders Army, an Odyssey across Three Continents* (Oxford: Osprey, 2015), 426ff.
54. See J. Davis, *The Jews of San Nicandro* (New Haven, CT: Yale University Press, 2010), 128–32. For the photo: ABLH, photographic fund, code 37720.
55. See TNA, WO 170/1770, War Diary, April 1944, May 1944, June 1944.
56. With regard to Menachem Shemi's artistic work from in 1944, see the site www.menachemshemi.org.
57. AYVJ, Zeiri Collection, correspondence, January 19, 1946.
58. Ibid., February 8, 1945.
59. Ibid.
60. Ibid., August 1, 1944.
61. See F. Del Canuto, "La ripresa delle attività sionistiche e delle organizzazioni ebraiche alla Liberazione (1944–1945)," *La Rassegna mensile di Israel*, 3rd series, no. 47 (January–June 1981): 209.
62. For the reconstruction of the atmosphere of the Jewish community in Naples right after the liberation, see B. Contini and L. Contini, eds., *Nino Contini (1906–1944): quel ragazzo in gamba di nostro padre. Diari dal confino e da Napoli liberata* (Florence: Giuntina, 2012), in particular 281ff. (with a reference to "maestro Zeiri").
63. Here I follow the memories of a big girl, Bice Foà: see B. Foà Chiaromonte, *Donna, ebrea e comunista* (Rome: Hapro srls, 2017), 69.
64. See C. S. Capogreco, *Ferramonti. La vita e gli uomini del più grande campo d'internamento fascista, 1940–1945* (Florence: Giuntina, 1987); C.

S. Capogreco, *I campi del duce. L'internamento civile nell'Italia fascista (1940-1943)* (Turin: Einaudi, 2004).

65. See K. Voigt, *Il rifugio precario. Gli esuli in Italia dal 1933 al 1945* (Florence: La Nuova Italia, 1993–96), in particular 2:3ff., 2:365ff.

66. For the vicissitudes of the Weintraud family, see ACDEC, schede Giusti, fasc. Iezzi Emidio e fasc. Maccia Guglielmo; AFYWR, various documents. In general, for the plight of persecuted Jewish children, see B. Maida, *La Shoah dei bambini. La persecuzione dell'infanzia ebraica in Italia, 1938–1945* (Turin: Einaudi, 2013).

67. See G. Weintraub, *Grazie*, Eurografica, Guardiagrele (Ch) 2003, passim.

68. AYVJ, Zeiri Collection, correspondence, October 1944.

69. Ibid., November, 1944. On the street urchins' harassment of women, see N. Lewis, *Napoli '44* (1978; Milan: Adelphi, 1998).

70. See AYVJ, November 12, 1944.

71. See Rebhun, *Due della Brigata*, 60ff.

72. See Nuriel, "Personal Testimony."

73. See AYVJ, Zeiri Collection, correspondence, November 4, 1944.

74. See M. Serra, *Malaparte. Vie et légendes* (Paris: Grasset, 2011), 327ff.

75. See P. Sands, *East West Street: On the Origins of "Genocide" and "Crimes Against Humanity"* (New York: Knopf, 2016), 218ff.

76. See Serra, *Malaparte*, 327 ff.

77. See D. Hofstadter, "Afterword," in C. Malaparte, *Kaputt* (New York: New York Review of Books, 2005), in particular 433–34.

78. C. Malaparte, *Kaputt* (Naples: Casella, 1944), 151–54. English edition: trans. Cesare Foligno (New York: E. P. Dutton), 93–94.

79. See D. Pohl, *Nationalsozialistische Judenverfolgung in Ostgalizien, 1941–1944. Organisation und Durchführung eines staatlichen Massenverbrechens* (Munich: Oldenbourg Verlag, 1997), 226ff.; R. Kuwalek, *Belzec. Le premier centre de mise à mort* (2010; Paris: Calmann-Lévy, 2013), 193–216; O. Bartov, *Erased: Vanishing Traces of Jewish Galicia in Present-Day Ukraine* (Princeton, NJ: Princeton University Press, 2007), 112ff.

80. "Letters from the Valley of Death," *Davar*, November 29, 1944.

81. AYVJ, Zeiri Collection, correspondence, December 3, 1944.

82. See AYVJ, series O.90, code 5263222.

83. AYVJ, Zeiri, correspondence, February 27, 1945.

84. See ibid., March 25, 1945.

85. Malaparte, *Kaputt*, 7.

86. See R. W. Baumer, *Aachen: The US Army's Battle for Charlemagne's City in World War II* (Mechaningsburg: Stackpole, 2015).

87. For the episode with Alfred, see the short article with no byline, *The National Jewish Monthly* 59 (Sept. 1944–August 1945): 320–21.
88. See Zeiri Sarner, "My German Family."
89. See M. Beckman, *The Jewish Brigade: An Army with Two Masters, 1944–45* (Staplehurst: Spellmount, 2009), 92ff.
90. AYVJ, Zeiri Collection, correspondence, April 12, 1945.
91. For the most varied European contexts, see C. Poujol, *L'Église de France et les enfants juifs. Des missions vaticanes à l'affaire Finaly (1944–1953)* (Paris: Presses universitaires de France, 2013), in particular 191ff.; E. Nachmany Gafny, *Dividing Hearts: The Removal of Jewish Children from Gentile Families in Poland in the Immediate Post-Holocaust Years* (Jerusalem: Yad Vashem, 2009), 185ff.; A. Tornielli and M. Napolitano, *Pacelli, Roncalli e i battesimi della Shoah* (Casale Monferrato: Piemme, 2005), 47ff.
92. On the cultural activities surrounding the Jewish Brigade, see B. Migliau and G. Piattelli, *La Brigata ebraica in Italia, 1943–1945. Attraverso il Mediterraneo per la libertà: manifesti, fotografie, documenti in mostra alla Cascina Farsetti di Villa Doria Pamphili*, Rome, June 13–29 2003, Litos, Rome 2003.
93. See F. Francesconi, "Lo spoglio di archivi americani per lo studio dei profughi e della ricostruzione: un primo bilancio," in *Per ricostruire e ricostruirsi: Astorre Mayer e la rinascita ebraica tra Italia e Israele*, ed. M. Paganoni (Milan: Franco Angeli, 2000), 134.
94. J. Roper, "Mob Spat on Duce's Body," *The Palestine Post*, May 1, 1945.
95. Oz, *A Tale of Love and Darkness*, 20.
96. See L. M. Mausbly, *Fascism, Architecture, and the Claiming of Modern Milan, 1922–1943* (Toronto: University of Toronto Press, 2014), 41ff., 126–28.
97. On the rage against the effigies of Mussolini, see S. Luzzatto, *Il corpo del duce. Un cadavere tra immaginazione, storia e memoria* (Turin: Einaudi, 1998), 35–37. For the bust of Il Duce in the Palazzo Odescalchi, see the memoir of Marcello Cantoni in ACDEC, Fondo M. Cantoni, b. 3, fasc. 5, Via Unione 5.
98. See (with caution) L. Cavalli and C. Strada, *Nel nome di Matteotti. Materiali per una storia delle Brigate Matteotti in Lombardia, 1943–45* (Milan: Franco Angeli, 1982), 39ff.
99. See ACDEC, Fondo Antifascisti, 4A, fasc. D. M. Levi.
100. See ACDEC, Fondo Vicissitudini dei singoli, fasc. 412, F. Levi.
101. See R. Hamaui, *Ebrei a Milano. Due secoli di storia fra integrazione e discriminazioni* (Bologna: il Mulino, 2016), 185ff.

102. See S. Minerbi, *Raffaele Cantoni. Un ebreo fra D'Annunzio e il sionismo* (Rome: Bonacci, 1992), 148ff.
103. See ACDEC, Fondo Vicissitudini dei singoli, fasc. 412, passim.
104. ACDEC, Fondo Soccorso ebraico, b. 1, fasc. 6, Comitato assistenza profughi israeliti di Milano; ACDEC, Fondo Soccorso ebraico, b. 3, fasc. 28, David Mario Levi; ACDEC, Fondo Antifascisti, 4A, fasc. D. M. Levi (for the quote as well).
105. See C. Villani, "Milano, via Unione 5. Un centro di accoglienza per «displaced persons» ebree nel secondo dopoguerra," *Studi storici* 2 (2009): 333–70. By the same author, and particularly important for the study of the movements at the borders, see the PhD thesis: C. Villani, "Infrangere le frontiere. L'arrivo delle *displaced persons* ebree in Italia (1945–1948): flussi, vie d'ingresso e politiche d'accoglienza," Università di Trento, 2010, especially 256ff.
106. AYVJ, Zeiri Collection, correspondence, May 2 and 15, 1945.
107. See AFDH, various documents and photographs.
108. AYVJ, Zeiri Collection, correspondence, May 2 and 15, 1945.
109. Ibid.

5. THE DROWNED AND THE SAVED

1. See Eliach, *There Once Was a World*, 604–5.
2. See M. Pollack, *Paesaggi contaminati. Per una nuova mappa della memoria in Europa* (2014), trans. M. Maggioni (Rovereto: Keller, 2016), 90ff.
3. See Aviel, *A Village Named Dowgalishok*, in particular 116–18.
4. See ibid., 126ff.
5. See ibid., 140ff.
6. See A. Levine, *Fugitives of the Forest. The Heroic Story of Jewish Resistance and Survival During the Second World War* (1998; New York: Lyons, 2009), 215ff. For the general context, see A. Ferrara, "La nostra deportazione rappresentò la nostra salvezza: il 'displacement' degli ebrei dell'Occidente sovietico (1939–1949)," in G. *Naufraghi della pace. Il 1945, i profughi e le memorie divise d'Europa*, ed. Crainz, R. Pupo, and S. Salvatici (Rome: Donzelli, 2008), 127–42.
7. See Aviel, *A Village Named Dowgalishok*, 153ff.
8. See ibid., 170.
9. See ibid., 172ff.
10. See Bauer, *The Death of the Shtetl*, 147–48.

11. See D. Porat, *The Fall of a Sparrow: The Life and Times of Abba Kovner* (Redwood City, CA: Stanford University Press, 2009), notably 57ff.
12. See Eliach, *There Once Was a World*, 636–37.
13. See Aviel, *A Village Named Dowgalishok*, 204ff.
14. See Levine, *Fugitives of the Forest*, 226–27.
15. See P. Levi, *Se non ora, quando?* (Turin: Einaudi, 1982); A. Appelfeld, *Storia di una vita* (1999), trans. O. Bannet and R. Scardi (Milan: Guanda, 2008), 55ff., 65ff., 102ff.
16. A. Appelfeld, *Il partigiano Edmond* (2012), trans. E. Loewenthal (Milan: Guanda, 2017), 193.
17. See Aviel, *A Village Named Dowgalishok*, 108.
18. See ibid., 211–12.
19. See Eliach, *There Once Was a World*, 637–38.
20. See Bauer, *The Death of the Shtetl*, 131.
21. See Levine, *Fugitives of the Forest*, 226–27.
22. See Aviel, *A Village Named Dowgalishok*, 220ff.
23. See Eliach, *There Once Was a World*, 647–49; Z. Barmats, *Heroism in the Forest: The Jewish Partisans of Belarus* (Tel Aviv: Kotarim International, 2013), 91–92.
24. See Aviel, *A Village Named Dowgalishok*, 277ff.
25. See Bauer, *The Death of the Shtetl*, 151.
26. See Aviel, *A Village Named Dowgalishok*, 290–92.
27. See ibid., 295–98. For the whole story of Avraham Lipkunski and his family, see the 2010 documentary *But Who Could I Pray For? The Story of Avraham Aviel*, Yad Vashem, International School for Holocaust Studies, Witnesses and Education program (accessible on YouTube, and available through the Yad Vashem Web Store: https://www.yadvashem.org/education/testimony-films/avraham-aviel.html).
28. See Wexler, *J'étais cet enfant*, 181.
29. See ABLH, photo collection, code 7798.
30. See R. J. Van Pelt, *Lodz and Getto Litzmannstadt*, 57ff.
31. See Wexler, *J'étais cet enfant*, 175ff. For the shoe factory, see G. J. Horwitz, *Ghettostadt*, 200.
32. O. Rosenfeld, *In the Beginning Was the Ghetto*, ed. H. Loewy (Evanston, IL: Northwestern University Press, 2002), 267–77, 275–76.
33. Ibid., 276.
34. Wexler, *J'étais cet enfant*, 193.
35. See L. Dobroszycki, ed., *The Chronicle of the Lodz Ghetto, 1941–1944* (New Haven, CT: Yale University Press, 1987), 499–500 (events of June

7–9, 1944); I. Trunk, *Lodz Ghetto: A History* (1962; Bloomington: Indiana University Press, 2006), 398.

36. Wexler, *J'étais cet enfant*, 194.
37. See ibid., 195–96.
38. Ibid., 198.
39. See H. Yablonka, *Survivors of the Holocaust: Israel after the War* (1999; New York: Palgrave MacMillan, 2014), 185ff; B. Cohen, *Israeli Holocaust Research* (New York: Routledge, 2013), 16–17.
40. See P. Levi, "Il re dei giudei" (1977), in *Lilìt e altri racconti* (1981), *Opere complete*, ed. M. Belpoliti (Turin: Einaudi, 2016), 2:292–97.
41. See Wexler, *J'étais cet enfant*, 209.
42. See G. Didi-Huberman, *Immagini, malgrado tutto* (2003; Milan: Raffaello Cortina, 2005), 15.
43. See Horwitz, *Ghettostadt*, 69–70.
44. Wexler, *J'étais cet enfant*, 209–23.
45. See ibid., 227.
46. L. Shelley, ed., *The Union Kommando in Auschwitz: The Auschwitz Munition Factory through the Eyes of Its Former Slave Laborers* (Lanham, MD: University Press of America, 1996).
47. See D. Blatman, *Le marce della morte. L'olocausto dimenticato dell'ultimo esodo dai lager* (2008; Milan: Rizzoli, 2009), 102–23.
48. Wexler, *J'étais cet enfant*, 238ff.
49. Ibid., 244–50.
50. Ibid., 259ff.
51. See R. L. Braham, *The Politics of Genocide: The Holocaust in Hungary*, condensed edition (Detroit: Wayne State University Press, 2000), 119–21.
52. See P. M. A. Cywinski, *Non c'è una fine. Trasmettere la memoria della Shoah* (2012; Turin: Bollati Boringhieri, 2017), 84ff.
53. See B. Gutterman and I. Gutman, eds., *Album Auschwitz*, Italian edition, ed. M. Pezzetti (Turin: Einaudi, 2008).
54. On the liquidation of the ghetto in Nagyszőlős and on the teacher Ortutay, see R. Segal, *Genocide in the Carpathians: War, Social Breakdown, and Mass Violence, 1914–1945* (Redwood City, CA: Stanford University Press, 2016), 95–96. Various details based on the memoirs of the surviving Weisz brothers in Papp, *Outcasts*, 142ff., 182ff.
55. The memories of Suti Weisz regarding his deportation to Birkenau, the death march, and his and Vilmos's vicissitudes between Mauthausen and Gunskirchen are mainly conveyed in two lectures given by him

NOTES 375

(under his Israeli identity of Yitzhak Livnat) at the University of Haifa on November 24, 2014, and January 7, 2016 (henceforth cited as "Livnat, Haifa Conference 2014" and "Livnat, Haifa Conference 2016," respectively).

56. Livnat, Haifa Conference 2014, minute 33.

57. Ibid.

58. Livnat, Haifa Conference 2016, minute 43.

59. For the reconstruction of the vicissitudes of the Liberman sisters from the liquidation of the Zdolbuniv ghetto to the integration into the community of Zachodnia Street in Łódź, I have largely relied on the narrative (based on memories of the Liberman sisters) contained in A. Aviel, *Freedom and Loneliness* (Tel Aviv: Kotarim International, 2008). Here, specifically 237–38.

60. See Bauer, *The Death of the Shtetl*, 123–26.

61. See Aviel, *Freedom and Loneliness*, 239.

62. On the dynamics of the liquidation of the Zdolbuniv ghetto, see D. K. Huneke, *The Moses of Rovno: The Stirring Story of Fritz Graebe, a German Christian Who Risked His Life to Lead Hundreds of Jews to Safety during the Holocaust* (New York: Presidio Press and Ballantine Books, 1990), 83–84. For context, see M. Zeitlin, "The Last Stands of Jews in the Small Towns Ghettos of German-Occupied Poland, 1941–1943," in *Society, History, and the Global Human Condition. Essays in Honor of Irving M. Zeitlin*, ed. Z. Baber and J. M. Bryant (Lanham, MD: Lexington, 2010), 33ff.

63. See J. Struk, *Photographing the Holocaust: Interpretations of the Evidence* (London: Tauris, 2004), 71–72.

64. Aviel, *Freedom and Loneliness*, 240ff.

65. See ibid., 247–48.

66. See K. C. Berkhoff, *Harvest of Despair: Life and Death in Ukraine Under Nazi Rule* (Cambridge, MA: Harvard University Press, 2008), 233ff., 266.

67. See Aviel, *Freedom and Loneliness*, 247–48.

68. See Berkhoff, *Harvest of Despair*, 253ff.

69. See Aviel, *Freedom and Loneliness*, 252ff.

70. See ibid., 258ff.

71. See Berkhoff, *Harvest of Despair*, 266.

72. See Aviel, *Freedom and Loneliness*, 283–84.

73. See M. Scott, *Yanks Meet Reds: Recollections of U.S. and Soviet Vets from the Linkup in World War II* (Santa Barbara, CA: Capra, 1988).

74. See Aviel, *Freedom and Loneliness*, 285–86.

75. See S. Redlich, *Life in Transit: Jews in Postwar Lodz, 1945–1950* (Boston: Academic Studies Press, 2010), 29ff.
76. See ibid., 33ff.
77. See Aviel, *Freedom and Loneliness*, 286–87.
78. See J. T. Gross, *La peur. L'antisémitisme en Pologne après Auschwitz* (2006; Paris: Calmann-Lévy, 2010), in particular 67ff.
79. See Redlich, *Life in Transit*, 59ff.
80. See ibid., 70–71.
81. The deposition of Adela Liberman is contained in AŻIHV, collection 301, doc. 872 (trans. Magdalena Bialas).
82. See Huneke, *The Moses of Rovno*, 34ff.
83. On the impossibility of reliable testimony of the victims, see R. Hilberg, *L'Holocauste: les sources de l'histoire* (2001; Paris: Gallimard, 2001), 52–54.
84. See B. J. Lifton, *The King of Children* (London: Pan, 1988), 315ff.; B. Engelking and J. Leociak, eds., *The Warsaw Ghetto: A Guide to the Perished City* (New Haven, CT: Yale University Press, 2009), 327, 607.
85. See ABLH, Nina Eckhajzer Boniówka Collection, code 29661.
86. See AŻIHV, collection 301, doc. 1528.
87. See M. Hochberg-Mariánska, *Dzjeci Oskarzaja* (Kraków: Wiedzna. 1947), 7–11; trans. in M. Hochberg-Mariánska and N. Grüss, eds., *The Children Accuse* (London: Vallentine Mitchell, 2005), 7–11.

6. THE HOUSE OF MUSSOLINI

1. AYVJ, Zeiri Collection, correspondence, June 2, 1945.
2. Ibid.
3. On the division of tasks in via Eupili during the summer of 1945, see also ACDEC, M. Cantoni Fund, b. 2, fasc. 4; A. Sarano, "Raffaele Cantoni nei miei ricordi," in *La Rassegna mensile di Israel*, April 1978, 252ff.
4. AYVJ, Zeiri Collection, correspondence, June 2, 1945.
5. See ACDEC, Antifascisti Collection, 4A, fasc. D. M. Levi.
6. See S. Minerbi, *Raffaele Cantoni. Un ebreo fra D'Annunzio e il sionismo* (Rome: Bonacci, 1992), 148ff.
7. AYVJ, Zeiri Collection, correspondence, June 12, 1945.
8. See Hamaui, *Ebrei a Milano*, 149ff.
9. AYVJ, Zeiri Collection, correspondence, June 12, 1945.
10. Ibid.

11. With regard to Varadi the Italian animator of Zionism, see A. Marzano, *Una terra per rinascere. Gli ebrei italiani e l'emigrazione in Palestina prima della guerra (1920–1940)* (Genoa: Marietti, 2003). For a biographical profile, see S. Galli, "Ricordo d'un collaboratore: Max Varadi," *Rivista di studi politici internazionali* 71, no. 4 (October–December 2004): 96–100. On the Zionist activities of Varadi before the outbreak of World War II, see also C. Forti and V. H. Luzzatti, *Palestina in Toscana. Pionieri ebrei nel Senese (1934–1938)* (Florence: Aska edizioni, 2009), 28ff. Memory elements on the meeting between Max Varadi and Matilde Cassin are in A. Pezzana, ed., *Quest'anno a Gerusalemme. Gli ebrei italiani in Israele* (Florence: Giuntina, 2008), 88ff.

12. On the Jewish relief networks and on the role of Raffaele Cantoni and Matilde Cassin, see S. Antonini, *DelAsEm. Storia della più grande organizzazione ebraica italiana di soccorso durante la seconda guerra mondiale* (Genoa: De Ferrari editore, 2000).

13. See Voigt, *Il rifugio precario*, 2:501–2; M. Longo Adorno, *Gli ebrei fiorentini dall'emancipazione alla Shoà* (Florence: Giuntina, 2003), 105ff.

14. On the Swiss experience of Cantoni and Cassin, see D. Grosser, *Refugees and Rescuers in Fascist and Post War Italy (1933–1946)*, manuscript, April 2016.

15. The Swiss period of Matilde Cassin is documented in various letters (some of which by Raffaele Cantoni) contained in AFVG, various documents. The same family archive contains the photograph of Matilde reproduced in the text, taken in Weggis in the early months of 1945.

16. ACDEC, Antifascisti Collection, 4A, fasc. D. M. Levi.

17. Ibid.

18. See AYVJ, Zeiri Collection, correspondence, letters of June 6, 1945, and June 12, 1945.

19. Ibid.

20. Ibid.

21. See ACDEC, Comunità Collection, b. 4, fasc. 10/2, minutes from June 28, 1945.

22. See ACDEC, Comunità Collection b. 4, fasc. 10/2, minutes of June 28, 1945. On the role of the Joint up until the Liberation, see Y. Bauer, *American Jewry and the Holocaust: The American Jewish Joint Distribution Committee, 1939–1945* (Detroit: Wayne State University Press, 1981). On the Joint after the Liberation of Italy, see Y Bauer, *Out of the Ashes: The Impact of American Jews on Post-Holocaust European Jewry* (Oxford: Pergamon, 1989); for Italy and Selvino, see pp. 245–51. For the activities

of UNRRA for children, see N. Stargardt, *Witnesses of War. Children's Lives under the Nazis* (New York: Knopf, 2005), 352ff. For the quotes of Haim Luftman, see AFSTA, interview 2008, 22–23.

23. See K. Lowe, *Il continente selvaggio. L'Europa alla fine della seconda guerra mondiale* (2012; Rome: Laterza, 2013) 208ff.; I. Buruma, *Anno Zero. Una storia del 1945* (2013; Milan: Mondadori, 2015), 171ff.

24. AYVJ, Zeiri Collection, letters, May 12, 1945.

25. See ACDEC, Comunità fund, b. 8, fasc. 19, subfasc. 5.

26. AYVJ, Zeiri collection, letters, May 12, 1945.

27. Ibid., June 13, 1945.

28. On the birth of the alpine colony of Sciesopoli, see G. Tiraboschi, *Selvino. La storia, la cronaca, le memorie* (Bergamo: Corponove, 2008), 187ff. The photograph of Sciesopoli in the thirties is taken from the iconographic material collected in a research of the E. Amaldi high school of Alzano Lombardo, available online on the institute's website (www.liceoamaldi.gov.it).

29. AYVJ, Zeiri Collection, correspondence, June 13, 1945.

30. See S. Baldi, "Opera Pia Fondazione Tonoli e Melloni," in *Istituto di Assistenza ai Minori e agli Anziani. Memorie e immagini di assistenza e di solidarietà* (Milan: Nexo, 2003), 25ff.

31. See AISEC, Cln Sesto S. Giovanni Collection, b. 3, fasc. 3/11.

32. See Minerbi, *Raffaele Cantoni*, 152.

33. See ACDEC, M. Cantoni Collection, b. 2, subfasc. 5.

34. AYVJ, Zeiri Collection, letters, June 13, 1945.

35. Ibid., June 26, 1945.

36. See Lifton, *The King of Children*, 268ff.

37. AYVJ, Zeiri Collection, correspondence, June 26, 1945.

38. Ibid., n.d. (but early June-late July 1945).

39. Ibid.

40. See AYVJ, O.90, code 5263222 (letter n. 250).

41. Ibid. (letter n. 261).

42. AYVJ, Zeiri Collection, correspondence, July 17, 1945.

43. Ibid.

44. For the centrality of the Brennero Pass for illegal immigration operations, see the memoirs of a major emissary, Efraim Dekel, cited here in their English version: E. Dekel, *Bri'ha: Flight to the Homeland* (New York: Herzl, 1972), in particular 278–79.

45. Haim Luftman's interview (with his Israeli name, Haim Sarid) with interviewer Lea Furst of the Yad Vashem institute, released (in Hebrew) in Tel Aviv, December 2, 2008, was translated into English and transcribed

for family members. Hereafter, it is cited with the mention: "AFSTA, interview 2008." For the reconstruction of the events of Haim Luftman, I have largely relied on this retrospective testimony of his.

46. See Z. Pakula, *The Jews of Poznan* (London: Vallentine Mitchell, 2003), in particular 19ff.

47. See AFSTA, interview 2008.

48. See ibid.

49. See Minerbi, *Raffaele Cantoni*, 164; A. Marzano, *Post-Shoah Relief and Rehabilitation: The Hakhsharot for Jewish DPs in Italy (1945–1948)*, paper presented at the conference Italian Jews in Context: Relations, Exchanges, Networks, CUNY-Columbia University, New York, March 9–10, 2015, 11. For a summary, see A. Marzano, "The 'Hachsharot' for Jewish Displaced Persons in Italy, 1945–1948," in *In Response to an Italian Captain. "Aliya Bet" from Italy, 1945–1948*, ed. R. Bonfil (Tel Aviv: Eretz Israel Museum, 2016), 49e–56e.

50. See Y. Gelber, "The Meeting between the Jewish Soldiers from Palestine Serving in the British Army and 'She'erit Hapletah,'" in *She'erit Hapletah*, ed. I. Gutman and A. Saf (Jerusalem: Yad Vashem, 1990), 10ff.; D. Porat, "One Side of a Jewish Triangle in Italy: The Encounter of Italian Jews with Holocaust Survivors and with Hebrew Soldiers and Zionist Representatives in Italy, 1944–1946," in *Israeli Society, the Holocaust and Its Survivors* (London: Vallentine Mitchell, 2008), 181–205; E. Salerno, *Mossad base Italia. Le azioni, gli intrighi, le verità nascoste* (Milan: il Saggiatore, 2010), 29ff.

51. See A. Sereni, *I clandestini del mare. L'emigrazione ebraica in terra d'Israele dal 1945 al 1948* (1973; Milan: Mursia, 2006).

52. See Bondy, *Enzo Sereni*, 426ff.

53. See ACDEC, b. 2, fasc. 4.

54. For two direct accounts on the activities of Aliyah Beth in Via Cantù, see Sereni, *I clandestini del mare*, 23ff.; G. Morpurgo, *Il violino liberato* (Milan: Mursia, 2008), 20ff.

55. AFSTA, interview 2008.

56. See M. Wyman, *DPs: Europe's Displaced Persons, 1945–1951* (Ithaca, NY: Cornell University Press, 1998), 97–98.

57. See Hilberg, *L'Holocauste*, 52.

58. See M. Myers Feinstein, *Holocaust Survivors in Postwar Germany, 1945–1957* (Cambridge: Cambridge University Press, 2009), 39; A. J. Patt, *Finding Home and Homeland. Jewish Youth and Zionism in the Aftermath of the Holocaust* (Detroit: Wayne State University Press, 2009), 3ff.

59. For the reference to Shmuel Milchman, see his memoir (in Hebrew): S. Milchman and C. Garti, *Il ragazzo da laggiù. Memorie di luce e di ombra*, partially reproduced in a site edited by the archivist Bernardino Pasinelli and dedicated to the historical memory of Sciesopoli (www.sciesopoli.com, accessed July 2017).

60. See Beckman, *The Jewish Brigade*, 120ff.; Porat, *The Fall of a Sparrow*, 204ff.

61. See Minerbi, *Raffaele Cantoni*, 158–60.

62. See Gelber, "The Meeting," 19.

63. See Y. Bauer, *Flight and Rescue: Brichah* (New York: Random House, 1970). See also the studies collected in T. Albrich and R. W. Zweig, eds., *Escape through Austria: Jewish Refugees and the Austrian Road to Palestine* (New York: Routledge, 2002).

64. See Bauer, *Flight and Rescue*, 66ff., 97ff.

65. Y. Grodzinsky, *In the Shadow of the Holocaust: The Struggle between Jews and Zionists in the Aftermath of World War II* (Monroe, ME: Common Courage, 2005), 31–38.

66. Ibid.

67. See quotes in Bauer, *Flight and Rescue*, 101.

68. See the quotes gathered in Segev, *The Seventh Million*, 117–18.

69. See I. Zertal, *Israele e la Shoah. La nazione e il culto della tragedia* (2002; Turin: Einaudi, 2007), 24ff.

70. Cited in Segev, *The Seventh Million*, 120.

71. AFSTA, interview 2008.

72. Ibid.

73. See Weintraub, *Grazie*, 124–25.

74. See ACDEC, Comunità Collection, b. 4, fasc. 10/1; ACS, Ministero dell'Interno, Direzione generale Pubblica Sicurezza, cat. 4A bis, b. 222.

75. On the hobbies of Piazzatorre, see V. Paggi, *Vicolo degli azzimi. Dal ghetto di Pitigliano al miracolo economico* (Rimini: Panozzo editore, 2013), 189ff. For the photo of Piazzatorre, see AFDH, various documents and photos.

76. AYVJ, Zeiri Collection, correspondence, August 11, 1945.

77. Ibid., August 27, 1945.

78. Ibid.

79. Ibid.

80. See Sereni, *I clandestini*, 27, 51.

81. AYVJ, Zeiri Collection, correspondence, September 10, 1945.

82. See ibid.

83. ACDEC, Comunità fund. b. 7, fasc. 15, Allies (1945).
84. On the role of Gorini, see ACDEC, M. Cantoni fund, b. 2, subfasc. 5/2, via Unione 5. For a first historiographical assessment on the Jewish colony of Sciesopoli, see the text of M. Cavallarin, "Sciesopoli (1945–1948): il contrappasso, la genesi, i nomi," published as an introduction to the graphic novel by A. Scandella, *Aliyah Beth. Sciesopoli: il ritorno alla vita di 800 bambini ebrei sopravvissuti alla Shoah (1945–1948)* (Milan: Unicopli, 2016), 8–22.
85. AYVJ, Zeiri Collection, correspondence, September 10, 1945.
86. Ibid.
87. Ibid.

7. A REPUBLIC OF ORPHANS

1. For the photo of Moshe in his office, see (at time stamp 2:29) the video posted on YouTube in December 2015 and titled (in Hebrew) *I bambini di Selvino*, which corresponds to an episode of popular Israeli TV show *See the World*.
2. AYVJ, Zeiri Collection, correspondence, October 4, 1945.
3. Ibid.
4. Ibid., October 3, 1945.
5. Ibid., October 21, 1945.
6. On the engagement of Reuven and Noga, see the photographic documentation contained in AFDH, various documents.
7. The quotes of Yaakov Meriash are taken from the transcription of a conversation I had with him in Kibbutz Erez on June 21, 2014, hereafter cited as Meriash, conversation with the author, 2014.
8. The quotes from Noga Cohen Donath are taken from the transcription of a conversation I had with her in Haifa on June 20, 2014.
9. See AFDH, various documents.
10. On the Friedrich family, see F. Falk, *Le comunità israelitiche di Fiume e Abbazia tra le due guerre* (Rome: Litos, 2012), under the surname entry.
11. See A. Megged, *Il viaggio verso la Terra promessa. La storia dei bambini di Selvino* (1985; Milan: Mazzotta, 1997), 22–23.
12. A. Tory, *Surviving the Holocaust: The Kovno Ghetto Diary*, ed. M. Gilbert and D. Porat (Cambridge, MA: Harvard University Press, 1990), 309–11.

13. AYVJ, Zeiri Collection, correspondence, October 15, 1945.
14. See A. Berger, "Munkács: A Jewish World That Was," PhD dissertation, University of Sydney, 2009, 13ff.; K. Čapková, *Czechs, Germans, Jews? National Identity and the Jews of Bohemia* (New York: Berghahn, 2012), 224–25.
15. See AYVJ, Zeiri Collection, correspondence, October 15, 1945.
16. See the documentation contained in AJDCNY, Italy, Refugees.
17. AYVJ, Zeiri Collection, correspondence, January 17, 1946.
18. On the Nembro-Selvino carriage road (unpaved until the 1950s), see G. Tiraboschi, *Selvino. La storia, la cronaca, le memorie* (Bergamo: Corponove, 2008), 297ff. The photograph of the street is taken from AMITY, Selvino Collection, doc. 4802.5.
19. See Aviel, *Freedom and Loneliness*, 136–37. Also, I am referring to the transcription of a conversation I had with Adam Wexler in Rishon-LeZion on June 16, 2014, henceforth, cited as Wexler, conversation with the author, 2014.
20. AYVJ, Zeiri Collection, correspondence, December 27, 1945.
21. See ibid., letters of October 3 and 4, 1945.
22. Ibid., October 12, 1945.
23. For the letters of Matilde Cassin to Moshe Zeiri, see AYVJ, series O.75, code 1299.
24. AYVJ, Zeiri Collection, correspondence, letter of December 14, 1945.
25. On the first legal departures from Italy to Palestine in 1945, see S. Kokkonen, *The Jewish Refugees in Postwar Italy, 1945–1951: The Way to Eretz Israel* (Saarbrücken: Lap Lambert Academic, 2011), 133ff. On the refugee camps in Italy, see C. Di Sante, "I campi profughi in Italia (1943–1947)," in *Naufraghi della pace. Il 1945, i profughi e le memorie divise d'Europa*, ed. G. Crainz, R. Pupo, and S. Salvatici (Rome: Donzelli, 2008), 143–56; M. Ravagnan, "I campi 'Displaced Persons' per profughi ebrei stranieri in Italia (1945–1950)," in *Storia e Futuro. Rivista di storia e storiografia*, no. 30 (November 2012): 3ff. The PH.D. dissertation by Ravagnan is also worth of attention: "I profughi ebrei in Italia nel secondo dopoguerra (1945–1950)," Università di Bologna, 2010–11.
26. AYVJ, Zeiri Collection, correspondence, December 27, 1945.
27. Ibid. For the literary reference, see I. L. Peretz, "Bontsha il silenzioso," in *Il meglio dei racconti Yiddish*, ed. I. Howe and E. Greenberg (Milan: Mondadori, 1985), 1:179ff.
28. AYVJ, Zeiri Collection, correspondence, December 27, 1945.
29. Ibid.

30. See Bauer, *Flight and Rescue*, 105; L. Jockusch, *Collect and Record! Jewish Holocaust Documentation in Early Postwar Europe* (New York: Oxford University Press, 2012), 123.

31. See AYVJ, Zeiri Collection, correspondence, n.d. (but early November 1945) and November 19, 1945.

32. See Megged, *Il viaggio verso la Terra promessa*, 23ff.

33. AYVJ, Zeiri Collection, correspondence, October 27, 1945.

34. AFSTA, interview 2008.

35. For the episodes of Avraham between Poland and Lithuania, see Aviel, *A Village Named Dowgalishok*, 298ff. For Avraham's journey toward Italy and the meeting with Moshe, see Aviel, *Freedom and Loneliness*, 17–68.

36. See Aviel, *Freedom and Loneliness*, 17–68.

37. See ibid.

38. For the photograph of Avraham with two companions from Sciesopoli (Romek Shichor and Bracha Lifschitz), see AFATA, various documents.

39. See B. Wasserstein, *On the Eve: The Jews of Europe before the Second World War* (London: Profile, 2013), 25–26, as well as an abundant case study in Yiddish literature.

40. For the misadventures of Yaakov Meriash, see his book in Hebrew quoted in the text (edition not commercially available, 2012); information based mainly on Meriash, conversation with the author, 2014.

41. See D. Pohl, "The Murder of Ukraine's Jews under the German Military Administration and in the Reich Commissariat Ukraine," in *The Shoah in Ukraine: History, Memory, Memorialization*, ed. R. Brandon and W. Lower (Bloomington: Indiana University Press, 2008), 23ff. (for the massacre of Lutsk, 49ff.); T. Snyder, "The Life and Death of Western Volhynian Jewry, 1921–1945," in *The Shoah in Ukraine*, ed. Brandon and Lower, 77ff. (for the rare Jews saved from Lutsk, 91).

42. On the rescue of Shmulik Shulman by his good Pole, see his testimony contained in the documentary *If You Survive: The Story of Shmulik Shilo*, edited by Z. Nevo (Hebrew University of Jerusalem, 2013), minute 41.

43. For the arrival of Dov and Adam Wexler in Selvino, see Wexler, conversation with the author, 2014. On Adam's arrival and his stay in Selvino in general, also see his second autobiographical book (in Hebrew, published posthumously), Wexler, *A Larger Standpoint*, private edition, Rishon LeZion (2016), 6–32.

44. See S. Salvatici, *Senza casa e senza paese. Profughi europei nel secondo dopoguerra* (Bologna: il Mulino, 2008), in particular 41ff.

45. See D. Stone, *La liberazione dei campi. La fine della Shoah e le sue eredità* (2015; Turin: Einaudi, 2017), viiiff.

46. For the photo of Adam and Dov, see AFWRL, various documents.

47. Some moments of everyday life in Sciesopoli, in particular the morning flag-raising and gymnastics sessions, are documented in a Zionist propaganda video dating back to the autumn of 1946. They are accessible on YouTube (at the initiative of Tami Sharon) under the title *Beit Aliyat Hanoar "Sciesopoli," Selvino, Italy 1945–1948* (https://www.sciesopoli.com/en/news/video-su-sciesopoli-ebraica/, accessed July 2017).

48. For Dov's partnership with Haim Luftman and for Adam's partnership with Avraham Lipkunski, I relied on Wexler, conversation with the author, 2014.

49. For Suti Weisz's arrival in Selvino, see Papp, *Outcasts*, 215ff.; Livnat, Haifa conference 2014, minute 57. Suti's photo is taken from the Yad Vashem website, the International School for Holocaust Studies, "Interviews." (https://www.yadvashem.org/articles/interviews/yitshak-and-haim.html, accessed September 15, 2022).

50. For the arrival in Selvino of the Łódź group, see Megged, *Il viaggio verso la Terra promessa*, 67–68.

51. AYVJ, Zeiri Collection, correspondence, November 19, 1945.

52. See AFATA, various documents.

53. AYVJ, Zeiri Collection, correspondence, October 21, 1945.

54. On the division of labor in Sciesopoli, besides the numerous letters from Moshe's correspondence, see also Megged, *Il viaggio verso la Terra promessa*, 70–71.

55. The slogan "to build and be built" comes from the verse of a popular Zionist song: see E. Zakim, *To Build and Be Built: Landscape, Literature, and the Construction of Zionist Identity* (Philadelphia: University of Pennsylvania Press, 2006), 1–2.

56. See AYVJ, Zeiri Collection, correspondence, January 29, 1946.

57. For the timing of arrivals and departures of the Sciesopoli teaching staff, see ACSe, Folder 47, 1931–1949.

58. See AYVJ, Zeiri Collection, correspondence, November 19, 1945.

59. Ibid.

60. See B. Rosner and F. C. Tubach, *An Uncommon Friendship: From Opposite Sides of the Holocaust* (Berkeley: University of California Press, 2010), 156.

61. The fresco of fascist artist Daniele Fontana, *Scena d'assalto* (1934), is reproduced in E. Rollandini, "Dall'irredentismo al regime. Il lascito De

Eccher dall'Eco e i progetti decorativi per il Castello del Buonconsiglio e Palazzo Thun a Trento," in *Tempi della storia, tempi dell'arte. Cesare Battisti tra Vienna e Roma*, ed. L. Dal Prà (Trento: Autonomous Province of Trento, 2016), 495.

62. Details on the cinematographic activities of Sciesopoli are based on a testimony of the children of Amedeo Barbaglia (Giambattista, Mariella, and Rosanna), which I collected in Bergamo on October 27, 2014. The quote on the "Jewish truck" is taken from the transcription of this meeting, according to the words of Amedeo Barbaglia. See also, by Mariella Barbaglia, a letter from her published on October 31, 2010, by the newspaper *L'Eco di Bergamo*, under the editorial title "*Le mie giornate tra i bambini scampati al lager*" (My days among the children who escaped the concentration camp).

63. AYVJ, Zeiri Collection, letters, October 21, 1945.

64. The information about Laurel and Hardy is taken from the testimony of Angela Camozzi, a teacher at Selvino, quoted in S. Viola, "Venivano dai lager e qui ritrovarono il sorriso," *Gente*, February 6, 1995.

65. The formula "atheist of the Book" is taken from Oz e Oz-Salzberger, *Gli ebrei e le parole*, 50.

66. For the photo of the fictional Hasidic Jew on the stage of a show in Sciesopoli, see AMITY, Selvino Collection, doc. 060.

67. See Ben-Amos, *Israël. La fabrique de l'identité nationale*, 74. See also, and particularly regarding the kibbutzim, Y. Shavit and S. Sitton, *Staging and Stagers in Modern Jewish Palestine: The Creation of Festival Lore in a New Culture, 1882–1948* (Detroit: Wayne State University Press, 2004), 106ff.

68. AYVJ, Zeiri Collection, correspondence, November 28, 1945.

69. Ibid.

70. Ibid., n.d. (but early November 1945).

71. The personal files of UNRRA related to Selvino are kept in copy at ACDEC, Comunità Collection, fasc. 19/4, UNRRA cards.

72. For the conflict with Adam, see Wexler, conversation with the author, 2014.

73. AYVJ, Zeiri Collection, correspondence, n.d. (but early November 1945).

74. Meriash, conversation with the author, 2014.

75. For Alexander Czoban's retrospective testimony, see AFZSL, 1988 radio transcript.

76. See Aviel, *Freedom and Loneliness*, 109.

386   NOTES

77. On the collective protests, see Megged, *Il viaggio verso la Terra promessa*, 42.

78. See ibid., 36. See the testimony of Sara herself contained (at time stamp 11:00) in a video entitled (in Hebrew) *La storia di una casa: i bambini di Selvino* and filmed in large part at the kibbutz Tel Yitzhak, March 24, 1992, on the occasion of a meeting of former "children of Selvino" (the video is available on YouTube, with erroneous chronological indication, under the title "Sciesopoli return in 1983": https://www.sciesopoli.com/en/news/ritorno-a-selvino-1983/, accessed September 15, 2022).

79. See AFSTA, various documents.

8. LIFE AFTER DEATH

1. See his own retrospective testimony in P. Tarjan, ed., *Children Who Survived the Final Solution: By Twenty-Six Survivors* (New York: iUniverse, 2004), 137–45.

2. See Alexander Czoban's retrospective testimony in AFZSL, 1988 radio transcript.

3. For the kitchen photo: AJDCNY, Photo archive, Selvino Collection, code_03262_dt1.

4. For the quotes on the abundance in the kitchens of Sciesopoli, I refer to the transcriptions of my conversations with Alberto Cortinovis in Selvino on October 29, 2014; with Pierina Tiraboschi Ghilardi in Selvino on October 29, 2014; and with Giovanni Grigis in Selvino, on October 29, 2014.

5. See E. Gianini Belotti, *Pimpì oselì* (1995; Milan: Feltrinelli, 2010), in particular 126ff.

6. From my conversation with Alberto Cortinovis, October 29, 2014.

7. From my conversation with Pierina Tiraboschi Ghilardi, October 20, 2014. Selvino's postcard is reproduced from materials collected by the local researcher Aurora Cantini, available online (http://acantini.altervista.org, accessed July 2017).

8. The quote from the hairdresser Andrea Cortinovis is taken from an interview conducted by the ethnologist Riccardo Schwamenthal in Selvino on November 18, 1989, which can be heard on the website on Sciesopoli managed by Bernardino Pasinelli (www.sciesopoli.com).

9. From my conversation with Giovanni Grigis, October 29, 2014.

10. From my conversation with Alberto Cortinovis, October 29, 2014.

11. From my conversation with Giovanni Grigis, October 29, 2014.

12. On the importance of photographic portraits for young Jews in refugee camps, see the comments by A. Grossmann, *Jews, German, and Allies: Close Encounters in Occupied Germany* (Princeton, NJ: Princeton University Press, 2007), 204–5.

13. For the photo of the three girls in the village: AMITY, Selvino Collection, doc. 3591.2a. The quotes of the former girls of Sciesopoli are taken from the video entitled (in Hebrew) *La storia di una casa*.

14. For the biographical events of the Auerbach family and the Gurman family, see AUSCSF, Visual history archive, testimonies, respectively the interviews with Bobbi Maxman (1996) and Tsiporah Rekhtman (1997). For the compositions of the two families in Selvino, see ACSe, Folder 47, years 1931–1949, passim. Various information also in Megged, *Il viaggio verso la Terra promessa*, 78.

15. AYVJ, Zeiri Collection, correspondence, January 9, 1946.

16. See AJDCNY, Photo archive, Selvino Collection, code_07541_dt.

17. AYVJ, Zeiri Collection, August 16, 1946.

18. On the propaganda use of children's photographs in the immediate postwar period, see M. Gardet, "Introduction," in *Revue d'histoire de l'enfance "irrégulière"* 15 (2013), monographic issue *Enfances déplacées. (II) En temps de guerre*, 3ff.

19. AYVJ, Zeiri Collection, correspondence, January 9, 1946.

20. Ibid., February 10, 1946.

21. On the issue of UNRRA money, I relied on Wexler, conversation with the author, 2014.

22. AYVJ, Zeiri Collection, correspondence, November 12, 1945.

23. A. Appelfeld, *Oltre la disperazione*, trans. E. Loewenthal 1994 (Milan: Guanda, 2016), 52.

24. AYVJ, Zeiri Collection, correspondence, January 17, 1946.

25. Ibid., November 19, 1945.

26. Ibid., November 12, 1945.

27. Ibid., November 19, 1945.

28. Ibid., January 17, 1946.

29. For Reuven Kohen (now Kohen-Raz) as an internationally renowned specialist, see at least his contribution entitled *Psychobiological Aspects of Cognitive Growth* (New York: Academic, 1977).

30. Cited in Patt, *Finding Home and Homeland*, 300 (and, in general, 82–102).

31. See recollections by Sara Goldman and Aviva Czoban in the video (in Hebrew) *La storia di una casa*.

32. See Appelfeld, *Storia di una vita*, 81.

33. For the only two photos saved and for Avraham Lipkunski's prayers in Sciesopoli, I relied on the transcription of my conversation with him in Tel Aviv on June 17, 2014.

34. AYVJ, Zeiri Collection, correspondence, October 27, 1945.

35. Ibid.

36. See Wexler, conversation with the author, 2014.

37. AYVJ, Zeiri Collection, correspondence, n.d. (but early November 1945).

38. See Megged, *Il viaggio verso la Terra promessa*, 37.

39. Cited in ibid., 79.

40. For the abundance of snow in Selvino in the mid-twentieth century, see Belotti, *Pimpì oselì*, 63ff. For the photograph of Adam with skis on: AFWRL, various documents.

41. See Gardet, "Introduction," 2–3.

42. On Yiddish as a language of annihilation, see R. Ertel, "Écrits en yiddish," in *Autour d'Élie Wiesel. Une parole pour l'avenir*, ed. M. de Saint-Chéron (Paris: Odile Jacob, 1996), 23ff.

43. On Hebrew as the language of victory, see G. Rozier, *D'un pays sans amour* (Paris: Grasset, 2011), 292ff.

44. See Appelfeld, *Storia di una vita*, 110–11.

45. Agnon, *Una storia comune*, 115.

46. See Aviel, *Freedom and Loneliness*, 157.

47. See Meriash, conversation with the author, 2014, and numerous other retrospective testimonies of the former guests of Sciesopoli.

48. AMITY, Selvino Collection, doc. 3572.1.

49. AYVJ, Zeiri Collection, correspondence, October 27, 1945.

50. AYVJ, Zeiri Collection, correspondence, November 19, 1945.

51. For the title page of the *Nivenu* journal (no. 9, March 8, 1946), see AMITY, b. 18, doc. 2285–41305. The photo is mine.

52. On the newspapers published in the Jewish refugee camps after the Liberation of Italy, and in general on childhood voices, see B. Cohen, "The Children's Voice: Postwar Collection of Testimonies from Child Survivors of the Holocaust," *Holocaust and Genocide Studies* 21, no. 1 (2007): 73ff.; B. Cohen, "Young Witnesses in the DP Camps: Children's Holocaust Testimony in Context," *Journal of Modern Jewish Studies* 11, no. 1 (2012): 103ff.

53. AYVJ, Zeiri Collection, October 27, 1945.

54. Cited in Megged, *Il viaggio verso la Terra promessa*, 55.

55. Cited in ibid., 55–56.

56. See AYVJ, series O.39, code 3549664. On the Hasman family in the Łódź ghetto, see A. Eilenberg Eibeshitz, *Preserved Evidence: Ghetto Lodz* (Haifa: Institute for Holocaust Studies, 1998), 1:428ff.

57. AMITY, b. 18, doc. 2285–41305 (trans. Chiara Camarda).
58. Ibid., doc. 2285–41302 (trans. Chiara Camarda).
59. Cited in Megged, *Il viaggio verso la Terra promessa*, 73–74.
60. AMITY, b. 18, doc. 2285–41309 (trans. Chiara Camarda).
61. See AFLTA, various documents, manuscript dated by Selvino, January 15, 1946.
62. Ibid.
63. See Pollack, *Paesaggi*, 90ff.
64. AMITY, doc. 2285–41306 (trans. Chiara Camarda).

9. KIBBUTZ SELVINO?

1. On the legend of Jewish paratroopers, see J. Tydor Baumel-Schwartz, *Perfect Heroes: The World War II Parachutists and the Making of Israeli Collective Memory* (Madison: University of Wisconsin Press, 2010).
2. See P. H. Silverstone, *Our Only Refuge, Open the Gates! Clandestine Immigration to Palestine, 1938–1948*, online, undated (but 1999): (https://paulsilverstone.com/book/our-only-refuge-open-the-gates-clandestine-immigration-to-palestine-1938-1948/, accessed September 15, 2022). For the diplomatic front relating to relations between Italy and the United Kingdom, see A. J. Kochavi, *Post-Holocaust Politics: Britain, the United States, and Jewish Refugees, 1945–1948* (Chapel Hill: University of North Carolina Press, 2001), 235; and above all M. Toscano, *La "porta di Sion." L'Italia e l'immigrazione clandestina ebraica in Palestina, 1945–1948* (Bologna: il Mulino, 1990), 103–50.
3. See M. G. Enardu, "L'immigrazione illegale ebraica verso la Palestina e la politica estera italiana," *Storia delle Relazioni Internazionali* 2, no. 1 (1986): 147–66; M. G. Enardu, "L'Aliyah Bet nella politica estera italiana, 1945–1948," in *Italia Judaica, Gli ebrei nell'Italia unita 1870–1945* (Rome: Atti del IV convegno internazionale, Ministero per i Beni culturali e ambientali, 1993), 514–32; J. Markovizky, "The Italian Government's Response to the Problem of Jewish Refugees, 1945–1948," *Journal of Israeli History* 19, no. 1 (Spring 1998): 23–39; G. Romano, "'Gli indesiderabili.' L'Italia e l'immigrazione ebraica in Palestina, 1945–1948," *Nuova Storia Contemporanea* 4, no. 6 (2000): 81–96.
4. For the statistics regarding the illegal departures from Italy, see M. Toscano, "Italy and 'Aliya Bet,'" in *In Response to an Italian Captain: "Aliya Bet" from Italy, 1945–1948*, ed. R. Bonfil (Tel Aviv: Eretz Israel Museum, 2016), 23e. For maps of Italian departure points, see p. 26.
5. See Sereni, *I clandestini del mare*, 86–94.

6. Alterman's poems are reproduced in full, in English translation, in Bonfil, *In Response*, 4e–5e.

7. See L. Rosenberg-Friedman, "The Lady in the Black Dress: The Story of Ada Sereni, Commander of Illegal Immigration in Italy," in Bonfil, *In Response*, 36e–48e.

8. For the rearmament of the *Enzo Sereni* (originally called *Rondine*), its navigation, and its passengers, see L. Giacchero, *Una Rondine fa primavera. Un legno arenzanese verso la Terra Promessa* (Genoa: Antica Tipografia Ligure, 2013); L. Giacchero, *Come Rondine al nido. A bordo della nave "Rondine"* (Genoa: Antica Tipografia Ligure, 2016). For a database of illegal migrant Jews in British Palestine from 1945–48, see the site www.maapilim.org.il (accessed July 2017).

9. AYVJ, Zeiri correspondence, n.d. (but circa December 20, 1945).

10. See Aviel, *Freedom and Loneliness*, 152–53.

11. On Julek Reich, see chapter 5 of his book of memoirs (in Hebrew): Y. Reich, "You Lifted My Soul from the Underworld" (edition out of print, accessible at www.yoelreich.net, accessed July 2017).

12. See Megged, *Il viaggio verso la Terra promessa*, 37.

13. See Sereni, *I clandestini del mare*, 100ff. The photograph of the truck with the Sciesopoli boys heading toward the port of Vado Ligure is taken from a private archive. For the photography of *Enzo Sereni* and her passengers, see AJITA, Photo archive, code PH-8478.

14. See A. Appelfeld, *Il ragazzo che voleva dormire*, trans. E. Loewenthal (2009; Milan: Guanda, 2012), 42–43.

15. AFSTA, interview 2008.

16. See Berkowitz, *Western Jewry and the Zionist Project*, 109–110.

17. For the photo of the landing in Haifa: ABLH, photo collection, code 20521.

18. AFSTA, interview 2008.

19. Ibid.

20. For the statistics on the departures of Jews from Poland, see Redlich, *Life in Transit*, 54.

21. See Gross, *La Peur*, 67ff.

22. See Bauer, *Flight and Rescue*, 113ff.

23. On the American activities of Jacob Pat, see C. Collomp, *Résister au nazisme. Le Jewish Labor Committee, New York, 1934–1945* (Paris: Éditions du CNRS, 2016), in particular 275ff.

24. J. Pat, *Ashes and Fire* (New York: International Universities Press, 1947).

25. Ibid., 7–11. On the situation of the children, see J. B. Michlic, "Rebuilding Shattered Lives: Some Vignettes of Jewish Children's Lives in Early Postwar Poland," in *Holocaust Survivors: Resettlement, Memories, Identities*, ed. D. Ofer, F. S. Ouzan, and J. Tydor Baumel-Schwartz (New York: Berghahn, 2012), 46–87.

26. For the story of Shulamit Kacyzne, see a memoir (in Hebrew) of Shulamit herself dating back to 1955 and deposited in AYVJ, series O.3. code 642. For Shulamit's photo portrait, see ABMP, Sulamita Kacyzne Collection, various documents.

27. See Pat, *Ashes and Fire*, 17–20.

28. On Eugenio Reale as ambassador to Warsaw (and on the distrust of the PCI staff toward Shulamit Kacyzne), see E. Aga-Rossi and V. Zaslavsky, *Togliatti e Stalin. Il Pci e la politica estera staliniana negli archivi di Mosca* (Bologna: il Mulino, 1997), 258–60.

29. Pat, *Ashes and Fire*, 19.

30. On the singularity of the position of the Royal ambassador compared to those of other chancelleries, see Kochavi, *Post-Holocaust Politics*, 163.

31. See T. Piotrowski, *Poland's Holocaust: Ethnic Strife, Collaboration with Occupying Forces and Genocide in the Second Republic, 1918–1947* (Jefferson, NC: McFarland, 2007), 46–47.

32. For Reale's diplomatic correspondence, see ACS, Direzione generale della Pubblica Sicurezza, cat. A5G, 1944–1948, b. 4, with reference to a dispatch dated February 19, 1946. See also A. Villa, *Dai Lager alla terra promessa. La difficile reintegrazione nella "nuova Italia" e l'immigrazione verso il Medio Oriente (1945–1948)* (Milan: Guerini, 2005), 58–60.

33. ASMAE, Affari politici, Polonia 1946–1950, report of February 20, 1946.

34. Zeiri's correspondence with Gordonia's leaders is collected in AMITY, b. 37-7253; also, in AHTA, Selvino Collection, fasc.141–123.

35. AYVJ, Zeiri Collection, correspondence, January 2, 1946.

36. See AYVJ, series O.90, code 5263222.

37. AYVJ, Zeiri Collection, correspondence, January 9, 1946.

38. Ibid.

39. Ibid., January 17, 1946.

40. See ibid., January 9, 1946.

41. Ibid., March 31, 1946.

42. From my conversation with Alberto Cortinovis, October 29, 2014.

43. S. J. Zoltak, *My Silent Pledge: A Journey of Struggle, Survival and Remembrance* (Toronto: MiroLand, 2013), 147.

44. AUSHMM, Photo archives, item 66420, courtesy of Simon Frumkin.
45. See Zoltak, *My Silent Pledge*, 151.
46. See Tarjan, *Children Who Survived*, 145.
47. See Rosner and Tubach, *An Uncommon Friendship*, 158ff.
48. AYVJ, Zeiri Collection, correspondence, January 29, 1946.
49. See ibid., February 10, 1946.
50. For the architectural project of Sciesopoli and the director's room, see AIAMAM, folder *"Affitto alla Comunità israelitica di Milano,"* project by Vietti Violi (1932), cross-section, drawing n. 23.
51. See Tiraboschi, *Selvino*, 193–94.
52. AYVJ, Zeiri Collection, correspondence, March 31, 1946.
53. Ibid.
54. AYVJ, Zeiri Collection, correspondence, letters of April 16 and 20, 1946.
55. See Sereni, *I clandestini del mare*, 113ff.
56. For this and for the subsequent citations of the prefectures from La Spezia, see ACS, Ministero dell'Interno, Direzione generale della Pubblica Sicurezza, cat. A 16, Stranieri ed ebrei stranieri (1930–1956), b. 20, Emigrazione illegale, fasc. La Spezia.
57. On the *Fede* and *Fenice* crisis, see Toscano, *La "porta di Sion,"* 76–91; I. Zertal, *From Catastrophe to Power: Holocaust Survivors and the Emergence of Israel* (Berkeley: University of California Press, 1998), 17ff.
58. See Minerbi, *Raffaele Cantoni*, 177–78.
59. AYVJ, Zeiri Collection, correspondence, April 16, 1946.
60. See Toscano, *La "porta di Sion,"* 83.
61. The article from *Secolo liberale*, no byline, is dated April 6, 1946.
62. Some ideas in S. Fantini, *Notizie dalla Shoah. La stampa italana nel 1945* (Bologna: Pendragon, 2005).
63. For the correspondent's article, see M. Torelli, "Milleduecento ebrei su una nave che non parte," *Corriere della Sera*, April 7, 1946; M. Torelli, "Pasqua ebraica sul molo di La Spezia," *Corriere d'informazione* (afternoon edition of *Corriere della Sera*), April 19–20, 1946; in addition to the unsigned photo-news "Verso la terra promessa," *Corriere d'informazione*, April 22–23, 1946.
64. Torelli, "Pasqua ebraica."
65. On Eva Ginat, see her own autobiographical memoir: E. Nadler, *Massacre on the Baltic*, edition out of print (Australia, 1995).
66. Jewish by family origin and Waldensian by religious choice, Franco Fortini (born in 1917 as Franco Lattes) was the most lucid and profound of

the Italian chroniclers first sent to the docks of La Spezia, then among the sands of Bocca di Magra, where those saved from the Shoah were waiting for the opportunity to embark. See in particular his reportage entitled "Ebrei clandestini dalle nostre coste," *Corriere della Sera*, "La Lettura" section, September 14, 1946.

67. AYVJ, Zeiri Collection, correspondence, n.d. (but circa April 20, 1946).

68. AUCEI, "Enti vari," envelope 44Q, fasc. 63, "Selvino," document "Kinderheim in Selvino," n.d.; "Bericht," April 30, 1946.

69. Ibid., various documents in Hebrew (n.d.; trans. Nitza Zeiri Sarner).

70. Ibid.

71. AYVJ, Zeiri Collection, correspondence, letter n.d. (but circa April 20, 1946) and letter from May 5, 1946.

72. See S. Luzzatto, *Il corpo del duce. Un cadavere tra immaginazione, storia e memoria* (Turin: Einaudi, 1998), 98ff.

73. AYVJ, Zeiri Collection, correspondence, May 16, 1946.

74. See Megged, *Il viaggio verso la Terra promessa*, 81.

75. See the issue of the newspaper *Nivenu* in AMITY, Selvino Fund, doc. 2235–41301 (trans. Chiara Camarda).

76. With regard to the Feldafing camp, see Grossmann, *Jews, German, and Allies*, passim; Z. W. Mankowitz, *Life between Memory and Hope: The Survivors of the Holocaust in Occupied Germany* (Cambridge: Cambridge University Press, 2002), in particular 131–60.

77. AJDCJ, Geneva II, Box 321B-322A, file n. 28, May 22, 1946.

78. See C. Roth, "Review: 'A Consolation for the Tribulations of Israel' by Samuel Usque," *Jewish Social Studies* 28, no. 1 (January 1966): 43.

79. ABLH, Nina Eckhajzer Boniówka Collection, code 29661.

80. On the division of roles between Ben-Gurion and Begin and on Black Saturday, see A. Mayer, *Plowshares into Swords: From Zionism to Israel* (London: Verso, 2008), 159ff.; C. Enderlin, *Attraverso il ferro e il fuoco. La lotta clandestina per l'indipendenza di Israele (1936–1948)* (Turin: Utet, 2010), 163ff.; Hoffman, *Anonymous Soldiers*, 204–5.

81. On the change of political line by the Zionist leadership, see M. van Creveld, *La spada e l'ulivo. Storia dell'esercito israeliano* (2002; Rome: Carocci, 2004), 97ff.

82. See Zertal, *From Catastrophe to Power*, 129ff. In general, on the politics of Ben-Gurion, see A. Shlaim, *The Iron Wall: Israel and the Arab World* (2000; New York: Norton, 2014), 22ff.

83. Gross, *La Peur*, 121–59. On the Kielce pogrom as a symptom of persistent Polish antisemitism, see F. M. Cataluccio, *Vado a vedere se di là è meglio. Quasi un breviario mitteleuropeo* (Palermo: Sellerio, 2010), 253–72.
84. See Redlich, *Life in Transit*, 54.
85. See Kochavi, *Post-Holocaust Politics*, 174–75.
86. See F. Liebreich, *Britain's Naval and Political Reaction to the Illegal Immigration of Jews to Palestine, 1945–1948* (New York: Routledge, 2005), 135ff.
87. For the article (no byline) on the Zionist meeting in Milan, see "Manifestazione di Israeliti per l'emigrazione in Palestina," *Corriere della Sera*, July 3, 1946.
88. The photo of the demonstration in Milan is taken from Bonfil, *In Response*, 244.
89. AYVJ, Zeiri Collection, correspondence, July 8, 1946.
90. Ibid.
91. Ibid., July 22, 1946.

10. IN ISRAEL'S WATERS

1. See AFWRL, various documents (in Polish, trans. Magdalena Bialas). On the "first letters" of the Shoah victims to their respective surviving families, see R. Rozett and I. Nidam-Orvieto, eds., *After So Much Pain and Anguish: First Letters after Liberation* (Jerusalem: Yad Vashem, 2016).
2. AMITY, Selvino Collection, letter to the secretary of the *Chaver haqevutsot*, July 19, 1946 (in Hebrew, trans. Chiara Camarda).
3. Ibid., July 28, 1946 (in Hebrew, trans. Chiara Camarda).
4. AYVJ, series O.33, code 9707, July 20, 1946 (in Hebrew, trans. Chiara Camarda).
5. ACS, Interior Ministry, Direzione generale della Pubblica Sicurezza, cat. A 16, Stranieri ed ebrei stranieri (1930–1956), b. 20, Emigrazione illegale, fasc. La Spezia.
6. See K. Kimche, "Haifa under Curfew as 'Liberty Ships' Load Deportees," *Palestine Post*, August 14, 1946; "Indignation and Dismay in Haifa," *Palestine Post*, August 18, 1946.
7. See "Indignation and Dismay in Haifa," *Palestine Post*, August 18, 1946.
8. "Tear Gas Overcomes Deportees' Desperate Resistance," *Palestine Post*, August 19, 1946.

9. Ibid.

10. Ibid. See also S. Guebenlian, "Deportees in Cyprus," *Palestine Post*, August 20, 1946.

11. For the front page of the *New York Times*: J. L. Meltzer, "Cyprus Ship Forced Back to Haifa by Bomb Blasts," *New York Times*, August 19, 1946. On the international impact of the incident, see Zertal, *From Catastrophe to Power*, 169–70.

12. On the dynamics of the terrorist attack, see Aviel, *Freedom and Loneliness*, 197–98.

13. The formulation of "anonymous soldiers" is taken from the title of Hoffman, *Anonymous Soldiers*.

14. For the photo Inda (Ayala) Liberman's immigration certificate, see AFATA, various documents.

15. See A. Halamish, *The Exodus Affair: Holocaust Survivors and the Struggle for Palestine* (New York: Syracuse University Press, 1998).

16. On the Cyprus camps, see above all D. Ofer, "Holocaust Survivors as Immigrants: The Case of Israel and the Cyprus Detainees," *Modern Judaism* 16, no. 1 (1996): 1–23 (for the statistics on deportees, 2–3). Furthermore, see the doctoral thesis by B. Nikolic Arrivé, *Les camps d'internement pour réfugiés juifs à Chypre de 1946 à 1949: le partage des responsabilité* (Inalco, Paris, 2016).

17. See S. Guebenlian, "No Guards, No Disorders," *Palestine Post*, August 28, 1946.

18. AFATA, various documents.

19. For the activities of Avraham in the camp, see his recollections in Aviel, *Freedom and Loneliness*, 216–29. For the issues of *Nivenu Baderech*, see ABLH, Selvino fund, code Z 8/15-50.

20. AMITY, b. 18, 2285–7756 (from the minutes of a meeting held in Kibbutz Kfar Ruppin on October 25, 1947: see infra).

21. See Megged, *Il viaggio verso la Terra promessa*, 127.

22. See S. Guebenlian, "Cyprus Detainees' Bid for Freedom," *Palestine Post*, August 19, 1946; S. Guebenlian, "Deportees to Be Segregated," *Palestine Post*, August 26, 1946.

23. Y. Kaniuk, *Il comandante dell' "Exodus,"* trans. M. Rapin (1999; Turin: Einaudi, 2001), 110–11.

24. See M. Laub, *Last Barrier to Freedom: Internment of Jewish Holocaust Survivors on Cyprus, 1946–1949* (Berkeley, CA: Judah L. Magnes Museum, 1985), 89–91.

25. See Aviel, *Freedom and Loneliness*, 233.

26. See AFATA, various documents.

27. See Rosner and Tubach, *An Uncommon Friendship*, 157.

28. See the article with no byline (though initialed): F. L., "Poveri orfanelli, gli Ebrei di Selvino," *Corriere d'informazione*, September 24–25, 1946.

29. Ibid.

30. Ibid.

31. Ibid.

32. For Yehudit's arrival in Naples with Nitza, see the information from her British Palestinian passport, in AFZE, various documents.

33. AYVJ, correspondence, respectively, from letters of July 8, 1946; July 22, 1946; and August 29, 1946. The photograph of Yehudit's class in the snow of Selvino (Nitza is the little girl in the center of the group) is taken from a private archive. A moment of play in the snow is documented (at time stamp 8:00) in a Zionist propaganda film dating back to the autumn of 1946 and accessible on YouTube, at the initiative of Tami Sharon, under the title *Beit Aliyat Hanoar "Sciesopoli, Selvino Italy 1945–1948*: https://www.sciesopoli.com/en/news/video-su-sciesopoli-ebraica/.

34. On the division of children and young people by age group, see the documentation contained in AUCEI, "Enti vari," envelope 44Q, fasc. 70, "Selvino Class I-II-III-IV-V-VI."

35. Cited in Megged, *Il viaggio verso la Terra promessa*, 86–87.

36. See an untitled sidebar in the *Palestine Post*, October 24, 1946.

37. For this, I refer to the evocative literary reconstruction of Y. Kaniuk, *Postmortem*, trans. G. Sciloni (1992; Turin: Einaudi, 2002), in particular 108, 203.

38. Nitza's quote, "everybody's father," is taken from an interview by Nitza Zeiri Sarner conducted in London, November 14, 2013, by Italian researchers Marco Cavallarin and Patrizia Ottolenghi, edited by the Milan CDEC: *Nitza Zeiri Sarner: "Sciesopoli," 1945–1948*. The video is accessible on the website managed by Bernardino Pasinelli, www.sciesopoli.com; the quote at minute 7:00.

39. For Moshe's ID card, see AFZE, various documents.

40. AJDCNY, Italy, Refugees, Education, November 29, 1946.

41. See Antonini, *DelAsEm*, 320–23.

42. ACS, Ministero dell'Interno, Direzione generale della Pubblica Sicurezza, cat. A16, Stranieri ed ebrei stranieri (1930–1956), b. 21, fasc. 5, Residenti nelle varie province d'Italia, sub-fasc. Bergamo.

43. See E. Nachmany Gafny, *Dividing Hearts: The Removal of Jewish Children from Gentile Families in Poland in the Immediate Post Holocaust Years* (Jerusalem: Yad Vashem, 2009), 158.

44. AJDCNY, Italy, Refugees, 1945–46: A. Syngalowski, "The Question of Vocational Training of Jews in Europe. A Clarification," December 22, 1946, 8.

45. See "Another 500 from Cyprus," *Palestine Post*, December 20, 1947.

46. For Avraham's own voyage toward Kiryat Shmuel, see Aviel, *Freedom and Loneliness*, 305. For Avraham's diary, see AYVJ, series O.37, code 731, item 9781670, Lipkunski papers.

47. On the voyage of the *Ulua* (renamed *Chaim Arlorozov*), see J. M. Hochstein and M. S. Greenfield, *The Jews' Secret Fleet: The Untold Story of North American Volunteers Who Smashed the British Blockade* (Jerusalem: Gefen, 1987), 88ff.; Halamish, *The Exodus Affair*, 26ff.

48. See A. L. Eliav, *The Voyage of the Ulua* (New York: Funk and Wagnalls, 1969).

49. For the photo report (no byline) in *Corriere d'informazione*, see the issue of March 19–20, 1947.

50. Cited in Megged, *Il viaggio verso la Terra promessa*, 123.

51. Cited in ibid., 124–25.

52. For Suti Weisz's voyage by ship, I refer to the transcript of a conversation I had with him, between Tel Aviv and Haifa, on January 7, 2016.

53. See AJDCNY, Cyprus, Youth Camp, Statistics, June 1, 1947.

54. See A. Citron, "Ben Hecht's Pageant-Drama: 'A Flag Is Born,'" in *Staging the Holocaust: The Shoah in Drama and Performance*, ed. C. Schumacher (Cambridge: Cambridge University Press, 1998), 92–93. On the Zionist season of Hecht's production, see G. Alonge, *Scrivere per Hollywood: Ben Hecht e la sceneggiatura americana classica* (Venice: Marsilio, 2012), 106ff.

55. B. Hecht, *A Flag Is Born* (New York: American League for a Free Palestine, 1946), 21, 46–47. The photo of Marlon Brando on Broadway is by Eileen Darby, the LIFE Images Collection/Getty Images.

56. On the navigation and passengers of the *Theodor Herzl*, see the report by F.-J. Armorin, *Des Juifs quittent l'Europe* (1947), republished with a different title in F.-J. Armorin, *Terre promise, Terre interdite* (1947; Palestine: Éditions Tallandier, 2011).

57. See Zertal, *From Catastrophe to Power*, 145–46. For lifeline chains in Belgium and illegal emigration from Belgium to Palestine, see J. Déom, *La filière des ombres. L'odyssée des réfugiés juifs, Belgique-Palestine (1945–1948)* (Brussels: Fondation de la Mémoire contemporaine, 2015).

58. For the presence on the ship of Mathilde Szwarcman and for her past during the racial persecution, I relied on the emails she sent me, with her Israeli identity of Dalia Wexler, in spring 2017. Her presence is confirmed by the website www.maapilim.org.il.

59. See ACS, Ministero dell'Interno, Direzione generale della Pubblica Sicurezza, cat. A 16, Stranieri ed ebrei stranieri (1930–1956), b. 20, Emigrazione illegale, fasc. La Spezia. On the evolution of the Italian government's attitude, see Toscano, La "porta di Sion," 151ff.

60. See Kaniuk, Il comandante dell' "Exodus," 153–54.

61. See Halamish, The Exodus Affair, 75ff.

62. For the interview with Ada Sereni, see F. Petriccione, "Inconveniente a Caifa di non essere un 'terrier,'" Corriere d'informazione, June 25–26, 1947.

63. A few notes on Operation Michaelberg are in D. Tsimhoni, "Activity of the Yishuv on the Behalf of Iraqi Jewry, 1914–1948," in *Organizing Rescue: National Jewish Solidarity in the Modern Period*, ed. S. I. Troen and B. Pinkus (London: Frank Cass, 1992), 262. The photograph of the American twin-engine is taken from the site en.maapilim.org.il, under the entry: Operation Michaelberg: (http://maapilim.org.il/notebook.asp?lang/, accessed July 2017).

64. On the aircraft operation of Paestum, see ACS, Ministero dell'Interno, Direzione generale della Pubblica Sicurezza, cat. A 16, Stranieri ed ebrei stranieri (1930–1956), b. 20, Emigrazione illegale.

65. Petriccione, *Inconveniente a Caifa*.

66. Sereni, *I clandestini del mare*, 265.

67. For the circumstances of Sara Goldman's survival in Poland, saved by Polish Christians later recognized as Righteous Among the Nations, see the Yad Vashem website, in the database on the Righteous, the dossier on the Tarasiuk family of Dolha (Lublin district).

11. THE ROAD TO JERUSALEM

1. See information from his British Palestinian passport, in AFZE, various documents.

2. AJDCNY, Italy, children, May 20, 1947 (Theodor Sznejberg report); AJDCJ, Box 9 A-2, File C 54.053, June 26, 1947. For a comparison with the institute of Sciesopoli with similar French institutions, see K. Hazan, *Les orphelins de la Shoah. Les maisons de l'espoir (1944–1960)* (Paris: Les Belles Lettres, 2000).

3. See AJDCNY, Italy, Refugees, Joint correspondence and activity of the ORT, August 31, 1947. See, moreover: S. Kavanaugh, *ORT, the Second World War and the Rehabilitation of Holocaust Survivors* (London: Vallentine Mitchell, 2008), 107–8. For the photo of the Sciesopoli carpenter's workshop, see AMITY, Selvino Collection, doc. 011.

4. See AMITY, Selvino Collection, b. 18, doc. 7253 (trans. Chiara Camarda).
5. Ibid.
6. Appelfeld, *Oltre la disperazione*, 94.
7. See S. Kangisser Cohen, *Child Survivors of the Holocaust in Israel. "Finding Their Voice": Social Dynamics and Post-War Experiences* (Brighton: Sussex Academic Press, 2005), 5ff.; Bensoussan, *Israele, un nome eterno*, 47ff.
8. AYVJ, Zeiri Collection, correspondence, n.d. (but late June–early July 1945).
9. See Appelfeld, *Il ragazzo che voleva dormire*, 92.
10. See Segev, *The Seventh Million*, 183.
11. See Aviel, *Freedom and Loneliness*, 344.
12. See Yablonka, *Survivors of the Holocaust*, 188–89.
13. Cited in Segev, *The Seventh Million*, 179.
14. See Appelfeld, *Il ragazzo che voleva dormire*, 68–69.
15. See Appelfeld, *Oltre la disperazione*, 9ff.
16. AFSTA, interview 2008, 24ff.
17. Ibid.
18. See H. Near, *The Kibbutz Movement: A History*, vol. 2, *Crisis and Achievement, 1939–1995* (Portland: Littman Library of Jewish Civilization/Vallentine Mitchell, 1997), 158ff.
19. See Yablonka, *Survivors of the Holocaust*, 175ff. Also useful are D. Ofer, "Mending the Body, Mending the Soul: Members of Youth Aliyah Take a Look at Themselves and at Others," in *Holocaust Survivors: Resettlement, Memories, Identities*, ed. D. Ofer, F. S. Ouzan, and J. Tydor Baumel-Schwartz (New York: Berghahn, 2012), 128–65; M. Balf, "Holocaust Survivors on Kibbutzim: Resettling Unsettled Memories," in *Holocaust Survivors*, ed. Ofer, Ouzan, and Tydor Baumel-Schwartz, 166–85; A. Schein, "Rooting the Rootless: The Absorption of Holocaust Survivors in Israeli Rural Settlements," in *Holocaust Survivors*, ed. Ofer, Ouzan, and Tydor Baumel-Schwartz, 207–32.
20. See D. Pagis, *The Selected Poetry*, trans. S. Mitchell (Berkeley: University of California Press, 1989). On Pagis's youth, see also a painful autobiographical text, published posthumously: D. Pagis, *Papà*, trans. F. Dal Bo (Florence: Giuntina, 2014).
21. Livnat, Haifa conference, 2016.
22. See Papp, *Outcasts*, 257ff.
23. Livnat, Haifa conference, 2016.

24. See Yablonka, *Survivors of the Holocaust*, 197ff.

25. Information on Moshe's whereabouts between Czechoslovakia and Palestine can be found in his British Palestinian passport, in AFZE, various documents.

26. See editorial articles "4 Killed in Bank Robbery," *Palestine Post*, September 28, 1947, and "Ten Killed in Haifa Explosion," *Palestine Post*, September 30, 1947. For the quote from Moshe: AMITY, b.18, doc. 37–7253, letter from October 3, 1947 (in Hebrew; trans. Chiara Camarda).

27. AMITY, b.18, doc. 37–7253, letter from October 3, 1947 (in Hebrew; trans. Chiara Camarda).

28. On Haim Luftman's bags already packed, see AFSTA, interview 2008, 24.

29. AMITY, b.18, doc. 37–7253, Moshe's letter.

30. My reconstruction of the meeting at Kibbutz Kfar Ruppin is based on the minutes of the meeting itself: AMITY, b. 18, doc. 2285–7756 (in Hebrew; trans. Nitza Zeiri Sarner).

31. Ibid.

32. Ibid.

33. Information on Moshe's return journey can be found in his British Palestinian passport, in AFZE, various documents.

34. AHTA, Selvino Collection, doc. 5/63.

35. ACS, Ministero dell'Interno, Direzione generale della Pubblica Sicurezza, cat. A 16, Stranieri ed ebrei stranieri (1930-1956), b. 21, fasc. 5, Residenti nelle varie province d'Italia, sottofasc. Bergamo.

36. AFZSL, various documents and photographs.

37. On the events in Haifa and the death of Heinz Rebhun, see the editorial, "All Day Fray in Haifa," *Palestine Post*, January 16, 1948, and the sidebar with no byline, "8 Victims Buried," *Palestine Post*, January 19, 1948.

38. See Rebhun, *Ho inciampato e non mi sono fatta male*; Rebhun, *Due della Brigata*.

39. See sidebar with no byline, "2000 Casualties in Six Weeks," *Palestine Post*, January 18, 1948.

40. See B. Morris, *La prima guerra di Israele* (2007; Milan: Rizzoli, 2008), 112ff.

41. Cited in Lockman, *Comrades and Enemies*, 356–57.

42. See Bensoussan, *Israele, un nome eterno*, 48.

43. For the military story of the trio, see Aviel, *Freedom and Loneliness*, 368ff. For the photo of the trio in uniform: AFATA, various documents.

44. See Morris, *La prima guerra di Israele*, 182–84.

45. See van Creveld, *La spada e l'ulivo*, 127–28.

46. See Pappe, *Storia della Palestina moderna*, 158.

47. On the Israeli military operations of May 1948, see Morris, *La prima guerra di Israele*, 236ff. On the incipient ethnic cleansing, see I. Pappe, *The Ethnic Cleansing of Palestine* (2006; Rome: Fazi editore, 2008), 160ff. On the destruction of Palestinian villages, see W. Khalidi, *All That Remains: The Palestinian Villages Occupied and Depopulated by Israel in 1948* (Washington, DC: Institute for Palestine Studies, 1992).

48. For the military exploits of Moshe's children, see Megged, *Il viaggio verso la Terra promessa*, 154–55; for the trio on the Latrun salient, see Aviel, *Freedom and Loneliness*, 377ff.

49. On the conquest of Lydda (Lod) as black box of Zionism, see Shavit, *My Promised Land*, 108–9. For a leftist critique of Shavit's position, see N. Thrall, "Feeling Good about Feeling Bad," in *The Only Language They Understand: Forcing Compromise in Israel and Palestine* (2014; New York: Metropolitan, 2017), 77–93. For a less severe historical vision of the turning point in Lydda, see M. Bar-On, *Moshe Dayan: Israel's Controversial Hero* (New Haven, CT: Yale University Press, 2012), 34–36.

50. On Dayan as Degania's second born after the firstborn Baratz, see S. Teveth, *Moshe Dayan: The Soldier, the Man, the Legend* (London: Quartet, 1972), 12. On terror as order of the day, see Morris, *La prima guerra di Israele*, 360ff.; Shapira, *Israel*, 167–68.

51. See Morris, *La prima guerra di Israele*, 360ff.

52. Aviel, *Freedom and Loneliness*, 381.

53. See Morris, *La prima guerra di Israele*, 410–11.

54. See A. Tal, *Pollution in a Promised Land: An Environmental History of Israel* (Berkeley: University of California Press, 2002), 76ff.

55. For literary references to Oz's works, see at least A. Oz, *Una pantera in cantina*, trans. E. Loewenthal (1997; Milan: Feltrinelli, 2010), 90; A. Oz, *Tra amici*, trans. E. Loewenthal (2011; Milan: Feltrinelli, 2012), 110–11.

56. See B. Morris, *Esilio: Israele e l'esodo palestinese, 1947–1949* (2004; Milan: Rizzoli, 2005).

57. See B. Morris, *1948. Israele e Palestina tra guerra e pace* (Milan: Rizzoli, 2004).

58. See Segev, *The Seventh Million*, 161–62; Mayer, *Plowshares into Swords*, 174ff.

59. Cited in Shapira, *Israel*, 161.

60. See Morris, *La prima guerra di Israele*, 400ff.; Shapira, *Israel*, 169–70.

61. For a powerful literary evocation, see S. Yizhar, *Convoglio di mezzanotte*, trans. E. Loewenthal (1950; Rome: Elliot/Lit edizioni, 2013), in particular 101ff.

62. Y. Kaniuk, *1948*, trans. E. Loewenthal (2010; Florence: Giuntina, 2012), 138. Also see Y. Kaniuk, *Sazio di giorni*, trans. O. Bannet and R. Scardi (2012; Florence: Giuntina, 2014), 12–13.

63. On the idealization of Jimmy as the prototype of the Palmachnik, see Almog, *The Sabra*, 129, 260. *The Portrait of Dead Jimmy* by Menachem Shemi belongs to the collections of the Museum of Art Ein Harod.

64. See D. Porat, "Attitudes of the Young State of Israel toward the Holocaust and Its Survivors: A Debate over Identity and Values," in *Israeli Society, the Holocaust and Its Survivors* (London: Vallentine Mitchell, 2008), 404.

65. For this, I refer to the transcription of a conversation of mine with Alberto Cortinovis in Selvino on October 29, 2014.

66. ACDEC, Comunità fund, b. 33, fasc. 53.

67. ACS, cat. A 16, Stranieri ed ebrei stranieri (1930–1956), Movimento profughi da Bergamo a Napoli.

68. See ibid.

69. The timing of arrival in Haifa can be deduced from the British Palestinian passports of Moshe and Yehudit; see AFZE, various documents.

70. This is based on an email that Nitza Zeiri Sarner sent to me on May 30, 2016.

71. See Yablonka, *Survivors of the Holocaust*.

72. See Oz, *A Tale of Love and Darkness*, 14; Grossman, *See Under: Love*, 46.

73. On the security settlements of Tzeelim and Rosh Hanikra, see Z. Drory, *The Israeli Defense Forces and the Foundation of Israel: Utopia in Uniform* (London: Frank Cass, 2004), 98–100.

74. See ibid. The photograph of the first buildings of the Rosh Hanikra kibbutz, against the backdrop of the Mediterranean, dates back to 1949: Palmach archive, Yiftach 1st Bataillon, vol. 4, album 7/12 (available online: https://en.wikipedia.org/wiki/Rosh_HaNikra_(kibbutz), accessed September 15, 2022).

75. On the experience of Adam Wexler in the Nahal and his arrival in Tze'elim, see his memoirs (in Hebrew): Wexler, *A Larger Standpoint*, 132–55. For the wedding with Dalia (Mathilde Szwarcman), see Wexler, *A Larger Standpoint*, 168ff.

76. For an overview of the postwar Israeli context, see T. Segev, *1949: The First Israelis* (New York: Henry Holt, 1998).

77. See Y. Achouch and Y. Morvan, "The Kibbutz and 'Development Towns' in Israel: Zionist Utopias: Ideals Ensnared in a Tormented History," in Université Paris-Ouest Nanterre La Défense, Laboratoire Mosaïques, 2012 (http://www.jssj.org, accessed July 2017).

78. For the photograph of smiling girls and armed boys on a farm wagon, taken at Kibbutz Tzeelim around 1949–50, see AFBSR, various documents and materials.

79. See AFMA, various documents.

80. See Megged, *Il viaggio verso la Terra promessa*, 139–41.

81. For the Negev Theater and kibbutz companies in general, see H. Nagid, "Israel," in *The World Encyclopedia of Contemporary Theater*, ed. D. Rubin, P. Nagy, and P. Rouyer (New York: Routledge, 1994), 502ff.; O. Zohar, "Le théâtre dans le kibboutz et la société du kibboutz dans le théâtre," *REEH. Revue européenne des études hébraïques* 5 (2001): 84–94. For reference to Moshe's letter, see above, chap. 2, note 81.

IF YOU SURVIVE

1. For the YouTube video of the Tze'elim gathering, see *Children of Selvino: Spring Gathering 2016* (https://www.youtube.com/watch?v=Ppuu6INgpXU, accessed July 2017).

2. For the screen shot of Shmulik driving a tractor, see the Al Jazeera documentary *The Promised Land?* (see below, note 5), third episode, time stamp 1:55.

3. See Sternhell, *Nascita di Israele*, 80ff.

4. An English transcript of Shmulik Shilo's speech on May 1, 2008, is available on the Yad Vashem website: "Remembrance, Holocaust Remembrance Day, 2008": (https://www.yadvashem.org/remembrance/archive/address-on-behalf-of-the-survivors/shmuel-shilo.html, accessed July 2017). For the photo, see the same website.

5. Al Jazeera's English documentary is titled *The Promised Land?* and is accessible on the Al Jazeera website: (https://www.aljazeera.com/news/2008/5/8/israeli-voices-shmuel-shilo accessed July 2017). It aired in three episodes, on May 5, 12, and 19, 2008. Shmulik's quotes are taken both from the documentary itself and from parts of the interview filmed but edited; these are also accessible, in transcription, on the Al Jazeera website.

6. The quotes from Avi Shilo are taken from the notes of my conversation with him via Skype on June 19, 2017.

7. For this last quote by Shmulik, see the documentary *If You Survive: The Story of Shmulik Shilo*: (https://www.youtube.com/watch?v=kbdgeoig524, accessed September 15, 2022).

INDEX

Aachen, Germany, 119
Aarontchik, 166
Abruzzo, 113–14
Agnon, Shmuel Yosef, 12, 39–40, 237
al-Bassa, Palestine, 315
Aleichem, Sholem, 55
Alexandrovna, Ksenia, 152–53
Aliyah Beth: British administration in Palestine and, 270, 271; *Enzo Sereni* group and, 186–87, 247–52, 258; *Exodus* group and, 304–5; *Hannah Szenes* group and, 245–46; Italy and, 256, 264–67; *Katriel Jaffe* group and, 277–82; Operation Michaelberg and, 305–7; secret agents and, 175–76; Shilo on, 344–45; *Ulua* group and, 300–303
Allied Military Government, 126, 184
Alterman, Nathan, 72, 102, 246, 259
alumni, Sciesopoli: Atlit detention camp and, 251–52, 298–99; Cyprus internment camps and, 282–87, 298–99, 301, 302, 321–22; gathering of, 341–42; kibbutzim and, 312–19, 334–35, 336–38; Kibbutz Selvino dream and, 309, 312, 319–23, 336–37; War for Independence and, 327–28, 329. See also *specific Sciesopoli alumni*
Amatore Sciesa Club, 122, 124–25, 168, 262
American Jewish Joint Distribution Committee: Benghazi Hebrew school and, 106; Cypriot camps and, 302–3; European Jews and, 87, 166, 179; Kopychyntsi and, 68; Youth Aliyah House and, 186–87, 197, 269, 309, 334; Zeiri and, 171, 228, 256, 295–96
Anders, Władysław, 110, 120
antisemitism: in Germany, 34, 47–48, 51–54; in Poland, 30, 42, 43, 157, 159, 252–53
Appelfeld, Aharon, 134, 229, 237, 249, 312, 313
Arab Liberation Army, 327
Arab Revolt, 61–62, 71–72, 75, 315
Arabs: British administration and, 75, 95; civil war and, 324–26, 327; as laborers, 43, 45, 64, 269; liberation movement of, 60–62, 71–72, 75, 315; in Libya, 103; Palestine civil war and, 324–26, 327–29; refugees, 330, 331; Sciesopoli alumni and, 299, 315; War of Independence and, 329, 330, 331

INDEX

Arab villages of Judea, 330
Arendt, Hannah, 56
Ariovitz, Elke "Todras," 132–33, 134
arms trafficking, 175
Army Group Rear Area Command, 84
Ashes and Fire (Pat), 253
Asner, Haim, 135
Asner, Itchele, 135
Asner, Yankl, 135
Atlit detention camp, 251–52, 298–99, 334
Auerbach, Avraham, 226–27
Auerbach, Bronka, 227, 233–34, 249, 287, 307
Auschwitz: Łódź ghetto liquidation and, 142–43, 147; march from, 145–46, 149–50; postwar, 255; Weisz family at, 146–49; Wexler family at, 143–45. *See also* Birkenau
Auschwitz Album, The, 147
Austerlitz (Sebald), 14
Avanti!, 210
Aviel, Avraham, 338. *See also* Lipkunski, Avraham
Aviel, Ayala, 338. *See also* Liberman, Inda, 338
Avuka kibbutz, 313, 320, 321
Ayelet Hashachar kibbutz, 40, 43, 69, 75, 320

Babel, Isaac, 10–11
Babyn Yar massacre, 85
Balam, Zippora, 277, 287, 338
Bander, Yaakov, 287
Banella, Bazar, 222–23
baptism, 120–21
Baratz, Yosef: about, 62–63, 183, 299; holidays and, 67; *Story of Degania*, 63; Zeiri and, 208, 261, 311, 320
Barbaglia, Amedeo, 210, 219
Batia, 194, 227, 228
Battle of Mishmar Haemek, 327
Bayt-Nattif, 330–31
Beer, Mordechai, 88

Beersheva, 331–32
Begin, Menachem, 271, 319
Beit Midrash, 31–32
Belgium, 296
Belzec extermination camp, 116–17
Benghazi, Libya, 101–4, 105–8
Ben-Gurion, David: about, 40; British and, 75, 95, 105, 125; on sabon, 314; terrorism and, 271; wars and, 327, 328
Bergamo, Italy, 179, 184, 297, 323–234. *See also* Selvino, Italy
Bergmann, Moshe, 86
Berkovitz, Aharke, 135
Berkowitz, Hans, 52
Berkowitz, Rachel, 47, 48, 52
Berkowski, Isaac, 86
Betar, 30–31, 35–36, 75, 76
Bialik, Nahman, 25–27, 31, 72–73, 74–75, 182, 232, 338
Bible, the, 67, 210
Birkenau: camp of, 190, 204, 248–49; postwar, 255; ramp of, 143, 146–47, 148–49, 174, 190. *See also* Auschwitz
Bisozky, Eliezer, 61
Bizet, Georges, 289
Black Box (Oz), 7
black boxes, 3, 5, 330
Black Saturday, 271
Black Washerwomen in Benghazi (Shemi), 108
blue boxes, 61
Bogliasco Jewish camp, 276, 277, 278, 301
Boim, Shmuel, 251, 269
Bolak, 201
Bologna, Italy, 120
Bolsheviks, 36, 83–84, 86
Boniówka, Izabela, 158–59
Boniówka, Nina, 158–59, 207, 252, 266, 270
Book of the Shoah, 3
Boy Who Wanted to Sleep, The (Appelfeld), 249

Brando, Marlon, 303
Brandt, 24
breasts, 234
Brembana Valley, 171
Bricha, 177, 252
British administration of Palestine: Arab Revolt and, 72, 75; civil war and, 326; identity cards and, 44–45; immigration and, 251, 270–72, 278–79, 285–87; immigration quotas and, 39, 75, 105, 175, 194, 272–73, 275; terrorism against, 271, 319; White Paper and, 75, 105, 175
British Army: illegal immigration and, 280–81, 299–300; Indian Pioneers of, 280; in Italy, 120, 124, 174, 175, 264; Jewish Brigade of, 118, 120, 173, 177; Nuriel and, 114–15; in Palestine during WWII, 92–93, 105; Palestinian volunteers and, 94–95. *See also* British Royal Engineers
British Mandate in Palestine, 22, 328
British Navy, 246, 250, 278, 300, 304–5
British Royal Engineers: about, 95; demobilization of, 256; in Egypt, 96–101; illegal immigration and, 175, 279–80; in Italy during war, 108–14, 117–21, 124–27, 179; in Italy postwar, 191, 256, 263, 266–68; in Libya, 101–4, 105–8. *See also* Zeiri, Moshe as a Royal Engineer
"Building and being built" slogan, 207
Bundists, 81, 82, 252
Buslik, Eliezer, 86
bus war, 324–25

Calatrava, Santiago, 1
Camarda, Chiara, 6–7
cameras, 101, 224
Cantoni, Raffaele, 123, 161–65, 169–70, 183, 193, 264
Carmen (Bizel), 289
Case del Fascio, 123

Cassin, Matilde "Rachel": about, 164; Jewish children summer camp and, 168–69, 180; Varadi and, 192–93, 298; Via Eupili Jewish School and, 160–61, 164, 165; Youth Aliyah House and, 186, 188, 189, 192–93, 206; Zeiri and, 161, 164, 192–93, 206, 257
Center for the Diaspora, 177, 183, 194, 228, 261, 267
Cerrone, Pesach, 341
Certificate, The (Singer), 43–44
Cesena, Italy, 120
Chaplin, Charlie, 101
chicken incident, 77–78
Children Accuse, 159
cinema, 209–10
civil war in Palestine, 324–29
Clandestini del mare (Sereni), 176
Cohen, Noga, 188, 189, 206, 342
Cologne, Germany, 48–49, 50, 52, 120
Colombo, Yoseph, 170
communal life: kibbutzim, *see* kibbutzim; at Youth Aliyah House, 214–15
compassion, 63, 299
Consolation of the Tribulations of Israel (Usque), 270
Corriere della Sera, 115–16, 265–66, 272, 289–91, 296, 301
Corriere d'informazione, 305, 306
Cortinovis, Alberto, 259–60
Cortinovis, Andrea, 221
Cut Tree and the New Tree, The (Meriash), 189
Cyprus internment camps, 272, 278–79, 282–87, 298–99, 300–305, 310–11, 321–23
Czechoslovakia, 36–37
Czoban, Alexander, 215, 277, 285, 315–16
Czoban, Aviva, 231, 301

Davar, 53–54, 76, 116, 246
Dayan, Moshe, 330

De Amicis, Edmondo, 290
Degania kibbutz, 40, 62, 208, 320, 330
De Gasperi, Alcide, 255, 264, 290
Dembinski, Szaya, 167
demonstrations and protests, public, 264, 266, 272–73, 279, 285–86
detention camp in Palestine, 251–52, 298–99, 334
Dinur, Ben-Zion, 53
Dizengoff Prize, 106, 121
Donath, Reuven: about, 99–101, 125, 244; *Kinderlach fon Selvino* and, 320; Youth Aliyah House alumni gathering and, 342; Youth Aliyah House and, 188, 189, 206, 224, 234, 289; Zeiri and, 320
Donath Cohen, Noga, 188, 189, 206, 342
Dugalishok, Poland, 27, 87, 129, 131–32, 134
Duvdevani, Yechiel, 99, 110, 178, 197

Eastern Front, 85, 118, 137
Egypt, 93, 95–96, 107, 328
Egyptian army, 328, 332
Eichmann, Adolf, 57
Eichmann trial, 89–91
Ein Harod kibbutz, 41
Einsatzgruppen, 84–85, 116–17
Eišiškės, 87
Eliav, Lova, 97, 300–301
emigration of Jews. *See* migration to Palestine
Empire Heywood, 279–82, 283, 287
Empire Rival, 279–80, 287
Enzo Sereni, 247–52, 258, 315
equality, gender, 60, 66, 321
Exodus affair, 282, 304–5

Fede, 264, 265–67, 270, 271, 277
Feldafing camp, 269
Fenice, 264, 266–67, 270, 271, 277
Fetter Moshe, 191, 215, 249, 320
Feuchtwanger, Lion, 52–53

Fighting Pioneer Youth, 335, 346
Final Solution, about, 3, 14, 87, 105, 143, 177, 226
Finkelstein, Chaia, 329
Finkelstein, Israel, 329
Finkelstein, Shalom, 242, 301–2, 329, 333
Fisher, Miriam, 251
Flag Is Born, A (Hecht), 303
Flamholtz, Yeshayahu, 157, 205
food, 215–16, 219–21
Forverts, 20, 34
Forward, The, 20, 34
France, 296
Frank, Hans, 115
Freier, Recha, 55, 56, 57, 176
Freier, Shalhevet, 176, 249, 264
Friedrich, Liliana, 189
Friedrich der Große hotel, 155–56
Frumkin, Simcha, 260

Galicia region of Poland, 10–12, 83, 116–17, 137. *See also specific villages of*
Gallichi, Luciana, 114, 325
gangs, Jewish, 130–31, 132–36
Garfinkel, Chana, 226, 341, 342
Gelbart, Gersham, 269–70
German Jews, 47–50, 53–58. *See also specific German Jews*
Germany: antisemitism in, 34, 47–48, 51–54; cooperation of Zionism by, 57–58; surrender of, 125. *See also specific cities of*
Ghetto Fighter's House, 142, 270, 318
Gianini Belotti, Elena, 220–21
Ginat, Eva, 207, 266
Givat-Brenner kibbutz, 65, 75, 110
Goldhammer, Pinkus, 167
Goldman, Elka, 307
Goldman, Ester, 307
Goldman, Lea, 216, 307
Goldman, Leibel, 307
Goldman, Mikhael, 307

Goldman, Sara, 216, 287, 307, 335
Goldman, Yaakov, 307
Goldstein, Dvora, 241
Gordon, Aharon David, 21, 62
Gordonia movement: about, 15, 21–22, 40, 62, 337; Flamholtz and, 157; Hashomer Hatzair and, 178, 263, 267; kibbutzim and, 40, 62, 63; Polish Jews and, 252, 256; Youth Aliyah House, 208, 256, 259, 303
Gorini, Luigi, 184
Gothic Line, 120
Gotthard, 145–46
Grigis, Emilio "Ciusca," 224–26
Grigis, Flaminio, 219
Grigis, Giovanni, 223–24
Grossman, David, 68–69, 334–35
guilt, 93, 230
Gunskirchen subcamp, 150
Gures, Etka, 135
Gures, Sara, 135
Gurman, Batia, 227–28
Gurman, Zippora, 227
Gusen camp, 145–46

Habima Theater School, 70, 73, 74, 106
Habsburg Empire, 11, 23
Haganah, 75, 271, 318, 326, 327, 328–29, 332
Hager, Zippora, 190–91, 208, 276, 284–85
Haifa, Palestine: illegal immigration and, 250, 278–81, 284, 299–300, 302, 303, 305; May Day celebration in, 269; terrorism in, 319; war in, 324, 326, 327–28, 331
Haim, Hafetz, 27
Haimowitz, Yissachar, 99, 177, 183, 197
Handel, George Frideric, 117
Hanita bell, 316
Hannah Szenes, 245–46
Hanukkah, 47, 48, 67, 117, 210–12, 298
Harel Brigade, 329, 330, 332

Hashomer Hatzair, 178, 256, 259, 263
Hasman, Adela, 241
Hasman, Avraham, 241–42
Hasman, Cesia, 241
Hasman, Dvora, 241
Hasman, Mordechai, 242
Hasman, Yehoshua, 242
Heart (De Amicis), 290
Hebrew language, 17–18, 55–56, 236–37, 239–40, 314
Hebrew school in Benghazi, 103, 106, 108
Hechaluz, 21, 22–23
Hecht, Ben, 303
Hefetz, Liebke, 135
Henrietta Szold, 278–79
Herzl, Theodor, 17, 18, 22–23, 36
Himmler, Heinrich, 158
Histadrut, 40, 53, 62, 92, 105, 178, 264
Hitler, Adolf, 53, 55
Hitlerjugend, 35
holidays, 67, 210–12. *See also specific holidays*
Hollander, Yaakov, 241, 277, 287
Holocaust, about, 3, 14, 87, 105, 143, 177, 226
Horthy, Miklós, 148
Hoter-Yishai, Aharon, 177–78
Hulda kibbutz, 40
Hungarian Jews, 36–37, 146–47, 150. *See also specific Hungarian Jews*
Hungary, 36–37, 148
hunger, 215–16, 219–21, 266, 316
hunger strikes, 264, 266, 279

If Not Now, When? (Levi), 133
If You Survive: The Story of Shmulik Shilo, 345, 346
illegal immigration of Jews. *See* Aliyah Beth
immigration certificates, 43, 55–56, 57, 194, 272, 287
immigration of Jews. *See* Aliyah Beth; migration to Palestine

Indian Pioneers of the British Army, 280
integration in kibbutzim, 312–19, 334–35, 336–37
International Institute for Holocaust Research, 3
internment of illegal migrants. *See* Cyprus internment camps
In the Heart of the Seas (Agnon), 39–40
Irgun, 75, 76, 271, 319
Israel, birth of State of, 282, 328–29, 333
Israel Museum, 5
Italian front, 118, 120
Italian Jews, 36, 110, 112–13, 162, 255. *See also specific Italian Jews*
Italian Navy, 277–78
Italy: German occupation of, 105–6, 113; liberation of, 108, 110, 111–12; Mussolini and, 121–22; postwar, 253, 256; solidarity with Palestine of, 272–73, 289
"I Will Remember" (Finkelstein), 302

Jabotinsky, Vladimir Ze'ev, 30, 35, 36, 75–76
Jadu concentration camp, 102
Jaffa, Palestine, 45, 61
Jaffa oranges, 45, 64–65, 92, 251
Janowo, Poland, 31–33, 34–35, 77, 137
Janusz Korczak Orphan House, 158, 170, 183, 187, 206
Jewish Agency, 58, 120, 264, 271
Jewish Brigade of British Army, 118, 120, 173, 177
Jewish gangs of Eastern Europe, 130–31, 132–36
Jewish Historical Commission, 157–58, 159
Jewish Infantry Brigade Group, 118, 120, 173, 177
Jewish National Fund, 17, 61, 93

Jewish Organization for the Rehabilitation through Training (ORT), 21, 52, 298, 310
Jewish Refugee Assistance Committee, 123–24
Jewish school in Milan, 162–66, 168, 291
Jewish school in Naples, 112–13, 117
Jewish Soldiers' Club, 121, 176
Jews and Words (Oz), 7
Jews of Brehove and Nagyszőlőa, 147
Jews of San Nicandro Garganico, 110–11
Joint, the. *See* American Jewish Joint Distribution Committee
Judas Maccabaeus (Handel), 117
Judenboykott, 47–48
Jüdische Rundschau, 55
Jugend-Alijah, 55–58, 176
Julich family, 70
Jungle, The (Sinclair), 209

Kacyzne, Alter, 12–13, 17, 19–20, 34, 83–84, 253–54
Kacyzne, Hana, 83, 84
Kacyzne, Shulamit, 83, 84, 253–55
Kafka, Franz, 16
Kagan, Renia, 142
Kaniuk, Yoram, 286, 332
Kaputt (Malaparte), 115–16, 119
Karaolos internment camp, 279, 282, 284–87, 300, 302–4, 322–23
Katriel Jaffe, 278, 279–85
Katz, Alter, 251
Katz family, 167
Katznelson, Berl, 54, 76, 300
Kfar Ruppin kibbutz, 313, 318, 320–21
Kibbutz Avuka, 313, 320, 321
Kibbutz Ayelet Hashachar, 40, 43, 69, 75, 320
Kibbutz Degania, 40, 62, 208, 320, 330
Kibbutz Ein Harod, 41

Kibbutz Givat-Brenner, 65, 75, 110
Kibbutz Hanita: about, 72, 315; *Kinderlach fon Selvino* summit and, 321, 322, 323; Sciesopoli orphans at, 259, 268–69, 315, 316, 318–19, 334, 335; Zeiri and, 106
Kibbutz Hulda, 40
kibbutzim: about, 60, 63–64, 66–67; Arab Revolt and, 72; integration into, 312–19, 334–35, 336–37; movement of, 23, 40, 63; Shoah orphans and, 167, 172, 258–59; Youth Aliyah House alumni and, 337–38; Zeiri on, 117–18. *See also specific kibbutzim*
Kibbutz Kfar Ruppin, 313, 318, 320–21
Kibbutz Merhavia, 313, 317, 318
Kibbutz Mishmar Haemek, 327–28
Kibbutz Mishmar Hasharon, 311, 313, 314, 318, 320, 321
Kibbutz Ramat Yohanan, 313, 321
Kibbutz Rosh Hanikra, 335, 337
Kibbutz Selvino dream, 309, 312, 319–23, 336–37
Kibbutz Tze'elim, 336, 337, 339, 341–42
Kielce, Poland, 272, 274
Kinderlach fon Selvino summit, 320–23, 329
King David, 25–26, 182
King David Hotel, 271
King David in the Cave (Bailik), 74–75
Kingdom of Galacia and Lodomiria, 11
Kiryat Anavim, 333
Kiryat Shmuel, 299
Kissin, Abraham, 190
Kissin, Pesia, 190, 233
Klein, Gershon, 251
Kleiner, David, 9–10, 13, 67
Kleiner, Moshe: aliyah of, 42–45; childhood of, 9, 10, 11, 12–14, 16–17, 19; name changes of, 44–45; Zionism and, 20–21, 22, 23–24. *See also* Zeiri, Moshe, about

Kleiner, Rivka: aliyah of, 39, 40–41, 43; childhood of, 9, 10; Lubianiker family and, 15–17; Nuriel and, 115; Tarbut and, 18
Kleiner, Zippora, 9–10, 13, 23–24, 42, 67–70
Kluczyńska, Halina, 154–55
Kohen, Reuven, 99, 110, 230–31
Kommando Union, 144–45
Koopermintz, Victor, 61
Kopeyka, Yosef, 25
Kopychyntsi, Poland, 2, 11–13, 17, 68, 83, 116–17
Koralniks, Sheinke, 90
Koralniks, Shlomo, 90
Korczak, Janusz, 41–42, 158, 170, 229
Korczak Orphan House, 158, 170, 183, 187, 206
Kornfeld, Haim, 61
Krajowa, Armia, 134, 135
Krampf, Rudolf, 157–58
Krampf, Shlomo, 322, 329, 339
Krausman, Josef, 167
Kripo, 140–42, 143
Kun, Béla, 36
Kutner, Avraham, 207, 252, 287, 338
kvutzas, about, 45
Kvutzat-Shiller: Meyer at, 60; Sciesopoli orphans and, 259, 334; Zeiri and, 45, 64, 74–75, 167, 258, 262, 320

Laiberg, Lea, 251
Landau, Abraham, 251
Lanfranchi, Ferruccio, 289–91
languages, 235–37; Hebrew, 17–18, 55–56, 236–37, 239–40, 314; Yiddish, 235–36, 239–40
La Spezia, Italy, 264–67, 270, 271, 277–78
Laypshe, 31, 35
Leiter, Miriam, 287

Le Journal Juif, 56
Leninski Komsomol Brigade, 133–36
"Letters from the Valley of Death," 116
"Let the Wind Hit You, Boys" (Alterman), 102
Levi, Davide Mario, 123–24, 161, 162, 164
Levi, Fausto, 123
Levi, Primo, 133, 202
Liberman, Adela "Adina": aliyah of, 277, 280, 282; as a fugitive, 152–54; at Karaolos camp, 285; language and, 236–37; liquidation of Zdolbuniv and, 151; in Łódź, 156–58; name change of, 237; *Nivenu* and, 239, 242–43; in Rivne, 24, 25, 85, 86–87; as a Third Reich volunteer, 154–56; at Youth Aliyah House, 207
Liberman, Feige, 24, 25, 86, 150–51, 152
Liberman, Inda "Ayala": aliyah of, 277, 280, 282; as a fugitive, 152–54; at Karaolos camp, 285; language and, 236–37; liquidation of Zdolbuniv and, 150–51; in Łódź, 156–58, 205; marriage of, 287–88; name change of, 237; *Nivenu* and, 239; in Rivne, 24, 25, 86–87; as a Third Reich volunteer, 154–56; at Youth Aliyah House, 207
Liberman, Meir, 24, 86, 150–51, 152
Libya, 101–4, 105–8
Libyan Jews, 102–4
Lichtenstein, Yeshayahu, 248, 251
Lida, Poland/Lithuania, 87
Lindau, Avraham, 321–22
Lipkunski, Avraham: aliyah of, 277, 280; at detention camps, 284–85, 298–99; in Dugalishok, 26–27, 28, 30–31; Jewish gangs and, 132–33, 135–36; journey to Youth Aliyah House of, 198–99; Kibbutz Tze'elim and, 336; *Kinderlach fon Selvino* and, 322; language and, 236–37; marriage of, 287–88; *Nivenu* and, 239, 244;

Palmach and, 315–16; photos and, 232; Pinchas Lipkunski and, 129–30, 136; in Raduń ghetto, 128–29; Raduń Jews massacre and, 87–88, 89–91; War for Independence and, 327, 329, 330; at Youth Aliyah House, 199–200, 201, 202–3, 215–16; as a Youth Aliyah House alumni, 338; Zeiri and, 311–12
Lipkunski, Moshe David, 27–28, 29–30, 87, 89, 129–30, 132, 134
Lipkunski, Pinchas, 27–28, 30, 87–90, 128–31, 136
Lipkunski, Sara Mina Rakowski, 27, 28–29, 87, 129, 136, 232
Lipkunski, Yekutiel, 27, 87, 88
Lipkunski family, 26–30
Lipman, Gussie, 27
literature, 19–20, 24, 52–53, 209. *See also specific literature*
Lithuania, 27, 87
Livnat, Yitzhak, 149, 318, 341. *See also* Weisz, Sándor "Suti"
Lloyd Triestino, 55, 59
Lod, Palestine, 329–30
Łódź, Poland, 78–83, 156–57
Łódź ghetto, 79–83, 137, 140–41, 143, 147, 202
Łódź group at Youth Aliyah House, 204–5, 207, 213
Loewi, Marina, 180
Loewi, Siegbert, 180
Lombardi, Riccardo, 161
Löwendahl, Alfred, 119
Löwendahl, Benno, 50, 119
Löwendahl, Henrietta, 119
Lubianiker, Pinchas: about, 15–16, 21–22, 40, 62; Arab revolt and, 71–72; on effects of War for Independence, 326–27; Gordonia founding and, 21–22; immigration and, 178; secularism and, 297; Youth Aliyah House and, 208; Zeiri and, 262

Lubianiker, Zelig, 15
Lubianiker, Zvi, 22
Lubianiker family, 15–17, 21–22, 40
Lubinski, Yitzhak, 81, 82, 137, 140
Luftman, Haim: about, 173–75; aliyah of, 173–75, 249–52; kibbutz integration and, 315–17; in Magenta, 176, 179; May Day and, 269; Palmach and, 315–16; in Piazzatorre, 180; Youth Aliyah House and, 179–80, 198, 202, 213, 217; Zeiri and, 320
Lurie, Esther, 121
Lviv, Poland/Ukraine, 11, 20–21, 23, 83–84

Maccabi movement, 52
Magenta, Italy, 175, 176
Magenta Collection Center Command, 124
Magenta farming camp, 175–76, 179, 197, 249
Magenta gang, 197, 213
Magyars, 36–37
mail, 118, 258
Majafit, Simcha Hertz, 25
Malaparte, Curzio, 114, 115–16, 119
Manduzio, Donato, 110
Man Who Never Stopped Sleeping, The (Appelfeld), 313
Mapai, 40, 71–72, 76, 297
march from Auschwitz, 145–46, 149–50
Mariusz, 35
Marschall, Georg, 158
Matteotti Brigades, 122–24, 161
Mauthausen concentration camp, 145, 149–50
May Day celebrations, 268–69, 312
mental health, 178, 207, 231
Merhavia kibbutz, 313, 317, 318
Meriash, Yaakov: aliyah of, 277, 280; at Karaolos camp, 285; Kibbutz Tze'elim and, 336; *Nivenu* and, 239; War for Independence and, 327, 329;
at Youth Aliyah House, 188–89, 199–200, 201, 215, 217; as Youth Aliyah House alumnus, 338, 341; Zeiri and, 311–12
Meyer, Heinrich, 48, 49–51, 57, 68, 69, 70, 293–94
Meyer, Jacques, 48, 52
Meyer, Trude: aliyah of, 55, 57–58–60; in Cologne, 47, 48, 50–52, 57; name change of, 66; romance with Zeiri of, 65–66. *See also* Zeiri, Yehudit
Meyer, Wilhelmina, 48, 68, 69, 70, 119
Meyerson, Golda, 264, 331
migration to Palestine: British administration and, 251, 270–72, 278–79, 285–87; immigration certificates and, 43, 55–56, 57, 194, 272, 287; Jabotinsky and, 30; legal European Jew, 15, 22, 30, 43, 54–57; quotas of, 39, 75, 105, 175, 194, 272–73, 275. *See also* Aliyah Beth; aliyah of *under specific names*
Milan, Italy, about, 122–27, 161, 168, 176, 272–73
Milanese Jews, 123–24, 213
Milan Jewish school, 160–68, 170–71, 291
Milchman, Shmuel, 177
Military Academy of Modena, 174
Mishmar Haemek kibbutz, 327–28
Mishmar Hasharon kibbutz, 311, 313, 314, 318, 320, 321
Mizoch, Ukraine, 151–52
Monte Cassino, Italy, 110
Moshe, Jakob, 129
Mossad secret services, 271
Mussman, Fania, 24, 25, 59
Mussolini, Benito, 121–22, 125, 168, 262, 268
Mussolini House, 2, 179–80, 183, 262. *See also* Sciesopoli
"My First Letter to My Uncles and Aunts in Tel Aviv" (Hasman), 241–42

INDEX

Nača forest, 130–31, 132, 134–35
Nagyszölös, Hungary, 36–37, 203–4
Nagyszölös Jews, 146–49
name changes, 44–45, 66, 120, 149, 237, 288, 318
Naples, Italy, 111–14
National Liberation Committee of Northern Italy, 169–70
national mourning, Palestinian, 93–94
Nazis, 34, 54, 56–57
Negev Desert, 335, 337–38
Negev Theater, 340
New York Times, 281
Niecała Street radio post, 82–83, 137, 139, 140–42
Nivenu, 239–44, 285
Nivenu Baderech, 285
Nordau, Max, 51
"not a word" on the past, 237–39, 241–42, 244, 314–15
Nudelman, Lila, 339
Nuriel, Yosef, 115

Oder-Neisse line, 155
Opera Pia Bergamasca, 185
Opera Pia Fanciulli Gracili, 169
Operation Dani, 329–30
Operation Erez, 329
Operation Maccabi, 329
Operation Michaelberg, 305–7
Operation Yiftach, 329
Operation Yitzhak, 329
Operation Yoav, 331–32
Oppermanns, The (Feuchtwanger), 52–53
oranges, Jaffa, 45, 64–65, 92, 251
Orphan House in Warsaw, 158, 170, 183, 187, 206
orphans, Sciesopoli: about, 177, 234–36; childhoods of, 207–9; illegal immigration of, 247–52, 256, 258–59, 300–303; kibbutzim and, 167, 172, 258–59, 312–19, 334–35, 336–37;

marriages of, 287–88; Piazzatorre camp and, 180–82, 184–85; rebirth of, 235–39, 290; success of, 337; trauma of, 229–31; Zionist Congress and, 297–98. *See also* Youth Aliyah House; *specific orphans*
ORT (Jewish Organization for the Rehabilitation through Training), 21, 52, 298, 310
Ortutay, Victor, 148, 243
"Our Word" (*Nivenu*), 239–44, 285
Oz, Amos, 7, 24–25, 59, 86, 122, 331, 334
Oz-Salzberger, Fania, 7

Pagis, Dan, 317
Palazzo Odescalchi, 122, 123, 161, 168
Palestine: in 1942, 92–95; about, 22–23, 39; Arab Revolt in, 61–62, 71–72, 75, 315; British Army in, 92–93, 105; British Mandate in, 22, 328; civil war in, 324–29; Italian solidarity with, 272–73, 289; legal migration of European Jews to, 22, 30, 43, 54–57; partition plan for, 326; White Paper on, 75, 105, 175; Zionism and, 75–76. *See also* Aliyah Beth; British administration of Palestine; War for Independence
Palestine Post, The, 122, 279–80, 282–84, 298, 325
Palmach: *Katriel Jaffe* and, 279, 281; Sciesopoli alumni and, 315–16; terrorism and, 271; War for Independence and, 326–27, 329–30, 331–32
Pan Doktor the, 41–42, 158, 170, 229
paramilitary training, 259–60
Partisan Edmond, The (Appelfeld), 134
Pashigoda, Haim, 61
Passover, 13, 95–96, 266
Pat, Jacob, 252–53, 254, 256
Peled, Avrami, 13, 184
Perach, Zalman, 282

Perényi, 37
Peretz, I. L., 98, 195
Petacci, Claretta, 121–22
photographs as propaganda, 228–29, 271
photographs by Ciusca, 224–26
Piazzatorre: foreign orphans at, 183–84, 185, 194; summer camp at, 171, 180–83, 197
Piłsudski, Józef, 30
Polak, Rivka, 231, 251
Poland: about, 2, 11, 20–21, 27, 87; antisemitism in, 30, 42, 43, 157, 159, 252–53; Molotov-Ribbentrop pact and, 83; Soviet occupation of, 83–84, 86, 87, 118. *See also specific cities and ghettos of*
Police Order No. 5, German, 113
Polish Army, 78, 110, 120
Polish Jews: about, 20, 22; Italy and, 256, 296; postwar, 177, 252–53, 256, 272. *See also specific Polish cities, ghettos, and Jews*
Polish Resistance, 130–31, 132–36, 137
Polonia Palace, 253
Polonka massacre, 201
"Poor Little Orphans, the Jews of Selvino" (Lanfranchi), 289–91
Post Office, The (Tagore), 158, 266
Po Valley, Italy, 125
Praszkier, Baruch, 80
propaganda, Zionist, 11, 17, 22, 36, 61, 228, 241, 299
protests and demonstrations, public, 264, 266, 272–73, 279, 285–86
Purim, 38, 67, 210–11

quotas, immigration, 39, 75, 105, 175, 194, 272–73, 275

radio post on Niecała Street, 81–83, 137–43
radio SWIT, 137

Raduń, Lithuania, 87, 88–89, 136, 198
Raduń Jews massacre, 88–91, 128–29
Rakotz, Aharon, 251
Rakowski, Sara Mina, 27, 28–29, 87, 129, 136, 232. *See also* Lipkunski, Sara Mina Rakowski
Rakowski family, 27, 88
Ramat Yohanan kibbutz, 313, 321
Ratmanski, Lea, 226
Reale, Eugenio, 255–56, 296
Rebhun, Heinz, 101, 114, 325
Rebhun, Miriam, 325
rebirth of Shoah orphans, 235–39, 290
Red Army: Eastern front and, 137; Jewish gangs and, 133–36; Liberman sisters and, 156; Lipkunski and, 198; in Poland, 83, 87, 88, 118, 133–36; Torgau Offensive and, 155
Red Cavalry (Babel), 10, 11
refugees, Arab, 330, 331
refugees, Jewish: about, 176–77, 234–35; in Italy, 113, 123–24, 166, 197; mental health of, 178, 207, 231; Polish, 156–57; in "their own country," 103; Zionism and, 177–78. *See also* orphans, Sciesopoli; *specific refugees*
Reggiani family, 220
Reich, Julek, 248, 251
Reichsbund judischer Frontsoldaten (RjF), 50
Reiss, Issachar, 86
Revisionist Zionists, 30, 35, 76, 326
Rhine campaign, 119–20
Righteous Among the Nations, 113–14, 159, 180
Ringer, Pinchas, 280, 338
ritual slaughter, 33, 34, 78
Rivne, Poland/Ukraine, 24–25, 84–87, 153, 158
RjF (Reichsbund judischer Frontsoldaten), 50
Rogovski, Niomke, 135
Rommel, Erwin, 102

Roper, James, 121–22
Rosenberg, Mrs., 148–49
Rosenfeld, Oskar, 139–40, 142
Rosh Hanikra kibbutz, 335, 337
Rosh Hashanah, 13, 184–85
Rosner, Baruch, 209, 239, 260–61
Rosner, Bernard, 167
Rossellini, Roberto, 114
Rotenburg, Ruth, 226
Rothenberg, Moshe, 25
Rotsztejn, Beyle, 144
Rotsztejn, Shayke, 144
Rotsztejn, Volf, 144
Royal Engineers. *See* British Royal Engineers
Royal Navy, 246, 250, 278, 300, 304–5
Rozenboym, Liebish, 151
Rozenboym, Meir, 151
Rudniki forest, 130–31
Rumkowski, Haim, 79, 80, 140, 142–43
Rundbaken, Wiktor, 82
Ruppin, Arthur, 58
Ruthenia, Hungary/Czechoslovakia, 36–37

sabon term, 314
sabras: about, 63, 326; British Army and, 94; Shoah survivors and, 313–14, 317, 334–35, 336–37; War for Independence and, 326, 332–33, 334–35, 336–37
San Nicandro Garganico, Italy, 110–11
Savaldi, Bruno, 110, 161
saved who save, 2, 120, 134, 282
scabies epidemic, 233–34
Schuminer, Chava, 44
Sciesopoli: house of, 168–70, 179–80, 183–84, 186, 209, 262; Jewish school at, *see* Youth Aliyah House; orphans of, *see* orphans, Sciesopoli
Sebald, W. G., 14
Secolo liberale, 265
secret service of Palestine, 175–76, 271

secularism: Shoa orphans' education and, 297–98; at Youth Aliyah House, 193, 210, 231–32, 267–68
security settlements, 335–36, 337
See Under: Love (Grossman), 68–69, 334–35
Selvino, Italy, 2, 168, 179–80, 183, 218–26. *See also* Youth Aliyah House
Selvino kibbutz dream, 309, 312, 319–23, 336–37
Senio River battle, 120
Sereni, Ada, 176, 247, 305–7
Sereni, Emilio, 110, 306
Sereni, Enzo, 56, 65, 68, 110, 176
745th Company of the Royal Engineers. *See* British Royal Engineers
Sevlus, 37
sex, 232–33
Shabbat, 67, 210, 267
Shafrir, Malka, 233–34, 248–49, 251, 319
Shambadal, David, 61
Sharett, Moshe, 120, 271
Shemi, Aharon "Jimmy," 332–33
Shemi, Menachem, 106–8, 111, 121, 332
Shichor, Romek, 277, 285, 287, 298–99
Shilo, Avi, 342, 345–46
Shilo, Shmulik, 339, 343–46. *See also* Shulman, Shmulik
Shoah, about, 3, 14, 87, 105, 143, 177, 226
shrine of Kiryat Anavim, 333
Shrine of the Book, 5
shtetl pole versus urban pole, 20
Shulman, Shmulik: aliyah of, 277, 280; documentary on, 345, 346; at Karaolos camp, 285, 287; Kibbutz Tze'elim and, 336, 339, 342–44; *Kinderlach fon Selvino* summit and, 320–22, 323, 339; Negev Theater and, 340; *Nivenu* and, 239, 241; War for Independence and, 327, 329; at Youth Aliyah House, 200–201; Zeiri and, 345–46
Shulman family, 200–201
Siegfried Line, 119

Sierakowiak, Dawid, 80
silence on the past, 237–39, 241–42, 244, 314–15
Sinclair, Upton, 109
Singer, Isaac Bashevis, 43–44
Singer, Israel Joshua, 19, 33
"soap bars" term, 314
soccer, 221
Soleh, Arieh, 190, 200, 208, 227, 320
Soleh, Yehudit, 227, 228
Solel Boneh Company, 92, 96, 99, 125, 175, 176, 179. See also British Royal Engineers
Sonderkommando, 143, 144–45
"Song of the Platoons" (Alterman), 72, 259
Sosenki forest massacre, 85–87, 158
Soviet Union: occupation of Poland by, 83–84, 86, 87, 136; Red Army of, see Red Army
Spivak, Lea, 277, 301, 321
Srebnik, Szymon, 157
SS, German, 57, 84, 135–36, 144
stamp collecting, 218
State of Israel birth, 282, 328–29, 333
Steel and Iron (Singer), 33
Steinberg, Aharon, 241
Steinberg family, 25
Stern, Mordecai, 241
Story of Degania, The (Baratz), 63
Strong and the Weak, The (Kacyzne), 20
SWIT radio, 137
Szenes, Hannah, 245
Szwarcman, Mathilde, 304

Tageschronik, 140
Tagore, Rabindranath, 158, 266
Tale of Love and Darkness, A (Oz), 24–25, 86, 334
Tarbut, 17–18, 25
Tarvisio Pass, 177
Taub family, 167
Teatro alla Scala, 289

Teitelbaum, Anita, 277, 280, 282, 299
Tel Aviv: about, 70, 73–74, 326; violence in, 61, 271, 319
Tel Aviv-Jerusalem road, 329
terrorism by Zionists, 75, 271, 303, 319, 326, 330
Tessler, Villi, 203
theater, the, 16–18, 73–75, 303, 339–40
Theodor Herzl, 303–4
Todras, 132–33, 134
Togliatti, Palmiro, 255
Tonoli Melloni Foundation, 170, 184
Topel, Moshe, 82, 140
Torelli, Milziade, 265–66
Torgau Offensive, 155
"To the Bird" (Bialik), 26–27, 31, 72–73, 338
trauma, 92–93, 229–31
Treaty of Trianon, 37
trials of war criminals, 89, 91–92, 157–58
Turani family, 220
Twenty-Second Zionist Congress, 297–98, 308
Twischor family, 25
Tzahal, 332, 345–46
Tze'elim kibbutz, 336, 337, 339, 341–42

Ukraine, 2, 11, 36, 87, 137, 151–52. See also specific cities of
Ukranian volunteers for the Third Reich, 153–54
Ulua, 300–301, 320
Unger, Moshe "Fetter Moshe," 191, 215, 249, 320
Union Jack, 125
Union of Italian Jewish Communities, 194, 264
United Nations, 166
United Nations Relief and Rehabilitation Administration (UNRRA), 166, 197, 213, 256, 269
Usque, Samuel, 270

van Gogh, Vincent, 209
Varadi, Max, 164, 192–93, 298
Ventitré, 278, 279–80, 284
vessels, discharged, 176
Via Cantù, 176
Via Capella Vecchia Jewish school, 112–13, 117
Via Eupili Jewish school, 162–66, 167, 168, 171–72, 291
Via Unione, 122–23, 124–27, 161, 167, 175, 233
Villa Comunale, 114
Vilnius, Poland/Lithuania, 20, 27–28, 87
Vittorio, Colonel, 123–24, 161, 162, 164
Volhynia region, 24, 83, 84–85, 87
voluntary orphanhood, 21, 53, 93
Vynohradiv, Ukraine, 36

Wannsee Conference, 87
War for Independence: about, 328–32, 336–37; Selvino alumni in, 329; Shoah survivors in, 332–33, 336–37
Warsaw, Poland: about, 20, 156, 253; ghetto diary of, 5–6; ghetto of, 99, 115, 137
Warsaw Orphan's House, 41–42, 170–71
weapons depot at Magenta, 175
Wehrmacht, 133, 134–35
Weichsel Union Metalwerke, 144
Weintraub, Helga, 113–14, 180
Weintraub, Isaac, 113–14, 180
Weiss-Livnat International Program in Holocaust Studies, 318
Weisz, Aliz, 37–39, 147, 148, 203–4
Weisz, Bandi, 37–39, 147, 203
Weisz, Hedi, 37–39, 147, 148, 204
Weisz, Icuka, 37–39, 147, 148–49, 243–44
Weisz, Sándor "Suti": aliyah of, 302; at Auschwitz-Birkenau, 146–50; in Hungary/Czechoslovakia, 37–39; kibbutz integration and, 317–18; name change of, 149, 237; *Nivenu* and, 243–44; at Youth Aliyah House, 203–4. *See also* Livnat, Yitzhak
Weisz, Terez, 37–39, 147, 243
Weisz, Vilmos, 37–39, 147, 150
Western Front, 118, 119–20, 137
Wexler, Adam: aliyah of, 301; at Auschwitz-Birkenau, 143–45; extended family of, 275–76; immigration exclusion of, 277; in Janowo, 31, 33–34, 35, 36; Kibbutz Selvino summit and, 321; Kibbutz Tze'elim and, 335–36; in Kolumna, 77–78; in Łódź, 79–81, 137–38, 140–42, 143; march from Auschwitz and, 145–46; marriage of, 304; at Youth Aliyah House, 201–3, 213–14, 218, 247; as a Youth Aliyah House alumnus, 338; Zeiri and, 233, 320
Wexler, Arieh, 276
Wexler, Dalia, 338
Wexler, David, 78, 79, 140, 142, 143
Wexler, Dov: aliyah of, 247, 251; at Auschwitz-Birkenau, 144–45; in Janowo, 31, 33–34, 35, 36; at Kibbutz Rosh Hanikra, 335; in Kolumna, 77; in Łódź, 80, 139, 141–42, 143; march from Auschwitz and, 145–46; marriage of, 287, 307; Palmach and, 315–16; War for Independence and, 327–28, 329, 331–32; at Youth Aliyah House, 201–2, 213–14, 217
Wexler, Gitel, 275
Wexler, Henoch: death of, 140, 143; in Janowo, 32–33, 34–35; in Kolumna, 77, 78; in Łódź, 78–79, 82; radio incident and, 137–39, 141
Wexler, Karol, 82, 141, 275
Wexler, Mindel: death of, 143; in Jenowo, 31, 33; in Kolumna, 77, 78; in Łódź, 139, 141–42
Wexler, Rosa, 142

Wexler, Ruth, 275
Wexler, Shaya: death of, 140, 143; in Janowo, 31, 32, 35, 36; in Łódź, 78, 81; radio incident and, 137, 139–40
Wexler, Shendil, 276
Wexler, Shimek, 82, 141, 275
Wexler, Shmuel, 275
Wexler, Uzi, 338
Wexler, Yankl, 82, 140, 143
Wexler, Yosef, 31, 32, 35–36, 78, 79
Wexler, Zosha, 141, 275
Wexler radio, 81–83, 137–42
White Paper of the British government on Palestine, 75, 105, 175
White Poles, 135, 136
Widawski, Chaim, 82, 140–41
Women's International Zionist Organization (WIZO), 25
World War I, 10–11, 22, 33, 37, 50

Yaakov, Abraham, 13, 184
Yad Vashem, 1, 3–6, 93, 180, 344
Yagur, 278–79
Yakar, Yehuda, 13, 184
Yiddish language, 235–36, 239–40
Yiftach Brigade, 329
Youth Aliyah House: about, 308–9; about children of, 226–28, 229–31; children arrivals to, 196–97, 198–205, 296–97; children departures from, 194–96 (see also Youth Aliyah House: illegal immigration from); closing of, 333–34; conflicts at, 212–16, 228–29; escapes from, 197; extracurricular acculturation at, 209–12; food at, 215–16, 219–21; founding of, 183–84, 186–88; illegal immigration from, 247–52, 256, 258–59, 300–303; Joint and, 296, 309–10; language and, 236–37; Łódź group at, 204–5, 207, 213; management of, 205–7, 256–57, 289, 308–9; Meriash on, 188–89; military training at, 259–60; name changes and, 237; *Nivenu* and, 239–40; privileges at, 216–17; protest of students of, 272–73; scabies epidemic at, 233–34; second anniversary of, 323; secularism at, 193, 210, 231–32, 267–68; Selvino village and, 218–23; sex and, 232–33; Shilo on, 344; silence on the past at, 237–39; staff of, 190–93, 208 (see also *specific staff*); vocational training at, 207, 310–11; Wexler on, 276; Zionism and, 207–8

Zachodnia Street shelter, 156–57, 159, 205
Zarach, 195
Zawadski, 77
Zdolbuniv, Ukraine, 86, 87, 150–52
Zeidmann, Franka, 86
Zeidmann, Shmuel, 86
Zeiri, Avner, 189, 309, 323
Zeiri, Moshe, about: as an actor, 73, 74–75, 182; background and overview of, 1–2, 45; Capri trip of, 118–19; Cassin and, 161, 164, 192–93, 206, 257; collection of letters of, 2–5, 6–7, 353nn1–2; Joint and, 171, 228, 256, 293–96; Kibbutz Selvino dream of, 309, 312, 316–17, 319–20; *Kinderlach fon Selvino* summit and, 322–23; as a laborer, 64, 73–74; Milan's Jewish schools and, 160–65, 167–73; mother and, 67; as a newlywed, 68, 70–71, 72–73, 74; Piazzatorre camp and, 180–82, 184–85; plans of, 165–67, 171–72; as a *tarbutnik*, 64, 97, 166; writing of, 229; Yehudit romance with, 65–66; Yehudit's move to Italy and, 262–63, 308, 309. See also Kleiner, Moshe; Zeiri, Moshe and Youth Aliyah House; Zeiri, Moshe as a Royal Engineer

Zeiri, Moshe and Youth Aliyah House: alumni care and, 310–12; children arrivals and departure and, 194–96, 199, 205; closing and, 334; conflicts and, 213–14, 215–16; Cyprus internment camps and, 310–11, 322–23; Donath on, 342; extracurricular acculturation and, 209–12; as father of children there, 294–95; founding, 183–84, 186–88, 189; illegal immigration and, 247, 276, 289; Italian solidarity and, 273–74; Lanfranchi on, 290–91; management of, 206–7, 256–57, 289, 308–9; *Nivenu* and, 239–41, 242; orphans and kibbutzim and, 258–59, 313; orphans' trauma and, 229–31; propaganda and, 228; secularism and, 267–68; silence on the past and, 237–39, 242; staff and, 190, 193, 227; Zionism and, 260–61, 297–98

Zeiri, Moshe as a Royal Engineer: in Egypt, 96–101; in Italy, 110, 112–14, 117–21, 126–27, 256, 263, 266–68; on leave, 104–5, 109; in Libya, 101–4, 105–6; overview of, 2, 96

Zeiri, Nitza: birth of, 95, 96; childhood of, 104, 262–63, 291–92, 294, 324; at Yad Vashem, 1, 3–7; Youth Aliyah House alumni gathering and, 341

Zeiri, Tali, 7, 189

Zeiri, Yehudit: background and overview of, 2; Moshe in Milan and, 165, 172–73; Moshe in the army and, 117–18; move to Italy of, 257–58, 262–63, 274, 291–92, 308–9; as a newlywed, 68, 70–71; Youth Aliyah House and, 292–93, 294, 309, 334. *See also* Meyer, Trude

Zeiri Collection, 2–5, 6–7, 353nn1–2

Zionism: Baratz and, 62–63; "black box" of, 329–30; British White Paper and, 75–76; emigration criterion and, 55–56; faction conflict of, 271; guilt and, 93; Hungary and, 36; Jabotinsky and, 30; Liberman family and, 25; in literature, 52–53; Lubianiker family and, 15–17; in Lviv, 20–21; orphans and, 182–83, 247, 256; propaganda of, 11, 17, 22, 36, 61, 228, 241, 299; refugees and, 103–4, 177–78; Revisionist, 30, 35, 76, 326; terrorism and, 75, 271, 303, 319, 326, 330; Twenty-Second Congress of, 297–98; vision of, 61; Weisz family and, 38; Wexler family and, 35–36; Yiddish and, 236; Youth Aliyah House and, 207–8. *See also* Gordonia movement; *under specific persons*

Zoltak, Shie, 260

Zugman, Dov, 218, 260

SERGIO LUZZATTO is Professor and the Emiliana Pasca Noether Chair in Modern Italian History at the University of Connecticut. Three of his books on Italian history (*The Body of Il Duce*, 2005; *Padre Pio*, 2010; *Primo Levi's Resistance*, 2016) have been translated into English.

STASH LUCZKIW is a New York–born poet and translator based in Italy.